Great Issues
in American
History

*

*From the Revolution to the
Civil War, 1765-1865*

GREAT ISSUES IN AMERICAN HISTORY

From the Revolution to the Civil War, 1765-1865

✳ EDITED BY ✳

Richard Hofstadter

VINTAGE BOOKS
A DIVISION OF RANDOM HOUSE
New York

*

To My Father

*

Preface

THESE documentary selections are intended to provide a generous sampling from the major political controversies in American history. I hope that the general introductions, together with the headnotes supplied for each selection, will serve to set the documents in their historical context in such a way as to make it possible for a reader with a modest knowledge of American history to read them profitably and without further supplement. But the volumes have been planned with special concern for the interests and needs of undergraduates who will have occasion to use them in connection with a textbook or a general survey of American history. With this in mind, I have not tried to make my general introductions into a collective history of American politics, nor even into histories of the particular issues I have chosen to illustrate; they are simply brief glosses on a few issues of central importance. They will serve their purpose if they refresh the memory of the general reader and assist the student in establishing the links between these sources and his other readings.

It has been my purpose to concentrate on political controversy. I have not tried to include the texts of statutes, which are available in reference books and are usually well summarized for the student's purposes in general books; nor have I—except in the cases of a few documents whose special importance seemed to demand their inclusion —reprinted purely illustrative materials. Almost everything in these volumes can be described as argumentative. These documents reproduce the words of major actors of American political history—whether judges, statesmen, legislative bodies, or private individuals of influence—engaged in debating issues of central importance. It has not been possible to include all the historical issues that may be considered important. To achieve such inclusiveness seems less desirable than that every issue selected should be discussed in some depth in the chosen documents, and that opposing views should be adequately represented.

Of necessity, the documents have been edited, and the ellipses indicate omitted portions. But I have tried to avoid snippets. Where severe selection from a larger text has been necessary, enough has been included in each case to give a coherent sample of the original argument at the point at which the author was stating the novel or essential portions of his case. Some small amount of modernization has been imposed on most documents written before about 1815.

I am grateful to my wife, Beatrice Kevitt Hofstadter, who generously took time from her own work in progress to help me collate and edit these documents and prepare the commentaries; and to Gerald and Dorothy Stearn for editorial assistance at every stage in the preparation of the manuscript.

March, 1958   R. H.

Contents

PART I: REVOLUTION AND INDEPENDENCE

PART II: THE CONSTITUTION

PART III: FEDERALISTS AND REPUBLICANS

PART IV: REPUBLICAN DIPLOMACY

PART V: THE JACKSONIAN ERA

PART VI: SLAVERY AND EXPANSION

PART VII: SECESSION, CIVIL WAR,
AND EMANCIPATION

Great Issues
in American
History

∗

*From the Revolution to the
Civil War, 1765-1865*

✳ PART I ✳

Revolution and Independence

✳ ✳ ✳ ✳ ✳ ✳ ✳

BY 1763, when the French and Indian War ended, the American colonies had grown to be a strong and thriving part of the British empire, whose people were passionately concerned to manage their own affairs. In the past they had been accustomed to a large measure of regulation of their trade by Parliament. But some of the inconvenient regulations, notably those on the trade with the French West Indies, had been regularly evaded by smugglers, and British officials had dealt very indulgently with violators of the law. Parliament had never taxed the colonists for the sake of revenue. Taxes, in the form of duties, had been imposed in the course of regulating trade, but these taxes were not passed to raise money, and it was understood that they were only incidental to regulation.

After 1763, the successive ministries that set policy in London felt that England could no longer afford to be as easy-going as in the past. The empire was expensive; costly wars had been fought to acquire and defend it; still more money would have to be laid out in the future to garrison it. From the British point of view, much of the outlay had been made in the interests of the colonies, and the home government felt it to be only just that the colonists should share in the immense tax burden borne by British subjects at home. Moreover, when smuggling, which had been tolerated before the war, continued to be carried on during hostilities, it became an act of treason. Therefore, in 1764 Parliament passed the Sugar Act, which was intended to end this illegal trade as well as to produce a revenue, and in 1765 passed the Stamp Act, which it was hoped would raise £ 60,000 a year.

For the Americans this new and firmer policy could hardly have come at a more inauspicious time. The presence of the French in Canada had always driven the colonists toward the mother country. Now, with the common enemy expelled, the colonists felt free to assert themselves. The Sugar Act and the Stamp Act found them in the midst of a post-war business depression and in a touchy mood. The colonists had always had to struggle to improve a currency supply that was inadequate to their needs; now the new taxes threatened to make this struggle even harder. Moreover, the illegal West Indies trade had long been one of the best sources of business profits and hard money for the northern colonies. Southern planters too, who were continually in debt to their British merchant creditors, were beginning to feel restive. And the Stamp Act, which affected all colonies in the same way, united them around a common grievance. The devices used to enforce the Sugar Act gave American merchants a legal issue which shrewd colonial lawyers were quick to exploit. In the past, colonial smugglers, when brought to trial, could look forward to almost certain acquittal. American juries would not convict them. Now violators were to be tried in the vice-admiralty courts, which had no juries. The Americans felt that by losing the benefit of jury trials they were deprived of one of the fundamental rights of Englishmen, acquired over long centuries of struggle for liberty.

In the decade following 1765, several measures of Parliament provided the colonists with a wide variety of grievances. But among all these, none occupied so prominent a place in the literature of American protest as the question of taxation. Taxation without representation became the central issue, the focal symbol which expressed the entire American feeling of discontent. One reason why, among all the matters at issue, taxation was given such importance was that here the colonists felt sure that their position was supported by British constitutional doctrine and prevailing ideas of natural rights. Since they had never before paid revenue-raising taxes, it was possible for them to feel victimized by a vicious innovation. English lawyers had long agreed that it was a violation of both natural rights and of the British constitution to tax a man without his consent, given directly or through his representatives. This was the position stated in the Resolutions of the Stamp Act Congress of 1765 (Document 1).

A standard British rebuttal of the colonial cry of "taxation without representation" was the doctrine of "virtual representation," exemplified here by the pamphleteer, Soame Jenyns (Document 2). The exponents of virtual representation pointed out that there were many Englishmen living in boroughs unrepresented in Parliament; they argued that these Englishmen, and along with them those who lived in the colonies, were virtually represented by the members of Parliament chosen by other constituents. In effect, those who represented some could represent all. Most American spokesmen, however, agreed with Daniel Dulany in his widely read protest against the Stamp Act (Document 3) that virtual representation had no meaning or value for Americans; and there were many Whig leaders in England—among them the elder Pitt in his famous speech against the Stamp Act (Document 4)—who heartily agreed with them, and celebrated American resistance to illegal taxation as a contribution to the rights of all Englishmen.

English merchants, who suffered from the boycotts by means of which the colonists implemented their protests, combined with English friends of the colonists like Pitt and his followers to force the repeal of the Stamp Act. But they did not succeed, as Pitt hoped, in getting Parliament to disavow the principle of taxation. Subsequent taxation acts were designed to exploit the weaknesses in the colonial argument. That is, if the colonists admitted the legality of taxes imposed to regulate trade but rejected those passed solely and frankly to raise money, why not devise taxes which would in fact raise money but which would look like trade regulations? Such was the reasoning behind the Townshend Acts of 1767, which imposed duties on a variety of colonial imports.

But the colonists really wanted to be exempted from all taxation by Parliament, not merely to have their legalistic distinctions observed. The most famous American statement against the Townshend Acts—John Dickinson's *Letters from a Farmer* (Document 5)—pointed out that these measures were unacceptable because whatever their form, their *purpose* was to raise revenue. But this was not a dependable solution. How could the colonists decide what purpose governed the mind of Parliament when it passed a law? In the end, they found it better to advance from this position to the unequivocal stand, expressed in the Declaration and Resolves of the First Continental Congress, 1774, (Document 6) that no taxation of any kind was legitimate without their consent.

The repeal in 1770 of the Townshend duties (except for that on tea, maintained to uphold the principle of Parliamentary taxation) led to a relative lull in colonial agitation for a few years—though even this lull was disturbed by the "Boston Massacre" and other incidents. However, the attempt of Parliament to bail the vast East India Company out of its financial difficulties, by giving its tea a privileged position in the American market, re-opened old issues that had been set aside but never resolved. Universal resistance to the acceptance of this tea was dramatized by the Boston Tea Party, which provoked the Boston Port Act and the other "Intolerable Acts" of the spring of 1774. The crisis now entered a new phase: now the colonists felt their rights and liberties were being invaded in many ways.

While some of the colonists began to advocate a complete break, the Loyalists in America found effective spokesmen for their side. One of the most eloquent of these, Daniel Leonard, argued that the principles invoked by the patriots would lead to anarchy (Document 7). John Adams, in his answer to Leonard (Document 8), expressed a different conception, one toward which a number of thoughtful Americans, including Thomas Jefferson and James Wilson, were tending. Such men had arrived at the conclusion that the Americans should be united to Britain not through any obligation to Parliament, of which they should be completely independent, but solely through loyalty to the crown. This anticipation of what later came to be Dominion status was too much in advance of its time. British government was too corrupt and irregular to undertake daring and constructive innovations, and there were men in England who shared Samuel Johnson's feeling that "the Americans are a nation of convicts and deserve anything we give them short of hanging." To be sure, there were men like Edmund Burke, who, for expediency's sake, preferred to deal with the colonists in a spirit of magnanimity (Document 9) rather than to stand on abstract assertions of Parliamentary right. There were also men like Adam Smith (Document 10) and Josiah Tucker, who soberly calculated the economic value of colonies and warned of the costs of trying to keep them.

In April 1775, the battles of Lexington and Concord took place. By July, the Second Continental Congress was explaining to the world why the Americans had been driven to take up arms, and was threatening to call in foreign intervention (Document 11). However, when the colonists did begin to fight, it was not to win independence but only to defend their rights. Fighting broke out without their having planned it, much less having decided what end they were fighting for. For well over a year, while both sides were futilely attempting to state acceptable terms of peace, Americans discussed what it was that they were fighting for. As the months went by, the logic of those who looked for a restoration of the imperial relationship grew weaker and less persuasive. The case for complete separation was forcefully stated by Thomas Paine in his *Common Sense* (Document 12). A number of Loyalists leaped into the propaganda struggle with answers to Paine in which the dangers of war and the disadvantages of independence were fully reviewed (Document 13). But in July 1776, the movement for independence prevailed, and the Congress committed American arms to this goal (Document 14).

DOCUMENT 1

RESOLUTIONS OF THE STAMP ACT CONGRESS, OCTOBER 19, 1765

On June 6, 1765, the Massachusetts House of Representatives, on the motion of James Otis, resolved to propose an intercolonial meeting to resist the Stamp Act. On June 8 it sent a circular letter to the assemblies of the other colonies inviting them to meet at New York the following October "to consider of a general and united, dutiful, loyal and humble representation of their condition to His Majesty and the Parliament; and to implore relief." Of the thirteen colonies which later took part in the Revolution, nine sent delegates. New Hampshire, Virginia, North Carolina, and Georgia were unrepresented; the last three were prevented by their governors from electing delegates, but New Hampshire gave its approval to the Congress after the proceedings were over. These resolutions were the chief accomplishment of the Congress. Two early drafts of the resolutions in the hand of John Dickinson of Pennsylvania suggest that the credit for the text should go to him, though some historians have concluded that they were drawn up by John Cruger, the mayor of New York. The principal issue that divided the twenty-seven delegates was whether to modify the rebellious tone of their denial of Parliament's authority to tax; this could be done by acknowledging explicitly what authority Parliament did have over the colonies. In the end this proved impossible because the more radical delegates were afraid of conceding too much. The extent of the concession they were willing to make is registered in the rather vague wording of the first resolution.

The members of this Congress, sincerely devoted, with the warmest sentiments of affection and duty to His Majesty's Person and Government, inviolably attached to the present happy establishment of the Protestant succession, and with minds deeply impressed by a sense of the present and impending misfortunes of the British colonies on this continent; having considered as maturely as time will permit the circumstances of the said colonies, esteem it our indispensable duty to make the following declarations of our humble opinion, respecting the most essential rights and liberties of the colonists, and of the grievances under which they labour, by reason of several late Acts of Parliament.

I. That His Majesty's subjects in these colonies, owe the same allegiance to the Crown of Great–Britain, that is owing from his subjects born within the realm, and all due subordination to that august body the Parliament of Great Britain.

II. That His Majesty's liege subjects in these colonies, are entitled to all the inherent rights and liberties of his natural born subjects within the kingdom of Great–Britain.

III. That it is inseparably essential to the freedom of a people, and the undoubted right of Englishmen, that no taxes be imposed on them, but with their own consent, given personally, or by their representatives.

IV. That the people of these colonies are not, and from their local circumstances cannot be, represented in the House of Commons in Great–Britain.

V. That the only representatives of the people of these colonies, are persons chosen therein by themselves, and that no taxes ever have been, or can be constitutionally imposed on them, but by their respective legislatures.

VI. That all supplies to the Crown, being free gifts of the people, it is unreasonable and inconsistent with the principles and spirit of the British Constitution, for the people of Great–Britain to grant to His Majesty the property of the colonists.

VII. That trial by jury is the inherent and invaluable right of every British subject in these colonies.

VIII. That the late Act of Parliament, entitled, *An Act for granting and applying certain Stamp Duties, and other Duties, in the British colonies and plantations in America, etc.,* by imposing taxes on the inhabitants of these colonies, and the said Act, and several other Acts, by extending the jurisdiction of the courts of Admiralty beyond its ancient limits, have a manifest tendency to subvert the rights and liberties of the colonists.

IX. That the duties imposed by several late Acts of Parliament, from the peculiar circumstances of these colonies, will be extremely burthensome and grievous; and from the scarcity of specie, the payment of them absolutely impracticable.

X. That as the profits of the trade of these colonies ultimately center in Great–Britain, to pay for the manufactures which they are obliged to take from thence, they eventually contribute very largely to all supplies granted there to the Crown.

XI. That the restrictions imposed by several late Acts of Parliament, on the trade of these colonies, will render them unable to purchase the manufactures of Great–Britain.

XII. That the increase, prosperity, and happiness of these colonies, depend on the full and free enjoyment of their rights and liberties, and an intercourse with Great–Britain mutually affectionate and advantageous.

XIII. That it is the right of the British subjects in these colonies, to petition the King, or either House of Parliament.

Lastly, That it is the indispensable duty of these colonies, to the best of sovereigns, to the mother country, and to themselves, to endeavour by a loyal and dutiful address to his Majesty, and humble applications to both Houses of Parliament, to procure the repeal of the Act for granting and applying certain stamp duties, of all clauses of any other Acts of Parliament, whereby the jurisdiction of the Admiralty is extended as aforesaid, and of the other late Acts for the restriction of American commerce.

DOCUMENT 2

SOAME JENYNS, *THE OBJECTIONS TO THE TAXATION . . . CONSIDER'D,*
1765

Soame Jenyns, a minor poet and a member of Parliament from 1741 to 1780, was a member of the Board of Trade and Plantations when he wrote this pamphlet, the full title of which was The Objections to the Taxation of our American Colonies by the Legislature of Great Britain, briefly consider'd. *In this excerpt he argues the case for Parliament's right to tax the colonies, and states briefly the theory of virtual representation.*

The right of the Legislature of Great–Britain to impose taxes on her American Colonies, and the expediency of

exerting that right in the present conjuncture, are propositions so indisputably clear, that I should never have thought it necessary to have undertaken their defence, had not many arguments been lately flung out, both in papers and conversation, which with insolence equal to their absurdity deny them both. As these are usually mixt up with several patriotic and favorite words such as Liberty, Property, Englishmen, etc., which are apt to make strong impressions on that more numerous part of mankind, who have ears but no understanding, it will not, I think, be improper to give them some answers: to this, therefore, I shall singly confine myself, and do it in as few words as possible, being sensible that the fewest will give least trouble to myself and probably most information to my reader.

The great capital argument, which I find on this subject, and which, like an Elephant at the head of a Nobob's army, being once overthrown, must put the whole into confusion, is this; that no Englishman is, or can be taxed, but by his own consent: by which must be meant one of these three propositions; either that no Englishman can be taxed without his own consent as an individual; or that no Englishman can be taxed without the consent of the persons he chuses to represent him; or that no Englishman can be taxed without the consent of the majority of all those, who are elected by himself and others of his fellow-subjects to represent them. Now let us impartially consider, whether any one of these propositions are in fact true: if not, then this wonderful structure which has been erected upon them, falls at once to the ground, and like another Babel, perishes by a confusion of words, which the builders themselves are unable to understand.

First then, that no Englishman is or can be taxed but by his own consent as an individual: this is so far from being true, that it is the very reverse of truth; for no man that I know of is taxed by his own consent; and an Englishman, I believe, is as little likely to be so taxed, as any man in the world.

Secondly, that no Englishman is or can be taxed but by the consent of those persons whom he has chose to represent him; for the truth of this I shall appeal only to the candid representatives of those unfortunate counties which produce cyder, and shall willingly ,acquiesce under their determination.

Lastly, that no Englishman is, or can be taxed, without the consent of the majority of those, who are elected by himself, and others of his fellow-subjects, to represent them. This is certainly as false as the other two; for every Englishman is taxed, and not one in twenty represented: copyholders, leaseholders, and all men possessed of personal property only, chuse no representatives; Manchester, Birmingham, and many more of our richest and most flourishing trading towns send no members to parliament, consequently cannot consent by their representatives, because they chuse none to represent them; yet are they not Englishmen? or are they not taxed?

I am well aware, that I shall hear Locke, Sidney, Selden, and many other great names quoted to prove that every Englishman, whether he has a right to vote for a representative, or not, is still represented in the British Parliament; in which opinion they all agree: on what principle of common sense this opinion is founded I comprehend not, but on the authority of such respectable names I shall acknowledge its truth; but then I will ask one question, and on that I will rest the whole merits of the cause: Why does not this imaginary representation extend to America, as well as over the whole island of Great–Britain? If it can travel three hundred miles, why not three thousand? if it can jump over rivers and mountains, why cannot it sail over the ocean? If the towns of Manchester and Birmingham sending no representatives to parliament, are notwithstanding there represented, why are not the cities of Albany and Boston equally represented in that assembly? Are they not alike British subjects? are they not Englishmen? or are they only Englishmen when they sollicit for protection, but not Englishmen when taxes are required to enable this country to protect them?

But it is urged, that the Colonies are by their charters placed under distinct Governments, each of which has a legislative power within itself, by which alone it ought to be taxed; that if this privilege is once given up, that liberty which every Englishman has a right to, is torn from them, they are all slaves, and all is lost.

The liberty of an Englishman, is a phrase of so

various a signification, having within these few years been
used as a synonymous term for blasphemy, bawdy,
treason, libels, strong beer, and cyder, that I shall not
here presume to define its meaning; but I shall venture to
assert what it cannot mean; that is, an exemption from
taxes imposed by the authority of the Parliament of Great
Britain; nor is there any charter, that ever pretended to
grant such a privilege to any colony in America; and had
they granted it, it could have had no force; their charters
being derived from the Crown, and no charter from the
Crown can possibly supersede the right of the whole
legislature: their charters are undoubtedly no more than
those of all corporations, which impower them to make
byelaws, and raise duties for the purposes of their own
police, for ever subject to the superior authority of parliament; and in some of their charters, the manner of exercising these powers is specified in these express words,
"according to the course of other corporations in Great–
Britain": and therefore they can have no more pretence to
plead an exemption from this parliamentary authority,
than any other corporation in England.

It has been moreover alleged, that, though Parliament
may have power to impose taxes on the Colonies, they
have no right to use it, because it would be an unjust tax;
and no supreme or legislative power can have a right to
enact any law in its nature unjust: to this, I shall only
make this short reply, that if Parliament can impose no
taxes but what are equitable, and the persons taxed are
to be the judges of that equity, they will in effect have no
power to lay any tax at all. No tax can be imposed exactly
equal on all, and if it is not equal, it cannot be just: and if
it is not just, no power whatever can impose it; by which
short syllogism, all taxation is at an end; but why it should
not be used by Englishmen on this side the Atlantic, as
well as by those on the other, I do not comprehend. . . .

DOCUMENT 3

DANIEL DULANY, *CONSIDERATIONS,*
OCTOBER, 1765

Daniel Dulany of Annapolis, Maryland, had studied law in England at the Middle Temple, and was considered, at least by one fellow Marylander, Charles Carroll, to be "indisputably the best lawyer on this continent." He wrote this pamphlet, entitled Considerations on the Propriety of Imposing Taxes in the British Colonies, for the Purpose of raising a Revenue, by Act of Parliament, *in opposition to the Stamp Act. Here he argued that virtual representation was empty and meaningless; that the colonies not only were not but could not be represented in Parliament; and that taxation without representation was a breach of the English common law. His arguments were widely read in America, and in England were drawn upon by William Pitt in his plea for repeal of the Stamp Act (Document 4).*

I shall undertake to disprove the supposed similarity of situation, whence the same kind of Representation is deduced of the inhabitants of the colonies, and of the *British* non-electors; and, if I succeed, the Notion of a *virtual representation* of the colonies must fail, which, in Truth is a mere cob-web, spread to catch the unwary, and intangle the weak. I would be understood. I am upon a question of *propriety,* not of power; and though some may be inclined to think it is to little purpose to discuss the one, when the other is irresistible, yet are they different considerations; and, at the same time that I invalidate the claim upon which it is founded, I may very consistently recommend a submission to the law, whilst it endures. . . .

Lessees for years, copyholders, proprietors of the public funds, inhabitants of Birmingham, Leeds, Halifax and Manchester, merchants of the City of London, or members of the corporation of the East India Company, are, *as such,* under no personal incapacity to be electors; for they may acquire the right of election, and there are *actually* not only a considerable number of electors in each of the classes of lessees for years etc., but in many of them, if not all, even members of Parliament. The interests therefore of the non-electors, the electors, and the representatives, are individually the same; to say nothing of the connection among neighbours, friends and relations. The security of the non-electors against oppression, is that their oppression will fall also upon the electors and the representatives. The one can't be injured and the other indemnified.

Further, if the non-electors should not be taxed by the British Parliament, they would not be taxed *at all;* and it would be iniquitous, as well as a solecism in the political system, that they should partake of all the benefits resulting from the imposition and application of taxes, and derive an immunity from the circumstances of not being qualified to vote. Under this Constitution then, a double or virtual representation may be reasonably supposed. . . .

There is not that intimate and inseparable relation between the electors of Great–Britain and the inhabitants of the colonies, which must inevitably involve both in the same taxation; on the contrary, not a single actual elector in England, might be immediately affected by a taxation in America, imposed by a statute which would have a general operation and effect, upon the properties of the inhabitants of the colonies . . . wherefore the relation between the British Americans, and the English electors, is a knot too infirm to be relied on. . . .

It appears to me, that there is a clear and necessary Distinction between an Act imposing a tax for *the single purpose of revenue,* and those Acts which have been made for the *regulation of trade,* and have produced some revenue in consequence of their effect and operation as regulations of trade.

The colonies claim the privileges of British subjects —It has been proved to be inconsistent with those privileges, to tax them without their own consent, and it hath been demonstrated that a tax imposed by Parliament, is a tax without their consent.

The subordination of the colonies, and the authority of Parliament to preserve it, have been fully acknowledged. Not only the welfare, but perhaps the existence of the mother country, as an independent kingdom, may depend upon her trade and navigation, and these so far upon her intercourse with the colonies, that if this should be neglected, there would soon be an end to that commerce, whence her greatest wealth is derived, and upon which her maritime power is principally founded. From these considerations, the right of the *British Parliament* to regulate the trade of the colonies, may be justly deduced; a denial of it would contradict the admission of the subordination, and of the authority to preserve it, resulting from the nature of the relation between the mother country and her colonies. It is a common, and frequently the most proper method to regulate trade by duties on imports and exports. The authority of the mother country to regulate the trade of the colonies being unquestionable, what regulations are the most proper, are to be of course submitted to the determination of the Parliament; and if an *incidental revenue,* should be produced by such regulations; these are not therefore unwarrantable.

A right to impose an internal tax on the colonies, without their consent *for the single purpose of revenue,* is denied, a right to regulate their trade without their consent is admitted. The imposition of a duty may, in some instances, be the proper regulation. If the claims of the mother country and the colonies should seem on such an occasion to interfere, and the point of right to be doubtful, (which I take to be otherwise) it is easy to guess that the determination will be on the side of power, and the inferior will be constrained to submit.

DOCUMENT 4

WILLIAM PITT, SPEECH ON THE STAMP ACT,
JANUARY 14, 1766

William Pitt the elder, later Earl of Chatham, had won great glory in his first ministry, which had laid the

*basis of victory in the Seven Years' War. He had re-
signed in 1761, and was absent from the House of
Commons when the Stamp Act was passed. Although
he firmly upheld Parliament's right to legislate for the
colonies, he agreed with the Americans that this right
did not extend to taxation. When the Stamp Act's
enforcement or repeal was before the House, Pitt
was bedridden with one of his fierce and painful attacks of gout, but he said to a friend: "If I can crawl,
or be carried, I will deliver my mind and heart upon
the state of America." The powerful speech from
which this selection is taken was an answer to Prime
Minister George Grenville, his brother-in-law, who
persisted in defending the stamp duties. The Marquess
of Rockingham wrote to King George III the day after
Pitt's speech: "The events of yesterday in the House of
Commons have shown the amazing power and influence which Mr. Pitt has whenever he takes part in
debate." The speech added new intensity to the ad-
miration Americans already had for its author. Ships,
towns, and babies were named after him, and one
rhymester wrote:*

> *I thank thee, Pitt, for all thy glorious strife
> Against the foes of LIBERTY and life.*

Gentlemen,—Sir [to the speaker], I have been charged with
giving birth to sedition in America. They have spoken their
sentiments with freedom against this unhappy act, and
that freedom has become their crime. Sorry I am to hear
the liberty of speech in this house, imputed as a crime.
But the imputation shall not discourage me. It is a liberty
I mean to exercise. No gentleman ought to be afraid to
exercise it. It is a liberty by which the gentleman who
calumniates it might have profited, by which he ought to
have profited. He ought to have desisted from his project.
The gentleman tells us, America is obstinate; America is
almost in open rebellion. I rejoice that America has
resisted. Three millions of people so dead to all feelings
of liberty, as voluntarily to submit to be slaves, would
have been fit instruments to make slaves of the rest. I

come not here armed at all points, with law cases and acts of parliament, with the statute book doubled down in dogs'-ears, to defend the cause of liberty: if I had, I myself would have cited the two cases of Chester and Durham. I would have cited them, to have shown that even under former arbitrary reigns, parliaments were ashamed of taxing a people without their consent, and allowed them representatives. Why did the gentleman confine himself to Chester and Durham? He might have taken a higher example in Wales; Wales, that never was taxed by parliament till it was incorporated. I would not debate a particular point of law with the gentleman. I know his abilities. I have been obliged to his diligent researches: but, for the defence of liberty, upon a general principle, upon a constitutional principle, it is a ground upon which I stand firm; on which I dare meet any man. The gentleman tells us of many who are taxed, and are not represented. The India Company, merchants, stock-holders, manufacturers. Surely many of these are represented in other capacities, as owners of land, or as freemen of boroughs. It is a misfortune that more are not equally represented: but they are all inhabitants, and as such, are they not virtually represented? . . . they have connections with those that elect, and they have influence over them. The gentleman mentioned the stock-holders: I hope he does not reckon the debts of the nation as a part of the national estate. Since the accession of King William, many ministers, some of great, others of more moderate abilities, have taken the lead of government. (He then went through the list of them, bringing it down till he came to himself, giving a short sketch of the characters of each of them.)

None of these thought, or ever dreamed, of robbing the colonies of their constitutional rights. That was reserved to mark the era of the late administration: not that there were wanting some, when I had the honour to serve his Majesty, to propose to me to burn my fingers with an American stamp-act. With the enemy at their back, with our bayonets at their breasts, in the day of their distress, perhaps the Americans would have submitted to the imposition; but it would have been taking an ungenerous and unjust advantage. The gentleman boasts of his bounties to America. Are not those bounties intended finally for the benefit of this kingdom? If they are not, he has mis-applied the national treasures. I am no courtier of America; I stand up for this kingdom. I maintain, that the parliament has a right to bind, to restrain America. Our legislative power over the colonies is sovereign and supreme. When it ceases to be sovereign and supreme, I would advise every gentleman to sell his lands, if he can, and embark for that country. When two countries are connected together, like England and her colonies, without being incorporated, the one must necessarily govern; the greater must rule the less; but so rule it, as not to contradict the fundamental principles that are common to both. If the gentleman does not understand the difference between external and internal taxes, I cannot help it; but there is a plain distinction between taxes levied for the purposes of raising a revenue, and duties imposed for the regulation of trade, for the accommodation of the subject; although, in the consequences, some revenue might incidentally arise from the latter.

The gentleman asks, when were the colonies emancipated? But I desire to know, when were they made slaves. But I dwell not upon words. When I had the honour of serving his Majesty, I availed myself of the means of information which I derived from my office: I speak, therefore, from knowledge. My materials were good; I was at pains to collect, to digest, to consider them; and I will be bold to affirm, that the profits to Great Britain from the trade of the colonies, through all its branches, is two millions a year. This is the fund that carried you triumphantly through the last war. . . . You owe this to America: this is the price that America pays you for her protection. And shall a miserable financier come with a boast, that he can bring a pepper-corn into the exchequer, to the loss of millions to the nation? I dare not say, how much higher these profits may be augmented. Omitting the immense increase of people by natural population, in the northern colonies, and the emigration from every part of Europe, I am convinced the whole commercial system of America may be altered to advantage. You have prohibited where you ought to have encouraged, encouraged where you ought to have prohibited. Improper restraints have been laid on the continent, in favour of the islands.

You have but two nations to trade with in America. Would you had twenty! Let acts of parliament in consequence of treaties remain, but let not an English minister become a custom-house officer for Spain, or for any foreign power. Much is wrong; much may be amended for the general good of the whole. . . .

The gentleman must not wonder he was not contradicted, when, as the minister, he asserted the right of parliament to tax America. I know not how it is, but there is a modesty in this House, which does not choose to contradict a minister. I wish gentlemen would get the better of this modesty. Even that chair, Sir, sometimes looks towards St. James's. If they do not, perhaps the collective body may begin to abate of its respect for the representative. . . .

A great deal has been said without doors of the power, of the strength of America. It is a topic that ought to be cautiously meddled with. In a good cause, on a sound bottom, the force of this country can crush America to atoms. I know the valour of your troops. I know the skill of your officers. There is not a company of foot that has served in America out of which you may not pick a man of sufficient knowledge and experience to make a governor of a colony there. But on this ground, on the Stamp Act, when so many here will think a crying injustice, I am one who will lift up my hands against it.

In such a cause, your success would be hazardous. America, if she fell, would fall like the strong man. She would embrace the pillars of the state, and pull down the constitution along with her. Is this your boasted peace? Not to sheathe the sword in its scabbard, but to sheathe it in the bowels of your countrymen? Will you quarrel with yourselves, now the whole House of Bourbon is united against you? . . .

The Americans have not acted in all things with prudence and temper. They have been wronged. They have been driven to madness by injustice. Will you punish them for the madness you have occasioned? Rather let prudence and temper come first from this side. I will undertake for America, that she will follow the example. There are two lines in a ballad of Prior's, of a man's behaviour to his wife, so applicable to you and your colonies, that I cannot help repeating them:—

> "Be to her faults a little blind;
> Be to her virtues very kind."

Upon the whole, I will beg leave to tell the House what is really my opinion. It is, that the Stamp–Act be repealed absolutely, totally, and immediately; that the reason for the repeal should be assigned, because it was founded on an erroneous principle. At the same time, let the sovereign authority of this country over the colonies be asserted in as strong terms as can be devised, and be made to extend to every point of legislation whatsoever: that we may bind their trade, confine their manufactures, and exercise every power whatsoever—except that of taking money out of their pockets without their consent.

DOCUMENT 5

JOHN DICKINSON, LETTERS II AND IV FROM *LETTERS FROM A FARMER*, 1767–8

John Dickinson, one of the outstanding members of the Philadelphia bar, and a man of moderate views, had been a leader of the opposition to the Stamp Act. In December 1767, he began to publish in the Pennsylvania Chronicle *a series of anonymous letters, subsequently published as a pamphlet entitled* Letters from a Farmer in Pennsylvania to the Inhabitants of the British Colonies *(1768). The letters, evoked by the Townshend Acts, were felt to be a signal statement of the American constitutional position, and they won Dickinson much applause. Influential though it was, Dickinson's argument was soon by-passed. It rested upon his assumption that the purpose of Parliament, when it passed a law, was the basis of that law's legitimacy. He defined a tax as an imposition "for the sole purpose of levying money." If a law was intended to raise money, it could be classified as a tax, and was therefore constitutionally unacceptable, no matter if, like the Townshend Acts, it was put forth in the form of a trade regulation. But the implication that the colonists could determine or define the purposes of Parliament presented too many difficulties for the colonial argument to rest long at this position.*

Letter II

There is another late act of parliament, which appears to me to be unconstitutional, and as destructive to the liberty of these colonies, as that mentioned in my last letter; that is, the act for granting the duties on paper, glass, &c. [the Townshend Act].

The parliament unquestionably possesses a legal authority to regulate the trade of Great–Britain and all her colonies. Such an authority is essential to the relation between a mother country and her colonies; and necessary for the common good of all. He, who considers these provinces as states distinct from the British empire, has very slender notions of justice, or of their interests. We are but parts of a whole; and therefore there must exist a power somewhere to preside, and preserve the connection in due order. This power is lodged in the parliament; and we are as much dependent on Great–Britain, as a perfectly free people can be on another.

I have looked over every statute relating to these colonies, from their first settlement to this time; and I find every one of them founded on this principle, till the Stamp–Act administration. All before, are calculated to regulate trade, and preserve or promote a mutually beneficial intercourse between the several constituent parts of the empire; and though many of them imposed duties on trade, yet those duties were always imposed with design to restrain the commerce of one part, that was injurious to another, and thus to promote the general welfare. The raising a revenue thereby was never intended . . . Never did the British parliament, till the period above mentioned, think of imposing duties in America, FOR THE PURPOSE OF RAISING A REVENUE. . . .

Here we may observe an authority expressly claimed

and exerted to impose duties on these colonies; not for the regulation of trade; not for the preservation or promotion of a mutually beneficial intercourse between the several constituent parts of the empire, heretofore the sole objects of parliamentary institutions; but for the single purpose of levying money upon us.

This I call an innovation; and a most dangerous innovation. It may perhaps be objected, that Great–Britain has a right to lay what duties she pleases upon her exports, and it makes no difference to us, whether they are paid here or there.

To this I answer. These colonies require many things for their use, which the laws of Great–Britain prohibit them from getting any where but from her. Such are paper and glass.

That we may be legally bound to pay any general duties on these commodities relative to the regulation of trade, is granted; but we being obliged by the laws to take from Great–Britain, any special duties imposed on their exportation to us only, with intention to raise a revenue from us only, are as much taxes, upon us, as those imposed by the Stamp–Act.

What is the difference in substance and right whether the same sum is raised upon us by the rates mentioned in the Stamp–Act, on the use of paper, or by these duties, on the importation of it. It is only the edition of a former book, shifting a sentence from the end to the beginning. . . .

Some persons perhaps may say, that this act lays us under no necessity to pay the duties imposed, because we may ourselves manufacture the articles on which they are laid; whereas by the Stamp–Act no instrument of writing could be good, unless made on British paper, and that too stamped.

I am told there are but two or three glass-houses on this continent, and but very few paper-mills; and suppose more should be erected, a long course of years must elapse, before they can be brought to perfection. This continent is a country of planters, farmers, and fishermen; not of manufacturers. The difficulty of establishing particular manufactures in such a country, is almost insuperable. . . .

Great—Britain has prohibited the manufacturing iron and steel in these colonies, without any objection being made to her right of doing it. The like right she must have to prohibit any other manufacture among us. Thus she is possessed of an undisputed precedent on that point. This authority, she will say, is founded on the original intention of settling these colonies; that is, that we should manufacture for them, and that they should supply her with materials. . . .

Here then, my dear country men ROUSE yourselves, and behold the ruin hanging over your heads. If you ONCE admit, that Great—Britain may lay duties upon her exportations to us, for the purpose of levying money on us only, she then will have nothing to do, but to lay those duties on the articles which she prohibits us to manufacture— and the tragedy of American liberty is finished. . . . If Great—Britain can order us to come to her for necessaries we want, and can order us to pay what taxes she pleases before we take them away, or when we land them here, we are as abject slaves as France and Poland can shew in wooden shoes, and with uncombed hair.

Letter IV

An objection, I hear, has been made against my second letter, which I would willingly clear up before I proceed. "There is," say these objectors, "a material difference between the Stamp—Act and the late Act for laying a duty on paper, &c., that justifies the conduct of those who opposed the former, and yet are willing to submit to the latter. The duties imposed by the Stamp—Act were internal taxes; but the present are external, and therefore the parliament may have a right to impose them."

To this I answer, with a total denial of the power of parliament to lay upon these colonies any "tax" whatever.

This point, being so important to this, and to succeeding generations, I wish to be clearly understood.

To the word "tax," I annex that meaning which the constitution and history of England require to be annexed to it; that is—that it is an imposition on the subject, for the sole purpose of levying money. . . .

Whenever we speak of "taxes" among Englishmen, let us therefore speak of them with reference to the principles on which, and the intentions with which they have been established. . . .

In the national, parliamentary sense insisted on, the word "tax" was certainly understood by the congress at New–York, whose resolves may be said to form the American "bill of rights."

The third, fourth, fifth, and sixth resolves are, thus expressed.

[Here Dickinson quoted the resolves of the Stamp Act Congress. See Document 1.]

Here is no distinction made between internal and external taxes. It is evident from the short reasoning thrown into these resolves, that every imposition "to grant to his Majesty the property of the colonies," was thought a "tax"; and that every such imposition, if laid any other way, than "with their consent, given personally, or by their representatives," was not only "unreasonable, and inconsistent with the principles and spirit of the British constitution," but destructive "to the freedom of a people."

Such persons therefore as speak of internal and external "taxes," I pray may pardon me, if I object to that expression, as applied to the privileges and interests of these colonies. There may be internal and external IMPOSITIONS, founded on different principles, and having different tendencies, every "tax" being an imposition, tho' every imposition is not a "tax." But all taxes are founded on the same principles; and have the same tendency.

External impositions, for the regulation of our trade, do not "grant to his Majesty the property of the colonies." They only prevent the colonies acquiring property, in things not necessary, in a manner judged to be injurious to the welfare of the whole empire. But the last statute respecting us, "grants to his Majesty the property of the colonies," by laying duties on the manufactures of Great–Britain which they MUST take, and which she settled on them, on purpose that they SHOULD take.

DOCUMENT 6

FIRST CONTINENTAL CONGRESS, DECLARATION AND RESOLVES,

OCTOBER 14, 1774

The first Continental Congress met at Philadelphia on September 5, 1774, in reaction to the "Intolerable Acts." All the colonies except Georgia were represented. A committee, which included John Adams, was appointed to draw up a declaration of the rights of the colonies. Adams drew up such a statement, and John Sullivan of New Hampshire prepared a list of cases in which they had been violated. The framers of the Declaration and Resolves were uncertain, according to Adams, as to whether they should "recur to the law of nature, as well as to the British constitution, and our American charters and grants." The radicals, including Adams, wanted to appeal to natural law; the conservatives held that the constitution offered guarantees enough. Adams chose to appeal to both. But, despite the reference to "the immutable laws of nature," the burden of the argument rests mainly on the appeal to constitutional and charter guarantees. The fourth resolution, with its strong repudiation of "every idea of taxation, internal or external," troubled the more conciliatory delegates. Joseph Galloway of Pennsylvania had proposed a plan for an American legislature under a crown-appointed executive, which was rejected by a vote of six colonies to five. In adopting this strong statement instead, the Americans served notice on Parliament that they no longer felt bound by any of its laws beyond those for "the regulation of our external commerce." This too had been much debated, for conservatives and radicals would not agree on "what authority we should concede to Parliament." Note that Parliament's regulation of commerce is something to which the delegates "cheerfully consent" because it is to their mutual ad-

vantage, not because it is conceded to be Parliament's rightful prerogative.

Whereas, since the close of the last war, the British parliament, claiming a power of right to bind the people of America, by statute in all cases whatsoever, hath, in some acts expressly imposed taxes on them, and in others, under various pretences, but in fact for the purpose of raising a revenue, hath imposed rates and duties payable in these colonies, established a board of commissioners with unconstitutional powers, and extended the jurisdiction of courts of Admiralty, not only for collecting the said duties, but for the trial of causes merely arising within the body of a county.

And whereas, in consequence of other statutes, judges, who before held only estates at will in their offices, have been made dependent on the Crown alone for their salaries, and standing armies kept in times of peace. And it has lately been resolved in Parliament, that by force of a statute made in the thirty-fifth year of the reign of king Henry the eighth, colonists may be transported to England, and tried there upon accusations for treasons, and misprisions, or concealments of treasons committed in the colonies; and by a late statute, such trials have been directed in cases therein mentioned.

And whereas, in the last session of parliament, three statutes were made . . . [the Boston Port Act, the Massachusetts Government Act, the Administration of Justice Act] And another statute was then made [the Quebec Act] . . . All which statutes are impolitic, unjust, and cruel, as well as unconstitutional, and most dangerous and destructive of American rights.

And whereas, Assemblies have been frequently dissolved, contrary to the rights of the people, when they attempted to deliberate on grievances; and their dutiful, humble, loyal, & reasonable petitions to the crown for redress, have been repeatedly treated with contempt, by his majesty's ministers of state:

The good people of the several Colonies of New-hampshire, Massachusetts-bay, Rhode-island and Providence plantations, Connecticut, New-York, New-Jersey, Pennsylvania, Newcastle, Kent and Sussex on Delaware,

Maryland, Virginia, North-Carolina, and South Carolina, justly alarmed at these arbitrary proceedings of parliament and administration, have severally elected, constituted, and appointed deputies to meet and sit in general congress, in the city of Philadelphia, in order to obtain such establishment, as that their religion, laws, and liberties, may not be subverted:

Whereupon the deputies so appointed being now assembled, in a full and free representation of these Colonies, taking into their most serious consideration, the best means of attaining the ends aforesaid, do, in the first place, as Englishmen, their ancestors in like cases have usually done, for asserting and vindicating their rights and liberties, declare,

That the inhabitants of the English Colonies in North America, by the immutable laws of nature, the principles of the English constitution, and the several charters or compacts, have the following Rights:

Resolved, N. C. D.

1. That they are entitled to life, liberty, and property, & they have never ceded to any sovereign power whatever, a right to dispose of either without their consent.

2. That our ancestors, who first settled these colonies, were at the time of their emigration from the mother country, entitled to all the rights, liberties, and immunities of free and natural-born subjects, within the realm of England.

3. That by such emigration they by no means forfeited, surrendered, or lost any of those rights, but that they were, and their descendants now are, entitled to the exercise and enjoyment of all such of them, as their local and other circumstances enable them to exercise and enjoy.

4. That the foundation of English liberty, and of all free government, is a right in the people to participate in their legislative council: and as the English colonists are not represented, and from their local and other circumstances, cannot properly be represented in the British parliament, they are entitled to a free and exclusive power of legislation in their several provincial legislatures, where their right of representation can alone be preserved, in all cases of taxation and internal polity, subject only to the

negative of their sovereign, in such manner as has been heretofore used and accustomed. But, from the necessity of the case, and a regard to the mutual interest of both countries, we cheerfully consent to the operation of such acts of the British parliament, as are bona fide, restrained to the regulation of our external commerce, for the purpose of securing the commercial advantages of the whole empire to the mother country, and the commercial benefits of its respective members; excluding every idea of taxation, internal or external, for raising a revenue on the subjects in America, without their consent.

5. That the respective colonies are entitled to the common law of England, and more especially to the great and inestimable privilege of being tried by their peers of the vicinage, according to the course of that law.

6. That they are entitled to the benefit of such of the English statutes as existed at the time of their colonization; and which they have, by experience, respectively found to be applicable to their several local and other circumstances.

7. That these, his majesty's colonies, are likewise entitled to all the immunities and privileges granted and confirmed to them by royal charters, or secured by their several codes of provincial laws.

8. That they have a right peaceably to assemble, consider of their grievances, and petition the King; and that all prosecutions, prohibitory proclamations, and commitments for the same, are illegal.

9. That the keeping a Standing army in these colonies, in times of peace, without the consent of the legislature of that colony, in which such army is kept, is against law.

10. It is indispensably necessary to good government, and rendered essential by the English constitution, that the constituent branches of the legislature be independent of each other; that, therefore, the exercise of legislative power in several colonies, by a council appointed, during pleasure, by the crown, is unconstitutional, dangerous, and destructive to the freedom of American legislation.

All and each of which the aforesaid deputies, in behalf of themselves and their constituents, do claim, demand, and insist on, as their indubitable rights and liberties; which cannot be legally taken from them, altered or abridged by any power whatever, without their own consent, by their representatives in their several provincial legislatures.

In the course of our inquiry, we find many infringments and violations of the foregoing rights, which, from an ardent desire that harmony and mutual intercourse of affection and interest may be restored, we pass over for the present, and proceed to state such acts and measures as have been adopted since the last war, which demonstrate a system formed to enslave America.

Resolved, That the following acts of Parliament are infringements and violations of the rights of the colonists; and that the repeal of them is essentially necessary in order to restore harmony between Great–Britain and the American colonies, . . . viz.:

The several Acts of 4 Geo. 3, ch. 15, & ch. 34; 5 Geo. 3, ch. 25; 6 Geo. 3, ch. 52; 7 Geo. 3, ch. 41 & 46; 8 Geo. 3, ch. 22; which impose duties for the purpose of raising a revenue in America, extend the powers of the admiralty courts beyond their ancient limits, deprive the American subject of trial by jury, authorize the judges' certificate to indemnify the prosecutor from damages that he might otherwise be liable to, requiring oppressive security from a claimant of ships and goods seized, before he shall be allowed to defend his property, and are subversive of American rights.

Also the 12 Geo. 3, ch. 24, entitled "An act for the better securing his Majesty's dockyards, magazines, ships, ammunition, and stores," which declares a new offense in America, and deprives the American subject of a constitutional trial by jury of the vicinage, by authorizing the trial of any person, charged with the committing any offense described in the said act, out of the realm, to be indicted and tried for the same in any shire or county within the realm.

Also the three acts passed in the last session of parliament, for stopping the port and blocking up the harbour of Boston, for altering the charter & government of the Massachusetts-bay, and that which is entitled "An Act for the better administration of Justice," &c.

Also the act passed the same session for establishing the Roman Catholick Religion in the province of Quebec, abolishing the equitable system of English laws, and erecting a tyranny there, to the great danger, from so total a dissimilarity of Religion, law, and government of the neighbouring British colonies. . . .

Also the act passed the same session for the better providing suitable quarters for officers and soldiers in his Majesty's service in North-America.

Also, that the keeping a standing army in several of these colonies, in time of peace, without the consent of the legislature of that colony in which the army is kept, is against law.

To these grievous acts and measures Americans cannot submit, but in hopes that their fellow subjects in Great-Britain will, on a revision of them, restore us to that state in which both countries found happiness and prosperity, we have for the present only resolved to pursue the following peaceable measures: . . . 1st. To enter into a non-importation, non-consumption, and non-exportation agreement or association. 2. To prepare an address to the people of Great-Britain, and a memorial to the inhabitants of British America, & 3. To prepare a loyal address to his Majesty; agreeable to resolutions already entered into.

DOCUMENT 7

DANIEL LEONARD, MASSACHUSETTENSIS,
JANUARY 9, 1775

Daniel Leonard, who lived in Taunton, Massachusetts, and practiced law in Boston, was one of the wealthiest and most aristocratic barristers of his day. John Adams marveled at his gold lace and magnificent coach, in which, Adams said, not another lawyer in the entire province could presume to ride. Leonard was thoroughly Tory in his views. In 1774 the patriots, outraged at his espousal of the cause of the crown, drove him from his Taunton home to find refuge in Boston. There, between December 1774 and April 1775, Leonard published a series of weekly "Letters Addressed to the Inhabitants of the Province of Massa-

chusetts Bay" in the Massachusetts Gazette, in which, under the pen name of Massachusettensis, he argued the case for submission to the crown and warned of the dangers of rebellion. These letters constitute one of the ablest statements of the Loyalist case by an American.

January 9, 1775

The security of the people from internal rapacity and violence, and from foreign invasion, is the end and design of government. The simple forms of government are monarchy, aristocracy and democracy, that is, where the authority of the state is vested in one, a few, or the many. Each of these species of government has advantages peculiar to itself, and would answer the ends of government, where the persons intrusted with the authority of the state, always guided themselves by unerring wisdom and public virtue; but rulers are not always exempt from the weakness and depravity which make government necessary to society. Thus monarchy is apt to rush headlong into tyranny, aristocracy to beget faction and multiplied usurpations, and democracy to degenerate into tumult, violence and anarchy. A government formed upon these three principles in due proportion, is the best calculated to answer the ends of government, and to endure. Such a government is the British constitution, consisting of King, Lords and Commons, which at once includes the principal excellencies, and excludes the principal defects of the other kinds of government. It is allowed, both by Englishmen and foreigners to be the most perfect system that the wisdom of ages has produced. The distributions of power are so just, and the proportions so exact, as at once to support and controul each other. An Englishman glories in being subject to, and protected by, such a government. The colonies are a part of the British empire. The best writers upon the law of nations, tell us, that when a nation takes possession of a distant country, and settles there, that country though separated from the principal establishment, or mother country, naturally becomes a part of the state, equal with its ancient possessions. Two supreme or independent authorities cannot exist in the same state. It would be what is called *imperium in imperio,* the height of political absurdity. The analogy between the political and human bodies is great. Two independent authorities in a state would be like two distinct principles of volition and action in the human body, dissenting, opposing and destroying each other. If then we are a part of the British empire, we must be subject to the supreme power of the state which is vested in the estates of parliament, notwithstanding each of the colonies have legislative and executive powers of their own, delegated or granted to them, for the purposes of regulating their own internal police, which are subordinate to, and must necessarily be subject to the checks, controul and regulation of the supreme authority of the state.

This doctrine is not new, but the denial of it is. It is beyond a doubt that it was the sense both of the parent country, and our ancestors, that they were to remain subject to parliament. It is evident from the charter itself, and this authority has been exercised by parliament, from time to time, almost ever since the first settlement of the country, and has been expressly acknowledged by our provincial legislatures. It is not less our interest, than our duty, to continue subject to the authority of parliament, which will be more fully considered hereafter. The principal argument against the authority of parliament, is this, the Americans are entitled to all the privileges of an Englishman, it is the privilege of an Englishman to be exempt from all laws that he does not consent to in person, or by representative; The Americans are not represented in parliament, and therefore are exempt from acts of parliament, or in other words, not subject to its authority. This appears specious; but leads to such absurdities as demonstrate its fallacy. If the colonies are not subject to the authority of parliament, Great–Britain and the colonies must be distinct states, as completely so as England and Scotland were before the union, or as Great–Britain and Hanover are now; The colonies in that case will owe no allegiance to the imperial crown, and perhaps not to the person of the King, as the title of the crown is derived from an act of parliament, made since the settlement of this province, which act respects the imperial crown only. Let us waive this difficulty, and suppose allegiance due from the colonies to the person of the King of Great–Britain, he then appears in a new capacity, of King of America, or rather in several new capacities, of King of Massachusetts, King of Rhode–Island, King of Connecticut, &c., &c. For if our connexion with Great–Britain by the parliament be dissolved, we shall have none among ourselves, but each colony become as distinct from the others, as England was from Scotland, before the union. . . . But let us suppose the same prerogatives inherent in the several American crowns, as are in the imperial crown of Great–Britain, where shall we find the British constitution that we all agree we are entitled to? We shall seek for it in vain in our provincial assemblies. They are but faint sketches of the estates of parliament. The houses of representatives, or Burgesses, have not all the powers of the House of Commons, in the charter governments they have no more than what is expressly granted by their several charters. The first charters granted to this province did not impower the assembly to tax the people at all. Our Council Boards are as destitute of the constitutional authority of the House of Lords, as their several members are of the noble independance and splendid appendages of Peerage. The House of Peers is the bulwark of the British constitution, and through successive ages, has withstood the shocks of monarchy, and the sappings of Democracy, and the constitution gained strength by the conflict. Thus the supposition of our being independent states, or exempt from the authority of parliament, destroys the very idea of our having a British constitution. The provincial constitutions, considered as subordinate, are generally well adapted to those purposes of government, for which they were intended, that is, to regulate the internal police of the several colonies; but have no principle of stability within themselves, they may support themselves in moderate times, but would be merged by the violence of turbulent ones, and the several colonies become wholly monarchial, or wholly republican, were it not for the checks, controuls, regulations, and support of the supreme authority of the empire. Thus the argument that is drawn from their first principle of our being entitled to English liberties, destroys the principle itself, it deprives us of the Bill of Rights, and all the benefits resulting from the revolution of English laws, and of the British constitution.

Our patriots have been so intent upon building up American rights, that they have overlooked the rights of Great—Britain, and our own interest. Instead of proving that we are entitled to privileges that our fathers knew our situation would not admit us to enjoy, they have been arguing away our most essential rights. If there be any grievance, it does not consist in our being subject to the authority of parliament, but in our not having an actual representation in it. Were it possible for the colonies to have an equal representation in Parliament, and were refused it upon proper application, I confess I should think it a grievance; but at present it seems to be allowed by all parties, to be impracticable, considering the colonies are distant from Great—Britain a thousand transmarine leagues. If that be the case, the right or privilege, that we complain of being deprived of, is not withheld by Britain, but the first principles of government, and the immutable laws of nature, render it impossible for us to enjoy it. . . . Allegiance and protection are reciprocal. It is our highest interest to continue a part of the British empire; and equally our duty to remain subject to the authority of parliament. Our own internal police may generally be regulated by our provincial legislatures, but in national concerns, or where our own assemblies do not answer the ends of government with respect to ourselves, the ordinance or interposition of the great council of the nation is necessary. In this case, the major must rule the minor. After many more centuries shall have rolled away, long after we, who are now bustling upon the stage of life, shall have been received to the bosom of mother earth, and our names are forgotten, the colonies may be so far increased as to have the balance of wealth, numbers and power, in their favour, the good of the empire make it necessary to fix the seat of government here; and some future George, equally the friend of mankind with him that now sways the British sceptre, may cross the Atlantic, and rule Great—Britain, by an American parliament.

DOCUMENT 8

JOHN ADAMS, NOVANGLUS,

FEBRUARY 6, 1775

This was part of John Adams's answer to Daniel Leonard's letters "On my return from Congress," Adams recalled, "I found the Massachusetts Gazette teeming with political speculations, and Massachusettensis shining like the moon among the lesser stars." He set to work at once to answer Leonard in his own series of letters, signing himself Novanglus. Adams here provides a forceful statement of the view many Americans had arrived at—that the authority of Parliament did not in any respect cross the ocean, and that the sole bond that united the colonists to Great Britain was a common loyalty to the crown. The remarks here quoted by Adams for the sake of refutation are all those of Daniel Leonard.

February 6, 1775.

I agree, that "two supreme and independent authorities cannot exist in the same state," any more than two supreme beings in one universe; And, therefore, I contend, that our provincial legislatures are the only supreme authorities in our colonies. Parliament, notwithstanding this, may be allowed an authority supreme and sovereign over the ocean, which may be limited by the banks of the ocean, or the bounds of our charters; our charters give us no authority over the high seas. Parliament has our consent to assume a jurisdiction over them. And here is a line fairly drawn between the rights of Britain and the rights of the colonies, namely, the banks of the ocean, or low-water mark; the line of division between common law, and civil or maritime law. . . .

"If then, we are a part of the British empire, we must be subject to the supreme power of the state, which is vested in the estates in parliament."

Here, again, we are to be conjured out of our senses

by the magic in the words "British empire," and "supreme power of the state." But, however it may sound, I say we are not a part of the British empire; because the British government is not an empire. The governments of France, Spain, &c. are not empires, but monarchies, supposed to be governed by fixed fundamental laws, though not really. The British government is still less entitled to the style of *an empire*. It is a limited monarchy. If Aristotle, Livy, and Harrington knew what a republic was, the British constitution is much more like a republic than an empire. They define a republic to be a *government of laws, and not of men*. If this definition is just, the British constitution is nothing more nor less than a republic, in which the king is first magistrate. This office being hereditary, and being possessed of such ample and splendid prerogatives, is no objection to the government's being a republic, as long as it is bound by fixed laws, which the people have a voice in making, and a right to defend. An empire is a despotism, and an emperor a despot, bound by no law or limitation but his own will; it is a stretch of tyranny beyond absolute monarchy. For, although the will of an absolute monarch is law, yet his edicts must be registered by parliaments. Even this formality is not necessary in an empire. . . .

"If the colonies are not subject to the authority of parliament, Great Britain and the colonies must be distinct states, as completely so as England and Scotland were before the union, or as Great Britain and Hanover are now." There is no need of being startled at this consequence. It is very harmless. There is no absurdity at all in it. Distinct states may be united under one king. And those states may be further cemented and united together by a treaty of commerce. This is the case. We have, by our own express consent, contracted to observe the Navigation Act, and by our implied consent, by long usage and uninterrupted acquiescence, have submitted to the other acts of trade, however grievous some of them may be. This may be compared to a treaty of commerce, by which those distinct states are cemented together, in perpetual league and amity. . . .

The only proposition in all this writer's long string of pretended absurdities, which he says follows from the position that we are distinct states, is this: That, "as the king must govern each state by its parliament, those several parliaments would pursue the particular interest of its own state; and however well disposed the king might be to pursue a line of interest that was common to all, the checks and control that he would meet with would render it impossible." Every argument ought to be allowed its full weight; and therefore candor obliges me to acknowledge, that here lies all the difficulty that there is in this whole controversy. There has been, from first to last, on both sides of the Atlantic, an idea, an apprehension that it was necessary there should be some superintending power, to draw together all the wills, and unite all the strength of the subjects in all the dominions, in case of war, and in the case of trade. The necessity of this, in case of trade, has been so apparent, that, as has often been said, we have consented that parliament should exercise such a power. In case of war, it has by some been thought necessary. But, in fact and experience, it has not been found so. . . . The inconveniences of this were small, in comparison of the absolute ruin to the liberties of all which must follow the submission to parliament, in all cases, which would be giving up all the popular limitations upon the government. . . .

But, admitting the proposition in its full force, that it is absolutely necessary there should be a supreme power, coextensive with all the dominions, will it follow that parliament, as now constituted, has a right to assume this supreme jurisdiction? By no means.

A union of the colonies might be projected, and an American legislature; for, if America has 3,000,000 people, and the whole dominions 12,000,000, she ought to send a quarter part of all the members to the house of commons; and instead of holding parliaments always at Westminister, the haughty members for Great Britain must humble themselves, one session in four, to cross the Atlantic, and hold the parliament in America.

There is no avoiding all inconveniences in human affairs. The greatest possible, or conceivable, would arise from ceding to parliament power over us without a representation in it. . . . The least of all would arise from going on as we began, and fared well for 150 years, by letting parliament regulate trade, and our own assemblies all other matters. . . .

But perhaps it will be said, that we are to enjoy the British constitution in our supreme legislature, the parliament, not in our provincial legislatures. To this I answer, if parliament is to be our supreme legislature, we shall be under a complete oligarchy or aristocracy, not the British constitution, which this writer himself defines a mixture of monarchy, aristocracy, and democracy. For king, lords, and commons, will constitute one great oligarchy, as they will stand related to America, as much as the decemvirs did in Rome; with this difference for the worse, that our rulers are to be three thousand miles off. . . . If our provincial constitutions are in any respect imperfect, and want alteration, they have capacity enough to discern it, and power enough to effect it, without interposition of parliament. . . . America will never allow that parliament has any authority to alter their constitution at all. She is wholly penetrated with a sense of the necessity of resisting it at all hazards. . . . The question we insist on most is, not whether the alteration is for the better or not, but whether parliament has any right to make any alteration at all. And it is the universal sense of America, that it has none. . . .

That a representation in parliament is impracticable, we all agree; but the consequence is, that we must have a representation in our supreme legislatures here. This was the consequence that was drawn by kings, ministers, our ancestors, and the whole nation, more than a century ago, when the colonies were first settled, and continued to be the general sense until the last peace; and it must be the general sense again soon, or Great Britain will lose her colonies. . . .

"It is our highest interest to continue a part of the British empire; and equally our duty to remain subject to the authority of parliament," says Massachusettensis.

We are a part of the British dominions, that is, of the King of Great Britain, and it is our interest and duty to continue so. It is equally our interest and duty to continue subject to the authority of parliament, in the regulation of our trade, as long as she shall leave us to govern our internal policy, and to give and grant our own money, and no longer. . . .

DOCUMENT 9

EDMUND BURKE, SPEECH ON CONCILIATION WITH AMERICA,

MARCH 22, 1775

Edmund Burke had become a Whig leader soon after his first speech in the House of Commons, delivered in January 1766. In October 1774, after he had been invited to stand for Parliament for the city of Bristol, he told his prospective constituents: "To reconcile British superiority with American liberty shall be my great object." Unlike Pitt and so many other contemporaries, Burke professed little interest in the much-argued abstract questions of right and constitutionality. He believed that, while Parliament had a right to tax the colonies, it was impracticable and inexpedient to do so. To attempt to crush American resistance would be disastrous to both British and American liberties, and he hoped not to risk such a disaster by an intransigent stand on the powers of Parliament. His famous speech on conciliation was inspired by Lord North's belated and inadequate conciliatory gesture—the offer to exempt from imperial taxation for revenue any colony that would voluntarily make a satisfactory offer for the support of civil and military government. Because this proposal did not specify the amounts which the various colonies might be expected to deliver, and because in the meantime the colonies were being held in duress with fleets and armies, Burke thought Lord North's gesture was ignominious—"a method of ransom by auction."

To restore order and repose to an empire so great and so distracted as ours is, merely in the attempt, an undertaking that would ennoble the flights of the highest genius, and obtain pardon for the efforts of the meanest understanding. Struggling a good while with these thoughts, by degrees I felt myself more firm. I derived, at length, some confidence from what in other circumstances usually produces timidity. I grew less anxious, even from the idea of my own insignificance. For, judging of what you are by what you ought to be, I persuaded myself that you would not reject a reasonable proposition because it had nothing but its reason to recommend it. . . .

The proposition is peace. Not peace through the medium of war; not peace to be hunted through the labyrinth of intricate and endless negotiations; not peace to arise out of universal discord, fomented from principle, in all parts of the empire; not peace to depend on the juridical determination of perplexing questions, or the precise marking the shadowy boundaries of a complex government. It is simple peace, sought in its natural course and in its ordinary haunts. . . .

Let the colonies always keep the idea of their civil rights associated with your government—they will cling and grapple to you, and no force under heaven will be of power to tear them from their allegiance. But let it be once understood that your government may be one thing and their privileges another, that these two things may exist without any mutual relation—the cement is gone, the cohesion is loosened, and everything hastens to decay and dissolution. As long as you have the wisdom to keep the sovereign authority of this country as the sanctuary of liberty, the sacred temple consecrated to our common faith, wherever the chosen race and sons of England worship freedom, they will turn their faces towards you. The more they multiply, the more friends you will have, the more ardently they love liberty, the more perfect will be their obedience. Slavery they can have anywhere. It is a weed that grows in every soil. They may have it from Spain, they may have it from Prussia. But until you become lost to all feeling of your true interest and your natural dignity, freedom they can have from none but you. This is the commodity of price, of which you have the monopoly. This is the true Act of Navigation, which binds to you the commerce of the colonies, and through them secures to you the wealth of the world. Deny them this participation of freedom, and you break that sole bond which originally made, and must still preserve, the unity of the empire. Do not entertain so weak an imagination as that your registers and your bonds, your affidavits and your sufferances, your cockets and your clearances, are what form the great securities of your commerce. Do not dream that your letters of office, and your instructions, and your suspending clauses are the things that hold together the great contexture of this mysterious whole. These things do not make your government. Dead instruments, passive tools as they are, it is the spirit of the English communion that gives all their life and efficacy to them. It is the spirit of the English constitution which, infused through the mighty mass, pervades, feeds, unites, invigorates, vivifies every part of the empire, even down to the minutest member.

Is it not the same virtue which does every thing for us here in England? Do you imagine, then, that it is the Land–Tax Act which raises your revenue? that it is the annual vote in the Committee of Supply, which gives you your army? or that it is the Mutiny Bill which inspires it with bravery and discipline? No! surely, no! It is the love of the people; it is their attachment to their government, from the sense of the deep stake they have in such a glorious institution, which gives you your army and your navy, and infuses into both that liberal obedience without which your army would be a base rabble and your navy nothing but rotten timber.

All this, I know well enough, will sound wild and chimerical to the profane herd of those vulgar and mechanical politicians who have no place among us: a sort of people who think that nothing exists but what is gross and material, and who, therefore, far from being qualified to be directors of the great movement of empire, are not fit to turn a wheel in the machine. But to men truly initiated and rightly taught, these ruling and master principles, which in the opinion of such men as I have mentioned have no substantial existence, are in truth everything, and all in all. Magnanimity in politics is not seldom the truest wisdom; and a great empire and little minds go ill together. If we are conscious of our situation, and glow with zeal to fill our places as becomes our station and ourselves, we ought to auspicate all our public proceedings on America with the old warning of the Church, *Sursum corda!* We ought to elevate our minds to the greatness of that trust to which the order of Providence has called us. By adverting to the dignity of this high calling, our ancestors have turned a savage wilderness into a glorious empire, and have made the most extensive and the only honorable conquests, not by destroying, but by promoting the wealth, the number, the happiness of the human race. Let us get an American revenue as we have got an American empire. English privileges have made it all that it is; English privileges alone will make it all it can be.

DOCUMENT 10

ADAM SMITH, THE COST OF EMPIRE, 1776

Adam Smith had retired from a professorship at Glasgow University and was living in France in 1764–5 when he began his great work, The Wealth of Nations. *The book was being written all during the years of strife between Britain and her colonies, but it was not published until 1776. In the passages which follow, Smith points to the impossibility of monopolizing the benefits of colonies, and pessimistically calculates the cost of empire, but the book appeared too late to have any effect upon British policy. Because the Declaration of Independence and* The Wealth of Nations, *the political and economic repudiations of empire and mercantilism, appeared in the same year, historians have often designated 1776 as one of the turning points in modern history. The end of this selection, the eloquent exhortation to the rulers of Britain to awaken from their grandiose dreams of empire, is the closing passage of Smith's book.*

The countries which possess the colonies of America, and which trade directly to the East Indies, enjoy, indeed, the whole show and splendour of this great commerce. Other countries, however, notwithstanding all the invidious restraints by which it is meant to exclude them, frequently enjoy a greater share of the real benefit of it. The colonies of Spain and Portugal, for example, give more real encouragement to the industry of other countries than to that of Spain and Portugal. . . .

After all the unjust attempts, therefore, of every country in Europe to engross to itself the whole advantage of the trade of its own colonies, no country has yet been able to engross to itself anything but the expense of supporting in time of peace, and of defending in time of war; the oppressive authority which it assumes over them. The inconveniencies resulting from the possession of its colonies, every country has engrossed to itself completely. The advantages resulting from their trade it has been obliged to share with many other countries.

At first sight, no doubt, the monopoly of the great commerce of America naturally seems to be an acquisition of the highest value. To the undiscerning eye of giddy ambition, it naturally presents itself amidst the confused scramble of politics and war, as a very dazzling object to fight for. The dazzling splendour of the object, however, the immense greatness of the commerce, is the very quality which renders the monopoly of it hurtful, or which makes one employment, in its own nature necessarily less advantageous to the country than the greater part of other employments, absorb a much greater proportion of the capital of the country than what would otherwise have gone to it. . . .

It is not contrary to justice that . . . America should contribute towards the discharge of the public debt of Great Britain. . . . a government to which several of the colonies of America owe their present charters, and consequently their present constitution; and to which all the colonies of America owe the liberty, security, and property which they have ever since enjoyed. That public debt has been contracted in the defence, not of Great Britain alone, but of all the different provinces of the empire; the immense debt contracted in the late war in particular, and a great part of that contracted in the war before, were both properly contracted in defence of America. . . .

If it should be found impracticable for Great Britain to draw any considerable augmentation of revenue from any of the resources above mentioned; the only resource which can remain to her is a diminution of her expense. In the mode of collecting, and in that of expending the public revenue; though in both there may be still room for improvement; Great Britain seems to be at least as economical as any of her neighbours. The military establishment which she maintains for her own defence in time of peace, is more moderate than that of any European state which can pretend to rival her either in wealth or in power. None of those articles, therefore, seem to admit of any considerable reduction of expense. The expense of the peace establishment of the colonies was, before the commencement of the present disturbances, very considerable, and is an expense which may, and if no revenue can be drawn from them ought certainly to be saved altogether. This constant expense in time of peace, though very great, is insignificant in comparison with what the defence of the colonies has cost us in time of war. The last war, which was undertaken altogether on account of the colonies, cost Great Britain . . . upwards of ninety millions. The Spanish war of 1739 was principally undertaken on their account; in which, and in the French war that was the consequence of it, Great Britain spent upwards of forty millions, a great part of which ought justly to be charged to the colonies. In those two wars the colonies cost Great Britain much more than double the sum which the national debt amounted to before the commencement of the first of them. Had it not been for those wars that debt might, and probably would by this time, have been completely paid; and had it not been for the colonies, the former of those wars might not, and the latter certainly would not have been undertaken. It was because the colonies were supposed to be provinces of the British empire, that this expense was laid out upon them. But countries which contribute neither revenue nor military force towards the support of the empire, cannot be considered as provinces. They may perhaps be considered as appendages, as a sort of splendid and showy equipage of the empire. But if the empire can no longer support the expense of keeping up this equipage, it ought certainly to lay it down; and if it cannot raise its revenue in proportion to its expense, it ought at least, to accommodate its expense to its revenue.

If the colonies, notwithstanding their refusal to submit to British taxes, are still to be considered as provinces of the British empire, their defence in some future war may cost Great Britain as great an expense as it ever has done in any former war. The rulers of Great Britain have, for more than a century past, amused the people with the imagination that they possessed a great empire on the west side of the Atlantic. This empire, however, has hitherto existed in imagination only. It has hitherto been, not an empire, but the project of an empire; not a gold mine, but the project of a gold mine; a project which has cost, which continues to cost, and which, if pursued in the same way as it has been hitherto, is likely to cost, immense expense, without being likely to bring any profit; for the effects of the monopoly of the colony trade, it has been shown, are, to the great body of the people, mere loss instead of profit. It is surely now time that our rulers should either realise this golden dream, in which they have been indulging themselves, perhaps, as well as the people; or, that they should awake from it themselves, and endeavour to awaken the people. If the project cannot be completed, it ought to be given up. If any of the provinces of the British empire cannot be made to contribute towards the support of the whole empire, it is surely time that Great Britain should free herself from the expense of defending those provinces in time of war, and of supporting any part of their civil or military establishments in time of peace, and endeavour to accommodate her future views and designs to the real mediocrity of her circumstances.

DOCUMENT 11

SECOND CONTINENTAL CONGRESS, DECLARATION OF THE CAUSES AND NECESSITY OF TAKING UP ARMS,

JULY 6, 1775

When the second Continental Congress convened in May 1775, the battles of Lexington and Concord had already been fought, and an informally organized

American army was besieging General Gage's troops in Boston. It now became imperative either to plan and justify further operations or to give in. The Americans chose continued resistance. This statement of their case as it stood after the beginning of hostilities was assigned to a seven-man committee, but was chiefly the work of Thomas Jefferson and John Dickinson.

If it was possible for men, who exercise their reason to believe, that the Divine Author of our existence intended a part of the human race to hold an absolute property in, and an unbounded power over others, marked out by his infinite goodness and wisdom, as the objects of a legal domination never rightfully resistible, however severe and oppressive, the Inhabitants of these Colonies might at least require from the parliament of Great Britain some evidence, that this dreadful authority over them, has been granted to that body. But a reverence for our great Creator, principles of humanity, and the dictates of common sense, must convince all those who reflect upon the subject, that government was instituted to promote the welfare of mankind, and ought to be administered for the attainment of that end. The legislature of Great Britain, however, stimulated by an inordinate passion for a power, not only unjustifiable, but which they know to be peculiarly reprobated by the very constitution of that kingdom, and desperate of success in any mode of contest, where regard should be had to truth, law, or right, have at length, deserting those, attempted to effect their cruel and impolitic purpose of enslaving these Colonies by violence, and have thereby rendered it necessary for us to close with their last appeal from Reason to Arms.—Yet, however blinded that assembly may be, by their intemperate rage for unlimited domination, so to slight justice and the opinion of mankind, we esteem ourselves bound, by obligations of respect to the rest of the world, to make known the justice of our cause.

Our forefathers, inhabitants of the island of Great Britain, left their native land, to seek on these shores a residence for civil and religious freedom. At the expense of their blood, at the hazard of their fortunes, without the least charge to the country from which they removed, by unceasing labour, and an unconquerable spirit, they effected settlements in the distant and inhospitable wilds of America, then filled with numerous and warlike nations of barbarians. Societies or governments, vested with perfect legislatures, were formed under charters from the crown, and an harmonious intercourse was established between the colonies and the kingdom from which they derived their origin. The mutual benefits of this union became in a short time so extraordinary, as to excite astonishment. It is universally confessed, that the amazing increase of the wealth, strength, and navigation of the realm, arose from this source; and the minister, who so wisely and successfully directed the measures of Great Britain in the late war, publicly declared, that these colonies enabled her to triumph over her enemies.—Towards the conclusion of that war, it pleased our sovereign to make a change in his counsels.—From that fatal moment, the affairs of the British empire began to fall into confusion, and gradually sliding from the summit of glorious prosperity, to which they had been advanced by the virtues and abilities of one man, are at length distracted by the convulsions, that now shake it to its deepest foundations. The new ministry finding the brave foes of Britain, though frequently defeated, yet still contending, took up the unfortunate idea of granting them a hasty peace, and of then subduing her faithful friends.

These devoted colonies were judged to be in such a state, as to present victories without bloodshed, and all the easy emoluments of statuteable plunder.—The uninterrupted tenor of their peaceable and respectful behaviour from the beginning of colonization, their dutiful, zealous, and useful services during the war, though so recently and amply acknowledged in the most honourable manner by his majesty, by the late king, and by Parliament, could not save them from the meditated innovations.—Parliament was influenced to adopt the pernicious project, and assuming a new power over them, have, in the course of eleven years, given such decisive specimens of the spirit and consequences attending this power, as to leave no doubt concerning the effects of acquiescence under it. They have undertaken to give and grant our money without our consent, though we have ever exercised an exclusive right to dispose of our own property; statutes have been passed for extending the jurisdiction of courts of Admiralty and Vice–Admiralty beyond their ancient limits; for depriving us of the accustomed and inestimable privilege of trial by jury, in cases affecting both life and property; for suspending the legislature of one of the colonies; for interdicting all commerce to the capital of another; and for altering fundamentally the form of government established by charter, and secured by acts of its own legislature solemnly confirmed by the crown; for exempting the "murderers" of colonists from legal trial, and in effect, from punishment; for erecting in a neighbouring province, acquired by the joint arms of Great Britain and America, a despotism dangerous to our very existence; and for quartering soldiers upon the colonists in time of profound peace. It has also been resolved in parliament, that colonists charged with committing certain offences, shall be transported to England to be tried.

But why should we enumerate our injuries in detail? By one statute it is declared, that parliament can "of right make laws to bind us IN ALL CASES WHATSOEVER." What is to defend us against so enormous, so unlimited a power? Not a single man of those who assume it, is chosen by us; or is subject to our controul or influence; but, on the contrary, they are all of them exempt from the operation of such laws, and an American revenue, if not diverted from the ostensible purposes for which it is raised, would actually lighten their own burdens in proportion as they increase ours. We saw the misery to which such despotism would reduce us. We for ten years incessantly and ineffectually besieged the Throne as supplicants; we reasoned, we remonstrated with parliament, in the most mild and decent language. But Administration, sensible that we should regard these oppressive measures as freemen ought to do, sent over fleets and armies to enforce them. The indignation of the Americans was roused, it is true; but it was the indignation of a virtuous, loyal, and affectionate people. A Congress of Delegates from the United Colonies was assembled at Philadelphia, on the fifth day of last September. We resolved again to offer an humble and dutiful petition to the King, and also addressed our fellow-subjects of Great Britain. We have pursued every temperate, every respectful measure: we have even proceeded to break off

our commercial intercourse with our fellow-subjects, as the
last peaceable admonition, that our attachment to no nation
upon earth should supplant our attachment to liberty.—
This, we flattered ourselves, was the ultimate step of the
controversy: But subsequent events have shewn, how vain
was this hope of finding moderation in our enemies. . . .

Fruitless were all the entreaties, arguments, and eloquence of an illustrious band of the most distinguished
Peers, and Commoners, who nobly and strenuously asserted
the justice of our cause, to stay, or even to mitigate the
heedless fury with which these accumulated and unexampled outrages were hurried on. . . .

General Gage . . . on the 19th day of April,
sent out from that place a large detachment of his army,
who made an unprovoked assault on the inhabitants of the
said province, [Massachusetts] at the town of Lexington, as
appears by the affidavits of a great number of persons, some
of whom were officers and soldiers of that detachment,
murdered eight of the inhabitants, and wounded many
others. From thence the troops proceeded in warlike array
to the town of Concord, where they set upon another party
of the inhabitants of the same province, killing several
and wounding more, until compelled to retreat by the
country people suddenly assembled to repel this cruel aggression. Hostilities, thus commenced by the British troops,
have been since prosecuted by them without regard to
faith or reputation.—The inhabitants of Boston being confined within that town by the General their Governor, and
having, in order to procure their dismission, entered into a
treaty with him, it was stipulated that the said inhabitants
having deposited their arms with their own magistrates,
should have liberty to depart, taking with them their other
effects. They accordingly delivered up their arms, but in
open violation of honour, in defiance of the obligation of
treaties, which even savage nations esteemed sacred, the
Governor ordered the arms deposited as aforesaid, that
they might be preserved for their owners, to be seized by
a body of soldiers; detained the greatest part of the inhabitants in the town, and compelled the few who were
permitted to retire, to leave their most valuable effects
behind. . . .

The General, further emulating his ministerial masters, by a proclamation bearing date on the 12th day of June, after venting the grossest falsehoods and calumnies against the good people of these colonies, proceeds to "declare them all, either by name or description, to be rebels and traitors, to supersede the course of the common law, and instead thereof to publish and order the use and exercise of the law martial."—His troops have butchered our countrymen, have wantonly burnt Charlestown, besides a considerable number of houses in other places; our ships and vessels are seized; the necessary supplies of provisions are intercepted, and he is exerting his utmost power to spread destruction and devastation around him.

We have received certain intelligence, that General Carleton, the Governor of Canada, is instigating the people of that province and the Indians to fall upon us; and we have but too much reason to apprehend, that schemes have been formed to excite domestic enemies against us. In brief, a part of these colonies now feels and all of them are sure of feeling, as far as the vengance of administration can inflict them, the complicated calamities of fire, sword, and famine.—We are reduced to the alternative of chusing an unconditional submission to the tyranny of irritated ministers, or resistance by force.— The latter is our choice.—We have counted the cost of this contest, and find nothing so dreadful as voluntary slavery.—Honor, justice, and humanity, forbid us tamely to surrender that freedom which we received from our gallant ancestors, and which our innocent posterity have a right to receive from us. We cannot endure the infamy and guilt of resigning succeeding generations to that wretchedness which inevitably awaits them, if we basely entail hereditary bondage upon them.

Our cause is just. Our union is perfect. Our internal resources are great, and, if necessary, foreign assistance is undoubtedly attainable.—We gratefully acknowledge, as signal instances of the Divine favour towards us, that his Providence would not permit us to be called into this severe controversy, until we were grown up to our present strength, had been previously exercised in warlike operation, and possessed of the means of defending ourselves.— With hearts fortified with these animating reflections, we most solemnly, before God and the world, declare, that, exerting the utmost energy of those powers, which our beneficent Creator hath graciously bestowed upon us, the arms we have been compelled by our enemies to assume, we will, in defiance of every hazard, with unabating firmness and perseverance, employ for the preservation of our liberties; being with our [one] mind resolved to die freemen rather than to live Slaves.

Lest this declaration should disquiet the minds of our friends and fellow–subjects in any part of the empire, we assure them that we mean not to dissolve that Union which has so long and so happily subsisted between us, and, which we sincerely wish to see restored.—Necessity has not yet driven us into that desperate measure, or induced us to excite any other nation to war against them.— We have not raised armies with ambitious designs of separating from Great Britain, and establishing independent states. We fight not for glory or for conquest. We exhibit to mankind the remarkable spectacle of a people attacked by unprovoked enemies, without any imputation or even suspicion of offence. They boast of their privileges and civilization, and yet proffer no milder conditions than servitude or death.

In our own native land, in defence of the freedom that is our birth–right, and which we ever enjoyed till the late violation of it—for the protection of our property, acquired solely by the honest industry of our fore–fathers and ourselves, against violence actually offered, we have taken up arms. We shall lay them down when hostilities shall cease on the part of the aggressors, and all danger of their being renewed shall be removed, and not before.

With an humble confidence in the mercies of the supreme and impartial Judge and Ruler of the universe, we most devoutly implore his divine goodness to protect us happily through this great conflict, to dispose our adversaries to reconciliation on reasonable terms, and thereby to relieve the empire from the calamities of civil war.

By order of Congress
JOHN HANCOCK
President.

DOCUMENT 12

THOMAS PAINE, *COMMON SENSE,*
1776

Many men were talking about independence and a few wrote about it before Thomas Paine's Common Sense *appeared early in 1776. But no appeal for independence had an influence remotely comparable to that of this document, which quickly sold about 150,000 copies. Paine, by his own account, was half finished with the work in October 1775, when Benjamin Franklin offered Paine some of his own materials on the struggle then raging. ". . . as I supposed the doctor's design in getting out a history was to open the new year with a new system, I expected to surprise him with a production on that subject much earlier than he thought of; and without informing him of what I was doing, got it ready for the press as fast as I conveniently could, and sent him the first pamphlet that was printed off." Two republican scientists and fellow members of the American Philosophical Society, Benjamin Rush and David Rittenhouse, seem to have been among the very few contemporaries who knew of the work during its composition. Paine had read each part to Rush as he composed it. Rush claimed that he suggested the title and arranged publication. In the* Crisis, *a pamphlet published the following year, Paine summed up his own argument as follows: "The principal arguments in support of independence may be comprehended under the four following heads: 1st, The natural right of the continent to independence; 2d, Her interest in being independent; 3d, The necessity;—and 4th, The moral advantages arising therefrom." The sections excerpted here deal not with Paine's general political theory but with his application of it to the events of the hour.*

Volumes have been written on the subject of the struggle between England and America. Men of all ranks have embarked in the controversy, from different motives, and with various designs: but all have been ineffectual, and the period of debate is closed. Arms as a last resource decide the contest; the appeal was the choice of the king, and the continent has accepted the challenge. . . .

As much has been said of the advantages of reconciliation, which, like an agreeable dream, has passed away and left us as we were, it is but right that we should examine the contrary side of the argument, and inquire into some of them any material injuries which these colonies sustain, and always will sustain, by being connected with and dependent on Great Britain. To examine that connection and dependence on the principles of nature and common sense; to see what we have to trust to, if separated, and what we are to expect, if dependent.

I have heard it asserted by some, that as America hath flourished under her former connection with Great Britain, the same connection is necessary towards her future happiness, and will always have the same effect. Nothing can be more fallacious than this kind of argument. We may as well assert that because a child has thriven upon milk, that it is never to have meat, or that the first twenty years of our lives is to become a precedent for the next twenty. But even this is admitting more than is true; for I answer roundly, that America would have flourished as much, and probably much more, had no European power taken any notice of her. The commerce by which she hath enriched herself are the necessaries of life, and will always have a market while eating is the custom of Europe.

But she has protected us, say some. That she hath engrossed us is true, and defended the continent at our expense as well as her own is admitted; and she would have defended Turkey from the same motive, viz., for the sake of trade and dominion.

Alas! we have been long led away by ancient prejudices, and made large sacrifices to superstition. We have boasted the protection of Great Britain without considering that her motive was *interest,* not *attachment*; and that she did not protect us from *our enemies* on *our account,* but from her enemies on her own account, from those who had no quarrel with us on any *other account,* but who will always be our enemies on the *same account*. Let Britain waive her pretensions to the continent, or the continent throw off the dependence, and we should be at peace with France and Spain were they at war with Britain. The miseries of Hanover's last war ought to warn us against connections.

It hath lately been asserted in parliament, that the colonies have no relation to each other but through the parent country, *i.e.,* that Pennsylvania and the Jerseys, and so on for the rest, are sister colonies by way of England; this is certainly a very roundabout way of proving relationship, but it is the nearest and only true way of proving enmity (or enemyship, if I may so call it). France and Spain never were, nor perhaps ever will be our enemies as *Americans,* but as our being the *subjects of Great Britain.*

But Britain is the parent country, say some. Then the more shame upon her conduct. Even brutes do not devour their young, nor savages make war upon their families; wherefore, the assertion, if true, turns to her reproach; but it happens not to be true, or only partly so, and the phrase *parent* or *mother country* hath been jesuitically adopted by the king and his parasites, with a low papistical design of gaining an unfair bias on the credulous weakness of our minds. Europe, and not England, is the parent country of America. This new world hath been the asylum for the persecuted lovers of civil and religious liberty from *every part* of Europe. Hither have they fled, not from the tender embraces of a mother, but from the cruelty of the monster; and it is so far true of England, that the same tyranny which drove the first emigrants from home, pursues their descendants still.

In this extensive quarter of the globe, we forget the narrow limits of three hundred and sixty miles (the extent of England) and carry our friendship on a larger scale; we claim brotherhood with every European Christian, and triumph in the generosity of the sentiment. . . .

I challenge the warmest advocate for reconciliation to show a single advantage that this continent can reap, by being connected with Great Britain. I repeat the challenge, not a single advantage is derived. Our corn will fetch its price in any market in Europe, and our imported goods must be paid for, buy them where we will.

But the injuries and disadvantages we sustain by that connection are without number; and our duty to mankind at large, as well as to ourselves, instructs us to renounce the alliance: because any submission to, or dependence on, Great Britain, tends directly to involve this continent in European wars and quarrels, and sets us at variance with nations who would otherwise seek our friendship, and against whom we have neither anger nor complaint. As Europe is our market for trade, we ought to form no partial connection with any part of it. 'Tis the true interest of America to steer clear of European contentions, which she never can do while by her dependence on Britain she is made the makeweight in the scale of British politics.

Europe is too thickly planted with kingdoms to be long at peace, and whenever a war breaks out between England and any foreign power, the trade of America goes to ruin, *because of her connection with Britain*. The next war may not turn out like the last, and should it not, the advocates for reconciliation now will be wishing for separation then, because neutrality in that case would be a safer convoy than a man of war. Everything that is right or natural pleads for separation. The blood of the slain, the weeping voice of nature cries, 'TIS TIME TO PART. Even the distance at which the Almighty hath placed England and America is a strong and natural proof that the authority of the one over the other, was never the design of heaven. The time likewise at which the continent was discovered, adds weight to the argument, and the manner in which it was peopled, increases the force of it. The Reformation was preceded by the discovery of America, as if the Almighty graciously meant to open a sanctuary to the persecuted in future years, when home should afford neither friendship nor safety.

The authority of Great Britain over this continent is a form of government which sooner or later must have an end. And a serious mind can draw no true pleasure by looking forward, under the painful and positive conviction that what he calls "the present constitution" is merely temporary. . . .

Though I would carefully avoid giving unnecessary offense, yet I am inclined to believe, that all those who espouse the doctrine of reconciliation may be included within the following descriptions: Interested men, who are not to be trusted, weak men who *cannot* see, prejudiced men, who *will not* see, and a certain set of moderate men who think better of the European world than it deserves; and this last class, by an ill-judged deliberation, will be the cause of more calamities to this continent than all of the other three.

It is the good fortune of many to live distant from the scene of present sorrow; the evil is not sufficiently brought to *their* doors to make *them* feel the precariousness with which all American property is possessed. But let our imaginations transport us for a few moments to Boston; that seat of wretchedness will teach us wisdom, and instruct us forever to renounce a power in whom we can have no trust. The inhabitants of that unfortunate city, who but a few months ago were in ease and affluence, have now no other alternative than to stay and starve, or turn out to beg. Endangered by the fire of their friends if they continue within the city, and plundered by the soldiery if they leave it, in their present situation they are prisoners without the hope of redemption, and in a general attack for their relief they would be exposed to the fury of both armies. . . .

But if you say, you can still pass the violations over, then I ask, Hath your house been burnt? Hath your property been destroyed before your face? Are your wife and children destitute of a bed to lie on, or bread to live on? Have you lost a parent or a child by their hands, and yourself the ruined and wretched survivor? If you have not, then you are not a judge of those who have. But if you have, and can still shake hands with the murderers, then you are unworthy the name of husband, father, friend, or lover; and whatever may be your rank or title in life, you have the heart of a coward, and the spirit of a sycophant.

This is not inflaming or exaggerating matters, but

trying them by those feelings and affections which nature justifies, and without which we should be incapable of discharging the social duties of life, or enjoying the felicities of it. I mean not to exhibit horror for the purpose of provoking revenge, but to awaken us from fatal and unmanly slumbers, that we may pursue determinately some fixed object. 'Tis not in the power of England or of Europe to conquer America, if she does not conquer herself by *delay* and *timidity*. The present winter is worth an age if rightly employed, but if lost or neglected the whole continent will partake of the misfortune; and there is no punishment which that man doth not deserve, be he who, or what, or where he will, that may be the means of sacrificing a season so precious and useful. . . .

Every quiet method for peace hath been ineffectual. Our prayers have been rejected with disdain; and have tended to convince us that nothing flatters vanity or confirms obstinacy in kings more than repeated petitioning—and nothing hath contributed more than that very measure to make the kings of Europe absolute. Witness Denmark and Sweden. Wherefore, since nothing but blows will do, for God's sake let us come to a final separation, and not leave the next generation to be cutting throats under the violated unmeaning names of parent and child.

To say they will never attempt it again is idle and visionary; we thought so at the repeal of the stamp act, yet a year or two undeceived us; as well may we suppose that nations which have been once defeated will never renew the quarrel.

As to government matters, it is not in the power of Britain to do this continent justice: the business of it will soon be too weighty and intricate to be managed with any tolerable degree of convenience, by a power so distant from us, and so very ignorant of us; for if they cannot conquer us, they cannot govern us. To be always running three or four thousand miles with a tale or a petition, waiting four or five months for an answer, which, when obtained, requires five or six more to explain it in, will in a few years be looked upon as folly and childishness. There was a time when it was proper, and there is a proper time for it to cease.

Small islands not capable of protecting themselves are the proper objects for kingdoms to take under their care; but there is something very absurd in supposing a continent to be perpetually governed by an island. In no instance hath nature made the satellite larger than its primary planet; and as England and America, with respect to each other, reverse the common order of nature, it is evident that they belong to different systems. England to Europe: America to itself. . . .

But admitting that matters were now made up, what would be the event? I answer, the ruin of the continent.- And that for several reasons.

First. The powers of governing still remaining in the hands of the king, he will have a negative over the whole legislation of the continent. And as he hath shown himself such an inveterate enemy to liberty, and discovered such a thirst for arbitrary power, is he, or is he not, a proper person to say to these colonies, *You shall make no laws but what I please!* And is there any inhabitant in America so ignorant as not to know, that according to what is called the *present constitution,* this continent can make no laws but what the King gives leave to; and is there any man so unwise as not to see, that (considering what has happened) he will suffer no law to be made here but such as suits *his* purpose? We may be as effectually enslaved by the want of laws in America, as by submitting to laws made for us in England. After matters are made up (as it is called), can there be any doubt but the whole power of the Crown will be exerted to keep this continent as low and humble as possible? Instead of going forward we shall go backward, or be perpetually quarreling, or ridiculously petitioning. We are already greater than the King wishes us to be, and will he not hereafter endeavor to make us less? To bring the matter to one point, Is the power who is jealous of our prosperity, a proper power to govern us? Whoever says *No* to this question is an *independent,* for independency means no more than this, whether we shall make our own laws, or whether the king, the greatest enemy which this continent hath, or can have, shall tell us, *There shall be no laws but such as I like.*

But the King, you'll say, has a negative in England; the people there can make no laws without his consent. In point of right and good order, it is something very ridiculous that a youth of twenty-one (which hath often happened) shall say to several millions of people, older and wiser than himself, "I forbid this or that act of yours to be law." But in this place I decline this sort of reply, though I will never cease to expose the absurdity of it, and only answer that England being the king's residence and America not so, makes quite another case. The king's negative here is ten times more dangerous and fatal than it can be in England; for *there* he will scarcely refuse his consent to a bill for putting England into as strong a state of defense as possible, and in America he would never suffer such a bill to be passed. . . .

Secondly. That as even the best terms which we can expect to obtain can amount to no more than a temporary expedient, or a kind of government by guardianship, which can last no longer than till the colonies come of age, so the general face and state of things in the interim will be unsettled and unpromising. Emigrants of property will not choose to come to a country whose form of government hangs but by a thread, and who is every day tottering on the brink of commotion and disturbance; and numbers of the present inhabitants would lay hold of the interval to dispose of their effects, and quit the continent.

But the most powerful of all arguments is, that nothing but independence, *i.e.* a continental form of government, can keep the peace of the continent and preserve it inviolate from civil wars. I dread the event of a reconciliation with Britain *now,* as it is more than probable that it will be followed by a revolt somewhere or other, the consequences of which may be far more fatal than all the malice of Britain.

Thousands are already ruined by British barbarity; (thousands more will probably suffer the same fate). Those men have other feelings than us who have nothing suffered. All they *now* possess is liberty; what they before enjoyed is sacrificed to its service, and having nothing more to lose, they disdain submission. . . .

But where, say some, is the king of America? I'll tell you, friend, he reigns above, and doth not make havoc of mankind like the Royal Brute of Great Britain. Yet that we may not appear to be defective even in earthly honors, let a day be solemnly set apart for proclaiming the charter; let it be brought forth placed on the divine law, the Word of God; let a crown be placed thereon, by which the world may know, that so far as we approve of monarchy, that in America THE LAW IS KING. For as in absolute governments the king is law, so in free countries the law *ought* to BE king, and there ought to be no other. But lest any ill use should afterwards arise, let the crown at the conclusion of the ceremony be demolished, and scattered among the people whose right it is.

A government of our own is our natural right; and when a man seriously reflects on the precariousness of human affairs, he will become convinced, that it is infinitely wiser and safer to form a constitution of our own in a cool deliberate manner, while we have it in our power, than to trust such an interesting event to time and chance. . . .

Ye that tell us of harmony and reconciliation, can ye restore to us the time that is passed? Can ye give to prostitution its former innocence? Neither can ye reconcile Britain and America. The last cord now is broken; the people of England are presenting addresses against us. There are injuries which nature cannot forgive; she would cease to be nature if she did. As well can the lover forgive the ravisher of his mistress, as the continent forgive the murders of Britain. The Almighty hath implanted in us these unextinguishable feelings for good and wise purposes. They are the guardians of his image in our hearts. They distinguish us from the herd of common animals. The social compact would dissolve, and justice be extirpated from the earth, or have only a casual existence, were we callous to the touches of affection. The robber and the murderer would often escape unpunished, did not the injuries which our tempers sustain, provoke us into justice.

O ye that love mankind! Ye that dare oppose not only the tyranny but the tyrant, stand forth! Every spot of the old world is overrun with oppression. Freedom hath been hunted round the globe. Asia and Africa have long expelled her. Europe regards her like a stranger, and England hath given her warning to depart. O receive the fugitive, and prepare in time an asylum for mankind.

DOCUMENT 13

CHARLES INGLIS, *THE TRUE INTEREST OF AMERICA IMPARTIALLY STATED.*
1776

One of the best evidences of the power of Paine's Common Sense is the number of Loyalists who leaped to the counterattack. Some of these are better known to history than the Anglican clergyman Charles Inglis, but none made a more succinct statement of the forebodings of Loyalists. His anonymous counterblast against Paine was entitled, The True Interest of America Impartially Stated in Certain Strictures on a Pamphlet Intitled Common Sense. *Inglis had come to live in America in 1755 and, at the outbreak of hostilities, was attached to Trinity Church in New York City. Throughout the war he kept writing essays intended to convince the patriots that they were on the wrong track. But in 1783, when he was about to sail for exile in England, he declared: "I do not leave behind me an individual, against whom I have the smallest degree of resentment or ill–will."*

I think it no difficult matter to point out many advantages which will certainly attend our reconciliation and connection with Great–Britain, on a firm, constitutional plan. I shall select a few of these; and that their importance may be more clearly discerned, I shall afterwards point out some of the evils which inevitably must attend our separating from Britain, and declaring for independency. On each article I shall study brevity.

    1. By a reconciliation with Britain, a period would be put to the present calamitous war, by which so many lives have been lost, and so many more must be lost, if it continues. This alone is an advantage devoutly to be wished for. This author [Paine] says—"The blood of

the slain, the weeping voice of nature cries, 'Tis time to part." I think they cry just the reverse. The blood of the slain, the weeping voice of nature cries—It is time to be reconciled; it is time to lay aside those animosities which have pushed on Britons to shed the blood of Britons; it is high time that those who are connected by the endearing ties of religion, kindred and country, should resume their former friendship, and be united in the bond of mutual affection, as their interests are inseparably united.

2. By a Reconciliation with Great–Britain, Peace— that fairest offspring and gift of Heaven—will be restored. In one respect Peace is like health; we do not sufficiently know its value but by its absence. What uneasiness and anxiety, what evils, has this short interruption of peace with the parent-state, brought on the whole British empire! Let every man only consult his feelings—I except my antagonist—and it will require no great force of rhetoric to convince him, that a removal of those evils, and a restoration of peace, would be a singular advantage and blessing.

3. Agriculture, commerce, and industry would resume their wonted vigor. At present, they languish and droop, both here and in Britain; and must continue to do so, while this unhappy contest remains unsettled.

4. By a connection with Great–Britain, our trade would still have the protection of the greatest naval power in the world. England has the advantage, in this respect, of every other state, whether of ancient or modern times. Her insular situation, her nurseries for seamen, the superiority of those seamen above others—these circumstances to mention no other, combine to make her the first maritime power in the universe—such exactly is the power whose protection we want for our commerce. To suppose, with our author, that we should have no war, were we to revolt from England, is too absurd to deserve a confutation. I could just as soon set about refuting the reveries of some brain-sick enthusiast. Past experience shews that Britain is able to defend our commerce, and our coasts; and we have no reason to doubt of her being able to do so for the future.

5. The protection of our trade, while connected with Britain, will not cost us a *fiftieth* part of what it must cost,

were we ourselves to raise a naval force sufficient for this purpose.

6. Whilst connected with Great–Britain, we have a bounty on almost every article of exportation; and we may be better supplied with goods by her, than we could elsewhere. What our author says is true—"that our imported goods must be paid for, buy them where we will"; but we may buy them dearer, and of worse quality, in one place than another. The manufactures of Great–Britain confessedly surpass any in the world—particularly those in every kind of metal, which we want most; and no country can afford linens and woollens, of equal quality cheaper.

7. When a Reconciliation is effected, and things return into the old channel, a few years of peace will restore everything to its pristine state. Emigrants will flow in as usual from the different parts of Europe. Population will advance with the same rapid progress as formerly, and our lands will rise in value.

These advantages are not imaginary but real. They are such as we have already experienced; and such as we may derive from a connection with Great Britain for ages to come. Each of these might easily be enlarged on, and others added to them; but I only mean to suggest a few hints to the reader.

Let us now, if you please, take a view of the other side of the question. Suppose we were to revolt from Great–Britain, declare ourselves Independent, and set up a Republic of our own—what would be the consequence?— I stand aghast at the prospect—my blood runs chill when I think of the calamities, the complicated evils that must ensue, and may be clearly foreseen—it is impossible for any man to foresee them all. . . .

1. All our property throughout the continent would be unhinged; the greatest confusion, and most violent convulsions would take place. It would not be here, as it was in England at the Revolution in 1688. That revolution was not brought about by an defeazance or disannulling the right of succession. James II, by abdicating the throne, left it vacant for the next in succession; acordingly his eldest daughter and her husband stept in. Every other matter went on in the usual, regular way; and the constitution, instead of being dissolved, was strengthened.

But in case of our revolt, the old constitution would be totally subverted. The common bond that tied us together, and by which our property was secured, would be snapt asunder. It is not to be doubted but our Congress would endeavor to apply some remedy for those evils; but with all deference to that respectable body, I do not apprehend that any remedy in their power would be adequate, at least for some time. I do not chuse to be more explicit; but I am able to support my opinion.

2. What a horrid situation would thousands be reduced to who have taken the oath of allegiance to the King; yet contrary to their oath, as well as inclination, must be compelled to renounce that allegiance, or abandon all their property in America! How many thousands more would be reduced to a similar situation; who, although they took not that oath, yet would think it inconsistent with their duty and a good conscience to renounce their Sovereign; I dare say these will appear trifling difficulties to our author; but whatever he may think, there are thousands and thousands who would sooner lose all they had in the world, nay life itself, than thus wound their conscience. A Declaration of Independency would infallibly disunite and divide the colonists.

3. By a Declaration for Independency, every avenue to an accommodation with Great–Britain would be closed; the sword only could then decide the quarrel; and the sword would not be sheathed till one had conquered the other.

The importance of these colonies to Britain need not be enlarged on, it is a thing so universally known. The greater their importance is to her, so much the more obstinate will her struggle be not to lose them. The independency of America would, in the end, deprive her of the West–Indies, shake her empire to the foundation, and reduce her to a state of the most mortifying insignificance. Great–Britain therefore must, for her own preservation, risk every thing, and exert her whole strength, to prevent such an event from taking place. This being the case—

4. Devastation and ruin must mark the progress of this war along the sea coast of America. Hitherto, Britain has not exerted her power. Her number of troops and ships

of war here at present, is very little more than she judged expedient in time of peace—the former does not amount to 12,000 men—nor the latter to 40 ships, including frigates. Both she, and the colonies, hoped for and expected an accommodation; neither of them has lost sight of that desirable object. The seas have been open to our ships; and although some skirmishes have unfortunately happened, yet a ray of hope still cheered both sides that, peace was not distant. But as soon as we declare for independency, every prospect of this kind must vanish. Ruthless war, with all its aggravated horrors, will ravage our once happy land—our seacoasts and ports will be ruined, and our ships taken. Torrents of blood will be split, and thousands reduced to beggary and wretchedness.

This melancholy contest would last till one side conquered. Supposing Britain to be victorious; however high my opinion is of British Generosity, I should be exceedingly sorry to receive terms from her in the haughty tone of a conqueror. Or supposing such a failure of her manufactures, commerce and strength, that victory should incline to the side of America; yet who can say in that case, what extremities her sense of resentment and self-preservation will drive Great–Britain to? For my part, I should not in the least be surprized, if on such a prospect as the Independency of America, she would parcel out this continent to the different European Powers. Canada might be restored to France, Florida to Spain, with additions to each—other states also might come in for a portion. Let no man think this chimerical or improbable. The independency of America would be so fatal to Britain, that she would leave nothing in her power undone to prevent it. I believe as firmly as I do my own existence, that if every other method failed, she would try some such expedient as this, to disconcert our scheme of independency; and let any man figure to himself the situation of these British colonies, if only Canada were restored to France!

5. But supposing once more that we were able to cut off every regiment that Britain can spare or hire, and to destroy every ship she can send—that we could beat off any other European power that would presume to intrude upon this continent: Yet, a republican form of government

would neither suit the genius of the people, nor the extent of America.

In nothing is the wisdom of a legislator more conspicuous than in adapting his government to the genius, manners, disposition and other circumstances of the people with whom he is concerned. If this important point is overlooked, confusion will ensue; his system will sink into neglect and ruin. Whatever check or barriers may be interposed, nature will always surmount them, and finally prevail. It was chiefly by attention to this circumstance, that Lycurgus and Solon were so much celebrated; and that their respective republics rose afterwards to such eminence, and acquired such stability.

The Americans are properly Britons. They have the manners, habits, and ideas of Britons; and have been accustomed to a similar form of government. But Britons never could bear the extremes, either of monarchy or republicanism. Some of their Kings have aimed at despotism; but always failed. Repeated efforts have been made towards democracy, and they equally failed. Once indeed republicanism triumphed over the constitution; the despotism of one person ensued; both were finally expelled. The inhabitants of Great–Britain were quite anxious for the restoration of *royalty* in 1660, as they were for its expulsion in 1642, and for some succeeding years. If we may judge of future events by past transactions, in similar circumstances, this would most probably be the case of America, were a republican form of government adopted in our present ferment. After much blood was shed, those confusions would terminate in the despotism of some one successful adventurer; and should the Americans be so fortunate as to emancipate themselves from that thraldom, perhaps the whole would end in a limited monarchy, after shedding as much more blood. Limited monarchy is the form of government which is most favourable to liberty —which is best adapted to the genius and temper of Britons; although here and there among us a crackbrained zealot for democracy or absolute monarchy, may be sometimes found.

Besides the unsuitableness of the republican form to the genius of the people, America is too extensive for it. That form may do well enough for a single city, or small territory; but would be utterly improper for such a continent as this. America is too unwieldy for the feeble, dilatory administration of democracy. Rome had the most extensive dominions of any ancient republic. But it should be remembered, that very soon after the spirit of conquest carried the Romans beyond the limits that were proportioned to their constitution, they fell under a despotic yoke. A very few years had elapsed from the time of their conquering Greece and first entering Asia, till the battle of Pharsalia, where Julius Caesar put an end to the liberties of his country. . . .

But here it may be said—*That all the evils above specified, are more tolerable than slavery*. With this sentiment I sincerely agree—any hardships, however great, are preferable to slavery. But then I ask, is there no other alternative in the present case? Is there no choice left us but slavery, or those evils? I am confident there is; and that both may be equally avoided. Let us only shew a disposition to treat or negociate in earnest—let us fall upon some method to set a treaty or negociation with Great Britain on foot; and if once properly begun, there is moral certainty that this unhappy dispute will be settled to the mutual satisfaction and interest of both countries. For my part, I have not the least doubt about it. . . .

But a Declaration for Independency on the part of America, would preclude treaty intirely; and could answer no good purpose. We actually have already every advantage of Independency, without its inconveniences. By a Declaration of Independency, we should instantly lose all assistance from our friends in England. It would stop their mouths; for were they to say any thing in our favour, they would be deemed rebels, and treated accordingly.

Our author is much elated with the prospect of foreign succour, if we once declare ourselves Independent; and from thence promiseth us mighty matters. This, no doubt, is intended to spirit up the desponding—all who might shrink at the thought of America encountering, singly and unsupported, the whole strength of Great–Britain. I believe in my conscience, that he is as much mistaken in this, as in any thing else; and that this expectation is delusive, vain and fallacious. My reasons are these, and I submit them to the reader's judgment.

The only European power from which we can possibly receive assistance, is France. But France is now at peace with Great–Britain; and is it possible that France would interrupt that peace, and hazard a war with the power which lately reduced her so low, from a *disinterested* motive of aiding and protecting these Colonies? . . .

It is well known that some of the French and Spanish Colonists, not long since, offered to put themselves under the protection of England, and declare themselves Independent of France and Spain; but England rejected both offers. The example would be rather dangerous to states that have colonies—to none could it be more so than to France and Spain, who have so many and such extensive colonies. "The practice of courts are as much against us" in this, as in the instance our author mentions. Can any one imagine, that because we declared ourselves Independent of England, France would *therefore* consider us as really Independent! And before England had acquiesced, or made any effort worth mentioning to reduce us? Or can any one be so weak as to think, that France would run the risque of a war with England, unless she (France) were sure of some extraordinary advantage by it, in having the colonies under her *immediate jurisdiction?* If England will not protect us for our trade, surely France will not. . . .

America is far from being yet in a desperate situation. I am confident she may obtain honourable and advantageous terms from Great–Britain. A few years of peace will soon retrieve all her losses. She will rapidly advance to a state of maturity, whereby she may not only repay the parent state amply for all past benefits; but also lay under the greatest obligations. . . .

However distant humanity may wish the period; yet, in the rotation of human affairs, a period may arrive, when (both countries being prepared for it) some terrible disaster, some dreadful convulsion in Great–Britain, may transfer the seat of empire to this western hemisphere— where the British constitution, like the Phoenix from its parent's ashes, shall rise with youthful vigour and shine with redoubled splendor.

DOCUMENT 14

THE DECLARATION OF INDEPENDENCE,
JULY 4, 1776

*On June 7, Richard Henry Lee introduced into Con-
gress a resolution (adopted on July 2), which asserted
that "these United Colonies are, and of right ought to
be, free and independent States." While this resolution was being discussed, a committee, consisting of
John Adams, Benjamin Franklin, Thomas Jefferson,
Robert R. Livingston, and Roger Sherman was appointed to draft a Declaration of Independence. The
members of the committee asked Jefferson to prepare
a first draft, and this was accepted by the committee,
with some alterations suggested by Adams and Franklin. The committee's draft was adopted by Congress
on July 4, after a number of changes had been made.
The most important of these was the excision of a
passage indicting the slave trade. This, Jefferson wrote
at the time, "was struck out in complaisance to South
Carolina and Georgia, who had never attempted to restrain the importation of slaves, and who on the contrary still wished to continue it. Our Northern brethren
also I believe felt a little tender under those censures,
for tho' their people have very few slaves themselves
yet they had been pretty considerable carriers of them
to others." A formal parchment copy of the Declaration was available for signing on August 2, and most
of the 55 signatures were inscribed upon it on that
date. As late as November, Matthew Thornton of New
Hampshire, recently elected to Congress, became the
last to sign. The intention of the Declaration, Jefferson later wrote, was not to say something new, but
"to place before mankind the common sense of the
subject, in terms so plain and firm as to command
their assent. . . . Neither aiming at originality of principles or sentiments, nor yet copied from any particular and previous writing, it was intended to be an*

expression of the American mind." Although the other
early documents in this volume have been modernized,
the Declaration of Independence is here taken, as an
example of formal eighteenth–century styling, from
the parchment copy version.

THE DECLARATION OF INDEPENDENCE

The Unanimous Declaration of the Thirteen United
States of America

When in the Course of human events, it becomes necessary
for one people to dissolve the political bands, which have
connected them with another, and to assume among the
powers of the earth, the separate and equal station to
which the Laws of Nature and of Nature's God entitle
them, a decent respect to the opinions of mankind requires that they should declare the causes which impel
them to the separation.—We hold these truths to be
self–evident, that all men are created equal, that they
are endowed by their Creator with certain unalienable
Rights, that among these are Life, Liberty and the pursuit
of Happiness.—That to secure these rights, Governments
are instituted among Men, deriving their just powers from
the consent of the governed,—That whenever any Form
of Government becomes destructive of these ends, it is
the Right of the People to alter or to abolish it, and to
institute new Government, laying its foundation on such
principles and organizing its powers in such form, as to
them shall seem most likely to effect their Safety and
Happiness. Prudence, indeed, will dictate that Governments long established should not be changed for light
and transient causes; and accordingly all experience hath
shewn, that mankind are more disposed to suffer, while
evils are sufferable, than to right themselves by abolishing
the forms to which they are accustomed. But when a long
train of abuses and usurpations, pursuing invariably the
same Object evinces a design to reduce them under
absolute Despotism, it is their right, it is their duty, to
throw off such Government, and to provide new Guards for
their future security.—Such has been the patient sufferance of these Colonies; and such is now the necessity

which constrains them to alter their former Systems of Government. The history of the present King of Great Britain is a history of repeated injuries and usurpations, all having in direct object the establishment of an absolute Tyranny over these States. To prove this, let Facts be submitted to a candid world.—He has refused his Assent to Laws, the most wholesome and necessary for the public good.—He has forbidden his Governors to pass Laws of immediate and pressing importance, unless suspended in their operation till his Assent should be obtained; and when so suspended, he has utterly neglected to attend to them.—He has refused to pass other Laws for the accommodation of large districts of people, unless those people would relinquish the right of Representation in the Legislature, a right inestimable to them and formidable to tyrants only.—He has called together legislative bodies at places unusual, uncomfortable, and distant from the depository of their public Records, for the sole purpose of fatiguing them into compliance with his measures.—He has dissolved Representative Houses repeatedly, for opposing with manly firmness his invasions on the rights of the people.—He has refused for a long time, after such dissolutions, to cause others to be elected; whereby the Legislative powers, incapable of Annihilation, have returned to the People at large for their exercise; the State remaining in the meantime exposed to all the dangers of invasion from without, and convulsions within. —He has endeavoured to prevent the population of these States; for that purpose obstructing the Laws for Naturalization of Foreigners; refusing to pass others to encourage their migrations hither, and raising the conditions of new Appropriations of Lands.—He has obstructed the Administration of Justice, by refusing his Assent to Laws for establishing Judiciary powers.—He has made Judges dependent on his Will alone, for the tenure of their offices, and the amount and payment of their salaries.—He has erected a multitude of New Offices, and sent hither swarms of Officers to harrass our people, and eat out their substance.—He has kept among us, in times of peace, Standing Armies without the Consent of our legislatures.—He has affected to render the Military independent of and superior to the Civil power.—He has combined with others to subject us to a jurisdiction foreign to our constitution, and unacknowledged by our laws; giving his Assent to their Acts of pretended Legislation.—For quartering large bodies of armed troops among us:—For protecting them, by a mock Trial, from punishment for any Murders which they should commit on the Inhabitants of these States:—For cutting off our Trade with all parts of the world:—For imposing Taxes on us without our Consent:—For depriving us in many cases, of the benefits of Trial by Jury:—For transporting us beyond Seas to be tried for pretended offenses:—For abolishing the free System of English Laws in a neighboring Province, establishing therein an Arbitrary government, and enlarging its Boundaries so as to render it at once an example and fit instrument for introducing the same absolute rule into these Colonies:—For taking away our Charters, abolishing our most valuable Laws, and altering fundamentally the Forms of our Governments:—For suspending our own Legislatures, and declaring themselves invested with power to legislate for us in all cases whatsoever.—He has abdicated Government here, by declaring us out of his Protection and waging War against us.—He has plundered our seas, ravaged our Coasts, burnt our towns, and destroyed the lives of our people.—He is at this time transporting large Armies of foreign Mercenaries to compleat the works of death, desolation and tyranny, already begun with circumstances of Cruelty & perfidy scarcely paralleled in the most barbarous ages, and totally unworthy the Head of a civilized nation.—He has constrained our fellow Citizens taken Captive on the high Seas to bear Arms against their Country, to become the executioners of their friends and Brethren, or to fall themselves by their Hands.—He has excited domestic insurrections amongst us, and has endeavoured to bring on the inhabitants of our frontiers, the merciless Indian Savages, whose known rule of warfare, is an undistinguished destruction of all ages, sexes and conditions. In every stage of these Oppressions We have Petitioned for Redress in the most humble terms: Our repeated Petitions have been answered only by repeated injury. A Prince whose character is thus marked by every act which may define a Tyrant, is unfit to be the ruler of a free people. Nor have We been wanting in attentions to our

Brittish brethren. We have warned them from time to time of attempts by their legislature to extend an unwarrantable jurisdiction over us. We have reminded them of the circumstances of our emigration and settlement here. We have appealed to their native justice and magnanimity, and we have conjured them by the ties of our common kindred to disavow these usurpations, which would inevitably interrupt our connections and correspondence. They too have been deaf to the voice of justice and of consanguinity. We must, therefore, acquiesce in the necessity, which denounces our Separation, and hold them, as we hold the rest of mankind, Enemies in War, in Peace Friends.—

We, therefore, the Representatives of the united States of America, in General Congress, Assembled, appealing to the Supreme Judge of the world for the rectitude of our intentions do, in the Name, and by Authority of the good People of these Colonies, solemnly publish and declare, That these United Colonies are, and of Right ought to be Free and Independent States; that they are Absolved from all Allegiance to the British Crown, and that all political connection between them and the State of Great Britain, is and ought to be totally dissolved; and that as Free and Independent States, they have full Power to levy War, conclude Peace, contract Alliances, establish Commerce, and to do all other Acts and Things which Independent States may of right do.—And for the support of this Declaration, with a firm reliance on the protection of divine Providence, we mutually pledge to each other our Lives, our Fortunes and our sacred Honor.

[Names omitted]

✳ PART II ✳

The Constitution

WITH the successful conclusion of the American Revolution, one old problem of imperial organization migrated to the New World. The empire had been unable to keep the American states successfully organized; could they independently organize and discipline themselves? In 1777 Congress had adopted the Articles of Confederation, which were finally ratified by the states and made effective in 1781. But the Articles of Confederation hardly created a real government. It was styled only as "a firm league of friendship" among the states for "their common defence, the security of their liberties, and their mutual and general welfare." Many weaknesses impaired its effectiveness. The old issue of taxation made almost as much trouble for the Confederation as it had for Parliament. Under the Articles Congress could requisition funds from the state governments, but could not tax the people directly. Since the states did not fully honor these requisitions, Congress did not have money enough to pay the expenses of government, the public debt, and the costs of an adequate army and navy. Membership in Congress itself became a farce. Many able men refused to serve in it or, when chosen by their legislatures, failed to attend. The states waged tariff wars upon each other. Conflicts between debtors and creditors, which culminated in Shays' Rebellion of 1786, alarmed men who were concerned with the defense of property rights or the maintenance of public order. Commercial uncertainties were widely attributed to the weakness of the government.

A movement to strengthen the central government gathered force; among the proposals for change the most important was to give Congress the power to pass tariffs in order to raise sufficient funds to pay the public debt. But Americans, who had just fought a war over taxes, were suspicious of all attempts to raise money from them. And this, or any other basic change in the Articles of Confederation, was all but impossible because the consent of every state was necessary to pass any amendment. Men who suggested that the states confer over a change in government quickly excited the suspicion that they were scheming to establish an aristocracy and destroy American liberties (Document 1). In 1786 George Washington and John Jay (Document 2), who both strongly felt the need for more energetic government, expressed in their letters a feeling of disappointment and disillusion that was widespread among American leaders. When things looked gloomiest, the demand for a change finally met with a positive response. Virginia called a convention at Annapolis in September 1786, to which five states sent delegates. The delegates adopted a report drafted by Alexander Hamilton which pointed to "important defects in the system of Federal Government," and called for another convention to be held at Philadelphia the following May "to devise such further provisions as shall appear to them necessary to render the constitution of the Federal Government adequate to the exigencies of the Union." The Federal Convention, which met in May 1787, decided, however, to side-step this mandate: instead of recommending changes in the Articles, it began to consider plans for a wholly new instrument of government.

To induce the states to give up any significant portion of their sovereignty was immensely difficult. Voting in the Continental Congress and under the Articles of Confederation had always been based upon the principle: one state, one vote. The proposal of the large states that voting in the national legislature be proportioned to population outraged the small states and almost broke up the Convention (Document 3). Once this clash was settled by the "Great Compromise," in which the states have parity in the Senate and proportionate voting in the House, the remaining problems, knotty though they often were, yielded more readily to compromise. After four months of arduous debate and equally arduous work, the Convention reported the final draft of the Constitution (Document 4) to the Congress, which referred it to the states for action.

The ensuing debate in the states over ratification was often so heated, the rhetoric so full of anger and suspicion, that it is easy to forget that large numbers of men were genuinely puzzled about the right course of action, and that some did change their minds in the course of discussion. Among those who opposed the Constitution some believed, with Elbridge Gerry (Document 5), in the value of a stronger union, but would not accept the Constitution because they thought it embodied some dangerous details. The most widespread, and certainly the most significant, of the objections, which troubled Thomas Jefferson among others (Document 6), was the absence of a Bill of Rights. The Articles of Confederation, to be sure, had had no Bill of Rights, but those who wanted one now pointed out that the range of powers to be given to the proposed central government was much wider, and that guarantees of rights were therefore more necessary to protect individuals against the abuse of these powers. The opponents of the Constitution in the state ratifying conventions (Document 7) repeatedly and urgently demanded a Bill of Rights. It is doubtful whether the Constitution could have been ratified had its friends not promised that a Bill of Rights would soon be supplied—as indeed it was in 1791. These promises helped to dispel one fundamental objection. Others were answered with great skill in the speeches and pamphlets of the defenders of the Constitution. James Madison and Alexander Hamilton provided in *The Federalist* (Document 8) the most important and enduring statement of the Federalist argument. After the ratification of the Constitution in 1788, differences as to its adoption were quickly submerged and forgotten. But the instrument itself, being brief, had to be vague or equivocal on many points; and it was not long before the same generation that adopted the Constitution fell out once again over its scope and implications.

DOCUMENT 1

MASSACHUSETTS DELEGATES IN CONGRESS, LETTER ON A CONSTITUTIONAL CONVENTION,
SEPTEMBER 3, 1785

In 1785, when the Massachusetts legislature instructed its delegates to introduce a resolution into Congress calling for a constitutional convention, the delegates balked and sent home this letter explaining their refusal. Although they conceded that the existing state of affairs left much to be desired, the delegates were suspicious of any change in government that might give tyranny a foothold. In Massachusetts, and in several other states, such sentiment remained strong when the Constitution was presented for ratification. The Massachusetts convention ratified the new Constitution by the narrow margin of 187 to 168.

If an alteration, either temporary or perpetual, of the commercial powers of Congress, is to be considered by a Convention, shall the latter be authorized to revise the Confederation *generally,* or only for express purposes?—the great object of the Revolution was the establishment of good government, and each of the states, in forming their own, as well as the federal Constitution, have adopted republican principles. Notwithstanding this, plans have been artfully laid, and vigorously pursued, which, had they been successful, we think would inevitably have changed our republican governments, into baleful aristocracies. . . . What the effect then may be, of calling a Convention to revise the Confederation generally, we leave with your Excellency and the honorable Legislature to determine. We are apprehensive and it is our duty to declare it, that such a measure would produce thro'out the Union, an exertion of the friends of aristocracy, to send members who would promote a change of government: and we can form some judgment of the plan, which such members would report to Congress.—but . . . such have been the declamations of designing men against the Confederation generally . . . that we think there is great danger of a report which would invest Congress with powers that the honorable Legislature have not the most distant intention to delegate. Perhaps it may be said, this can produce no ill effect; because Congress may correct the report however exceptionable, or if passed by them, any of the states may refuse to ratify it— true it is, that Congress and the states have such powers, but would not such a report affect the tranquillity and weaken the government of the Union? We have already considered the operation of the report as it would respect Congress; and if animosities and parties would naturally arise from their rejecting it, how much would these be increased, if the report approved by Congress and some of the states, should be rejected by other states? Would there not be a danger of a party spirit's being thus more generally diffused and warmly supported?—far distant we know it to be from the honorable Legislature of Massachusetts, to give up a single principle of republicanism, but when a general revision shall have proceeded from their motion, and a report which to them may be highly offensive, shall have been confirmed by seven states in Congress, and ratified by several Legislatures, will not these be ready to charge Massachusetts with inconsistency, in being the first to oppose a measure which the state will be said to have originated? Massachusetts has great weight, and is considered as one of the most republican states in the Union; and when it is known, that the legislature have proposed a general revision, there can be no doubt that they will be represented as being convinced of the necessity of increasing generally the powers of Congress, and the opinion of the state will be urged with such art as to convince numbers that the Articles of Confederation are altogether exceptionable. Thus, whilst measures are taken to guard against the evils arising from the want of one or two particulars of power in Congress, we are in great danger of incurring the other extreme—"More power in Congress" has been the cry from all quarters, but especially of those whose views, not being confined to a government that will best promote the happiness of the people, are extended to one that will afford lucrative employments, civil and military. Such a government is an aristocracy, which would require a standing army and a numerous train of pensioners and placemen to prop and support its exalted administration. To recommend one's self to such an administration would be to secure an establishment for life and at the same time to provide for his posterity. These are pleasing prospects, which republican governments do not afford, and it is not to be wondered at that many persons of elevated views and idle habits in these states are desirous of the change. We are for increasing the power of Congress as far as it will promote the happiness of the people, but at the same time are clearly of opinion that every measure should be avoided which would strengthen the hands of the enemies to a free government. And that an administration of the present Confederation with all its inconveniences, is preferable to the Risque of general dissensions and animosities which may approach to anarchy and prepare the way to a ruinous system of government.

DOCUMENT 2

JOHN JAY AND GEORGE WASHINGTON ON THE CRISIS OF THE 1780's,

JUNE 27 AND AUGUST 1, 1786

These letters illustrate the feelings of a large number of conservative patriots about the inadequacies of the central government in the Confederation period. Jay and Washington were both advocates of a more vigorous government and their correspondence shows how shaken their earlier confidence was by the unsettled conditions of the 1780's.

John Jay to George Washington, June 27, 1786.

To oppose popular prejudices, to censure the proceedings, and expose the improprieties of States, is an unpleasant task, but it must be done. Our affairs seem to lead to some crisis, some revolution—something that I cannot foresee or conjecture. I am uneasy and apprehensive; more so than during the war. Then we had a fixed object, and though the means and time of obtaining it were often problematical, yet I did firmly believe we should ultimately succeed, because I was convinced that justice was with us. The case is now altered; we are going and doing wrong, and therefore I look forward to evils and calamities, but without being able to guess at the instrument, nature, or measure of them.

That we shall again recover, and things again go well, I have no doubt. Such a variety of circumstances would not, almost miraculously, have combined to liberate and make us a nation for transient and unimportant purposes. I therefore believe that we are yet to become a great and respectable people; but when or how, the spirit of prophecy can only discern.

There doubtless is much reason to think and to say that we are wofully and, in many instances, wickedly misled. Private rage for property suppresses public considerations, and personal rather than national interests have become the great objects of attention. Representative bodies will ever be faithful copies of their originals, and generally exhibit a checkered assemblage of virtue and vice, of abilities and weakness.

The mass of men are neither wise nor good, and the virtue like the other resources of a country, can only be drawn to a point and exerted by strong circumstances ably managed, or a strong government ably administered. New governments have not the aid of habit and hereditary respect, and being generally the result of preceding tumult and confusion, do not immediately acquire stability or strength. Besides, in times of commotion, some men will gain confidence and importance, who merit neither, and who, like political mountebanks, are less solicitous about the health of the credulous crowd than about making the most of their nostrums and prescriptions. . . .

What I most fear is, that the better kind of people, by which I mean the people who are orderly and industrious, who are content with their situations and not uneasy in their circumstances, will be led by the insecurity of property, the loss of confidence in their rulers, and the want of public faith and rectitude, to consider the charms of liberty as imaginary and delusive. A state of fluctuation and uncertainty must disgust and alarm such men, and

prepare their minds for almost any change that may promise them quiet and security.

George Washington to John Jay, August 1, 1786.

Your sentiments, that our affairs are drawing rapidly
to a crisis, accord with my own. What the event will be,
is also beyond the reach of my foresight. We have errors
to correct. We have probably had too good an opinion of
human nature in forming our confederation. Experience
has taught us, that men will not adopt and carry into
execution measures the best calculated for their own good,
without the intervention of a coercive power. I do not
conceive we can exist long as a nation without having
lodged some where a power, which will pervade the whole
Union in as energetic a manner as the authority of the
State governments extends over the several States.

To be fearful of investing Congress, constituted as
that body is, with ample authorities for national purposes,
appears to me the very climax of popular absurdity and
madness. Could Congress exert them for the detriment of
the public, without injuring themselves in an equal or
greater proportion? Are not their interests inseparably
connected with those of their constituents? By the rotation of appointment, must they not mingle frequently with
the mass of citizens? Is it not rather to be apprehended,
if they were possessed of the powers before described, that
the individual members would be induced to use them,
on many occasions, very timidly and inefficaciously for
fear of losing their popularity and future election? We
must take human nature as we find it. Perfection falls
not to the share of mortals. Many are of opinion, that
Congress have too frequently made use of the suppliant,
humble tone of requisition in applications to the States,
when they had a right to assert their imperial dignity and
command obedience. Be that as it may, requisitions are
a perfect nullity where thirteen sovereign, independent,
disunited States are in the habit of discussing and refusing
compliance with them at their option. Requisitions are
actually little better than a jest and a by-word throughout
the land. If you tell the legislatures they have violated
the treaty of peace, and invaded the prerogatives of the
confederacy, they will laugh in your face. What then is

to be done? Things cannot go on in the same train for ever. It is much to be feared, as you observe, that the better kind of people, being disgusted with the circumstances, will have their minds prepared for any revolution whatever. We are apt to run from one extreme into another. To anticipate and prevent disastrous contingencies would be the part of wisdom and patriotism.

What astonishing changes a few years are capable of producing. I am told that even respectable characters speak of a monarchical form of government without horror. From thinking proceeds speaking; thence to acting is often but a single step. But how irrevocable and tremendous! What a triumph for our enemies to verify their predictions! What a triumph for the advocates of despotism to find, that we are incapable of governing ourselves, and that systems founded on the basis of equal liberty are merely ideal and fallacious! Would to God, that wise measures may be taken in time to avert the consequences we have but too much reason to apprehend. . . .

DOCUMENT 3

DEBATE IN THE FEDERAL CONVENTION,
JUNE 9 AND 11, 1787

The delegates at the Federal Convention were, with a few exceptions, men convinced of the need for a stronger central government. But on innumerable questions concerning the exact powers such a government should have, its internal structure, and the relative powers of the states within it, they differed profoundly. Before any constitution could be drafted these differences had to be thrashed out and somehow compromised. Several issues provoked sharp debate, and one nearly broke up the Convention. This was the clash between the large and small states over the question of how the states would vote in the national legislature. In the Continental Congress and under the Articles of Confederation, each state had had one vote, regardless of population. The small state dele-

gates were now aroused by the proposal in the Virginia Plan that under the new constitution voting should be proportionate to numbers, an arrangement that would favor the large states—Virginia, Pennsylvania, and Massachusetts. In this selection the issue is argued by David Brearly of New Jersey (whose name is here misspelled in Madison's reports), by William Paterson of the same state, the proponent of the small states' counter-proposal, by James Wilson and Benjamin Franklin of Pennsylvania, and by Roger Sherman of Connecticut. Finally, the proposal devised in part by Franklin and presented by Sherman, was adopted on July 17, giving the large states their proportional vote in the House and the small states their equal vote in the Senate.

June 9

PATERSON: Moved that the Committee resume the clause relating to the rule of suffrage in the national legislature.

BREARLEY: Seconds him. He was sorry, he said, that any question on this point was brought into view. It had been much agitated in Congress at the time of forming the Confederation, and was then rightly settled by allowing to each sovereign state an equal vote. Otherwise, the smaller states must have been destroyed instead of being saved. The substitution of a ratio, he admitted, carried fairness on the face of it; but on a deeper examination was unfair and unjust. Judging of the disparity of the states by the quota of Congress, Virginia would have sixteen votes and Georgia but one. A like proportion to the others will make the whole number ninety. There will be three large states and ten small ones. The large states, by which he meant Massachusetts, Pennsylvania, and Virginia, will carry everything before them. It had been admitted, and was known to him from facts within New Jersey, that where large and small counties were united into a district for electing representatives for the district, the large counties always carried their point, and consequently the states would do so. Virginia with her sixteen votes will be a solid column indeed, a formidable phalanx. While Georgia with her solitary vote, and the other little states, will be obliged to throw themselves constantly into the scale of some large one in order to have any weight at all. He had come to the Convention with a view of being as useful as he could in giving energy and stability to the federal government. When the proposition for destroying the equality of votes came forward, he was astonished, he was alarmed. Is it fair, then, it will be asked, that Georgia should have an equal vote with Virginia? He would not say it was. What remedy, then? One only, that a map of the United States be spread out, that all the existing boundaries be erased, and that a new partition of the whole be made into thirteen equal parts.

PATERSON: Considered the proposition for a proportional representation as striking at the existence of the lesser states. He would premise, however, to an investigation of this question, some remarks on the nature, structure, and powers of the Convention. The Convention, he said, was formed in pursuance of an act of Congress; that this act was recited in several of the commissions, particularly that of Massachusetts, which he required to be read; that the amendment of the Confederacy was the object of all the laws and commissions on the subject; that the Articles of the Confederation were therefore the proper basis of all the proceedings of the Convention; that we ought to keep within its limits, or we should be charged by our constituents with usurpation; that the people of America were sharp-sighted and not to be deceived. But the commissions under which we acted were not only the measure of our power, they denoted also the sentiments of the states on the subject of our deliberation. The idea of a national government, as contradistinguished from a federal one, never entered into the mind of any of them; and to the public mind we must accommodate ourselves. We have no power to go beyond the federal scheme; and if we had, the people are not ripe for any other. We must follow the people; the people will not follow us. The *proposition* could not be maintained, whether considered in reference to us as a nation or as a confederacy. A confederacy supposes sovereignty in the members composing it and sovereignty supposes equality. If we are to be considered as a nation, all state distinctions must be abolished, the whole must be thrown into hotchpot, and when an equal division is made, then there may be fairly an equality of representation. . . .

Give the large states an influence in proportion to their magnitude, and what will be the consequences? Their ambition will be proportionally increased, and the small states will have everything to fear. . . .

He alluded to the hint thrown out by Mr. Wilson, of the necessity to which the large states might be reduced, of confederating among themselves by a refusal of the others to concur. Let them unite if they please, but let them remember that they have no authority to compel the others to unite. New Jersey will never confederate on the plan before the Committee. She would be swallowed up. He had rather submit to a monarch, to a despot, than to such a fate. He would not only oppose the plan here, but on his return home do everything in his power to defeat it there.

WILSON: Hoped, if the Confederacy should be dissolved, that a *majority*—nay, a *minority* of the states would unite for their safety. He entered elaborately into the defense of a proportional representation, stating for his first position, that, as all authority was derived from the people, equal numbers of people ought to have an equal number of representatives, and different numbers of people, different numbers of representatives. This principle had been improperly violated in the Confederation, owing to the urgent circumstances of the time. . . .

Are not the citizens of Pennsylvania equal to those of New Jersey? Does it require one hundred and fifty of the former to balance fifty of the latter? Representatives of different districts ought clearly to hold the same proportion to each other as their respective constituents hold to each other. If the small states will not confederate on this plan, Pennsylvania, and he presumed some other states, would not confederate on any other. We have been told that each state being sovereign, all are equal. So each man is naturally a sovereign over himself, and all men are therefore naturally equal. Can he retain this equality when he becomes a member of civil government? He cannot. As little can a sovereign state, when it becomes a member of a federal government. If

New Jersey will not part with her sovereignty, it is vain to talk of government. A new partition of the states is desirable, but evidently and totally impracticable.

June 11

SHERMAN: Proposed that the proportion of suffrage in the first branch should be according to the respective numbers of free inhabitants; and that in the second branch, or Senate, each state should have one vote and no more. He said, as the states would remain possessed of certain individual rights, each state ought to be able to protect itself, otherwise a few large states will rule the rest. The House of Lords in England, he observed, had certain particular rights under the constitution, and hence they have an equal vote with the House of Commons, that they may be able to defend their rights.

The question being about to be put, Dr. Franklin said he had thrown his ideas of the matter on a paper, which Mr. Wilson read to the Committee, in the words following:

"Mr. Chairman: It has given me great pleasure to observe that, till this point, the proportion of representation, came before us, our debates were carried on with great coolness and temper. If anything of a contrary kind has on this occasion appeared, I hope it will not be repeated; for we are sent here to *consult,* not to *contend,* with each other; and declarations of a fixed opinion, and of determined resolution never to change it, neither enlighten nor convince us. Positiveness and warmth on one side naturally beget their like on the other, and tend to create and augment discord and division, in a great concern wherein harmony and union are extremely necessary to give weight to our councils, and render them effectual in promoting and securing the common good.

"I must own that I was originally of opinion it would be better if every member of Congress, or our national council, were to consider himself rather as a representative of the whole than as an agent for the interests of a particular state; in which case the proportion of members for each state would be of less consequence, and it would not be very material whether they voted by states or individually. But as I find this is not to be expected, I now think the number of representatives should bear some proportion to the number of the represented; and that the decisions should be by the majority of members, not by the majority of the states. This is objected to from an apprehension that the greater states would then swallow up the smaller. I do not at present clearly see what advantage the greater states could propose to themselves by swallowing up the smaller, and therefore do not apprehend they would attempt it. . . .

"But, sir, in the present mode of voting by states, it is equally in the power of the lesser states to swallow up the greater; and this is mathematically demonstrable. Suppose, for example, that seven smaller states had each three members in the House, and the six larger to have one with another six members, and that, upon a question, two members of each smaller state should be in the affirmative, and one in the negative, they would make: affirmatives, 14; negatives, 7; and that all the larger states should be unanimously in the negative, they would make, negatives 36; in all, affirmatives, 14, negatives 43.

"It is, then, apparent that the fourteen carry the question against the forty-three, and the minority overpowers the majority, contrary to the common practice of assemblies in all countries and ages.

"The greater states, sir, are naturally as unwilling to have their property left in the disposition of the smaller as the smaller are to have theirs in the disposition of the greater. . . ."

DOCUMENT 4

THE CONSTITUTION OF THE UNITED STATES

The Federal Convention met at Philadelphia on May 14, 1787. After many weeks of debate, during which the "Great Compromise" between the large and small states surmounted the chief obstacle to ultimate agreement, the Convention had done enough of its work to draft a detailed Constitution. From July 26 to August 6 a select committee of five delegates labored to put the resolutions adopted by the Convention into preliminary form. From August 6 to September 10, its report was discussed in detail, clause by clause. On September 8 a second committee of five was appointed "to revise the style of and arrange the articles which had been agreed to by the house." On September 17, the Convention met in a final session, at which it adopted and signed the completed Constitution. Of the fifty-five delegates who had attended at various times, forty-two were present at the end, and all but three of these put their signatures to the document. Some members of the Convention, who were also members of Congress, immediately took the Constitution to New York where Congress was meeting, and on September 28, 1787, Congress referred the Constitution to the states for action. By June 21, 1788, nine states had ratified, and in theory the Constitution could go into effect; but the success of the Union was assured only by the subsequent ratifications of Virginia, June 25, and New York, June 26. North Carolina ratified on November 21, 1789, Rhode Island on May 29, 1790, completing the roster of the original thirteen states. The text below shows where provisions of the Constitution have been amended, and gives the date when each Amendment was passed by Congress and ratified by the necessary three-fourths of the states.

THE CONSTITUTION OF THE UNITED STATES OF AMERICA

We the people of the United States, in order to form a more perfect Union, establish justice, insure domestic tranquility, provide for the common defence, promote the general welfare, and secure the blessings of liberty to ourselves and our posterity, do ordain and establish this Constitution for the United States of America.

ARTICLE I

Section 1.   All legislative powers herein granted shall be vested in a Congress of the United States, which shall consist of a Senate and House of Representatives.

Section 2. 1. The House of Representatives shall be composed of members chosen every second year by the people of all the several States, and the Electors in each State shall have the qualifications requisite for electors of the most numerous branch of the State Legislature.

2. No person shall be a representative who shall not have attained to the age of twenty-five years, and been seven years a citizen of the United States, and who shall not, when elected, be an inhabitant of that State in which he shall be chosen.

3. Representatives and direct taxes[1] shall be apportioned among the several States which may be included within this Union, according to their respective numbers, which shall be determined by adding to the whole number of free persons, including those bound to service for a term of years, and excluding Indians not taxed, three fifths of all other persons.[2] The actual enumeration shall be made within three years after the first meeting of the Congress of the United States, and within every subsequent term of ten years, in such manner as they shall by law direct. The number of representatives shall not exceed one for every thirty thousand, but each State shall have at least one representative; and until such enumeration shall be made, the State of New Hampshire shall be entitled to chuse three, Massachusetts eight, Rhode–Island and Providence Plantations one, Connecticut five, New–York six, New Jersey four, Pennsylvania eight, Delaware one, Maryland six, Virginia ten, North Carolina five, South Carolina five, and Georgia three.

4. When vacancies happen in the representation from any State, the executive authority thereof shall issue writs of election to fill such vacancies.

5. The House of Representatives shall chuse their speaker and other officers; and shall have the sole power of impeachment.

Section 3. 1. The Senate of the United States shall be composed of two senators from each State, chosen by the legislature thereof,[3] for six years; and each senator shall have one vote.

[1] See the 16th Amendment.
[2] See the 14th Amendment.
[3] See the 17th Amendment.

2. Immediately after they shall be assembled in consequence of the first election, they shall be divided as equally as may be into three classes. The seats of the senators of the first class shall be vacated at the expiration of the second year, of the second class at the expiration of the fourth year, and of the third class at the expiration of the sixth year, so that one third may be chosen every second year; and if vacancies happen by resignation, or otherwise, during the recess of the legislature of any State, the executive thereof may make temporary appointments until the next meeting of the legislature, which shall then fill such vacancies.[4]

3. No person shall be a senator who shall not have attained to the age of thirty years, and been nine years a citizen of the United States, and who shall not, when elected, be an inhabitant of that State for which he shall be chosen.

4. The Vice President of the United States shall be President of the Senate, but shall have no vote, unless they be equally divided.

5. The Senate shall chuse their other officers and also a president pro tempore, in the absence of the Vice President, or when he shall exercise the office of President of the United States.

6. The Senate shall have the sole power to try all impeachments. When sitting for that purpose, they shall be on oath or affirmation. When the President of the United States is tried, the chief justice shall preside: and no person shall be convicted without the concurrence of two thirds of the members present.

7. Judgment in cases of impeachment shall not extend further than to removal from office, and disqualifications to hold and enjoy any office of honor, trust or profit under the United States: but the party convicted shall nevertheless be liable and subject to indictment, trial, judgment and punishment, according to law.

Section 4. 1. The times, places, and manner of holding elections for senators and representatives, shall be prescribed in each State by the legislature thereof; but the Congress may at any time by law make or alter such regulations, except as to the places of chusing senators.

[4] See the 17th Amendment.

2. The Congress shall assemble at least once in every year, and such meeting shall be on the first Monday in December, unless they shall by law appoint a different day.

Section 5. 1. Each House shall be the judge of the elections, returns and qualifications of its own members, and a majority of each shall constitute a quorum to do business; but a smaller number may adjourn from day to day, and may be authorized to compel the attendance of absent members, in such manner, and under such penalties as each House may provide.

2. Each House may determine the rules of its proceedings, punish its members for disorderly behaviour, and, with the concurrence of two thirds, expel a member.

3. Each House shall keep a journal of its proceedings, and from time to time publish the same, excepting such parts as may in their judgment require secrecy; and the yeas and nays of the members of either House on any question shall, at the desire of one fifth of those present, be entered on the journal.

4. Neither House, during the session of Congress, shall, without the consent of the other, adjourn for more than three days, nor to any other place than that in which the two Houses shall be sitting.

Section 6. 1. The senators and representatives shall receive a compensation for their services, to be ascertained by law, and paid out of the Treasury of the United States. They shall in all cases, except treason, felony, and breach of the peace, be privileged from arrest during their attendance at the session of their respective Houses, and in going to and returning from the same; and for any speech or debate in either House, they shall not be questioned in any other place.

2. No senator or representative shall, during the time for which he was elected, be appointed to any civil office under the authority of the United States, which shall have been created, or the emoluments whereof shall have been encreased, during such time; and no person holding any office under the United States shall be a member of either House during his continuance in office.

Section 7. 1. All bills for raising revenue shall originate in the House of Representatives; but the Senate may propose or concur with amendments as on other bills.

2. Every bill which shall have passed the House of Representatives and the Senate, shall, before it become a law, be presented to the President of the United States; if he approves he shall sign it, but if not he shall return it, with his objections to that House in which it shall have originated, who shall enter the objections at large on their journal, and proceed to reconsider it. If after such reconsideration two thirds of that House shall agree to pass the bill, it shall be sent, together with the objections, to the other House, by which it shall likewise be reconsidered, and if approved by two thirds of that House, it shall become a law. But in all such cases the votes of both Houses shall be determined by yeas and nays, and the names of the persons voting for and against the bill shall be entered on the journal of each House respectively. If any bill shall not be returned by the President within ten days (Sundays excepted) after it shall have been presented to him, the same shall be a law, in like manner as if he had signed it, unless the Congress by their adjournment prevent its return, in which case it shall not be a law.

3. Every order, resolution, or vote to which the concurrence of the Senate and the House of Representatives may be necessary (except on a question of adjournment) shall be presented to the President of the United States; and before the same shall take effect, shall be approved by him, or being disapproved by him, shall be repassed by two thirds of the Senate and House of Representatives, according to the rules and limitations prescribed in the case of a bill.

Section 8. The Congress shall have the power

1. To lay and collect taxes, duties, imposts, and excises, to pay the debts and provide for the common defence and general welfare of the United States; but all duties, imposts, and excises shall be uniform throughout the United States;

2. To borrow money on the credit of the United States;

3. To regulate commerce with foreign nations, and among the several States, and with the Indian tribes;

4. To establish an uniform rule of naturalization, and uniform laws on the subject of bankruptcies throughout the United States;

5. To coin money, regulate the value thereof, and of foreign coin, and fix the standard of weights and measures;

6. To provide for the punishment of counterfeiting the securities and current coin of the United States;

7. To establish post offices and post roads;

8. To promote the progress of science and useful arts, by securing for limited times to authors and inventors the exclusive right to their respective writings and discoveries;

9. To constitute tribunals inferior to the Supreme Court;

10. To define and punish piracies and felonies committed on the high seas, and offences against the law of nations;

11. To declare war, grant letters of marque and reprisal, and make rules concerning captures on land and water;

12. To raise and support armies, but no appropriation of money to that use shall be for a longer term than two years;

13. To provide and maintain a navy;

14. To make rules for the government and regulation of the land and naval forces;

15. To provide for calling forth the militia to execute the laws of the Union, suppress insurrections and repel invasions;

16. To provide for organizing, arming, and disciplining the militia, and for governing such part of them as may be employed in the service of the United States, reserving to the States respectively, the appointment of the officers, and the authority of training the militia according to the discipline prescribed by Congress;

17. To exercise exclusive legislation in all cases whatsoever, over such district (not exceeding ten miles square) as may, by cession of particular States, and the acceptance of Congress, become the seat of the government of the United States, and to exercise like authority over all places purchased by the consent of the legislature of the State in

which the same shall be, for the erection of forts, magazines, arsenals, dock–yards, and other needful buildings; and

18. To make all laws which shall be necessary and proper for carrying into execution the foregoing powers, and all other powers vested by this Constitution in the government of the United States, or in any department or officer thereof.

Section 9. 1. The migration or importation of such persons as any of the States now existing shall think proper to admit, shall not be prohibited by the Congress prior to the year one thousand eight hundred and eight, but a tax or duty may be imposed on such importation, not exceeding ten dollars for each person.

2. The privilege of the writ of habeas corpus shall not be suspended, unless when in cases of rebellion or invasion the public safety may require it.

3. No bill of attainder or ex post facto law shall be passed.

4. No capitation, or other direct, tax shall be laid, unless in proportion to the census or enumeration hereinbefore directed to be taken.[5]

5. No tax or duty shall be laid on articles exported from any State.

6. No preference shall be given by any regulation of commerce or revenue to the ports of one State over those of another: nor shall vessels bound to, or from, one State be obliged to enter, clear, or pay duties in another.

7. No money shall be drawn from the treasury, but in consequence of appropriations made by law; and a regular statement and account of the receipts and expenditures of all public money shall be published from time to time.

8. No title of nobility shall be granted by the United States: and no person holding any office of profit or trust under them, shall, without the consent of the Congress, accept of any present, emolument, office, or title, of any kind whatever, from any king, prince, or foreign State.

Section 10. 1. No State shall enter into any treaty, alliance, or confederation; grant letters of marque and reprisal; coin money; emit bills of credit; make any thing but

[5] See the 16th Amendment.

gold and silver coin a tender in payment of debts; pass any bill of attainder, ex post facto law, or law impairing the obligation of contracts, or grant any title of nobility.

2. No State shall, without the consent of the Congress, lay any imposts or duties on imports or exports, except what may be absolutely necessary for executing its inspection laws: and the net produce of all duties and imposts laid by any State on imports or exports, shall be for the use of the treasury of the United States; and all such laws shall be subject to the revision and control of the Congress.

3. No State shall, without the consent of the Congress, lay any duty of tonnage, keep troops, or ships of war in time of peace, enter into any agreement or compact with another State, or with a foreign power, or engage in war, unless actually invaded, or in such imminent danger as will not admit of delay.

ARTICLE II

Section 1. 1. The executive power shall be vested in a President of the United States of America. He shall hold his office during the term of four years, and, together with the Vice President, chosen for the same term, be elected, as follows:

2. Each State shall appoint, in such manner as the legislature thereof may direct, a number of electors, equal to the whole number of senators and representatives to which the State may be entitled in the Congress: but no senator or representative, or person holding an office of trust or profit under the United States, shall be appointed an elector.

The electors shall meet in their respective States, and vote by ballot for two persons, of whom one at least shall not be an inhabitant of the same State with themselves. And they shall make a list of all the persons voted for, and of the number of votes for each; which list they shall sign and certify, and transmit sealed to the seat of the government of the United States, directed to the president of the Senate. The president of the Senate shall, in the presence of the Senate and House of Representatives, open all the certificates, and the votes shall then be counted. The person having the greatest number of votes shall be the President, if such number be a majority of the whole number of electors appointed; and if there be more than one who have such majority, and have an equal number of votes, then the House of Representatives shall immediately chuse by ballot one of them for President; and if no person have a majority, then from the five highest on the list the said House shall in like manner chuse the President. But in chusing the President, the votes shall be taken by States, the representation from each State having one vote; a quorum for this purpose shall consist of a member or members from two thirds of the States, and a majority of all the States shall be necessary to a choice. In every case, after the choice of the President, the person having the greatest number of votes of the electors shall be the Vice President. But if there should remain two or more who have equal votes, the Senate shall chuse from them by ballot the Vice President.[6]

3. The Congress may determine the time of chusing the electors, and the day on which they shall give their votes; which day shall be the same throughout the United States.

4. No person except a natural born citizen, or a citizen of the United States, at the time of the adoption of this Constitution, shall be eligible to the office of President; neither shall any person be eligible to that office who shall not have attained to the age of thirty five years, and been fourteen years a resident within the United States.

5. In case of the removal of the President from office, or of his death, resignation, or inability to discharge the powers and duties of the said office, the same shall devolve on the Vice President, and the Congress may by law provide for the case of removal, death, resignation or inability, both of the President and Vice President, declaring what officer shall then act as President, and such officer shall act accordingly, until the disability be removed, or a President shall be elected.

6. The President shall, at stated times, receive for his services a compensation, which shall neither be increased nor diminished during the period for which he shall have been elected, and he shall not receive within that period any other emolument from the United States, or any of them.

7. Before he enter on the execution of his office, he

[6] Superseded by the 12th Amendment.

shall take the following oath or affirmation:—"I do solemnly swear (or affirm) that I will faithfully execute the office of President of the United States, and will to the best of my ability, preserve, protect and defend the Constitution of the United States."

Section 2. 1. The President shall be commander in chief of the army and navy of the United States, and of the militia of the several States, when called into the actual service of the United States; he may require the opinion, in writing, of the principal officer in each of the executive departments, upon any subject relating to the duties of their respective offices, and he shall have power to grant reprieves and pardons for offenses against the United States, except in cases of impeachment.

2. He shall have power, by and with the advice and consent of the Senate, to make treaties, provided two thirds of the senators present concur; and he shall nominate, and by and with the advice and consent of the Senate, shall appoint ambassadors, other public ministers and consuls, judges of the Supreme Court, and all other officers of the United States, whose appointments are not herein otherwise provided for, and which shall be established by law: but the Congress may by law vest the appointment of such inferior officers, as they think proper, in the President alone, in the courts of law, or in the heads of departments.

3. The President shall have power to fill up all vacancies that may happen during the recess of the Senate, by granting commissions which shall expire at the end of their next session.

Section 3. He shall from time to time give to the Congress information of the state of the Union, and recommend to their consideration such measures as he shall judge necessary and expedient; he may, on extraordinary occasions, convene both Houses, or either of them, and in case of disagreement between them with respect to the time of adjournment, he may adjourn them to such time as he shall think proper; he shall receive ambassadors and other public ministers; he shall take care that the laws be faithfully executed, and shall commission all the officers of the United States.

Section 4. The President, Vice President, and all civil officers of the United States, shall be removed from office on impeachment for, and conviction of, treason, bribery, or other high crimes and misdemeanors.

ARTICLE III

Section 1. The judicial power of the United States shall be vested in one Supreme Court, and in such inferior courts as the Congress may from time to time ordain and establish. The judges, both of the supreme and inferior courts, shall hold their offices during good behavior, and shall, at stated times, receive for their services, a compensation, which shall not be diminished during their continuance in office.

Section 2. 1. The judicial power shall extend to all cases, in law and equity, arising under this Constitution, the laws of the United States, and treaties made, or which shall be made, under their authority;—to all cases affecting ambassadors, other public ministers and consuls;—to all cases of admiralty and maritime jurisdiction;—to controversies to which the United States shall be a party;[7]— to controversies between two or more States;—between a State and citizens of another State;—between citizens of different States;—between citizens of the same State claiming lands under grants of different States, and between a State, or the citizens thereof, and foreign States, citizens or subjects.

2. In all cases affecting ambassadors, other public ministers and consuls, and those in which a State shall be party, the Supreme Court shall have original jurisdiction. In all the other cases before mentioned, the Supreme Court shall have appellate jurisdiction, both as to law and fact, with such exceptions, and under such regulations as the Congress shall make.

3. The trial of all crimes, except in cases of impeachment, shall be by jury; and such trial shall be held in the State where the said crimes shall have been committed; but when not committed within any State, the trial shall be at such place or places as the Congress may by law have directed.

Section 3. 1. Treason against the United States shall consist only in levying war against them, or in adhering to their enemies, giving them aid and comfort. No person

[7] See the 11th Amendment.

shall be convicted of treason unless on the testimony of two witnesses to the same overt act, or on confession in open court.

2. The Congress shall have power to declare the punishment of treason, but no attainder of treason shall work corruption of blood, or forfeiture except during the life of the person attainted.

ARTICLE IV

Section 1. Full faith and credit shall be given in each State to the public acts, records, and judicial proceedings of every other State. And the Congress may by general laws prescribe the manner in which such acts, records and proceedings shall be proved, and the effect thereof.

Section 2. 1. The citizens of each State shall be entitled to all privileges and immunities of citizens in the several States.[8]

2. A person charged in any State with treason, felony, or other crime, who shall flee from justice, and be found in another State, shall on demand of the executive authority of the State from which he fled, be delivered up to be removed to the State having jurisdiction of the crime.

3. No person held to service or labour in one State under the laws thereof, escaping into another, shall, in consequence of any law or regulation therein, be discharged from such service or labour, but shall be delivered up on claim of the party to whom such service or labour may be due.[9]

Section 3. 1. New States may be admitted by the Congress into this Union; but no new State shall be formed or erected within the jurisdiction of any other State; nor any State be formed by the junction of two or more States, or parts of States, without the consent of the legislatures of the States concerned as well as of the Congress.

2. The Congress shall have power to dispose of and make all needful rules and regulations respecting the territory or other property belonging to the United States; and nothing in this Constitution shall be so construed as to

[8] See the 14th Amendment, Sec. 1.
[9] See the 13th Amendment.

prejudice any claims of the United States, or of any particular State.

Section 4. The United States shall guarantee to every State in this Union a republican form of government, and shall protect each of them against invasion; and on application of the legislature, or of the executive (when the legislature cannot be convened) against domestic violence.

ARTICLE V

The Congress, whenever two thirds of both Houses shall deem it necessary, shall propose amendments to this Constitution, or, on the application of the legislatures of two thirds of the several States, shall call a convention for proposing amendments, which in either case, shall be valid to all intents and purposes, as part of this Constitution, when ratified by the legislatures of three fourths of the several States, or by conventions in three fourths thereof, as the one or the other mode of ratification may be proposed by the Congress; Provided that no amendment which may be made prior to the year one thousand eight hundred and eight shall in any manner affect the first and fourth clauses in the ninth section of the first article; and that no State, without its consent, shall be deprived of its equal suffrage in the Senate.

ARTICLE VI

1. All debts contracted and engagements entered into, before the adoption of this Constitution, shall be as valid against the United States under this Constitution, as under the Confederation.[10]

2. This Constitution, and the laws of the United States which shall be made in pursuance thereof; and all treaties made, or which shall be made, under the authority of the United States, shall be the supreme law of the land; and the Judges in every State shall be bound thereby, any thing in the Constitution or laws of any State to the contrary notwithstanding.

3. The senators and representatives before mentioned, and the members of the several State legislatures,

---

[10] See the 14th Amendment, Sec. 4.

and all executive and judicial officers, both of the United States and of the several States, shall be bound by oath or affirmation to support this Constitution; but no religious test shall ever be required as a qualification to any office or public trust under the United States.

ARTICLE VII

The ratification of the conventions of nine States shall be sufficient for the establishment of this Constitution between the States so ratifying the same.

Done in Convention by the unanimous consent of the States present the seventeenth day of September in the year of our Lord one thousand seven hundred and eighty seven, and of the independence of the United States of America the twelfth. In witness whereof we have hereunto subscribed our names.

[Names omitted]

*   *   *

Articles in addition to, and amendment of, the Constitution of the United States of America, proposed by Congress, and ratified by the legislatures of the several States, pursuant to the fifth article of the original Constitution.

AMENDMENTS

FIRST TEN AMENDMENTS PASSED BY CONGRESS
SEPT. 25, 1789. RATIFIED BY THREE-FOURTHS
OF THE STATES DECEMBER 15, 1791.

AMENDMENT I

Congress shall make no law respecting an establishment of religion, or prohibiting the free exercise thereof; or abridging the freedom of speech, or of the press; or the right of the people peaceably to assemble, and to petition the government for a redress of grievances.

AMENDMENT II

A well regulated militia, being necessary to the security of a free State, the right of the people to keep and bear arms, shall not be infringed.

AMENDMENT III

No soldier shall, in time of peace be quartered in any house, without the consent of the owner, nor in time of war, but in a manner to be prescribed by law.

AMENDMENT IV

The right of the people to be secure in their persons, houses, papers, and effects, against unreasonable searches and seizures, shall not be violated, and no warrants shall issue, but upon probable cause, supported by oath or affirmation, and particularly describing the place to be searched, and the persons or things to be seized.

AMENDMENT V

No person shall be held to answer for a capital, or otherwise infamous crime, unless on a presentment or indictment of a grand jury, except in cases arising in the land or naval forces, or in the militia, when in actual service in time of war or public danger; nor shall any person be subject for the same offence to be twice put in jeopardy of life or limb; nor shall be compelled in any criminal case to be a witness against himself, nor be deprived of life, liberty, or property, without due process of law; nor shall private property be taken for public use, without just compensation.

AMENDMENT VI

In all criminal prosecutions, the accused shall enjoy the right to a speedy and public trial, by an impartial jury of the State and district wherein the crime shall have been committed, which district shall have been previously ascertained by law, and to be informed of the nature and cause of the accusation; to be confronted with the witnesses against him; to have compulsory process for obtaining witnesses in his favor, and to have the assistance of counsel for his defence.

AMENDMENT VII

In suits at common law, where the value in controversy shall exceed twenty dollars, the right of trial by jury shall be preserved, and no fact tried by a jury shall be otherwise reëxamined in any court of the United States, than according to the rules of the common law.

AMENDMENT VIII

Excessive bail shall not be required, nor excessive fines imposed, nor cruel and unusual punishments inflicted.

AMENDMENT IX

The enumeration in the Constitution of certain rights shall not be construed to deny or disparage others retained by the people.

AMENDMENT X

The powers not delegated to the United States by the Constitution, nor prohibited by it to the States, are reserved to the States respectively, or to the people.

AMENDMENT XI

PASSED BY CONGRESS MARCH 5, 1794. RATIFIED JANUARY 8, 1798.

The judicial power of the United States shall not be construed to extend to any suit in law or equity, commenced or prosecuted against one of the United States by citizens of another State, or by citizens or subjects of any foreign State.

AMENDMENT XII

PASSED BY CONGRESS DECEMBER 9, 1803. RATIFIED SEPTEMBER 25, 1804.

The electors shall meet in their respective States, and vote by ballot for President and Vice President, one of whom, at least, shall not be an inhabitant of the same State with themselves; they shall name in their ballots the person voted for as President, and in distinct ballots, the person voted for as Vice President, and they shall make distinct lists of all persons voted for as President and of all persons voted for as Vice President, and of the number of votes for each, which lists they shall sign and certify, and transmit sealed to the seat of the government of the

United States, directed to the President of the Senate;—The President of the Senate shall, in the presence of the Senate and House of Representatives, open all the certificates and the votes shall then be counted;—The person having the greatest number of votes for President, shall be the President, if such number be a majority of the whole number of electors appointed; and if no person have such majority, then from the persons having the highest numbers not exceeding three on the list of those voted for as President, the House of Representatives shall choose immediately, by ballot, the President. But in choosing the President, the votes shall be taken by States, the representation from each State having one vote; a quorum for this purpose shall consist of a member or members from two thirds of the States, and a majority of all the States shall be necessary to a choice. And if the House of Representatives shall not choose a President whenever the right of choice shall devolve upon them, before the fourth day of March next following, then the Vice President shall act as President, as in the case of the death or other constitutional disability of the President. The person having the greatest number of votes as Vice President shall be the Vice President, if such number be a majority of the whole number of electors appointed, and if no person have a majority, then from the two highest numbers on the list, the Senate shall choose the Vice President; a quorum for the purpose shall consist of two thirds of the whole number of Senators, and a majority of the whole number shall be necessary to a choice. But no person constitutionally ineligible to the office of President shall be eligible to that of Vice President of the United States.

AMENDMENT XIII

PASSED BY CONGRESS FEBRUARY 1, 1865. RATIFIED DECEMBER 18, 1865.

Section 1. Neither slavery nor involuntary servitude, except as a punishment for crime whereof the party shall have been duly convicted, shall exist within the United States, or any place subject to their jurisdiction.

Section 2. Congress shall have power to enforce this article by appropriate legislation.

AMENDMENT XIV

PASSED BY CONGRESS JUNE 16, 1866. RATIFIED
JULY 28, 1868.

Section 1. All persons born or naturalized in the United States, and subject to the jurisdiction thereof, are citizens of the United States and of the State wherein they reside. No State shall make or enforce any law which shall abridge the privileges or immunities of citizens of the United States; nor shall any State deprive any person of life, liberty, or property, without due process of law; nor deny to any person within its jurisdiction the equal protection of the laws.

Section 2. Representatives shall be apportioned among the several States according to their respective numbers, counting the whole number of persons in each State, excluding Indians not taxed. But when the right to vote at any election for the choice of electors for President and Vice President of the United States, representatives in Congress, the executive and judicial officers of a State, or the members of the legislature thereof, is denied to any of the male inhabitants of such State, being twenty-one years of age, and citizens of the United States, or in any way abridged, except for participating in rebellion, or other crime, the basis of representation therein shall be reduced in the proportion which the number of such male citizens shall bear to the whole number of male citizens twenty-one years of age in such State.

Section 3. No person shall be a senator or representative in Congress, or elector of President and Vice President, or hold any office, civil or military, under the United States, or under any State, who having previously taken an oath, as a member of Congress, or as an officer of the United States, or as a member of any State legislature, or as an executive or judicial officer of any State, to support the Constitution of the United States, shall have engaged in insurrection or rebellion against the same, or given aid or comfort to the enemies thereof. But Congress may by a vote of two thirds of each House, remove such disability.

Section 4. The validity of the public debt of the United States, authorized by law, including debts incurred for payment of pensions and bounties for services in suppressing insurrection or rebellion, shall not be questioned. But neither the United States nor any State shall assume or pay any debt or obligation incurred in aid of insurrection or rebellion against the United States, or any claim for the loss or emancipation of any slave; but all such debts, obligations, and claims shall be held illegal and void.

Section 5. The Congress shall have power to enforce, by appropriate legislation, the provisions of this article.

AMENDMENT XV

PASSED BY CONGRESS FEBRUARY 27, 1869. RATIFIED MARCH 30, 1870.

Section 1. The right of citizens of the United States to vote shall not be denied or abridged by the United States or by any State on account of race, color, or previous condition of servitude.

Section 2. The Congress shall have power to enforce this article by appropriate legislation.

AMENDMENT XVI

PASSED BY CONGRESS JULY 12, 1909. RATIFIED FEBRUARY 25, 1913.

The Congress shall have power to lay and collect taxes on incomes, from whatever source derived, without apportionment among the several States. and without regard to any census or enumeration.

AMENDMENT XVII

PASSED BY CONGRESS MAY 16, 1912. RATIFIED MAY 31, 1913.

The Senate of the United States shall be composed of two senators from each State, elected by the people thereof, for six years; and each senator shall have one vote. The electors in each State shall have the qualifications requisite for electors of the most numerous branch of the State legislature.

When vacancies happen in the representation of any State in the Senate, the executive authority of such State shall issue writs of election to fill such vacancies: *Provided,* That the legislature of any State may empower the executive thereof to make temporary appointments until the people fill the vacancies by election as the legislature may direct.

This amendment shall not be so construed as to affect the election or term of any senator chosen before it becomes valid as part of the Constitution.

AMENDMENT XVIII [11]

PASSED BY CONGRESS DECEMBER 17, 1917. RATIFIED JANUARY 29, 1919.

After one year from the ratification of this article, the manufacture, sale, or transportation of intoxicating liquors within, the importation thereof into, or the exportation thereof from the United States and all territory subject to the jurisdiction thereof for beverage purposes is hereby prohibited.

The Congress and the several States shall have concurrent power to enforce this article by appropriate legislation.

This article shall be inoperative unless it shall have been ratified as an amendment to the Constitution by the legislatures of the several States, as provided in the Constitution, within seven years from the date of the submission hereof to the States by Congress.

AMENDMENT XIX

PASSED BY CONGRESS JUNE 5, 1919. RATIFIED AUGUST 26, 1920.

The right of citizens of the United States to vote shall not be denied or abridged by the United States or by any State on account of sex.

[11] Repealed by the 21st Amendment.

Congress shall have power to enforce this article by appropriate legislation.

AMENDMENT XX

PASSED BY CONGRESS MARCH 3, 1932. RATIFIED JANUARY 23, 1933.

Section 1. The terms of the President and Vice President shall end at noon on the 20th day of January, and the terms of Senators and Representatives at noon on the 3d day of January, of the years in which such terms would have ended if this article had not been ratified; and the terms of their successors shall then begin.

Section 2. The Congress shall assemble at least once in every year, and such meeting shall begin at noon on the 3d day of January, unless they shall by law appoint a different day.

Section 3. If, at the time fixed for the beginning of the term of the President, the President elect shall have died, the Vice President elect shall become President. If a President shall not have been chosen before the time fixed for the beginning of his term, or if the President elect shall have failed to qualify, then the Vice President elect shall act as President until a President shall have qualified; and the Congress may by law provide for the case wherein neither a President elect nor a Vice President elect shall have qualified, declaring who shall then act as President, or the manner in which one who is to act shall be selected, and such person shall act accordingly until a President or Vice President shall have qualified.

Section 4. The Congress may by law provide for the case of the death of any of the persons from whom the House of Representatives may choose a President whenever the right of choice shall have devolved upon them, and for the case of the death of any of the persons from whom the Senate may choose a Vice President whenever the right of choice shall have devolved upon them.

Section 5. Sections 1 and 2 shall take effect on the 15th day of October following the ratification of this article.

Section 6. This article shall be inoperative unless it shall have been ratified as an amendment to the Constitution by the legislatures of three-fourths of the several States within seven years from the date of its submission.

AMENDMENT XXI

PASSED BY CONGRESS FEBRUARY 20, 1933. RATIFIED DECEMBER 5, 1933.

Section 1. The Eighteenth Article of amendment to the Constitution of the United States is hereby repealed.

Section 2. The transportation or importation into any State, Territory, or possession of the United States for delivery or use therein of intoxicating liquors in violation of the laws thereof, is hereby prohibited.

Section 3. This article shall be inoperative unless it shall have been ratified as an amendment to the Constitution by conventions in the several States, as provided in the Constitution, within seven years from the date of the submission thereof to the States by the Congress.

AMENDMENT XXII

PASSED BY CONGRESS MARCH 12, 1947. RATIFIED MARCH 1, 1951.

No person shall be elected to the office of the President more than twice, and no person who has held the office of President, or acted as President, for more than two years of a term to which some other person was elected President shall be elected to the office of the President more than once.

But this article shall not apply to any person holding the office of President when this article was proposed by the Congress, and shall not prevent any person who may be holding the office of President, or acting as President, during the term within which this article becomes operative from holding the office of President or acting as President during the remainder of such term.

This article shall be inoperative unless it shall have been ratified as an amendment to the Constitution by the legislatures of three-fourths of the several States within seven years from the date of its submission to the States by the Congress.

DOCUMENT 5

ELBRIDGE GERRY, LETTER TO PRESIDENT OF SENATE AND SPEAKER OF HOUSE OF REPRESENTATIVES OF MASSACHUSETTS,

OCTOBER 18, 1787

Three men—Elbridge Gerry of Massachusetts, George Mason and Edmund Randolph of Virginia—stayed to the end of the Federal Convention but withheld their signatures from the Constitution. In this letter, reporting to the legislature of Massachusetts on the work of the Convention, Gerry expresses his objections to the Constitution with great succinctness. His complaint here "that there is no adequate provision for a representation of the people," after his words to the Convention: "The evils we experience flow from the excess of democracy," will suggest some of the complex problems of interpretation that confront students of the debate over the Constitution.

Gentlemen:

I have the honor to inclose, pursuant to my commission, the constitution proposed by the federal convention.

To this system I gave my dissent, and shall submit my objections to the honourable legislature.

It was painful for me, on a subject of such national importance, to differ from the respectable members who signed the constitution: But conceiving as I did, that the liberties of America were not secured by the system, it was my duty to oppose it.

My principal objections to the plan, are, that there is no adequate provision for a representation of the people—that they have no security for the right of election—that some of the powers of the legislature are ambiguous, and others indefinite and dangerous—that the executive is blended with, and will have an undue influence over, the legislature—that the judicial department will be oppressive—that treaties of the highest importance may be formed by the president with the advice of two–thirds of a quorum of the senate—and that the system is without the security of a bill of rights. These are objections which are not local, but apply equally to all the states.

As the convention was called for "the sole and express purpose of revising the articles of confederation, and reporting to congress, and the several legislatures, such alterations and provisions as shall render the federal constitution adequate to the exigencies of government, and the preservation of the union," I did not conceive that these powers extend to the formation of the plan proposed: but the convention being of a different opinion, I acquiesced in it, being fully convinced that to preserve the union, an efficient government was indispensably necessary; and that it would be difficult to make proper amendments to the articles of confederation.

The constitution proposed has few if any federal features; but is rather a system of national government. Nevertheless, in many respects, I think it has great merit, and by proper amendments, may be adapted to the "exigencies of government, and preservation of liberty."

DOCUMENT 6

THOMAS JEFFERSON, LETTER TO JAMES MADISON ON THE CONSTITUTION,

DECEMBER 20, 1787

Many men stood either violently for or violently against the Constitution. Thomas Jefferson, however, like a large number of other moderates, had mixed feelings. He had never liked the imperfect control of commerce under the Confederation, and he was unhappy with its failure to separate sufficiently the powers of executive, legislature, and judiciary. Yet he was not nearly so alarmed about conditions under the Confederation as some of his friends, nor so upset about Shays's Rebellion. He wrote to Madison in 1786 that he favored a constitution that would "make us one nation as to

foreign concerns, and keep us distinct in domestic
ones." He approved of the calling of the Federal Con-
vention, which he called "an assembly of demigods."
When the final results of the Convention's work
reached him in France, he wrote this letter on the
proposed Constitution to his friend Madison, which
gives the opinions of a man not entirely certain about
its worth. This letter is particularly valuable for its
cogent statement of the widespread view that the in-
clusion of a bill of rights was of the highest impor-
tance. Though Jefferson was expressing his real views
to Madison, he was probably toning down the inten-
sity of his misgivings. To another Virginian, Edward
Carrington, he wrote, December 21, 1787: "As to the
Constitution I find myself nearly a neutral. There is a
great mass of good in it, in a very desirable form: but
there is also to me a bitter pill or two."

Thomas Jefferson to James Madison, December 20, 1787

I like much the general idea of framing a government into Legislative, Judiciary and Executive. I like the
power given the Legislature to levy taxes; and for that
reason solely approve of the greater house being chosen
by the people directly. For tho' I think a house chosen by
them will be very illy qualified to legislate for the Union,
for foreign nations &c. yet this evil does not weigh against
the good of preserving inviolate the fundamental principle
that the people are not to be taxed but by representatives
chosen immediately by themselves. I am captivated by
the compromise of the opposite claims of the great and
little states, of the latter to equal, and the former to proportional influence. I am much pleased too with the
substitution of the method of voting by persons, instead
of that of voting by states: and I like the negative given
to the Executive with a third of either house, though I
should have liked it better had the Judiciary been associated
for that purpose, or invested with a similar and separate
power. There are other good things of less moment. I
will now add what I do not like. First the omission of a
bill of rights providing clearly and without the aid of
sophisms for freedom of religion, freedom of the press,
protection against standing armies, restriction against

monopolies, the eternal and unremitting force of the habeas corpus laws, and trials by jury in all matters of fact triable by the laws of the land and not by the law of Nations. . . . Let me add that a bill of rights is what the people are entitled to against every government on earth, general or particular, and what no just government should refuse, or rest on inference. The second feature I dislike, and greatly dislike, is the abandonment in every instance of the necessity of rotation in office and most particularly in the case of the President. Experience concurs with reason in concluding that the first magistrate will always be re-elected if the constitution permits it. He is then an officer for life. This once observed it becomes of so much consequence to certain nations to have a friend or a foe at the head of our affairs that they will interfere with money and with arms. . . . It may be said that if elections are to be attended with these disorders, the seldomer they are renewed the better. But experience shews that the only way to prevent disorder is to render them uninteresting by frequent changes. An incapacity to be elected a second time would have been the only effectual preventative. The power of removing him every fourth year by the vote of the people is a power which will not be exercised. The king of Poland is removable every day by the Diet, yet he is never removed.—Smaller objections are the Appeal in fact as well as law, and the binding all persons Legislative, Executive and Judiciary by oath to maintain that constitution. I do not pretend to decide what would be the best method of procuring the establishment of the manifold good things in this constitution, and of getting rid of the bad. Whether by adopting it in hopes of future amendment, or, after it has been duly weighed and canvassed by the people, after seeing the parts they generally dislike, and those they generally approve, to say to them "We see now what you wish. Send together your deputies again, let them frame a constitution for you omitting what you have condemned, and establishing the powers you approve. Even these will be a great addition to the energy of your government.". . . I own I am not a friend to a very energetic government. It is always oppressive. The late rebellion in Massachusetts has given more alarm than I think it should have done. Calculate that one rebellion in 13 states in the course of 11 years, is but one for each state in a century and a half. No country should be so long without one. Nor will any degree of power in the hands of government prevent insurrections. France with all it's despotism, and two or three hundred thousand men always in arms has had three insurrections in the three years I have been here in every one of which greater numbers were engaged than in Massachusetts and a great deal more blood was spilt. In Turkey, which Montesquieu supposes more despotic, insurrections are the events of every day. In England, where the hand of power is lighter than here [France], but heavier than with us they happen every half dozen years. Compare again the ferocious depredations of their insurgents with the order, the moderation and the almost self extinguishment of ours.—After all, it is my principle that the will of the Majority should always prevail. If they approve the proposed Convention in all it's parts, I shall concur in it chearfully, in hopes that they will amend it whenever they shall find it work wrong. I think our governments will remain virtuous for many centuries; as long as they are chiefly agricultural; and this will be as long as there shall be vacant lands in any part of America. When they get piled upon one another in large cities, as in Europe, they will become corrupt as in Europe. Above all things I hope the education of the common people will be attended to; convinced that on their good sense we may rely with the most security for the preservation of a due degree of liberty. . . .

DOCUMENT 7

DEBATE IN THE VIRGINIA RATIFYING CONVENTION,
JUNE 4 AND 5, 1788

In the ratifying conventions called by the several states, the merits and defects of the proposed system of government were thoroughly debated. Without the adherence of Virginia, the richest and most populous

state, the new government could hardly hope for
success. In no state was the subject more brilliantly
debated. The Virginia convention called forth the an-
alytical and oratorical talents of such men as Patrick
Henry, Henry ("Light-Horse Harry") Lee, John Mar-
shall, George Mason, Edmund Pendleton, Governor
Edmund Randolph, and George Wythe. In this selec-
tion some important objections to the new government
are set forth in the contrasting styles of Mason and
Henry.

June 4, 1788

MR. GEORGE MASON. Mr. Chairman, whether the
Constitution be good or bad, the present clause clearly
discovers that it is a national government, and no longer
a Confederation. I mean that clause which gives the first
hint of the general government laying direct taxes. The
assumption of this power of laying direct taxes does, of
itself, entirely change the confederation of the states into
one consolidated government. This power, being at discretion, unconfined, and without any kind of control, must
carry everything before it. The very idea of converting
what was formerly a confederation to a consolidated
government, is totally subversive of every principle which
has hitherto governed us. This power is calculated to
annihilate totally the state governments. Will the people of
this great community submit to be individually taxed by
two different and distinct powers? Will they suffer themselves to be doubly harassed? These two concurrent powers
cannot exist long together; the one will destroy the other:
the general government being paramount to, and in every
respect more powerful than the state governments, the
latter must give way to the former. Is it to be supposed
that one national government will suit so extensive a
country, embracing so many climates, and containing
inhabitants so very different in manners, habits, and customs? It is ascertained, by history, that there never was a
government over a very extensive country without destroying the liberties of the people: history also, supported by
the opinions of the best writers, shows us that monarchy
may suit a large territory, and despotic governments over

so extensive a country, but that popular governments can only exist in small territories. Is there a single example, on the face of the earth, to support a contrary opinion? Where is there one exception to this general rule? Was there ever an instance of a general national government extending over so extensive a country, abounding in such a variety of climates, etc., where the people retained their liberty? I solemnly declare that no man is a greater friend to a firm union of the American States than I am; but, sir, if this great end can be obtained without hazarding the rights of the people, why should we recur to such dangerous principles? Requisitions have been often refused, sometimes from an impossibility of complying with them; often from that great variety of circumstances which retards the collection of moneys; and perhaps sometimes from a wilful design of procrastinating. But why shall we give up to the national government this power, so dangerous in its nature, and for which its members will not have sufficient information? Is it not well known that what would be a proper tax in one state would be grievous in another? The gentleman who hath favored us with a eulogium in favor of this system, must, after all the encomiums he has been pleased to bestow upon it, acknowledge that our federal representatives must be unacquainted with the situation of their constituents. Sixty-five members cannot possibly know the situation and circumstances of all the inhabitants of this immense continent. When a certain sum comes to be taxed, and the mode of levying to be fixed, they will lay the tax on that article which will be most productive and easiest in the collection, without consulting the real circumstances or convenience of a country, with which, in fact, they cannot be sufficiently acquainted.

The mode of levying taxes is of the utmost consequence; and yet here it is to be determined by those who have neither knowledge of our situation, nor a common interest with us, nor a fellow-feeling for us. The subject of taxation differs in three-fourths, nay, I might say with truth, in four-fifths of the states. If we trust the national government with an effectual way of raising the necessary sums, it is sufficient: everything we do further is trusting the happiness and rights of the people. Why, then, should we give up this dangerous power of individual taxation? Why leave the manner of laying taxes to those who, in the nature of things, cannot be acquainted with the situation of those on whom they are to impose them, when it can be done by those who are well acquainted with it? If, instead of giving this oppressive power, we give them such an effectual alternative as will answer the purpose, without encountering the evil and danger that might arise from it, then I would cheerfully acquiesce; and would it not be far more eligible? I candidly acknowledge the inefficacy of the Confederation; but requisitions have been made which were impossible to be complied with—requisitions for more gold and silver than were in the United States. If we give the general government the power of demanding their quotas of the states, with an alternative of laying direct taxes in case of non–compliance, then the mischief would be avoided; and the certainty of this conditional power would, in all human probability, prevent the application, and the sums necessary for the Union would be then laid by the states, by those who know how it can best be raised, by those who have a fellow-feeling for us. Give me leave to say, that the sum raised one way with convenience and ease, would be very oppressive another way. Why, then, not leave this power to be exercised by those who know the mode most convenient for the inhabitants, and not by those who must necessarily apportion it in such manner as shall be oppressive? . . . To a government which, in the nature of things cannot but be defective, no powers ought to be given but such as are absolutely necessary. There is one thing in it which I conceive to be extremely dangerous. Gentlemen may talk of public virtue and confidence; we shall be told that the House of Representatives will consist of the most virtuous men on the continent, and that in their hands we may trust our dearest rights. This, like all other assemblies, will be composed of some bad and some good men; and, considering the natural lust of power so inherent in man, I fear the thirst of power will prevail to oppress the man, I fear the thirst of power will prevail to oppress the people. . . .

If such amendments be introduced as shall exclude danger, I shall most gladly put my hand to it. When such amendments as shall, from the best information, secure the great essential rights of the people, shall be agreed to by gentlemen, I shall most heartily make the greatest concessions, and concur in any reasonable measure to obtain the desirable end of conciliation and unanimity.

June 5, 1788

MR. HENRY. . . . I rose yesterday to ask a question which arose in my own mind. When I asked that question, I thought the meaning of my interrogation was obvious. The fate of this question and of America may depend on this. Have they said, We, the States? Have they made a proposal of a compact between States? If they had, this would be a confederation. It is otherwise most clearly a consolidated government. The question turns, sir, on that poor little thing—the expression, We, the *people,* instead of the *states,* of America. I need not take much pains to show that the principles of this system are extremely pernicious, impolitic, and dangerous. Is this a monarchy, like England—a compact between prince and people, with checks on the former to secure the liberty of the latter? Is this a confederacy, like Holland—an association of a number of independent states, each of which retains its individual sovereignty? It is not a democracy, wherein the people retain all their rights securely. Had these principles been adhered to, we should not have been brought to this alarming transition, from a confederacy to a consolidated government. We have no detail of these great considerations, which, in my opinion, ought to have abounded before we should recur to a government of this kind. Here is a resolution as radical as that which separated us from Great Britain. It is radical in this transition; our rights and privileges are endangered, and the sovereignty of the states will be relinquished: and cannot we plainly see that this is actually the case? The rights of conscience, trial by jury, liberty of the press, all your immunities and franchises, all pretensions to human rights and privileges, are rendered insecure, if not lost, by this change, so loudly talked of by some, and inconsiderately by others. Is this tame relinquishment of rights worthy of freemen? Is it worthy of that manly fortitude that ought to characterize republicans? . . . You are not to inquire how your trade may be increased, nor how you are to become a great and powerful people, but how your liberties can be secured; for liberty ought to be the direct end of your government. . . .

We are come hither to preserve the poor commonwealth of Virginia, if it can be possibly done: something must be done to preserve your liberty and mine. The Confederation, this same despised government, merits, in my opinion, the highest encomium. It carried us through a long and dangerous war; it rendered us victorious in that bloody conflict with a powerful nation; it has secured us a territory greater than any European monarch possesses: and shall a government which has been thus strong and vigorous, be accused of imbecility, and abandoned for want of energy? Consider what you are about to do before you part with the government. Take longer time in reckoning things; revolutions like this have happened in almost every country in Europe; similar examples are to be found in ancient Greece and ancient Rome—instances of the people losing their liberty by their own carelessness, and the ambition of a few. We are cautioned by the honorable gentleman, who presides, against faction and turbulence. I acknowledge that licentiousness is dangerous, and that it ought to be provided against: I acknowledge, also, the new form of government may effectually prevent it: yet there is another thing it will as effectually do—it will oppress and ruin the people.

There are sufficient guards placed against sedition and licentiousness; for, when power is given to this government to suppress these, or for any other purpose, the language it assumes is clear, express, and unequivocal; but when this Constitution speaks of privileges, there is an ambiguity, sir, a fatal ambiguity—an ambiguity which is very astonishing. In the clause under consideration there is the strangest language that I can conceive. I mean, when it says that there shall not be more representatives than one for every thirty thousand. Now, sir, how easy is it to evade this privilege! "The number shall not exceed one for every thirty thousand." This may be satisfied by one representative from each state. Let our numbers be ever so great, this immense continent may, by this artful expression, be reduced to have but thirteen representatives. . . .

Where is the danger? If, sir, there was any, I would recur to the American spirit to defend us; that spirit which has enabled us to surmount the greatest difficulties: to that illustrious spirit I address my most fervent prayer to prevent our adopting a system destructive to liberty. Let not gentlemen be told that it is not safe to reject this government. Wherefore is it not safe? We are told there are dangers, but those dangers are ideal; they cannot be demonstrated. To encourage us to adopt it, they tell us that there is a plain, easy way of getting amendments. When I come to contemplate this part, I suppose that I am mad, or that my countrymen are so. The way to amendment is, in my conception, shut. Let us consider this plain, easy way. [Constitution, Art. v]

Hence it appears that three fourths of the states must ultimately agree to any amendments that may be necessary. Let us consider the consequence of this. However uncharitable it may appear, yet I must tell my opinion—that the most unworthy characters may get into power, and prevent the introduction of amendments. Let us suppose—for the case is supposable, possible, and probable—that you happen to deal those powers to unworthy hands; will they relinquish powers already in their possession, or agree to amendments? Two thirds of the Congress, or of the state legislatures, are necessary even to propose amendments. If one third of these be unworthy men, they may prevent the application for amendments; but what is destructive and mischievous, is, that three fourths of the state legislatures, or of the state conventions, must concur in the amendments when proposed! In such numerous bodies, there must necessarily be some designing, bad men. To suppose that so large a number as three fourths of the states will concur, is to suppose that they will possess genius, intelligence, and integrity, approaching to miraculous. It would indeed be miraculous that they should concur in the same amendments, or even in such as would bear some likeness to one another; for four of the smallest states, that do not collectively contain one tenth part of the population of the United States, may

obstruct the most salutary and necessary amendments.
Nay, in these four states, six tenths of the people may
reject these amendments; and suppose that amendments
shall be opposed to amendments, which is highly probable,
—is it possible that three fourths can ever agree to the
same amendments? A bare majority in these four small
states may hinder the adoption of amendments; so that
we may fairly and justly conclude that one twentieth part
of the American people may prevent the removal of the
most grievous inconveniences and oppression, by refusing
to accede to amendments. A trifling minority may reject
the most salutary amendments. Is this an easy mode of
securing the public liberty? . . .

Shall we imitate the example of those nations who
have gone from a simple to a splendid government? Are
those nations more worthy of our imitation? What can
make an adequate satisfaction to them for the loss they
have suffered in attaining such a government—for the
loss of their liberty? If we admit this consolidated government, it will be because we like a great, splendid one.
Some way or other we must be a great and mighty empire;
we must have an army, and a navy, and a number of
things. When the American spirit was in its youth, the
language of America was different: liberty, sir, was then
the primary object. We are descended from a people
whose government was founded on liberty: our glorious
forefathers of Great Britain made liberty the foundation
of every thing. That country is become a great, mighty,
and splendid nation; not because their government is
strong and energetic, but, sir, because liberty is its direct
end and foundation. We drew the spirit of liberty from
our British ancestors: by that spirit we have triumphed
over every difficulty. But now, sir, the American spirit,
assisted by the ropes and chains of consolidation, is about
to convert this country into a powerful and mighty
empire. If you make the citizens of this country agree to
become the subjects of one great consolidated empire of
America, your government will not have sufficient energy
to keep them together. Such a government is incompatible
with the genius of republicanism. There will be no checks,
no real balances, in this government. What can avail your
specious, imaginary balances, your rope-dancing, chain-

rattling, ridiculous ideal checks and contrivances? But, sir, we are not feared by foreigners; we do not make nations tremble. Would this constitute happiness, or secure liberty? I trust, sir, our political hemisphere will ever direct their operations to the security of those objects.

Consider our situation, sir: go to the poor man, and ask him what he does. He will inform you that he enjoys the fruits of his labor, under his own fig-tree, with his wife and children around him, in peace and security. Go to every other member of society,—you will find the same tranquil ease and content; you will find no alarms or disturbances. Why, then, tell us of danger, to terrify us into an adoption of this new form of government? And yet who knows the dangers that this new system may produce? They are out of the sight of the common people: they cannot foresee latent consequences. I dread the operation of it on the middling and lower classes of people: it is for them I fear the adoption of this system. . . .

This Constitution is said to have beautiful features; but when I come to examine these features, sir, they appear to me horribly frightful. Among other deformities, it has an awful squinting; it squints towards monarchy; and does not this raise indignation in the breast of every true American?

Your President may easily become king. Your Senate is so imperfectly constructed that your dearest rights may be sacrificed by what may be a small minority; and a very small minority may continue forever unchangeably this government, although horridly defective. Where are your checks in this government? Your strongholds will be in the hands of your enemies. It is on a supposition that your American governors shall be honest, that all the good qualities of this government are founded; but its defective and imperfect construction puts it in their power to perpetrate the worst of mischiefs, should they be bad men; and, sir, would not all the world, from the eastern to the western hemisphere, blame our distracted folly in resting our rights upon the contingency of our rulers being good or bad? Show me that age and country where the rights and liberties of the people were placed on the sole chance of their rulers being good men, without a consequent loss of liberty! I say that the loss of that dearest privilege has ever followed, with absolute certainty, every such mad attempt. . . .

DOCUMENT 8

THE FEDERALIST,
NUMBERS 10 AND 15, 1787

The Federalist papers, generally considered the most important contribution to political thought made in America, were first published under the signature of "Publius" in the New York press, beginning on October 27, 1787. The essays appeared in book form in 1788, with an introduction by Hamilton, and subsequently in many editions and several languages. "Publius" was, of course, three men—Hamilton, Madison, and Jay; but Jay wrote only a few of the eighty-five articles, Hamilton and Madison the rest. The Federalist was not a detached or abstract inquiry into political theory but an instrument in the campaign for the adoption of the Constitution by New York state. Besides giving all the major arguments for the ratification of the Constitution, the authors also discussed many general problems of politics. In The Federalist *Number 10, published in the* New York Packet, *November 23, Madison shows how the evils of faction and the danger of majority tyranny can be avoided in an extensive union embracing many diverse interests. In Number 15, published in the* Independent Journal, *December 1, 1787, Hamilton reviews the inadequacy of the central government under the Articles of Confederation.*

James Madison,
The Federalist, Number 10

Among the numerous advantages promised by a well-constructed Union, none deserves to be more accurately developed than its tendency to break and control the violence of faction. The friend of popular governments never finds himself so much alarmed for their character and fate as when he contemplates their propensity to this dangerous vice. He will not fail, therefore, to set a due value on any plan which, without violating the principles to which he is attached, provides a proper cure for it. The instability, injustice, and confusion introduced into the public councils, have, in truth, been the mortal diseases under which popular governments have everywhere perished; as they continue to be the favorite and fruitful topics from which the adversaries to liberty derive their most specious declamations. The valuable improvements made by the American constitutions on the popular models, both ancient and modern, cannot certainly be too much admired; but it would be an unwarrantable partiality to contend that they have as effectually obviated the danger on this side as was wished and expected. Complaints are everywhere heard from our most considerate and virtuous citizens, equally the friends of public and private faith, and of public and personal liberty, that our governments are too unstable, that the public good is disregarded in the conflicts of rival parties, and that measures are too often decided, not according to the rules of justice and the rights of the minor party, but by the superior force of an interested and overbearing majority. However anxiously we may wish that these complaints had no foundation, the evidence of known facts will not permit us to deny that they are in some degree true. It will be found, indeed, on a candid review of our situation, that some of the distresses under which we labor have been erroneously charged on the operation of our governments; but it will be found, at the same time, that other causes will not alone account for many of our heaviest misfortunes; and, particularly, for that prevailing and increasing distrust of public engagements, and alarm for private rights, which are echoed from one end of the continent to the other. These must be chiefly, if not wholly, effects of the unsteadiness and injustice with which a factious spirit has tainted our public administrations.

By a faction, I understand a number of citizens, whether amounting to a majority or a minority of the whole, who are united and actuated by some common impulse of passion, or of interest, adverse to the rights of other citizens, or to the permanent and aggregate interests of the community.

There are two methods of curing the mischiefs of faction: the one, by removing its causes; the other, by controlling its effects.

There are again two methods of removing the causes of faction: the one, by destroying the liberty which is essential to its existence; the other, by giving to every citizen the same opinions, the same passions, and the same interests.

It could never be more truly said than of the first remedy, that it was worse than the disease. Liberty is to faction what air is to fire, an aliment without which it instantly expires. But it could not be less folly to abolish liberty, which is essential to political life, because it nourishes faction, than it would be to wish the annihilation of air, which is essential to animal life, because it imparts to fire its destructive agency.

The second expedient is as impracticable as the first would be unwise. As long as the reason of man continues fallible, and he is at liberty to exercise it, different opinions will be formed. As long as the connection subsists between his reason and his self-love, his opinions and his passions will have a reciprocal influence on each other; and the former will be objects to which the latter will attach themselves. The diversity in the faculties of men, from which the rights of property originate, is not less an insuperable obstacle to a uniformity of interests. The protection of these faculties is the first object of government. From the protection of different and unequal faculties of acquiring property, the possession of different degrees and kinds of property immediately results; and from the influence of these on the sentiments and views of the respective proprietors, ensues a division of the society into different interests and parties.

The latent causes of faction are thus sown in the nature of man; and we see them everywhere brought into different degrees of activity, according to the different circumstances of civil society. A zeal for different opinions concerning religion, concerning government, and many other points, as well of speculation as of practice; an attachment to different leaders ambitiously contending for pre-eminence and power; or to persons of other descriptions whose fortunes have been interesting to the human passions, have, in turn, divided mankind into parties, inflamed them with mutual animosity, and rendered them much more disposed to vex and oppress each other than to co-operate for their common good. So strong is this propensity of mankind to fall into mutual animosities that, where no substantial occasion presents itself, the most frivolous and fanciful distinctions have been sufficient to kindle their unfriendly passions and excite their most violent conflicts. But the most common and durable source of factions has been the various and unequal distribution of property. Those who hold and those who are without property have ever formed distinct interests in society. Those who are creditors, and those who are debtors, fall under a like discrimination. A landed interest, a manufacturing interest, a mercantile interest, a moneyed interest, with many lesser interests, grow up of necessity in civilized nations, and divide them into different classes actuated by different sentiments and views. The regulation of these various and interfering interests forms the principal task of modern legislation, and involves the spirit of party and faction in the necessary and ordinary operations of the government.

No man is allowed to be a judge in his own cause, because his interest would certainly bias his judgment and, not improbably, corrupt his integrity. With equal, nay with greater reason, a body of men are unfit to be both judges and parties at the same time; yet what are many of the most important acts of legislation but so many judicial determinations, not indeed concerning the rights of single persons, but concerning the rights of large bodies of citizens? And what are the different classes of legislators but advocates and parties to the causes which they determine? Is a law proposed concerning private debts? It is a question to which the creditors are parties on one side and the debtors on the other. Justice ought to hold the balance between them. Yet the parties are, and must be, themselves the judges; and the most numerous party, or, in other words, the most powerful faction, must be expected to prevail. Shall domestic manufactures be encouraged, and in what degree, by restrictions on foreign manufactures? are questions which would be differently decided by the landed and the manufacturing classes, and probably by neither with a sole regard to justice and the public good. The apportionment of taxes on the various descriptions of property is an act which seems to require the most exact impartiality; yet there is, perhaps, no legislative act in which greater opportunity and temptation are given to a predominant party to trample on the rules of justice. Every shilling with which they overburden the inferior number is a shilling saved to their own pockets.

It is in vain to say that enlightened statesmen will be able to adjust these clashing interests, and render them all subservient to the public good. Enlightened statesmen will not always be at the helm. Nor in many cases can such an adjustment be made at all without taking into view indirect and remote considerations, which will rarely prevail over the immediate interest which one party may find in disregarding the rights of another or the good of the whole.

The inference to which we are brought is that the *causes* of faction cannot be removed, and that relief is only to be sought in the means of controlling its *effects*.

If a faction consists of less than a majority, relief is supplied by the republican principle, which enables the majority to defeat its sinister views by regular vote. It may clog the administration, it may convulse the society; but it will be unable to execute and mask its violence under the forms of the Constitution. When a majority is included in a faction, the form of popular government, on the other hand, enables it to sacrifice to its ruling passion or interest both the public good and the rights of other citizens. To secure the public good and private rights against the danger of such a faction, and at the same time to preserve the spirit and the form of popular government, is then the great object to which our inquiries are directed. Let me add that it is the great desideratum by which this form of government can be rescued from the opprobrium under which it has so long labored, and be recommended to the esteem and adoption of mankind.

By what means is this object attainable? Evidently by one of two only: Either the existence of the same passion or interest in a majority at the same time must be prevented, or the majority, having such coexistent passion or interest, must be rendered, by their number and local situation, unable to concert and carry into effect schemes of oppression. If the impulse and the opportunity be suffered to coincide, we well know that neither moral nor religious motives can be relied on as an adequate control. They are not found to be such on the injustice and violence of individuals, and lose their efficacy in proportion to the number combined together, that is, in proportion as their efficacy becomes needful.

From this view of the subject it may be concluded that a pure democracy, by which I mean a society consisting of a small number of citizens, who assemble and administer the government in person, can admit of no cure for the mischiefs of faction. A common passion or interest will, in almost every case, be felt by a majority of the whole; a communication and concert result from the form of government itself; and there is nothing to check the inducements to sacrifice the weaker party or an obnoxious individual. Hence it is that such democracies have ever been spectacles of turbulence and contention; have ever been found incompatible with personal security or the rights of property; and have in general been as short in their lives as they have been violent in their deaths. Theoretic politicians, who have patronized this species of government, have erroneously supposed that by reducing mankind to a perfect equality in their political rights, they would, at the same time, be perfectly equalized and assimilated in their possessions, their opinions, and their passions.

A republic, by which I mean a government in which the scheme of representation takes place, opens a different prospect, and promises the cure for which we are seeking. Let us examine the points in which it varies from pure democracy, and we shall comprehend both the nature of the cure and the efficacy which it must derive from the Union.

The two great points of difference between a democracy and a republic are: first, the delegation of the government, in the latter, to a small number of citizens elected by the rest; secondly, the greater number of citizens, and greater sphere of country, over which the latter may be extended.

The effect of the first difference is, on the one hand,

to refine and enlarge the public views, by passing them through the medium of a chosen body of citizens, whose wisdom may best discern the true interest of their country, and whose patriotism and love of justice will be least likely to sacrifice it to temporary or partial considerations. Under such a regulation, it may well happen that the public voice, pronounced by the representatives of the people, will be more consonant to the public good than if pronounced by the people themselves, convened for the purpose. On the other hand, the effect may be inverted. Men of factious tempers, of local prejudices, or of sinister designs, may, by intrigue, by corruption, or by other means, first obtain the suffrages, and then betray the interests, of the people. The question resulting is, whether small or extensive republics are more favorable to the election of proper guardians of the public weal; and it is clearly decided in favor of the latter by two obvious considerations:

In the first place, it is to be remarked that, however small the republic may be, the representatives must be raised to a certain number, in order to guard against the cabals of a few; and that, however large it may be, they must be limited to a certain number, in order to guard against the confusion of a multitude. Hence, the number of representatives in the two cases not being in proportion to that of the two constituents, and being proportionally greater in the small republic, it follows that, if the proportion of fit characters be not less in the large than in the small republic, the former will present a greater option, and consequently a greater probability of a fit choice.

In the next place, as each representative will be chosen by a greater number of citizens in the large than in the small republic, it will be more difficult for unworthy candidates to practice with success the vicious arts by which elections are too often carried; and the suffrages of the people, being more free, will be more likely to center in men who possess the most attractive merit and the most diffusive and established characters.

It must be confessed that in this, as in most other cases, there is a mean, on both sides of which inconveniences will be found to lie. By enlarging too much the number of electors, you render the representative too little acquainted with all their local circumstances and lesser interests; as by reducing it too much, you render him unduly attached to these, and too little fit to comprehend and pursue great and national objects. The federal Constitution forms a happy combination in this respect; the great and aggregate interests being referred to the national, the local and particular to the State legislatures.

The other point of difference is, the greater number of citizens and extent of territory which may be brought within the compass of republican than of democratic government; and it is this circumstance principally which renders factious combinations less to be dreaded in the former than in the latter. The smaller the society, the fewer probably will be the distinct parties and interests composing it; the fewer the distinct parties and interests, the more frequently will a majority be found of the same party; and the smaller the number of individuals composing a majority, and the smaller the compass within which they are placed, the more easily will they concert and execute their plans of oppression. Extend the sphere, and you take in a greater variety of parties and interests; you make it less probable that a majority of the whole will have a common motive to invade the rights of other citizens; or, if such a common motive exists, it will be more difficult for all who feel it to discover their own strength and to act in unison with each other. Besides other impediments, it may be remarked that where there is a consciousness of unjust or dishonorable purposes, communication is always checked by distrust in proportion to the number whose concurrence is necessary.

Hence it clearly appears that the same advantage which a republic has over a democracy, in controlling the effects of faction, is enjoyed by a large over a small republic, is enjoyed by the Union over the States composing it. Does the advantage consist in the substitution of representatives whose enlightened views and virtuous sentiments render them superior to local prejudices and to schemes of injustice? It will not be denied that the representation of the Union will be most likely to possess these requisite endowments. Does it consist in the greater security afforded by a greater variety of parties against the event of any one party being able to outnumber and oppress the rest? In an equal degree does the increased variety of parties comprised within the Union increase this security. Does it, in fine, consist in the greater obstacles opposed to the concert and accomplishment of the secret wishes of an unjust and interested majority? Here, again, the extent of the Union gives it the most palpable advantage.

The influence of factious leaders may kindle a flame within their particular States, but will be unable to spread a general conflagration through the other States. A religious sect may degenerate into a political faction in a part of the Confederacy; but the variety of sects dispersed over the entire face of it must secure the national councils against any danger from that source. A rage for paper money, for an abolition of debts, for an equal division of property, or for any other improper or wicked project, will be less apt to pervade the whole body of the Union than a particular member of it; in the same proportion as such a malady is more likely to taint a particular county or district than an entire State.

In the extent and proper structure of the Union, therefore, we behold a republican remedy for the diseases most incident to republican government. And according to the degree of pleasure and pride we feel in being republicans ought to be our zeal in cherishing the spirit and supporting the character of Federalists.

Alexander Hamilton,
The Federalist, Number 15

In pursuance of the plan which I have laid down for the discussion of the subject, the point next in order to be examined is the "insufficiency of the present Confederation to the preservation of the Union." It may perhaps be asked what need there is of reasoning or proof to illustrate a position which is not either controverted or doubted, to which the understandings and feelings of all classes of men assent, and which in substance is admitted by the opponents as well as by the friends of the new Constitution. It must in truth be acknowledged that, however these may differ in other respects, they in general appear to harmonize in this sentiment, at least, that there are material imperfections in our national system, and that something is necessary to be done to rescue us from impending anarchy. The facts that support this opinion are no longer objects of speculation. They have forced themselves upon the sensibility of the people at large. . . .

We may indeed with propriety be said to have reached almost the last stage of national humiliation. There is scarcely anything that can wound the pride or degrade the character of an independent nation which we no not experience. Are there engagements to the performance of which we are held by every tie respectable among men? These are the subjects of constant and unblushing violation. Do we owe debts to foreigners and to our own citizens contracted in a time of imminent peril for the preservation of our political existence? These remain without any proper or satisfactory provision for their discharge. Have we valuable territories and important posts in the possession of a foreign power which, by express stipulations, ought long since to have been surrendered? These are still retained, to the prejudice of our interests, not less than of our rights. Are we in a condition to resent or to repel the aggression? We have neither troops, nor treasury, nor government.[1] Are we even in a condition to remonstrate with dignity? The just imputations on our own faith, in respect to the same treaty, ought first to be removed. Are we entitled by nature and compact to a free participation in the navigation of the Mississippi? Spain excludes us from it. Is public credit an indispensable resource in time of public danger? We seem to have abandoned its cause as desperate and irretrievable. Is commerce of importance to national wealth? Ours is at the lowest point of declension. Is respectability in the eyes of foreign powers a safeguard against foreign encroachments? The imbecility of our government even forbids them to treat with us. Our ambassadors abroad are the mere pageants of mimic sovereignty. Is a violent and unnatural decrease in the value of land a symptom of national distress? The price of improved land in most parts of the country is much lower than can be accounted for by the quantity of waste land at market, and can only be fully explained by that want of private and public confidence, which is so alarmingly prevalent among all ranks, and which has a

[1] "I mean for the Union."—Publius

direct tendency to depreciate property of every kind. Is private credit the friend and patron of industry? That most useful kind which relates to borrowing and lending is reduced within the narrowest limits, and this still more from an opinion of insecurity than from the scarcity of money. To shorten an enumeration of particulars which can afford neither pleasure nor instruction, it may in general be demanded, what indication is there of national disorder, poverty, and insignificance that could befall a community so peculiarly blessed with natural advantages as we are, which does not form a part of the dark catalogue of our public misfortunes?

This is the melancholy situation to which we have been brought by those very maxims and councils which would now deter us from adopting the proposed Constitution; and which, not content with having conducted us to the brink of a precipice, seem resolved to plunge us into the abyss that awaits us below. Here, my countrymen, impelled by every motive that ought to influence an enlightened people, let us make a firm stand for our safety, our tranquillity, our dignity, our reputation. Let us at last break the fatal charm which has too long seduced us from the paths of felicity and prosperity. . . .

The old adversaries of federal measures . . . admit that the government of the United States is destitute of energy, [but] they contend against conferring upon it those powers which are requisite to supply that energy. They seem still to aim at things repugnant and irreconcilable; at an augmentation of federal authority, without a diminution of State authority; at sovereignty in the Union, and complete independence in the members. They still, in fine, seem to cherish with blind devotion the political monster of an *imperium in imperio.* This renders a full display of the principal defects of the Confederation necessary, in order to show that the evils we experience do not proceed from minute or partial imperfections, but from fundamental errors in the structure of the building, which cannot be amended otherwise than by an alteration in the first principles and main pillars of the fabric.

The great and radical vice in the construction of the existing Confederation is in the principle of LEGISLATION *for* STATES *or* GOVERNMENTS, in their CORPORATE *or* COL-

LECTIVE CAPACITIES, and as contradistinguished from the INDIVIDUALS of which they consist. Though this principle does not run through all the powers delegated to the Union, yet it pervades and governs those on which the efficacy of the rest depends. Except as to the rule of apportionment, the United States has an indefinite discretion to make requisitions for men and money; but they have no authority to raise either by regulations extending to the individual citizens of America. The consequence of this is that, though in theory their resolutions concerning those objects are laws constitutionally binding on the members of the Union, yet in practice they are mere recommendations which the States observe or disregard at their option.

It is a singular instance of the capriciousness of the human mind that, after all the admonitions we have had from experience on this head, there should still be found men who object to the new Constitution for deviating from a principle which has been found the bane of the old, and which is in itself evidently incompatible with the idea of GOVERNMENT;—a principle, in short, which, if it is to be executed at all, must substitute the violent and sanguinary agency of the sword for the mild influence of the magistracy.

There is nothing absurd or impracticable in the idea of a league or alliance between independent nations for certain defined purposes precisely stated in a treaty regulating all the details of time, place, circumstance, and quantity; leaving nothing to future discretion; and depending for its execution on the good faith of the parties. Compacts of this kind exist among all civilized nations, subject to the usual vicissitudes of peace and war, of observance and non-observance, as the interests or passions of the contracting powers dictate. . . .

If the particular States in this country are disposed to stand in a similar relation to each other, and to drop the project of a general DISCRETIONARY SUPERINTENDENCE, the scheme would indeed be pernicious, and would entail upon us all the mischiefs which have been enumerated under the first head; but it would have the merit of being, at least, consistent and practicable. Abandoning all views towards a confederate government, this would bring us to a simple alliance offensive and defensive; and would place us in a situation to be alternative friends and enemies of each other, as our mutual jealousies and rivalships, nourished by the intrigues of foreign nations, should prescribe to us.

But if we are unwilling to be placed in this perilous situation; if we still will adhere to the design of a national government, or, which is the same thing, of a superintending power, under the direction of a common council, we must resolve to incorporate into our plan those ingredients which may be considered as forming the characteristic difference between a league and a government; we must extend the authority of the Union to the persons of the citizens—the only proper objects of government.

Government implies the power of making laws. It is essential to the idea of a law that it be attended with a sanction; or, in other words, a penalty or punishment for disobedience. If there be no penalty annexed to disobedience, the resolutions or commands which pretend to be laws will, in fact, amount to nothing more than advice or recommendation. This penalty, whatever it may be, can only be inflicted in two ways: by the agency of the courts and ministers of justice, or by military force; by the COERCION of the magistracy, or by the COERCION of arms. The first kind can evidently apply only to men; the last kind must, of necessity, be employed against bodies politic, or communities, or States. It is evident that there is no process of a court by which the observance of the laws can, in the last resort, be enforced. Sentences may be denounced against them for violations of their duty; but these sentences can only be carried into execution by the sword. In an association where the general authority is confined to the collective bodies of the communities that compose it, every breach of the laws must involve a state of war; and military execution must become the only instrument of civil obedience. Such a state of things can certainly not deserve the name of government, nor would any prudent man choose to commit his happiness to it.

There was a time when we were told that breaches by the States of the regulations of the federal authority were not to be expected; that a sense of common interest would preside over the conduct of the respective members, and would beget a full compliance with all the constitutional requisitions of the Union. This language, at the present day, would appear as wild as a great part of what we now hear from the same quarter will be thought, when we shall have received further lessons from that best oracle of wisdom, experience. It at all times betrayed an ignorance of the true springs by which human conduct is actuated, and belied the original inducements to the establishment of civil power. Why has government been instituted at all? Because the passions of men will not conform to the dictates of reason and justice, without constraint. Has it been found that bodies of men act with more rectitude or greater disinterestedness than individuals? The contrary of this has been inferred by all accurate observers of the conduct of mankind; and the inference is founded upon obvious reasons. Regard to reputation has a less active influence when the infamy of a bad action is to be divided among a number, than when it is to fall singly upon one. A spirit of faction, which is apt to mingle its poison in the deliberations of all bodies of men, will often hurry the persons of whom they are composed into improprieties and excesses for which they would blush in a private capacity.

In addition to all this there is in the nature of sovereign power an impatience of control, that disposes those who are invested with the exercise of it to look with an evil eye upon all external attempts to restrain or direct its operations. From this spirit it happens that, in every political association which is formed upon the principle of uniting in a common interest a number of lesser sovereignties, there will be found a kind of eccentric tendency in the subordinate or inferior orbs, by the operation of which there will be a perpetual effort in each to fly off from the common center. This tendency is not difficult to be accounted for. It has its origin in the love of power. Power controlled or abridged is almost always the rival and enemy of that power by which it is controlled or abridged. This simple proposition will teach us how little reason there is to expect that the persons entrusted with the administration of the affairs of the particular members of a confederacy will at all times be ready, with perfect good-humor and an unbiased regard to the public weal, to execute the resolutions or decrees of the general authority. The reverse of this results from the constitution of human nature.

If, therefore, the measures of the Confederacy cannot

be executed without the intervention of the particular administrations, there will be little prospect of their being executed at all. The rulers of the respective members, whether they have a constitutional right to do it or not, will undertake to judge of the propriety of the measures themselves. They will consider the conformity of the thing proposed or required to their immediate interests or aims; the momentary conveniences or inconveniences that would attend its adoption. All this will be done; and in a spirit of interested and suspicious scrutiny, without that knowledge of national circumstances and reasons of state which is essential to a right judgment; and with that strong predilection in favor of local objects which can hardly fail to mislead the decision. The same process must be repeated in every member of which the body is constituted; and the execution of the plans, framed by the councils of the whole, will always fluctuate on the discretion of the ill-informed and prejudiced opinion of every part. Those who have been conversant in the proceedings of popular assemblies; who have seen how difficult it often is, where there is no exterior pressure of circumstances, to bring them to harmonious resolutions on important points, will readily conceive how impossible it must be to induce a number of such assemblies, deliberating at a distance from each other, at different times, and under different impressions, long to co-operate in the same views and pursuits.

In our case, the concurrence of thirteen distinct sovereign wills is requisite, under the Confederation, to the complete execution of every important measure that proceeds from the Union. It has happened as was to have been foreseen. The measures of the Union have not been executed; the delinquencies of the States have, step by step, matured themselves to an extreme, which has at length arrested all the wheels of the national government and brought them to an awful stand. Congress at this time scarcely possesses the means of keeping up the forms of administration, till the States can have time to agree upon a more substantial substitute for the present shadow of a federal government. Things did not come to this desperate extremity at once. The causes which have been specified produced at first only unequal and disproportionate degrees of compliance with the requisitions of the Union. The greater deficiencies of some States furnished the pretext of example and the temptation of interest to the complying or to the least delinquent States. Why should we do more in proportion than those who are embarked with us in the same political voyage? Why should we consent to bear more than our proper share of the common burden? These were suggestions which human selfishness could not withstand, and which even speculative men, who looked forward to remote consequences, could not, without hesitation, combat. Each State, yielding to the persuasive voice of immediate interest or convenience, has successively withdrawn its support, till the frail and tottering edifice seems ready to fall upon our heads and to crush us beneath its ruins.

✳ PART III ✳

Federalists and Republicans

WHILE the framing and establishment of the Constitution absorbed the attention of the Founding Fathers, they were able to submerge their differences. But once the new government was set in operation, important differences quickly began to reassert themselves. Significantly, Madison and Hamilton, who had fought side by side in the battle for the Constitution, became political opponents. Jefferson, who had taken a moderate position on the Constitution, became the leader of opposition to measures passed under its authority.

Hamilton, the leading spirit in the Washington administration until his resignation in January 1795, was determined to make the new government strong and effective. Jefferson wanted to make it "wise and frugal." As Secretary of the Treasury, Hamilton formulated a program designed to attract the support of the wealthy by serving their interests. This program consisted of three main proposals: first, the establishment of the public credit on as sound a basis as possible, and the use of the public funds to supply circulating capital; second, the creation of a federally chartered national bank with the power to issue notes—a bank which would augment capital as well as lend to the federal government and facilitate its collections and payments; third, governmental encouragement of the development of manufactures, which would add to the country's internal diversification and its exploitation of its labor resources, and thus increase its economic independence and its total wealth. This program pleased the holders of public securities, investors, bankers, merchants, and speculators in land. It was far less attractive to many planters and farmers, who thought that they would be asked to pay otherwise unnecessary taxes simply to enable the government to carry on activities favorable to the moneyed classes.

From the beginning, then, Hamilton's program had a divisive effect. His desire to set public credit on a sound footing (Document 1) led him to propose two controversial measures: first, that all holders of the public debt, whether they were original purchasers or subsequent speculators, be paid in full; and second, that the debts of the states be assumed by the federal government and added to the obligations carried over from the Confederation. The first of these measures irritated those who, like Jefferson (Document 3) and Madison, felt that speculators who had bought public securities at a fraction of their face value should not receive payment at full value. Assumption of state debts was even more bitterly opposed; states which, like Virginia (Document 2), had already paid a large share of their debts felt that their funds would be conscripted to pay debts for states that had not been so prompt or scrupulous. This opposition was finally placated by a compromise in which Jefferson concurred, to his later regret (Document 3). Southern Congressmen accepted debt assumption in return for the promised removal of the national capital from the cities of the North (where governmental operations were deemed too susceptible to commercial pressures) to the District of Columbia.

The proposal to create a national bank led to another conflict between Jefferson and Hamilton (Documents 4 and 5) over the question of whether the Constitution endowed Congress with any such power. By deciding in favor of Hamilton's argument for a broad construction of the implied powers of Congress, Washington gave Hamilton's program another victory, which added still further to the irritation of Hamilton's opponents.

There had long been a school of thought, eloquently represented in Jefferson's *Notes on Virginia* (Document 6), which saw, in the growth of manufactures, large cities, and an urban working class, not a promise but a grave threat. Such a social change would destroy the simple, agrarian republicanism which many men considered to be the distinctively valuable American contribution to the development of civilization. To them, Hamilton's Report on Manufactures (Document 7) meant that they were being asked to make sacrifices to bring about a state of society less desirable than that which they already had. They succeeded in defeating those parts of Hamilton's program that were intended to develop manufactures: high protective duties, bounties and premiums, encouragement to invention, and the public construction of roads and canals.

When Washington's two-term presidency ended, political animosities, which had already reached a high pitch, expressed themselves in the formation of political parties. John Adams did not have Washington's unifying prestige, and during his administration quarrels over the American attitude toward the wars of the French Revolution (Part IV) became even more intense than those excited by Hamilton's proposals. Criticism of the Adams administration became so heated that the Federalists tried to suppress it altogether with the Alien and Sedition Acts of 1798. These measures were directed both against Adams's domestic opponents and against French and Irish immigrants, who usually sided with them. They made naturalization of immigrants intensely difficult, authorized more or less arbitrary deportation, and in loosely phrased language, proscribed criticism of the government or its officers, providing for severe fine and imprisonment. The Republicans immediately protested that these acts were despotic and unconstitutional. The Virginia and Kentucky Resolutions of 1798 (Document 8) not only argued the unconstitutionality of these particular acts, but claimed for the states the general right to interpret the constitutionality of acts of Congress and to protect their citizens against unconstitutional measures. These protests thus opened up an issue of constitutional interpretation even more explosive than that raised by the bank issue. A precedent was also set for future actions of the states against the powers of the federal government. Answers of the Northern legislatures to these resolutions (Document 9) suggest that this issue was drawn along sectional lines. But the Republicans were beginning to gain strength in the Northern states; and when New York, which had voted for Adams in 1796, swung to the Republican column in 1800, it tipped the balance and elected Jefferson.

Jefferson liked to refer to his election as "the revolution of 1800." Actually he was a man of moderate spirit, and his great First Inaugural Address (Document 10) showed that he shared the alarm already expressed by Washington in his Farewell Address (Part IV, Document 3) over the intense state of party feeling. The moderate tone of Jefferson's address anticipated a conciliatory policy, and indeed he left intact much of the Hamiltonian program. The method of funding the debt he felt to be fixed beyond alteration. The Bank of the United States was taken over rather than destroyed; and although its charter was allowed to expire in 1811, it was rechartered under Republican leadership in 1816. Frugality in government and some changes in tax policy were the primary deviations made by the Jeffersonians from Federalist domestic policy.

An acute controversy took place, however, over the federal judiciary. Long after both the executive and legislative branches of the government had been won by the Republicans, the judiciary remained in the hands of appointees of Washington and Adams; and long after Jeffersonian policies were being enacted, John Marshall, as Chief Justice of the Supreme Court continued to hand down major decisions that embodied Federalist law. The Federalist-dominated judiciary had already made itself highly unpopular with the Jeffersonians by its prejudiced handling of cases arising under the Alien and Sedition Acts. Jefferson, troubled by the inaccessibility of a judiciary appointed for life, hoped to tame the judiciary by making the impeachment of judges a political proceeding rather than indictment for "high crimes and misdemeanors," and thus to expose the justices to the influence of public opinion. However this device, so shocking to advocates of judicial independence, was proved to be ineffective by the failure of the impeachment of Justice Samuel Chase in 1805. The real victor in the fight over the judiciary was John Marshall, whose decision in *Marbury* v. *Madison* (Document 11) firmly asserted the right of the Supreme Court to declare Acts of Congress uncon-

stitutional. In other decisions Marshall continued to restrain the state governments, protect the sanctity of contracts, and enlarge the commerce power of the federal
government. Sixteen years after *Marbury* v. *Madison*,
Jefferson was still trying to find (Document 12) a tech-
nique for subjecting the judiciary to some measure of
democratic control.

DOCUMENT 1

ALEXANDER HAMILTON, REPORT ON THE PUBLIC CREDIT,

JANUARY 9, 1790

*In September 1789, Congress requested information
from the Secretary of the Treasury on the state of the
American public debt. By January 9, 1790, Hamilton
had drafted the first of his great reports, and on January 14 he submitted it to Congress. Although his argument against discriminating between original holders
and subsequent buyers of government securities
aroused strong opposition, his program was adopted,
substantially as he proposed it, within seven months.*

In the opinion of the Secretary, the wisdom of the House,
in giving explicit sanction to the proposition which has been
stated, cannot but be applauded by all who will seriously
consider, and trace through their obvious consequences,
these plain and undeniable truths:

That exigencies are to be expected to occur, in the
affairs of nations, in which there will be a necessity for
borrowing.

That loans in time of public danger, especially from
foreign war, are found an indispensable resource, even to
the wealthiest of them.

And that, in a country which, like this, is possessed of
little active wealth, or, in other words, little moneyed capital, the necessity for that resource must, in such emergencies, be proportionably urgent.

And as, on the one hand, the necessity for borrowing in particular emergencies cannot be doubtful, so, on the other, it is equally evident that, to be able to borrow upon good terms, it is essential that the credit of a nation should be well established.

For, when the credit of a country is in any degree questionable, it never fails to give an extravagant premium, in one shape or another, upon all the loans it has occasion to make. Nor does the evil end here; the same disadvantage must be sustained on whatever is to be bought on terms of future payment.

From this constant necessity of borrowing and buying dear, it is easy to conceive how immensely the expenses of a nation, in a course of time, will be augmented by an unsound state of the public credit. . . .

If the maintenance of public credit, then, be truly so important, the next inquiry which suggests itself is: By what means is it to be effected? The ready answer to which question is, by good faith; by a punctual performance of contracts. States, like individuals, who observe their engagements are respected and trusted, while the reverse is the fate of those who pursue an opposite conduct.

Every breach of the public engagements, whether from choice or necessity, is, in different degrees, hurtful to public credit. When such a necessity does truly exist, the evils of it are only to be palliated by a scrupulous attention, on the part of the Government, to carry the violation no further than the necessity absolutely requires, and to manifest, if the nature of the case admit of it, a sincere disposition to make reparation whenever circumstances shall permit. . . .

To justify and preserve their confidence; to promote the increasing respectability of the American name; to answer the calls of justice; to restore landed property to its due value; to furnish new resources, both to agriculture and commerce; to cement more closely the union of the States; to add to their security against foreign attack; to establish public order on the basis of an upright and liberal policy;—these are the great and invaluable ends to be secured by a proper and adequate provision, at the present period, for the support of public credit. . . .

The advantage to the public creditors, from the in-

creased value of that part of their property which consti-
tutes the public debt, needs no explanation.

But there is a consequence of this, less obvious, though
not less true, in which every other citizen is interested. It
is a well-known fact, that, in countries in which the national
debt is properly funded, and an object of established confidence, it answers most of the purposes of money. Trans-
fers of stock or public debt are there equivalent to payments in specie; or, in other words, stock, in the principal
transactions of business, passes current as specie. The same
thing would, in all probability, happen here under the like
circumstances.

The benefits of this are various and obvious:

First.—Trade is extended by it. . . .

Secondly.—Agriculture and manufactures are also
promoted by it. . . .

Thirdly.—The interest of money will be lowered by
it. . . .

And from the combination of these effects, additional
aids will be furnished to labor, to industry, and to arts of
every kind. . . .

Having now taken a concise view of the inducements
to a proper provision for the public debt, the next inquiry
which presents itself is: What ought to be the nature of
such a provision? This requires some preliminary discussions.

It is agreed, on all hands, that that part of the debt
which has been contracted abroad, and is denominated the
foreign debt, ought to be provided for according to the
precise terms of the contracts relating to it. The discussions
which can arise, therefore, will have reference essentially
to the domestic part of it, or to that which has been contracted at home. It is to be regretted that there is not the
same unanimity of sentiment on this part as on the other.

The Secretary has too much deference for the opinions
of every part of the community not to have observed one,
which has more than once made its appearance in the
public prints, and which is occasionally to be met with
in conversation. It involves this question: Whether a discrimination ought not to be made between original holders
of the public securities, and present possessors, by pur-

chase? Those who advocate a discrimination are for making a full provision for the securities of the former at their nominal value, but contend that the latter ought to receive no more than the cost to them, and the interest. And the idea is sometimes suggested of making good the difference to the primitive possessor.

In favor of this scheme it is alleged that it would be unreasonable to pay twenty shillings in the pound to one who had not given more for it than three or four. And it is added that it would be hard to aggravate the misfortune of the first owner, who, probably through necessity, parted with his property at so great a loss, by obliging him to contribute to the profit of the person who had speculated on his distresses.

The Secretary, after the most mature reflection on the force of this argument, is induced to reject the doctrine it contains, as equally unjust and impolitic; as highly injurious, even to the original holders of public securities; as ruinous to public credit.

It is inconsistent with justice, because, in the first place, it is a breach of contract—a violation of the rights of a fair purchaser.

The nature of the contract, in its origin, is that the public will pay the sum expressed in the security, to the first holder or his assignee. The intent in making the security assignable is, that the proprietor may be able to make use of his property, by selling it for as much as it may be worth in the market, and that the buyer may be safe in the purchase.

Every buyer, therefore, stands exactly in the place of the seller; has the same right with him to the identical sum expressed in the security; and, having acquired that right by fair purchase and in conformity to the original agreement and intention of the Government, his claim cannot be disputed without manifest injustice.

That he is to be considered as a fair purchaser, results from this: whatever necessity the seller may have been under, was occasioned by the Government, in not making a proper provision for its debts. The buyer had no agency in it, and therefore ought not to suffer. He is not even chargeable with having taken an undue advantage. He paid what the commodity was worth in the market, and took the risks of reimbursement upon himself. He, of course, gave a fair equivalent, and ought to reap the benefit of his hazard —a hazard which was far from inconsiderable, and which, perhaps, turned on little less than a revolution in government.

That the case of those who parted with their securities from necessity is a hard one, cannot be denied. But, whatever complaint of injury, or claim of redress, they may have, respects the Government solely. . . . But, though many of the original holders sold from necessity, it does not follow that this was the case with all of them. It may well be supposed that some of them did it either through want of confidence in an eventual provision, or from the allurements of some profitable speculation. How shall these different classes be discriminated from each other? . . .

Questions of this sort . . . demonstrate the injustice of a discrimination, even on the most subtile calculations of equity, abstracted from the obligation of contract.

The difficulties, too, of regulating the details of a plan for that purpose, which would have even the semblance of equity, would be found immense. . . .

It will be perceived, at first sight, that the transferable quality of stock is essential to its operation as money, and that this depends on the idea of complete security to the transferee, and a firm persuasion that no distinction can, in any circumstances, be made between him and the original proprietor. . . . It would be repugnant to an express provision of the Constitution of the United States. This provision is that "all debts contracted and engagements entered into before the adoption of that Constitution, shall be as valid against the United States under it as under the Confederation"; which amounts to a constitutional ratification of the contracts respecting the debt in the state in which they existed under the Confederation. And, resorting to that standard, there can be no doubt that the rights of assignees and original holders must be considered as equal. . . .

The Secretary, concluding that a discrimination between the different classes of creditors of the United States cannot, with propriety, be made, proceeds to examine whether a difference ought to be permitted to remain between them and another description of public creditors—

those of the States individually. The Secretary, after mature reflection on this point, entertains a full conviction
that an assumption of the debts of the particular States
by the Union, and a like provision for them as for those
of the Union, will be a measure of sound policy and substantial justice.

It would, in the opinion of the Secretary, contribute,
in an eminent degree, to an orderly, stable, and satisfactory
arrangement of the national finances. Admitting, as ought
to be the case, that a provision must be made, in some way
or other, for the entire debt, it will follow that no greater
revenues will be required whether that provision be made
wholly by the United States, or partly by them and partly
by the States separately. . . .

If all the public creditors receive their dues from one
source, distributed with an equal hand, their interest will be
the same. And, having the same interests, they will unite
in the support of the fiscal arrangements of the Government—as these, too, can be made with more convenience
where there is no competition. These circumstances combined will insure to the revenue laws a more ready and
more satisfactory execution. . . .

The result of the foregoing discussion is this: That
there ought to be no discrimination between the original
holders of the debt, and present possessors by purchase;
that it is expedient there should be an assumption of the
State debts by the Union; and that the arrears of interest
should be provided for on an equal footing with the principal. . . .

The interesting problem now occurs: Is it in the power
of the United States, consistently with those prudential
considerations which ought not to be overlooked, to make
a provision equal to the purpose of funding the whole debt,
at the rates of interest which it now bears, in addition to the
sum which will be necessary for the current service of the
Government?

The Secretary will not say that such a provision would
exceed the abilities of the country, but he is clearly of
opinion that to make it would require the extension of taxation to a degree and to objects which the true interest of the
public creditors forbids. It is, therefore, to be hoped, and
even to be expected, that they will cheerfully concur in

such modifications of their claims, on fair and equitable principles, as will facilitate to the Government an arrangement substantial, durable, and satisfactory to the community. The importance of the last characteristic will strike every discerning mind. No plan, however flattering in appearance, to which it did not belong, could be truly entitled to confidence. . . .

Persuaded, as the Secretary is, that the proper funding of the present debt will render it a national blessing, yet he is so far from acceding to the position, in the latitude in which it is sometimes laid down, that "public debts are public benefits"—a position inviting to prodigality and liable to dangerous abuse—that he ardently wishes to see it incorporated as a fundamental maxim in the system of public credit of the United States, that the creation of debt should always be accompanied with the means of extinguishment. . . .

DOCUMENT 2

VIRGINIA RESOLUTIONS ON THE ASSUMPTION OF STATE DEBTS,
DECEMBER 16, 1790

This protest against the assumption of the debts of the states was drawn up by Patrick Henry. It was passed by the Virginia Assembly on December 16, 1790, and agreed to by the Senate a week later. Hamilton thought he saw in it "the first symptom of a spirit which must either be killed, or will kill the Constitution of the United States."

The General Assembly of the Commonwealth of Virginia to the United States in Congress assembled.
Represent,
That it is with great concern they find themselves compelled, from a sense of duty, to call the attention of Congress to an act of their last session, intitled "An act making provision for the debt of the United States," which the General Assembly conceive neither policy, justice nor

the constitution warrants. Republican policy in the opinion of your memorialists could scarcely have suggested those clauses in the aforesaid act, which limit the right of the United States, in their redemption of the public debt. On the contrary they discern a striking resemblance between this system and that which was introduced into England, at the revolution; a system which has perpetuated upon that nation an enormous debt, and has moreover insinuated into the hands of the executive, an unbounded influence, which pervading every branch of the government, bears down all opposition, and daily threatens the destruction of everything that appertains to English liberty. The same causes produce the same effects! In an agricultural country like this, therefore to erect, and concentrate, and perpetuate a large monied interest, is a measure which your memorialists apprehend must in the course of human events produce one or other of two evils, the prostration of agriculture at the feet of commerce, or a change in the present form of foederal government, fatal to the existence of American liberty. . . .

During the whole discussion of the foederal constitution by the convention of Virginia, your memorialists were taught to believe "That every power not granted was retained," under this impression and upon this positive condition, declared in the instrument of ratification, the said government was adopted by the people of this Commonwealth; but your memorialists can find no clause in the constitution authorizing Congress to assume the debts of the states! As the guardians then of the rights and interests of their constituents, as sentinels placed by them over the ministers of the foederal government, to shield it from their encroachments, or at least to sound the alarm when it is threatened with invasion, they can never reconcile it to their consciences, silently to acquiesce in a measure, which violates that hallowed maxim: a maxim on the truth and sacredness of which the foederal government depended for its adoption in this Commonwealth. But this injudicious act not only deserves the censure of the General Assembly, because it is not warranted by the constitution of the United States, but because it is repugnant to an express provision of that constitution; this provision is "That all debts contracted and engagements entered into, before the adoption of this constitution, shall be as valid against the United States under this constitution, as under the confederation," which amounts to a constitutional ratification of the contracts respecting the state debts in the situation in which they existed under the confederation, and resorting to that standard, there can be no doubt that in the present question the rights of states as contracting parties with the United States must be considered as sacred.

The General Assembly of the Commonwealth of Virginia confide so fully in the justice and wisdom of Congress upon the present occasion, as to hope that they will revise and amend the aforesaid act generally, and repeal in particular, so much of it as relates to the assumption of the state debts.

DOCUMENT 3

THOMAS JEFFERSON, RECOLLECTIONS OF THE HAMILTONIAN SYSTEM,
FEBRUARY 4, 1818

During his period of office as Secretary of State, 1789–93, Jefferson wrote frequent memoranda about the increasingly intense differences within Washington's administration that eventually led to the formation of two distinct parties. A quarter of a century later he revised these Anas, or notes, and in these introductory remarks he sets down his version of Hamilton's political views and aspirations, and also of his foe's public credit policies.

I returned from that mission [to France] in the first year of the new government, having landed in Virginia in December, 1789, and proceeded to New York in March, 1790, to enter on the office of Secretary of State. Here, certainly, I found a state of things which, of all I had ever contemplated, I the least expected. I had left France in the first year of her revolution, in the fervor of natural rights, and zeal for reformation. My conscientious devotion to these rights could not be heightened, but it had been aroused and excited by daily exercise. The President received me cordially, and my colleagues and the circle of principal citizens apparently with welcome. The courtesies of dinner parties given me, as a stranger newly arrived among them, placed me at once in their familiar society. But I cannot describe the wonder and mortification with which the table conversations filled me. Politics was the chief topic, and a preference of kingly over republican government was evidently the favorite sentiment. An apostate I could not be, nor yet a hypocrite; and I found myself, for the most part, the only advocate on the republican side of the question, unless among the guests there chanced to be some member of that party from the legislative Houses. Hamilton's financial system had then passed. It had two objects; 1st, as a puzzle, to exclude popular understanding and inquiry; 2d, as a machine for the corruption of the legislature; for he avowed the opinion that man could be governed by one of two motives only, force or interest; force, he observed, in this country was out of the question, and the interests, therefore, of the members must be laid hold of, to keep the legislative in unison with the executive. And with grief and shame it must be acknowledged that his machine was not without effect; that even in this, the birth of our government, some members were found sordid enough to bend their duty to their interest, and to look after personal rather than public good.

It is well known that during the war the greatest difficulty we encountered was the want of money or means to pay our soldiers who fought, or our farmers, manufacturers and merchants who furnished the necessary supplies of food and clothing for them. After the expedient of paper money had exhausted itself, certificates of debt were given to the individual creditors, with assurance of payments so soon as the United States should be able. But the distresses of these people often obliged them to part with these for the half, the fifth, and even a tenth of their value; and speculators had made a trade of cozening them from the holders by the most fraudulent practices, and persuasions that they would never be paid. In the bill for funding and paying these, Hamilton made no difference between the original holders and the fraudulent purchasers of this paper. Great and just repugnance arose at putting these two classes of creditors on the same footing, and great exertions were used to pay the former the full value, and to the latter, the price only which they had paid, with interest. But this would have prevented the game which was to be played, and for which the minds of greedy members were already tutored and prepared. When the trial of strength on these several efforts had indicated the form in which the bill would finally pass, this being known within doors sooner than without, and especially than to those who were in distant parts of the Union, the base scramble began. Couriers and relay horses by land, and swift sailing pilot boats by sea, were flying in all directions. Active partners and agents were associated and employed in every state, town and country neighborhood, and this paper was bought up at five shillings, and even as low as two shillings in the pound, before the holder knew that Congress had already provided for its redemption at par. Immense sums were thus filched from the poor and ignorant, and fortunes accumulated by those who had themselves been poor enough before. Men thus enriched by the dexterity of a leader would follow of course the chief who was leading them to fortune, and become the zealous instruments of all his enterprises.

This game was over, and another was on the carpet at the moment of my arrival; and to this I was most ignorantly and innocently made to hold the candle. This fiscal maneuver is well known by the name of the Assumption. Independently of the debts of Congress, the states had during the war contracted separate and heavy debts; and Massachusetts particularly, in an absurd attempt, absurdly conducted, on the British post of Penobscott: and the more debt Hamilton could rake up, the more plunder for his mercenaries. This money, whether wisely or foolishly spent, was pretended to have been spent for general purposes, and ought, therefore, to be paid from the general purse. But it was objected that nobody knew what these debts were, what their amount, or what their proofs. No matter; we will guess them to be twenty millions. But of these twenty millions, we do not know how much should be reimbursed to one state, or how much to another. No matter; we will guess. And so another scramble was set on foot among the several states, and some got much, some little, some nothing. But the main object was obtained, the phalanx of the Treasury was reinforced by additional recruits. This measure produced the most bitter and angry contest ever known in Congress, before or since the Union of the states. I arrived in the midst of it. But a stranger to the ground, a stranger to the actors on it, so long absent as to have lost all familiarity with the subject, and as yet unaware of its object, I took no concern in it.

The great and trying question, however, was lost in the House of Representatives. So high were the feuds excited by this subject, that on its rejection business was suspended. Congress met and adjourned from day to day without doing anything, the parties being too much out of temper to do business together. The eastern members particularly, who, with Smith from South Carolina, were the principal gamblers in these scenes, threatened a secession and dissolution. Hamilton was in despair. As I was going to the President's one day, I met him in the street. He walked me backward and forward before the President's door for half an hour. He painted pathetically the temper into which the legislature had been wrought; the disgust of those who were called the creditor states; the danger of the *secession* of their members, and the separation of the states. He observed that the members of the administration ought to act in concert; that though this question was not of my department, yet a common duty should make it a common concern; that the President was the center on which all administrative questions ultimately rested, and that all of us should rally around him, and support, with joint efforts, measures approved by him; and that the question having been lost by a small majority only, it was probable that an appeal from me to the judgment and discretion of some of my friends might effect a change in the vote, and the machine of government, now suspended, might be again set into motion. I told him that I was really a stranger to the whole subject; that, not having yet informed myself of the system of finances adopted, I knew not how far this was a necessary sequence; that undoubtedly, if its rejection endangered a dissolution of our Union at this incipient stage, I should deem that the most unfortunate of all consequences, to avert which all partial and temporary evils should be yielded. I proposed to him, however, to dine with me the next day, and I would invite another friend or two, bring them into conference together, and I thought it impossible that reasonable men, consulting together coolly, could fail, by some mutual sacrifices of opinion, to form a compromise which was to save the Union.

The discussion took place. I could take no part in it but an exhortatory one, because I was a stranger to the circumstances which should govern it. But it was finally agreed that, whatever importance had been attached to the rejection of this proposition, the preservation of the Union and of concord among the states was more important, and that therefore it would be better that the vote of rejection should be rescinded, to effect which, some members should change their votes. But it was observed that this pill would be peculiarly bitter to the southern states, and that some concomitant measure should be adopted, to sweeten it a little to them. There had before been propositions to fix the seat of government either at Philadelphia, or at Georgetown on the Potomac; and it was thought that by giving it to Philadelphia for ten years, and to Georgetown permanently afterwards, this might, as an anodyne, calm in some degree the ferment which might be excited by the other measure alone. So two of the Potomac members (White and Lee, but White with a revulsion of stomach almost convulsive), agreed to change their votes, and Hamilton undertook to carry the other point. In doing this, the influence he had established over the eastern members, with the agency of Robert Morris with those of the middle states, effected his side of the engagement; and so the Assumption was passed, and twenty millions of stock divided among favored states, and thrown in as a pabulum to the stock–jobbing herd. This added to the number of votaries to the Treasury, and made its chief the master of every vote in the legislature, which might give to the government the direction suited to his political views.

I know well, and so must be understood, that nothing like a majority in Congress had yielded to this corruption. Far from it. But a division, not very unequal, had already taken place in the honest part of that body, between the parties styled republican and federal. The latter being monarchists in principle, adhered to Hamilton of course, as their leader in that principle, and this mercenary phalanx added to them, insured him always a majority in both Houses: so that the whole action of legislature was now under the direction of the Treasury. Still the machine was not complete. The effect of the funding system, and of the Assumption, would be temporary; it would be lost with the loss of the individual members whom it has enriched, and some engine of influence more permanent must be contrived, while these myrmidons were yet in place to carry it through all opposition. This engine was the Bank of the United States. All that history is known, so I shall say nothing about it. While the government remained at Philadelphia, a selection of members of both Houses were constantly kept as directors who, on every question interesting to that institution, or to the views of the federal head, voted at the will of that head; and, together with the stock-holding members, could always make the federal vote that of the majority. By this combination, legislative expositions were given to the Constitution, and all the administrative laws were shaped on the model of England, and so passed. And from this influence we were not relieved, until the removal from the precincts of the bank, to Washington.

Here then was the real ground of the opposition which was made to the course of administration. Its object was to preserve the legislature pure and independent of the executive, to restrain the administration to republican forms and principles, and not permit the Constitution to be construed into a monarchy, and to be warped, in practice, into all the principles and pollutions of their favorite English model. Nor was this an opposition to General Washington. He was true to the republican charge confided to him; and has solemnly and repeatedly protested to me, in our conversations, that he would lose the last drop of his blood in support of it; and he did this the oftener and with the more earnestness, because he knew my suspicions of Hamilton's designs against it, and wished to quiet them. For he was not aware of the drift or of the effect of Hamilton's schemes. Unversed in financial projects and calculations and budgets, his approbation of them was bottomed on his confidence in the man.

But Hamilton was not only a monarchist, but for a monarchy bottomed on corruption. In proof of this, I will

relate an anecdote, for the truth of which I attest the God
who made me. Before the President set out on his southern
tour in April, 1791, he addressed a letter of the fourth of
that month, from Mount Vernon, to the Secretaries of
States, Treasury, and War, desiring that if any serious and
important cases should arise during his absence, they would
consult and act on them. And he requested that the Vice-
President should also be consulted. This was the only occasion on which that officer was ever requested to take part
in a cabinet question. Some occasion for consultation arising, I invited those gentlemen (and the Attorney-General,
as well as I remember) to dine with me, in order to confer
on the subject. After the cloth was removed, and our
question agreed and dismissed, conversation began on other
matters and, by some circumstance, was led to the British
constitution, on which Mr. Adams observed, "Purge that
constitution of its corruption, and give to its popular
branch equality of representation, and it would be the
most perfect constitution ever devised by the wit of man."
Hamilton paused and said, "Purge it of its corruption, and
give to its popular branch equality of representation, and
it would become an *impracticable* government: as it stands
at present, with all its supposed defects, it is the most
perfect government which ever existed." And this was
assuredly the exact line which separated the political creeds
of these two gentlemen. The one was for two hereditary
branches and an honest elective one; the other, for a
hereditary king, with a House of Lords and Commons
corrupted to his will, and standing between him and the
people.

Hamilton was, indeed, a singular character. Of acute
understanding, disinterested, honest, and honorable in all
private transactions, amiable in society, and duly valuing
virtue in private life, yet so bewitched and perverted by
the British example as to be under thorough conviction
that corruption was essential to the government of a
nation. . . .

DOCUMENT 4

THOMAS JEFFERSON, OPINION ON THE CONSTITUTIONALITY OF THE BANK,

FEBRUARY 15, 1791

Washington, considering Hamilton's proposal for a national bank, sought the opinions of Hamilton, Jefferson, and Attorney-General Edmund Randolph on its constitutionality. Randolph's advice was equivocal, but the other two took definite stands. Jefferson prepared this brief and almost skeletal statement of his case against the bank in a very short time.

The bill for establishing a national bank, in 1791, undertakes, among other things:

1. To form the subscribers into a corporation.
2. To enable them in their corporate capacities to receive grants of lands; and so far is against the laws of *mortmain*.
3. To make *alien* subscribers capable of holding lands; and so far is against the laws of *alienage*.
4. To transmit these lands, on the death of a proprietor, to a certain line of successors; and so far changes the course of *descents*.
5. To put the lands out of the reach of forfeiture or escheat; and so far is against the laws of *forfeiture* and *escheat*.
6. To transmit personal chattels to successors in a certain line; and so far is against the laws of *distribution*.
7. To give them the sole and exclusive right of banking under the national authority; and so far is against the laws of *monopoly*.
8. To communicate to them a power to make laws paramount to the laws of the states; for so they must be construed to protect the institution from the control of the state legislatures; and so, probably, they will be construed.

I consider the foundation of the Constitution as laid on this ground—that *all powers not delegated to the United*

States, by the Constitution,˙nor prohibited by it to the states, are reserved to the states, or to the people (10th amend.). To take a single step beyond the boundaries thus specially drawn around the powers of Congress, is to take possession of a boundless field of power, no longer susceptible of any definition.

The incorporation of a bank, and the powers assumed by this bill, have not, in my opinion, been delegated to the United States by the Constitution.

I. *They are not among the powers specially enumerated.* For these are,—

1. A power to *lay taxes* for the purpose of paying the debts of the United States. But no debt is paid by this bill, nor any tax laid. Were it a bill to raise money, its origination in the Senate would condemn it by the Constitution.

2. "To borrow money." But this bill neither borrows money nor insures the borrowing it. The proprietors of the bank will be just as free as any other money-holders to lend or not to lend their money to the public. The operation proposed in the bill, first to lend them two millions, and then to borrow them back again, cannot change the nature of the latter act, which will still be a payment, and not a loan, call it by what name you please.

3. "To regulate commerce with foreign nations, and among the states, and with the Indian tribes." To erect a bank, and to regulate commerce, are very different acts. He who erects a bank creates a subject of commerce in its bills; so does he who makes a bushel of wheat, or digs a dollar out of the mines; yet neither of these persons regulates commerce thereby. To make a thing which may be bought and sold, is not to prescribe regulations for buying and selling. Besides, if this were an exercise of the power of regulating commerce, it would be void, as extending as much to the internal commerce of every state, as to its external. For the power given to Congress by the Constitution does not extend to the internal regulation of the commerce of a state . . . which remain exclusively with its own legislature; but to its external commerce only, that is to say, its commerce with another state, or with foreign nations, or with the Indian tribes. Accordingly the bill does not propose the measure as a "regulation of trade,"

but as "productive of considerable advantages to trade."
Still less are these powers covered by any other of the
special enumerations.

II. Nor are they within either of the general phrases,
which are the two following:—

1. "To lay taxes to provide for the general welfare of the
United States;" that is to say, "to lay taxes *for the purpose*
of providing for the general welfare;" for the laying of
taxes is the *power,* and the general welfare the *purpose*
for which the power is to be exercised. Congress are not
to lay taxes *ad libitum for any purpose they please;* but
only to *pay the debts or provide for the welfare of the
Union.* In like manner, they are not *to do anything they
please* to provide for the general welfare, but only *to lay
taxes* for that purpose. To consider the latter phrase, not
as describing the purpose of the first, but as giving a distinct
and independent power to do any act they please which
might be for the good of the Union, would render all the
preceding and subsequent enumerations of power completely useless. It would reduce the whole instrument to a
single phrase—that of instituting a Congress with power
to do whatever would be for the good of the United
States; and, as they would be the sole judges of the good
or evil, it would be also a power to do whatever evil they
pleased.

It is an established rule of construction, where a
phrase will bear either of two meanings, to give it that
which will allow some meaning to the other parts of the
instrument, and not that which will render all the others
useless. Certainly no such universal power was meant to
be given them. It was intended to lace them up straitly
within the enumerated powers, and those without which, as
means, these powers could not be carried into effect. It is
known that the very power now proposed *as a means,* was
rejected *as an end* by the Convention which formed the
Constitution. A proposition was made to them to authorize
Congress to open canals, and an amendatory one to empower them to incorporate. But the whole was rejected,
and óne of the reasons of objection urged in debate was,
that they then would have a power to erect a bank, which
would render great cities, where there were prejudices and

jealousies on that subject, adverse to the reception of the Constitution.

2. The second general phrase is, "to make all laws *necessary* and proper for carrying into execution the enumerated powers." But they can all be carried into execution without a bank. A bank therefore, is *not necessary,* and consequently not authorized by this phrase.

It has been urged that a bank will give great facility or convenience in the collection of taxes. Suppose this were true; yet the Constitution allows only the means which are "necessary," not those which are merely "convenient," for effecting the enumerated powers. If such a latitude of construction be allowed to this phrase as to give any non-enumerated power, it will go to every one; for there is no one which ingenuity may not torture into a *convenience in some way or other, to some one* of so long a list of enumerated powers. It would swallow up all the delegated powers, and reduce the whole to one power, as before observed. Therefore it was that the Constitution restrained them to the *necessary* means; that is to say, to those means without which the grant of the power would be nugatory. . . .

Perhaps, indeed, bank bills may be a more *convenient* vehicle than treasury orders. But a little *difference* in the degree of convenience cannot constitute the necessity which the Constitution makes the ground for assuming any non-enumerated power. . . .

Can it be thought that the Constitution intended that for a shade or two of *convenience,* more or less, Congress should be authorized to break down the most ancient and fundamental laws of the several states, such as those against mortmain, the laws of alienage, the rules of descent, the acts of distribution, the laws of escheat and forfeiture, and the laws of monopoly?

Nothing but a necessity invincible by other means, can justify such a prostitution of laws, which constitute the pillars of our whole system of jurisprudence. Will Congress be too strait-laced to carry the Constitution into honest effect, unless they may pass over the foundation–laws of the state governments, for the slightest convenience of theirs?

The negative of the President is the shield provided by the Constitution to protect against the invasions of the legislature; 1. *The rights of the executive;* 2. *Of the judiciary;* 3. *Of the states and state legislatures.* The present is the case of a right remaining exclusively with the states, and is, consequently, one of those intended by the Constitution to be placed under his protection.

It must be added, however, that, unless the President's mind, on a view of everything which is urged for and against this bill, is tolerably clear that it is unauthorized by the Constitution; if the *pro* and the *con* hang so evenly as to balance his judgment, a just respect for the wisdom of the legislature would naturally decide the balance in favor of their opinion. It is chiefly for cases where they are clearly misled by error, ambition, or interest, that the Constitution has placed a check in the negative of the President.

DOCUMENT 5

ALEXANDER HAMILTON, OPINION ON THE CONSTITUTIONALITY OF THE BANK,

FEBRUARY 23, 1791

Hamilton drew up his answer to Washington's request much more deliberately than Jefferson. He had the additional advantage that the papers of Randolph and Jefferson, received by Washington, had been forwarded to him in order that he might have before him the arguments he must answer. In his opinion on the bank, he laid down the classical arguments of those who have favored an effective central government and national power. John Marshall incorporated these arguments in his decision on the bank in the case of McCulloch v. Maryland, 1819.

In entering upon the argument it ought to be premised that the objections of the Secretary of State and the Attorney-General are founded on a general denial of the authority of the United States to erect corporations. The latter, indeed, expressly admits, that if there be anything in the bill which is not warranted by the Constitution, it is the clause of incorporation.

Now it appears to the Secretary of the Treasury that this *general principle* is *inherent* in the very *definition* of government, and *essential* to every step of the progress to be made by that of the United States, namely: That every power vested in a government is in its nature *sovereign*, and includes, by *force* of the *term*, a right to employ all the *means* requisite and fairly applicable to the attainment of the *ends* of such power, and which are not precluded by restrictions and exceptions specified in the Constitution, or not immoral, or not contrary to the *essential ends* of political society.

If it would be necessary to bring proof to a proposition so clear, as that which affirms that the powers of the federal government, as to *its objects,* were sovereign, there is a clause of its Constitution which would be decisive. It is that which declares that the Constitution, and the laws of the United States made in pursuance of it, . . . shall be the *supreme law of the land.* The power which can create the *supreme law of the land,* in any case, is doubtless *sovereign* as to such case.

This general and indisputable principle puts at once an end to the *abstract* question, whether the United States have power to erect a corporation; that is to say, to give a *legal* or *artificial capacity* to one or more persons, distinct from the *natural.* For it is unquestionably incident to *sovereign power* to erect corporations, and consequently to *that* of the United States, in *relation* to the *objects* intrusted to the management of the government. The difference is this: where the authority of the government is general, it can create corporations in *all cases;* where it is confined to certain branches of legislation, it can create corporations *only* in those cases.

It is not denied that there are *implied* as well as *express powers,* and that the *former* are as effectually delegated as the *latter.* And for the sake of accuracy it shall be mentioned, that there is another class of powers, which may be properly denominated *resulting powers.* It will not be doubted, that if the United States should make a conquest of any of the territories of its neighbours, they would possess sovereign jurisdiction over the conquered territory. This would be rather a result from the whole mass of the powers of the government, and from the nature of political society, than a consequence of either of the powers specially enumerated. . . .

It is conceded that *implied powers* are to be considered as delegated equally with *express ones*. Then it follows, that as a power of erecting a corporation may as well be *implied* as any other thing, it may as well be employed as an *instrument* or *means* of carrying into execution any of the specified powers, as any other *instrument* or *means* whatever. The only question must be, in this, as in every other case, whether the means to be employed, or, in this instance, the corporation to be erected, has a natural relation to any of the acknowledged objects or lawful ends of the government. Thus a corporation may not be erected by Congress for superintending the police of the city of Philadelphia, because they are not authorized to *regulate* the *police* of that city. But one may be erected in relation to the collection of taxes, or to the trade with foreign countries, or to the trade between the States, or with the Indian tribes; because it is the province of the federal government to *regulate* those objects, and because it is incident to a general *sovereign* or *legislative* power to *regulate* a thing, to employ all the means which relate to its regulation to the best and greatest advantage.

Through this mode of reasoning respecting the right of employing all the means requisite to the execution of the specified powers of the government, it is to be objected, that none but necessary and proper means are to be employed; and the Secretary of State maintains, that no means are to be considered *necessary* but those without which the grant of the power would be *nugatory*. . . .

It is essential to the being of the national government, that so erroneous a conception of the meaning of the word *necessary* should be exploded.

It is certain, that neither the grammatical nor popular sense of the term requires that construction. According to both, *necessary* often means no more than *needful, requisite, incidental, useful,* or *conducive to.* . . . And it is the true one in which it is to be understood as used in the Constitution. The whole turn of the clause containing it indicates, that it was the intent of the Convention, by that clause, to give a liberal latitude to the exercise of the specified powers. The expressions have peculiar comprehensiveness. They are, "to make all *laws* necessary and proper for *carrying into execution* the *foregoing powers,* and *all other powers,* vested by the Constitution in the *government* of the United States, or in any *department* or *officer* thereof."

To understand the word as the Secretary of State does, would be to depart from its obvious and popular sense, and to give it a restrictive operation, an idea never before entertained. It would be to give it the same force as if the word *absolutely* or *indispensably* had been prefixed to it. . . .

The *degree* in which a measure is necessary, can never be a *test* of the legal right to adopt it; that must be a matter of opinion, and can only be a *test* of expediency. The *relation* between the *measure* and the *end;* between the *nature* of the *means* employed towards the execution of a power, and the object of that power, must be the criterion of constitutionality, not the more or less of *necessity* or *utility.* . . .

This restrictive interpretation of the word *necessary* is also contrary to this sound maxim of construction; namely, that the powers contained in a constitution of government, especially those which concern the general administration of the affairs of a country, its finances, trade, defence &c., ought to be construed liberally in advancement of the public good. . . . The means by which national exigencies are to be provided for, national inconveniences obviated, national prosperity promoted, are of such infinite variety, extent, and complexity, that there must of necessity be great latitude of discretion in the selection and application of those means. Hence, consequently, the necessity and propriety of exercising the authorities intrusted to a government on principles of liberal construction. . . .

But the doctrine which is contended for is not chargeable with the consequences imputed to it. It does not affirm that the National Government is sovereign in all respects, but that it is sovereign to a certain extent; that it is, to the extent of the objects of its specified powers.

It leaves, therefore, a criterion of what is constitutional, and of what is not so. This criterion is the *end*, to which the measure relates as a *means*. If the *end* be clearly comprehended within any of the specified powers, and if the measure have an obvious relation to that *end*, and is not forbidden by any particular provision of the Constitution, it may safely be deemed to come within the compass of the national authority. There is also this further criterion, which may materially assist the decision; Does the proposed measure abridge a pre-existing right of any State or of any individual? If it does not, there is a strong presumption in favor of its constitutionality, and slighter relations to any declared object of the Constitution may be permitted to turn the scale. . . .

It is presumed to have been satisfactorily shown in the course of the preceding observations:

1. That the power of the government, as to the objects intrusted to its management, is, in its nature, sovereign.

2. That the right of erecting corporations is one inherent in, and inseparable from, the idea of sovereign power.

3. That the position, that the government of the United States can exercise no power but such as is delegated to it by its Constitution, does not militate against this principle.

4. That the word *necessary*, in the general clause, can have no *restrictive* operation derogating from the force of this principle; indeed, that the degree in which a measure is or is not *necessary*, cannot be a *test* of *constitutional right*, but of *expediency only*.

5. That the power to erect corporations is not to be considered as an *independent* or *substantive* power, but as an *incidental* and *auxiliary* one, and was therefore more properly left to implication than expressly granted.

6. That the principle in question does not extend the power of the government beyond the prescribed limits, because it only affirms a power to *incorporate* for purposes *within the sphere* of the *specified powers*.

And lastly, that the right to exercise such a power in certain cases is unequivocally granted in the most *positive* and *comprehensive* terms. . . .

A hope is entertained that it has, by this time, been made to appear, to the satisfaction of the President, that a bank has a natural relation to the power of collecting taxes—to that of regulating trade—to that of providing for the common defence—and that, as the bill under consideration contemplates the government in the light of a joint proprietor of the stock of the bank, it brings the case within the provision of the clause of the Constitution which immediately respects the property of the United States.

Under a conviction that such a relation subsists, the Secretary of the Treasury, with all deference, conceives, that it will result as a necessary consequence from the position, that all the specified powers of government are sovereign, as to the proper objects; that the incorporation of a bank is a constitutional measure; and that the objections taken to the bill, in this respect, are ill-founded. . . .

DOCUMENT 6

THOMAS JEFFERSON, THE IMPORTANCE OF AGRICULTURE,
1784

The only full-length book Jefferson ever wrote was his Notes on Virginia, originally written in answer to inquiries made of him by the Secretary of the French Legation in Philadelphia, and first published in Paris, 1784. The book was much esteemed at home and abroad for its encyclopedic information. But in this famous passage, Jefferson soon moves from the business of reporting facts to a deeply felt statement of his civic beliefs, in which he voices his love of husbandry and his fear of the influence of manufactures and large cities.

The political economists of Europe have established it as a principle that every state should endeavor to manufacture for itself; and this principle, like many others, we transfer to America, without calculating the difference of circumstance which should often produce a difference of result. In Europe the lands are either cultivated, or locked up against the cultivator. Manufacture must therefore be resorted to of necessity, not of choice, to support the surplus of their people. But we have an immensity of land courting the industry of the husbandman. Is it best then that all our citizens should be employed in its improvement, or that one half should be called off from that to exercise manufactures and handicraft arts for the other? Those who labor in the earth are the chosen people of God, if he ever had a chosen people, whose breasts he has made his peculiar deposit for substantial and genuine virtue. It is the focus in which he keeps alive that sacred fire, which otherwise might escape from the face of the earth. Corruption of morals in the mass of cultivators is a phenomenon of which no age nor nation has furnished an example. It is the mark set on those who, not looking up to heaven, to their own soil and industry, as does the husbandmen, for their subsistence, depend for it on the casualties and caprice of customers. Dependence begets subservience and venality, suffocates the germ of virtue, and prepares fit tools for the designs of ambition. This, the natural progress and consequence of the arts, has sometimes perhaps been retarded by accidental circumstances; but, generally speaking, the proportion which the aggregate of the other classes of citizens bears in any state to that of its husbandmen is the proportion of its unsound to its healthy parts, and is a good enough barometer whereby to measure its degree of corruption. While we have land to labor then, let us never wish to see our citizens occupied at a workbench, or twirling a distaff. Carpenters, masons, smiths, are wanting in husbandry; but, for the general operations of manufacture, let our workshops remain in Europe. It is better to carry provisions and materials to workmen there than bring them to the provisions and materials, and with them their manners and principles. The loss by the transportation of commodities across the Atlantic will be made up in happiness and permanence of government. The mobs of great cities add just so much to the support of pure government, as sores do to the strength of the human body. It is the manners and spirit of a people which preserve a republic in vigor. A degeneracy in these is a canker which soon eats to the heart of its laws and constitution. . . .

DOCUMENT 7

ALEXANDER HAMILTON, REPORT ON THE SUBJECT OF MANUFACTURES,

DECEMBER 5, 1791

In January 1790, the House requested Hamilton to draw up a plan to encourage manufactures, with the object of making the United States independent of other nations, especially in military supplies. During the following year, Hamilton, though busy with many other concerns, assiduously collected information from a wide range of sources throughout the world. From this wealth of material he drew the last of his famous reports. Hamilton's report went far beyond the scope of his mandate from the House. With remarkable grasp of economic matters, he set forth the advantages of a manufacturing system, and with remarkable prescience he forecast changes which came with the later growth of manufactures. But clearly as Hamilton anticipated the benefits of manufacturing industry, he also anticipated the evils of modern industrialism—and without the slightest humanitarian forebodings. One of the advantages, for instance, that he saw in British cotton manufacturing was that it made use of the labor of "women and children, and many of them of a very tender age."

The expediency of encouraging manufactures in the United States . . . appears at this time to be pretty generally admitted. The embarrassments which have obstructed the progress of our external trade, have led to serious reflections on the necessity of enlarging the sphere of our domestic commerce. The restrictive regulations, which, in foreign markets, abridge the vent of the increasing surplus of our agricultural produce . . . beget an earnest desire that a more extensive demand for that surplus may be created at home. . . .

To affirm that the labor of the manufacturer is unproductive, because he consumes as much of the produce of land as he adds value to the raw material which he manufactures, is not better founded than it would be to affirm that the labor of the farmer, which furnishes materials to the manufacturer, is unproductive, because he consumes an equal value of manufactured articles. Each furnishes a certain portion of the produce of his labor to the other, and each destroys a corresponding portion of the produce of the labor of the other. In the meantime, the maintenance of two citizens, instead of one, is going on; the State has two members instead of one; and they, together, consume twice the value of what is produced from the land. . . .

It is now proper to proceed a step further, and to enumerate the principal circumstances from which it may be inferred that manufacturing establishments not only occasion a positive augmentation of the produce and revenue of the society, but that they contribute essentially to rendering them greater than they could possibly be without such establishments. These circumstances are:

1. The division of labor.
2. An extension of the use of machinery.
3. Additional employment to classes of the community not ordinarily engaged in the business.
4. The promoting of emigration from foreign countries.
5. The furnishing greater scope for the diversity of talents and dispositions, which discriminate men from each other.
6. The affording a more ample and various field for enterprise.
7. The creating, in some instances, a new, and securing, in all, a more certain and steady demand for the surplus produce of the soil.

Each of these circumstances has a considerable influence upon the total mass of industrious effort in a community; together, they add to it a degree of energy and effect which is not easily conceived. . . .

1. *As to the division of labor*

It has justly been observed, that there is scarcely any thing of greater moment in the economy of a nation than the proper division of labor. The separation of occupations causes each to be carried to a much greater perfection than it could possibly acquire if they were blended. This arises principally from three circumstances:

1st. The greater skill and dexterity naturally resulting from a constant and undivided application to a single object. . . .

2d. The economy of time, by avoiding the loss of it, incident to a frequent transition from one operation to another of a different nature. . . .

3d. An extension of the use of machinery. A man occupied on a single object will have it more in his power, and will be more naturally led to exert his imagination, in devising methods to facilitate and abridge labor, than if he were perplexed by a variety of independent and dissimilar operations. . . .

2. *As to an extention of the use of machinery, a point which, though partly anticipated, requires to be placed in one or two additional lights*

The employment of machinery forms an item of great importance in the general mass of national industry. It is an artificial force brought in aid of the natural force of man; and, to all the purposes of labor, is an increase of hands, an accession of strength, unencumbered too by the expense of maintaining the laborer. May it not, therefore, be fairly inferred, that those occupations which give greatest scope to the use of this auxiliary, contribute most to the general stock of industrious effort, and, in consequence, to the general product of industry? . . .

3. *As to the additional employment of classes of the community not originally engaged in the particular business*

This is not among the least valuable of the means by which manufacturing institutions contribute to augment the general stock of industry and production. In places where those institutions prevail, besides the persons regularly engaged in them, they afford occasional and extra employment to industrious individuals and families, who are willing to devote the leisure resulting from the intermissions of their ordinary pursuits to collateral labors, as a resource for multiplying their acquisitions or their enjoyments. The husbandman himself experiences a new source of profit and support from the increased industry of his wife and daughters, invited and stimulated by the demands of the neighboring manufactories.

It is worthy of particular remark that, in general, women and children are rendered more useful, and the latter more early useful, by manufacturing establishments, than they would otherwise be. Of the number of persons employed in the cotton manufactories of Great Britain, it is computed that four sevenths, nearly, are women and children, of whom the greatest proportion are children, and many of them of a very tender age. . . .

4. *As to the promoting of emigration from foreign countries*

Men reluctantly quit one course of occupation and livelihood for another, unless invited to it by very apparent and proximate advantages. Many who would go from one country to another, if they had a prospect of continuing with more benefit the callings to which they have been educated, will often not be tempted to change their situation by the hope of doing better in some other way. Manufacturers who, listening to the powerful invitations of a better price for their fabrics or their labor, of greater cheapness of provisions and raw materials, of an exemption from the chief part of the taxes, burthens, and restraints which they endure in the Old World, of greater personal independence and consequence, under the operation of a more equal government, and of what is far more precious than mere religious toleration, a perfect equality of religious privileges, would probably flock from Europe to the United States, to pursue their own trades or professions, if they were once made sensible of the advantages they would enjoy, and were inspired with an assurance of encouragement and employment, will, with difficulty, be induced to transplant themselves, with a view to becoming cultivators of land. . . .

5. *As to the furnishing greater scope for the diversity of talents and dispositions, which discriminate men from each other*

If there be any thing in a remark often to be met with, namely, that there is, in the genius of the people of this country, a peculiar aptitude for mechanic improvements, it would operate as a forcible reason for giving opportunities to the exercise of that species of talent, by the propagation of manufactures.

6. *As to the affording a more ample and various field for enterprise*

The spirit of enterprise, useful and prolific as it is, must necessarily be contracted or expanded, in proportion to the simplicity or variety of the occupations and productions which are to be found in a society. It must be less in a nation of mere cultivators, than in a nation of cultivators and merchants; less in a nation of cultivators and merchants, than in a nation of cultivators, artificers, and merchants.

7. *As to the creating, in some instances, a new, and securing, in all, a more certain and steady demand for the surplus produce of the soil*

This is among the most important of the circumstances which have been indicated. It is a principal means by which the establishment of manufactures contributes to an augmentation of the produce or revenue of a country, and has an immediate and direct relation to the prosperity of agriculture.

It is evident that the exertions of the husbandman will be steady or fluctuating, vigorous or feeble, in proportion to the steadiness or fluctuation, adequateness or inadequateness, of the markets on which he must depend for the vent of the surplus which may be produced by his labor; and that such surplus, in the ordinary course of things, will be greater or less in the same proportion. . . .

This idea of an extensive domestic market for the surplus produce of the soil, is of the first consequence. It is, of all things, that which most effectually conduces to a flourishing state of agriculture. If the effect of manufactories should be to detach a portion of the hands which would otherwise be engaged in tillage, it might possibly cause a smaller quantity of lands to be under cultivation; but, by their tendency to procure a more certain demand for the surplus produce of the soil, they would, at the same time, cause the lands which were in cultivation to be better improved and more productive. And while, by their influence, the condition of each individual farmer would be meliorated, the total mass of agricultural production would probably be increased. For this must evidently depend as much upon the degree of improvement, if not more, than upon the number of acres under culture. . . .

The foregoing considerations seem sufficient to establish, as general propositions, that it is the interest of nations to diversify the industrious pursuits of the individuals who compose them; that the establishment of manufactures is calculated not only to increase the general stock of useful and productive labor, but even to improve the state of agriculture in particular,—certainly to advance the interests of those who are engaged in it. . . .

DOCUMENT 8

VIRGINIA AND KENTUCKY RESOLUTIONS, 1798

These resolutions were adopted by the legislatures of the two states as a protest against the Alien and Sedition Acts. The Kentucky Resolutions were written by Jefferson and introduced into the legislature by John Breckenridge. The Virginia Resolutions were written by Madison and introduced into the legislature by John Taylor. These documents were the fountainhead of all subsequent resistance by the states to the encroachments of the federal government. Here it is forcefully asserted that the federal government was created by a compact between the states and not directly by the people as a whole. In these resolutions an attempt is also made to set the states up as legitimate judges of the constitutionality of federal laws, a role soon to be assumed more firmly and successfully by the Supreme Court (See Document 11). Opposition to these Resolutions was quickly expressed by the Federalists everywhere. Even in Virginia a group of

Federalists in the House of Delegates signed a pro-
test against the resolutions of their own state in which
these "treasonable resolutions" were accused of hav-
ing been designed "to subvert the Constitution and to
introduce discord and anarchy." In 1799 Madison
tried to explain that the declarations of both Virginia
and Kentucky were "expressions of opinion, unaccom-
panied with any other effect than what they may pro-
duce on opinion by exciting reflection." However, in
response to Jefferson's desires the Kentucky legislature
in 1799 adopted further resolutions, answering various
state replies to the original resolutions, in which it was
firmly stated that the states had the right to judge of
infractions of the Constitution, and "That a nullifica-
tion of those sovereignties, of all unauthorized acts
done under color of that instrument is the rightful
remedy." The constitutional issue did not come to a
head, only because the Alien and Sedition Acts ex-
pired in 1800. Jefferson's election in that year made
their re-enactment unthinkable.

KENTUCKY RESOLUTIONS
November 16, 1798

I. *Resolved*, that the several States composing the
United States of America, are not united on the principle
of unlimited submission to their general government; but
that by compact under the style and title of a Constitution
for the United States and of amendments thereto, they
constituted a general government for special purposes, delegated to that government certain definite powers, reserving
each State to itself, the residuary mass of right to their
own self-government; and that whensoever the general
government assumes undelegated powers, its acts are un-
authoritative, void, and of no force: That to this compact
each State acceded as a State, and is an integral party, its
co-States forming, as to itself, the other party: That the
government created by this compact was not made the
exclusive or final judge of the extent of the powers delegated to itself; since that would have made its discretion,
and not the Constitution, the measure of its powers; but
that as in all other cases of compact among parties having

no common Judge, each party has an equal right to judge for itself, as well of infractions as of the mode and measure of redress. . . .

III. *Resolved,* that it is true as a general principle, and is also expressly declared by one of the amendments to the Constitution that "the powers not delegated to the United States by the Constitution, nor prohibited by it to the States, are reserved to the States respectively, or to the people;" and that no power over the freedom of religion, freedom of speech, or freedom of the press being delegated to the United States by the Constitution, nor prohibited by it to the States, all lawful powers respecting the same did of right remain, and were reserved to the States, or to the people: That thus was manifested their determination to retain to themselves the right of judging how far the licentiousness of speech and of the press may be abridged without lessening their useful freedom, and how far those abuses which cannot be separated from their use should be tolerated rather than the use be destroyed; and thus also they guarded against all abridgment by the United States of the freedom of religious opinions and exercises, and retained to themselves the right of protecting the same, as this State, by a law passed on the general demand of its citizens, had already protected them from all human restraint or interference: And that in addition to this general principle and express declaration, another and more special provision has been made by one of the amendments to the Constitution which expressly declares, that "Congress shall make no law respecting an establishment of religion, or prohibiting the free exercise thereof, or abridging the freedom of speech, or of the press," thereby guarding in the same sentence, and under the same words, the freedom of religion, of speech, and of the press insomuch, that whatever violates either, throws down the sanctuary which covers the others, and that libels, falsehoods, defamation equally with heresy and false religion, are withheld from the cognizance of Federal tribunals. That therefore [the Sedition Act], which does abridge the freedom of the press, is not law, but is altogether void and of no effect.

IV. *Resolved,* that alien friends are under the jurisdiction and protection of the laws of the State wherein they are; that no power over them has been delegated to the United States, nor prohibited to the individual States distinct from their power over citizens; and it being true as a general principle [Alien Act of June 22, 1798], which assumes power over alien friends not delegated by the Constitution, is not law, but is altogether void and of no force. . . .

VI. *Resolved,* that the imprisonment of a person under the protection of the laws of this Commonwealth on his failure to obey the simple order of the President to depart out of the United States, as is undertaken by the said act entitled "An act concerning aliens," is contrary to the Constitution, one amendment to which has provided, that "no person shall be deprived of liberty without due process of law," and that another having provided "that in all criminal prosecutions, the accused shall enjoy the right to a public trial by an impartial jury, to be informed of the nature and cause of the accusation, to be confronted with the witnesses against him, to have compulsory process for obtaining witnesses in his favour, and to have the assistance of counsel for his defense," the same act undertaking to authorize the President to remove a person out of the United States, who is under the protection of the law, on his own suspicion, without accusation, without jury, without public trial, without confrontation of the witnesses against him, without having witnesses in his favour, without defense, without counsel, is contrary to these provisions also of the Constitution, is therefore not law, but utterly void, and of no force. That transferring the power of judging any person, who is under the protection of the laws, from the courts to the President of the United States, as is undertaken by the same act concerning aliens, is against the article of the Constitution which provides, that "the judicial power of the United States shall be vested in courts, the judges of which shall hold their offices during good behavior," and that the said act is void for that reason also and it is further to be noted, that this transfer of judiciary power is to that magistrate of the general government who already possesses all the executive, and a qualified negative in all the legislative powers.

VII. *Resolved,* that the construction applied by the general government (as is evinced by sundry of their proceedings) to those parts of the Constitution of the United States which delegate to Congress a power to lay and collect taxes, duties, imposts, and excises: to pay the debts, and provide for the common defense, and general welfare of the United States, and to make all laws which shall be necessary and proper for carrying into execution the powers vested by the Constitution in the government of the United States, or any department thereof, goes to the destruction of all the limits prescribed to their power by the Constitution: That words meant by that instrument to be subsidiary only to the execution of the limited powers ought not to be so construed as themselves to give unlimited powers, nor a part so to be taken as to destroy the whole residue of the instrument: That the proceedings of the general government under color of these articles will be a fit and necessary subject for revisal and correction at a time of greater tranquillity, while those specified in the preceding resolutions call for immediate redress. . . .

IX. *Resolved,* lastly, that the Governor of this Commonwealth be, and is hereby authorized and requested to communicate the preceding Resolutions to the Legislatures of the several States, to assure them that this Commonwealth considers Union for specified National purposes, and particularly for those specified in their late Federal Compact, to be friendly to the peace, happiness, and prosperity of all the States: that faithful to that compact according to the plain intent and meaning in which it was understood and acceded to by the several parties, it is sincerely anxious for its preservation: that it does also believe, that to take from the States all the powers of self-government, and transfer them to a general and consolidated government, without regard to the special delegations and reservations solemnly agreed to in that compact, is not for the peace, happiness, or prosperity of these States: And that, therefore, this Commonwealth is determined, as it doubts not its co-States are, tamely to submit to undelegated and consequently unlimited powers in no man or body of men on earth. . . . That the friendless alien has indeed been selected as the safest subject of a first experiment, but the citizen will soon follow, or rather has already followed: for, already has a sedition act

marked him as its prey: that these and successive acts of
the same character, unless arrested on the threshold, may
tend to drive these States into revolution and blood, and
will furnish new calumnies against Republican governments, and new pretexts for those who wish it to be
believed, that man cannot be governed but by a rod of
iron: that it would be a dangerous delusion were a confidence in the men of our choice to silence our fears for
the safety of our rights: that confidence is everywhere the
parent of despotism: free government is founded in
jealousy and not in confidence; it is jealousy and not confidence which prescribes limited Constitutions to bind
down those whom we are obliged to trust with power:
that our Constitution has accordingly fixed the limits
to which and no further our confidence may go; and
let the honest advocate of confidence read the alien
and sedition acts, and say if the Constitution has not been
wise in fixing limits to the government it created, and
whether we should be wise in destroying those limits; let
him say what the government is if it be not a tyranny,
which the men of our choice have conferred on the
President, and the President of our choice has assented to
and accepted over the friendly strangers, to whom the
mild spirit of our country and its laws had pledged
hospitality and protection: that the men of our choice have
more respected the bare suspicions of the President than
the solid rights of innocence, the claims of justification,
the sacred force of truth, and the forms and substance of
law and justice. In questions of power then let no more be
heard of confidence in man, but bind him down from
mischief by the claims of the Constitution. That this
Commonwealth does therefore call on its co–States for
an expression of their sentiments on the acts concerning
aliens, and for the punishment of certain crimes herein
before specified, plainly declaring whether these acts are
or are not authorized by the Federal Compact. And it
doubts not that their sense will be so announced as to
prove their attachment unaltered to limited government,
whether general or particular, and that the rights and
liberties of their co–States will be exposed to no dangers
by remaining embarked on a common bottom with their
own: That they will concur with this Commonwealth in

considering the said acts so palpably against the Constitution as to amount to an undisguised declaration, that the compact is not meant to be the measure of the powers of the general government, but that it will proceed in the exercise over these States of all powers whatsoever: That they will view this as seizing the rights of the States and consolidating them in the hands of the general government with a power assumed to bind the States (not merely in cases made Federal) but in all cases whatsoever, by laws made, not with their consent, but by others against their consent: That this would be to surrender the form of government we have chosen, and to live under one deriving its powers from its own will, and not from our authority; and that the co–States, recurring to their natural right in cases not made Federal, will concur in declaring these acts void and of no force, and will each unite with this Commonwealth in requesting their repeal at the next session of Congress.

VIRGINIA RESOLUTIONS
December 24, 1798

Resolved, That the General Assembly of Virginia doth unequivocally express a firm resolution to maintain and defend the Constitution of the United States, and the Constitution of this state, against every aggression either foreign or domestic; and that they will support the Government of the United States in all measures warranted by the former.

That this Assembly most solemnly declares a warm attachment to the union of the states, to maintain which it pledges all its powers; and that, for this end, it is their duty to watch over and oppose every infraction of those principles which constitute the only basis of that union, because a faithful observance of them can alone secure its existence and the public happiness.

That this Assembly doth explicitly and peremptorily declare, that it views the powers of the Federal Government as resulting from the compact to which the states are parties, as limited by the plain sense and intention of the instrument constituting that compact, as no further valid than they are authorized by the grants enumerated in that compact; and that, in case of a deliberate, palpable, and dangerous exercise of other powers, not granted by the said compact, the states, who are parties thereto, have the right, and are in duty bound, to interpose, for arresting the progress of the evil, and for maintaining, within their respective limits, the authorities, rights, and liberties, appertaining to them.

That the General Assembly doth also express its deep regret, that a spirit has, in sundry instances, been manifested by the Federal Government to enlarge its powers by forced constructions of the constitutional charter which defines them; and that indications have appeared of a design to expound certain general phrases (which, having been copied from the very limited grant of powers in the former Articles of Confederation, were the less liable to be misconstrued) so as to destroy the meaning and effect of the particular enumeration which necessarily explains and limits the general phrases, and so as to consolidate the states, by degrees, into one sovereignty, the obvious tendency and inevitable consequence of which would be, to transform the present republican system of the United States into an absolute, or, at best, a mixed monarchy.

That the General Assembly doth particularly PRO-TEST against the palpable and alarming infractions of the Constitution, in the two late cases of the "Alien and Sedition Acts," passed at the last session of Congress; the first of which exercises a power nowhere delegated to the Federal Government, and which, by uniting legislative and judicial powers to those of [the] executive, subverts the general principles of free government, as well as the particular organization and positive provisions of the Federal Constitution; and the other of which acts exercises, in like manner, a power not delegated by the Constitution, but, on the contrary, expressly and positively forbidden by one of the amendments thereto,—a power which, more than any other, ought to produce universal alarm, because it is levelled against the right of freely examining public characters and measures, and of free communication among the people thereon, which has ever been justly deemed the only effectual guardian of every other right.

That this state having, by its Convention which ratified the Federal Constitution, expressly declared that, among other essential rights, "the liberty of conscience and of the press cannot be cancelled, abridged, restrained, or modified, by any authority of the United States," and from its extreme anxiety to guard these rights from every possible attack of sophistry and ambition, having, with other states, recommended an amendment for that purpose, which amendment was, in due time, annexed to the Constitution,—it would mark a reproachful inconsistency, and criminal degeneracy, if an indifference were now shown to the palpable violation of one of the rights thus declared and secured, and to the establishment of a precedent which may be fatal to the other.

That the good people of this commonwealth, having ever felt and continuing to feel the most sincere affection for their brethren of the other states; the truest anxiety for establishing and perpetuating the union of all; and the most scrupulous fidelity to that Constitution, which is the pledge of mutual friendship, and the instrument of mutual happiness, the General Assembly doth solemnly appeal to the like dispositions in the other states, in confidence that they will concur with this Commonwealth in declaring, as it does hereby declare, that the acts aforesaid are unconstitutional; and that the necessary and proper measures will be taken *by each* for co-operating with this state, in maintaining unimpaired the authorities, rights, and liberties, reserved to the states respectively, or to the people. . . .

DOCUMENT 9

THE LEGISLATURE OF RHODE ISLAND ON THE VIRGINIA RESOLUTIONS,

FEBRUARY 1799

The Virginia and Kentucky Resolutions provoked counter-statements from every state north of the Potomac, of which these by Rhode Island are representative. All the replies sharply rejected the principles set forth by Jefferson and Madison, and in all of them the alleged right of the state legislatures to find an act

*of Congress unconstitutional was flatly repudiated.
Like this statement, most of the replies referred to the
right of the Supreme Court to exercise this function.*

Certain resolutions of the Legislature of Virginia, passed
on the 21st of December last, being communicated to
this Assembly,—

1. *Resolved,* That, in the opinion of this legislature,
the second section of the third article of the Constitution
of the United States, in these words, to wit,—"The judicial
power shall extend to all cases arising under the laws of
the United States,"—vests in the Federal Courts, exclusively, and in the Supreme Court of the United States,
ultimately, the authority of deciding on the constitutionality of any act or law of the Congress of the United
States.

2. *Resolved,* That for any state legislature to assume
that authority would be—

1st. Blending together legislative and judicial powers;

2d. Hazarding an interruption of the peace of the
states by civil discord, in case of a diversity of opinions
among the state legislatures; each state having, in that
case, no resort, for vindicating its own opinions, but the
strength of its own arm;

3d. Submitting most important questions of law to
less competent tribunals; and,

4th. An infraction of the Constitution of the United
States, expressed in plain terms.

3. *Resolved,* That, although, for the above reasons,
this legislature, in their public capacity, do not feel themselves authorized to consider and decide on the constitutionality of the Sedition and Alien laws, (so called,) yet
they are called upon, by the exigency of this occasion, to
declare that, in their private opinions, these laws are within
the powers delegated to Congress, and promotive of the
welfare of the United States.

4. *Resolved,* That the governor communicate these
resolutions to the supreme executive of the state of Virginia, and at the same time express to him that this
legislature cannot contemplate, without extreme concern
and regret, the many evil and fatal consequencies which

may flow from the very unwarrantable resolutions aforesaid of the legislature of Virginia, passed on the twenty-first day of December last.

DOCUMENT 10

THOMAS JEFFERSON, FIRST INAUGURAL ADDRESS,
MARCH 4, 1801

This address, one of Jefferson's most felicitous works, is memorable as a consummation of eighteenth-century elegance in style, as well as for its conciliatory tone and its restatement of republican principles. To the seventy-eight year old revolutionary leader, Samuel Adams, Jefferson wrote a few weeks after its delivery: "I addressed a letter to you, my very dear and ancient friend, on the 4th of March: not indeed to you by name, but through the medium of some of my fellow citizens, whom occasion called on me to address. In meditating the matter of that address, I often asked myself, is this exactly in the spirit of the patriarch, Samuel Adams? Is it as he would express it? Will he approve of it?"

Friends and Fellow-Citizens:

Called upon to undertake the duties of the first executive office of our country, I avail myself of the presence of that portion of my fellow-citizens which is here assembled to express my grateful thanks for the favor with which they have been pleased to look toward me, to declare a sincere consciousness that the task is above my talents, and that I approach it with those anxious and awful presentiments which the greatness of the charge and the weakness of my powers so justly inspire. A rising nation, spread over a wide and fruitful land, traversing all the seas with the rich productions of their industry, engaged in commerce with nations who feel power and forget right, advancing rapidly to destinies beyond the reach of mortal eye—when I contemplate these transcendent objects, and see the honor, the happiness, and the hopes of this beloved country committed to the issue and the auspices of this day, I shrink from the contemplation, and humble myself before the magnitude of the undertaking. Utterly, indeed, should I despair did not the presence of many whom I here see remind me that in the other high authorities provided by our Constitution I shall find resources of wisdom, of virtue, and of zeal on which to rely under all difficulties. To you, then, gentlemen, who are charged with the sovereign functions of legislation, and to those associated with you, I look with encouragement for that guidance and support which may enable us to steer with safety the vessel in which we are all embarked amidst the conflicting elements of a troubled world.

During the contest of opinion through which we have passed the animation of discussions and of exertions has sometimes worn an aspect which might impose on strangers unused to think freely and to speak and to write what they think; but this being now decided by the voice of the nation, announced according to the rules of the Constitution, all will, of course, arrange themselves under the will of the law, and unite in common efforts for the common good. All, too, will bear in mind this sacred principle, that though the will of the majority is in all cases to prevail, that will to be rightful must be reasonable; that the minority possess their equal rights, which equal law must protect, and to violate would be oppression. Let us, then, fellow-citizens, unite with one heart and one mind. Let us restore to social intercourse that harmony and affection without which liberty and even life itself are but dreary things. And let us reflect that, having banished from our land that religious intolerance under which mankind so long bled and suffered, we have yet gained little if we countenance a political intolerance as despotic, as wicked, and capable of as bitter and bloody persecutions. During the throes and convulsions of the ancient world, during the agonizing spasms of infuriated man, seeking through blood and slaughter his long-lost liberty, it was not wonderful that the agitation of the billows should reach even this distant and peaceful shore; that this should be more felt and feared by some and less by others, and should divide opinions as to measures of safety. But every difference of opinion is not a difference of principle. We have called by different names brethren of the same principle. We are all Republicans, we are all Federalists. If there be any among us who would wish to dissolve this Union or to change its republican form, let them stand undisturbed as monuments of the safety with which error of opinion may be tolerated where reason is left free to combat it. I know, indeed, that some honest men fear that a republican government can not be strong, that this Government is not strong enough; but would the honest patriot, in the full tide of successful experiment, abandon a government which has so far kept us free and firm on the theoretic and visionary fear that this Government, the world's best hope, may by possibility want energy to preserve itself? I trust not. I believe this, on the contrary, the strongest Government on earth. I believe it the only one where every man, at the call of the law, would fly to the standard of the law, and would meet invasions of the public order as his own personal concern. Sometimes it is said that man can not be trusted with the government of himself. Can he, then, be trusted with the government of others? Or have we found angels in the forms of kings to govern him? Let history answer this question.

Let us, then, with courage and confidence pursue our own Federal and Republican principles, our attachment to union and representative government. Kindly separated by nature and a wide ocean from the exterminating havoc of one quarter of the globe; too high-minded to endure the degradations of the others; possessing a chosen country, with room enough for our descendants to the thousandth and thousandth generation; entertaining a due sense of our equal right to the use of our own faculties, to the acquisitions of our own industry, to honor and confidence from our fellow-citizens, resulting not from birth, but from our actions and their sense of them; enlightened by a benign religion, professed, indeed, and practiced in various forms, yet all of them inculcating honesty, truth, temperance, gratitude, and the love of man; acknowledging and adoring an overruling Providence, which by all its dispensations proves that it delights in the happiness of man here and his greater happiness hereafter—with all these blessings, what more is necessary to make us a happy and a prosperous people? Still one thing more, fellow-citizens—a wise and frugal Government, which shall restrain men from injuring one another, shall leave them otherwise free to regulate their own pursuits of industry and improvement, and shall not take from the mouth of labor the bread it has earned. This is the sum of good government, and this is necessary to close the circle of our felicities.

About to enter, fellow-citizens, on the exercise of duties which comprehend everything dear and valuable to you, it is proper you should understand what I deem the essential principles of our Government, and consequently those which ought to shape its Administration. I will compress them within the narrowest compass they will bear, stating the general principle, but not all its limitations. Equal and exact justice to all men, of whatever state or persuasion, religious or political; peace, commerce, and honest friendship with all nations, entangling alliances with none; the support of the State governments in all their rights, as the most competent administrations for our domestic concerns and the surest bulwarks against anti-republican tendencies; the preservation of the General Government in its whole constitutional vigor, as the sheet anchor of our peace at home and safety abroad; a jealous care of the right of election by the people—a mild and safe corrective of abuses which are lopped by the sword of revolution where peaceable remedies are unprovided; absolute acquiescence in the decisions of the majority, the vital principle of republics, from which is no appeal but to force, the vital principle and immediate parent of despotism; a well-disciplined militia, our best reliance in peace and for the first moments of war, till regulars may relieve them; the supremacy of the civil over the military authority; economy in the public expense, that labor may be lightly burthened; the honest payment of our debts and sacred preservation of the public faith; encouragement of agriculture, and of commerce as its handmaid; the diffusion of information and arraignment of all abuses at the bar of the public reason; freedom of religion; freedom of the press, and freedom of person under the protection of the habeas corpus, and trial by juries impartially selected. These principles form the bright constellation which has gone before us and guided our steps through an age of revolution and reformation. The wisdom of our sages and blood of our heroes have been devoted to their attainment. They should be the creed of our political faith, the text of civic instruction, the touchstone by which to try the services of those we trust; and should we wander from them in moments of error or of alarm, let us hasten to retrace our steps and to regain the road which alone leads to peace, liberty, and safety.

I repair, then, fellow-citizens, to the post you have assigned me. With experience enough in subordinate offices to have seen the difficulties of this the greatest of all, I have learnt to expect that it will rarely fall to the lot of imperfect man to retire from this station with the reputation and the favor which bring him into it. Without pretensions to that high confidence you reposed in our first and greatest revolutionary character, whose preëminent services had entitled him to the first place in his country's love and destined for him the fairest page in the volume of faithful history, I ask so much confidence only as may give firmness and effect to the legal administration of your affairs. I shall often go wrong through defect of judgment. When right, I shall often be thought wrong by those whose positions will not command a view of the whole ground. I ask your indulgence for my own errors, which will never be intentional, and your support against the errors of others, who may condemn what they would not if seen in all its parts. The approbation implied by your suffrage is a great consolation to me for the past, and my future solicitude will be to retain the good opinion of those who have bestowed it in advance, to conciliate that of others by doing them all the good in my power, and to be instrumental to the happiness and freedom of all.

Relying, then, on the patronage of your good will, I advance with obedience to the work, ready to retire from it whenever you become sensible how much better choice it is in your power to make. And may that Infinite Power which rules the destinies of the universe lead our councils to what is best, and give them a favorable issue for your peace and prosperity.

DOCUMENT 11

MARBURY v. MADISON,
1803

*At a time when the Republicans were planning to cut
down the power of the federal judiciary, Chief Justice
John Marshall handed down this decision, which establishes the power of the Court to declare acts of
Congress unconstitutional. In accordance with an act
of 1801, empowering the president to appoint justices
of the peace for five-year terms in any number that he
saw fit, John Adams, just before leaving the White
House, hurriedly nominated forty-two men to fill
such posts. They were confirmed by the Senate, and
their commissions were signed but, in the rush of the
closing hours of the Adams administration, were not
actually delivered. On the ground that too many justices had been created, Jefferson, upon taking office,
withheld the commissions of seventeen. Only four of
the seventeen, including one William Marbury,
thought it worth while to bring suit to force Secretary
of State James Madison to deliver the commissions
without which they could not assume these rather insignificant judicial posts. But Marbury's appeal for a
writ of mandamus ordering such delivery became the
occasion for a major judicial coup on Marshall's part.
To outward appearances, so far as the substantive result was concerned, the case of the Federalists was
given away; for Marshall held that, though Marbury
was entitled to his commission, the Court lacked the
jurisdiction to issue the writ he sued for. But Section
13 of the Judiciary Act of 1789 had given the Court
this jurisdiction; and, in refusing to exercise it, Marshall found Section 13 inconsistent with Article III
of the Constitution, and therefore unconstitutional. At
the moment of a seeming refusal to assume power, he
thus asserted in the most sweeping fashion the authority of the Court. The opinion occasioned little comment at the time, even from the hostile Republicans.*

They may have been satisfied by their substantive victory in the case; but in any case they were soon preoccupied by the Louisiana Purchase and the renewal of the European war. But by 1807, during the trial of Aaron Burr, Jefferson was again gravely concerned. He wrote to District Attorney George Hay: "I have long wished for a proper occasion to have the gratuitous opinion in Marbury v. Madison brought before the public, and denounced as not law; and I think the present a fortunate one, because it occupies such a place in the public attention."

MARSHALL, C. J. . . . The first object of enquiry is,

Has the applicant a right to the commission he demands? . . .

Mr. Marbury, . . . since his commission was signed by the president, and sealed by the secretary of state, was appointed; and as the law creating the office, gave the officer a right to hold for five years, independent of the executive, the appointment was not revocable; but vested in the officer legal rights, which are protected by the laws of his country.

To withhold his commission, therefore, is an act deemed by the court not warranted by law, but violative of a vested legal right.

2. This brings us to the second enquiry: which is,

If he has a right, and that right has been violated, do the laws of his country afford him a remedy? . . .

It is . . . the opinion of the Court,

1st. That by signing the commission of Mr. Marbury, the President of the United States appointed him a justice of peace for the county of Washington in the district of Columbia; and that the seal of the United States, affixed thereto by the secretary of state, is conclusive testimony of the verity of the signature, and of the completion of the appointment; and that the appointment conferred on him a legal right to the office for the space of five years.

2dly. That, having this legal title to the office, he has a consequent right to the commission; a refusal to deliver which, is a plain violation of that right, for which the laws of his country afford him a remedy.

It remains to be enquired whether,

3dly. He is entitled to the remedy for which he applies. This depends on

1st. The nature of the writ applied for, and

2dly. The power of this court. . . .

This, then, is a plain case for a *mandamus,* either to deliver the commission, or a copy of it from the record; and it only remains to be enquired,

Whether it can issue from this court.

The act to establish the judicial courts of the United States authorizes the supreme court "to issue writs of *mandamus,* in cases warranted by the principles and usages of law, to any courts appointed, or persons holding office, under the authority of the United States."

The secretary of state, being a person holding an office under the authority of the United States, is precisely within the letter of the description; and if this court is not authorized to issue a writ of *mandamus* to such an officer, it must be because the law is unconstitutional, and therefore, absolutely incapable of conferring the authority and assigning the duties which its words purport to confer and assign.

The constitution vests the whole judicial power of the United States in one supreme court, and such inferior courts as congress shall, from time to time, ordain and establish. This power is expressly extended to all cases arising under the laws of the United States; and consequently, in some form, may be exercised over the present case; because the right claimed is given by a law of the United States.

In the distribution of this power, it is declared, that "the supreme court shall have original jurisdiction in all cases affecting ambassadors, other public ministers and consuls, and those in which a state shall be a party. In all other cases, the supreme court shall have appellate jurisdiction." . . .

If it had been intended to leave it in the discretion of the legislature to apportion the judicial power between the supreme and inferior courts according to the will of that body, it would certainly have been useless to have proceeded further than to have defined the judicial power, and the tribunals in which it should be vested. The subsequent part of the section is mere surplusage, is entirely without meaning, if such is to be the construction. If congress remains at liberty to give this court appellate jurisdiction, where the constitution has declared their jurisdiction shall be original; and original jurisdiction where the constitution has declared it shall be appellate; the distribution of jurisdiction, made in the constitution, is form without substance.

It cannot be presumed, that any clause in the constitution is intended to be without effect; and therefore such a construction is inadmissible, unless the words require it. . . .

The authority, therefore, given to the supreme court, by the act establishing the judicial courts of the United States, to issue writs of *mandamus* to public officers, appears not to be waranted by the constitution; and it becomes necessary to inquire whether a jurisdiction so conferred can be exercised.

The question whether an act repugnant to the constitution can become the law of the land, is a question deeply interesting to the United States; but, happily, not of an intricacy proportioned to its interest. It seems only necessary to recognize certain principles supposed to have been long and well established, to decide it.

That the people have an original right to establish for their future government such principles as, in their opinion, shall most conduce to their own happiness, is the basis on which the whole American fabric has been erected. The exercise of this original right is a very great exertion, nor can it, nor ought it to be frequently repeated. The principles therefore so established are deemed fundamental. And as the authority from which they proceed is supreme and can seldom act, they are designed to be permanent.

This original and supreme will organizes the government, and assigns to different departments their respective powers. It may either stop here or establish certain limits not to be transcended by those departments. The government of the United States is of the latter description. The powers of the legislature are defined and limited; and that those limits may not be mistaken or forgotten, the constitution is written. To what purpose are powers limited, and to what purpose is that limitation committed to writing, if these limits may, at any time, be passed by those intended to be restrained? The distinction between a government with limited and unlimited powers is abolished if those limits do not confine the persons on whom they are imposed and if acts prohibited and acts allowed are of equal obligation. It is a proposition too plain to be contested, that the constitution controls any legislative act repugnant to it; or, that the legislature may alter the constitution by an ordinary act.

Between these alternatives there is no middle ground. The constitution is either a superior paramount law, unchangeable by ordinary means, or it is on a level with ordinary legislative acts, and, like other acts, is alterable when the legislature shall please to alter it. If the former part of the alternative be true, then a legislative act contrary to the constitution is not law; if the latter part be true, then written constitutions are absurd attempts, on the part of the people, to limit a power in its own nature illimitable.

Certainly all those who have framed written constitutions contemplate them as forming the fundamental and paramount law of the nation, and consequently the theory of every such government must be that an act of the legislature repugnant to the Constitution is void. This theory is essentially attached to a written constitution, and is consequently to be considered, by this court, as one of the fundamental principles of our society. It is not, therefore, to be lost sight of in the further consideration of this subject.

If an act of the legislature repugnant to the constitution is void, does it, notwithstanding its invalidity, bind the courts and oblige them to give it effect? Or, in other words, though it be not law, does it constitute a rule as operative as if it was a law? This would be to overthrow in fact what was established in theory, and would seem, at first view, an absurdity too gross to be insisted on. It shall, however, receive a more attentive consideration.

It is emphatically the province and duty of the judicial department to say what the law is. Those who apply the rule to particular cases must of necessity expound and interpret that rule. If two laws conflict with each other, the courts must decide on the operation of each.

So if a law be in opposition to the constitution; if both the law and the constitution apply to a particular case, so that the court must either decide that case conformably to the law, disregarding the constitution, or conformably to the constitution, disregarding the law, the court must determine which of these conflicting rules governs the case. This is of the very essence of judicial duty. If, then, the courts are to regard the constitution, and the constitution is superior to any ordinary act of the legislature, the constitution, and not such ordinary act, must govern the case to which they both apply.

Those, then, who controvert the principle that the constitution is to be considered in court as a paramount law, are reduced to the necessity of maintaining that courts must close their eyes on the constitution and see only the law. This doctrine would subvert the very foundation of all written constitutions. It would declare that an act which, according to the principles and theory of our government, is entirely void, is yet, in practice, completely obligatory. It would declare that if the legislature shall do what is expressly forbidden, such act, notwithstanding the express prohibition, is in reality effectual. It would be giving to the legislature a practical and real omnipotence with the same breath which professes to restrict their powers within narrow limits. It is prescribing limits and declaring that those limits may be passed at pleasure.

That it thus reduces to nothing what we have deemed the greatest improvement on political institutions, a written constitution, would of itself be sufficient, in America, where written constitutions have been viewed with so much reverence, for rejecting the construction. But the peculiar expressions of the constitution of the United States furnish additional arguments in favor of its rejection.

The judicial power of the United States is extended to all cases arising under the constitution.

Could it be the intention of those who gave this power to say that in using it the constitution should not be looked into? That a case arising under the constitution should be decided without examining the instrument under which it arises? This is too extravagant to be maintained.

In some cases, then, the constitution must be looked

into by the judges. And if they can open it at all, what part of it are they forbidden to read or to obey?

There are many other parts of the constitution which serve to illustrate this subject.

It is declared that "no tax or duty shall be laid on articles exported from any state." Suppose a duty on the export of cotton, of tobacco, or of flour, and a suit instituted to recover it, ought judgment to be rendered in such a case? Ought the judges to close their eyes on the constitution, and only see the law?

The constitution declares "that no bill of attainder or *ex post facto* law shall be passed." If, however, such a bill should be passed, and a person should be prosecuted under it, must the court condemn to death those victims whom the constitution endeavors to preserve?

"No person," says the constitution, "shall be convicted of treason unless on the testimony of two witnesses to the same overt act, or on confession in open court." Here the language of the constitution is addressed especially to the courts. It prescribes, directly for them, a rule of evidence not to be departed from. If the legislature should change that rule, and declare one witness, or a confession out of court, sufficient for conviction, must the constitutional principle yield to the legislative act?

From these, and many other selections which might be made, it is apparent that the framers of the constitution contemplated that instrument as a rule for the government of courts, as well as of the legislature. Why otherwise does it direct the judges to take an oath to support it? This oath certainly applies in an especial manner to their conduct in their official character. How immoral to impose it on them if they were to be used as the instruments, and the knowing instruments, for violating what they swear to support!

The oath of office, too, imposed by the legislature, is completely demonstrative of the legislative opinion on this subject. It is in these words: "I do solemnly swear that I will administer justice without respect to persons, and do equal right to the poor and to the rich; and that I will faithfully and impartially discharge all the duties incumbent on me as ————, according to the best of my abilities and understanding, agreeably to the constitution and laws of the

United States." Why does a judge swear to discharge his duties agreeably to the constitution of the United States, if that constitution forms no rule for his government?—if it is closed upon him, and cannot be inspected by him? If such be the real state of things, this is worse than solemn mockery. To prescribe, or to take this oath, becomes equally a crime.

It is also not entirely unworthy of observation, that in declaring what shall be the *supreme* law of the land, the constitution itself is first mentioned, and not the laws of the United States generally, but those only which shall be made in pursuance of the constitution, have that rank.

Thus, the particular phraseology of the constitution of the United States confirms and strengthens the principle, supposed to be essential to all written constitutions, that a law repugnant to the constitution is void, and that courts, as well as other departments, are bound by that instrument.

DOCUMENT 12

THOMAS JEFFERSON ON THE SUPREME COURT,
SEPTEMBER 6, 1819

Jefferson never ceased to be troubled by the supremacy of an unchecked federal judiciary. After a number of Marshall's opinions favoring national authority and private rights had followed each other in close succession, notably McCulloch v. Maryland *and* Dartmouth College v. Woodward, *both decided in 1819, Jefferson's letters contained frequent anguished references to the Court's power. This selection is from a letter to a fellow opponent of the federal judiciary, Judge Spencer Roane of Virginia. Some Republicans had argued that the Court's right to pass on the unconstitutionality of acts of Congress was legitimate in so far as it bore on the co-ordination of the three main branches of the federal government, but not as it bore on the fundamental distribution of powers between the state and federal governments. Jefferson thought that even this conceded too much, and that each of the three departments should have equal power to decide on constitutionality—an opinion that was echoed by Andrew Jackson in his famous veto of the recharter of the Bank of the United States (see Part V, Document 10). Having found impeachment an inadequate weapon against the justices of the Supreme Court, Jefferson was now looking for more effective ways of checking men whom he described as "the corps of sappers and miners, steadily working to undermine the independent rights of the states, and to consolidate all power in the hands of [the federal] government." His remark here that the Constitution was but "wax in the hands of the Judiciary" presages Charles Evans Hughes's observation, over a century later: "We are under a Constitution, but the Constitution is what the judges say it is." In a subsequent letter (to James Pleasants, December 26, 1821) Jefferson proposed that the judges be appointed not for life, but for terms of six years (like the terms of Senators) and reappointed by the president with the concurrence of both houses of Congress. This, he thought, might provide an adequate popular check on the Judiciary.*

The revolution of 1800 . . . was as real a revolution in the principles of our government as that of 1776 was in its form; not effected indeed by the sword, as that, but by the rational and peaceable instrument of reform, the suffrage of the people. The nation declared its will by dismissing functionaries of one principle, and electing those of another, in the two branches, executive and legislative, submitted to their election. Over the judiciary department, the Constitution had deprived them of their control. That, therefore, has continued the reprobated system, and . . . after twenty years' confirmation of the federated system by the voice of the nation, declared through the medium of elections, we find the judiciary on every occasion, still driving us into consolidation.

In denying the right they usurp of exclusively explaining the Constitution, I go further than you do, if I understand rightly your quotation from *The Federalist*, of an opinion that "the judiciary is the last resort in relation *to the other departments* of the government, but not in relation to the rights of the parties to the compact under which the Judiciary is derived." If this opinion be sound, then indeed is our Constitution a complete *felo de se*. For intending to establish three departments, co-ordinate and independent, that they might check and balance one another, it has given, according to this opinion, to one of them alone, the right to prescribe rules for the government of the others, and to that one too, which is unelected by, and independent of the nation. For experience has already shown that the impeachment it has provided is not even a scarecrow. . . . The Constitution, on this hypothesis, is a mere thing of wax in the hands of the judiciary, which they may twist and shape into any form they please. It should be remembered, as an axiom of eternal truth in politics, that whatever power in any government is independent, is absolute also; in theory only, at first, while the spirit of the people is up, but in practice, as fast as that relaxes. Independence can be trusted nowhere but with the people in mass. They are inherently independent of all but moral law. My construction of the Constitution is . . . that each department is truly independent of the others, and has an equal right to decide for itself what is the meaning of the Constitution in the cases submitted to its action; and especially, where it is to act ultimately and without appeal.

✳ PART IV ✳

Republican Diplomacy

IN *Common Sense*, Thomas Paine had predicted that immunity from Europe's wars would be one of the main benefits of American independence. Not long after independence was achieved, however, the Americans discovered that neither their economic interests nor their political passions could be easily detached from European affairs. As early as 1793 the wars precipitated by the French Revolution confronted Washington's administration with serious problems. America's treaty with France, made in 1778, and originating from our own Revolution, seemed to demand that the United States now come to France's support. The discussion of proper American policy toward this treaty foreshadowed from the very beginning the ways in which Federalists and Jeffersonians would differ for years to come. The entire Federalist system, as Hamilton had designed it, depended upon the trade with Britain from which governmental revenues were derived. If material interest were not enough, prejudice also pointed in the same direction. To many Federalists the British government still represented authority and order, ideals which they felt were menaced by the democracy of both America and France. Their opponents, the Jeffersonians, however, did not care so much about trade or tariffs or public credit as they did about the balance of European interests in America, which they hoped to exploit for the benefit of American security and expansion. Even more, to the Jeffersonians Britain represented monarchy, oppressive authority, and arbitraiy taxation, and they tended still to harbor the resentments of the Revolutionary War. France, on the contrary, seemed to them to be fighting for the rights of man for which they had themselves fought so short a time ago. The difference between Federalist and Republican thus became, in a considerable degree, the difference between what contemporaries called "Anglomen" and "Gallomen."

Upon the outbreak of war in 1793, Washington was again confronted by opposing advice from Hamilton and Jefferson. Hamilton urged open repudiation of the French treaty and the issuance of a proclamation of neutrality, on the ground that the treaty had been made with Louis XVI, not with the Republic which succeeded him. Jefferson insisted that the treaty was as binding with the Republic as it had been with the monarchy, and should not be repudiated. But he did not favor American involvement on the side of France, because the French had not lived up to the treaty to the extent of helping the United States remove British troops from garrisons on American soil. This, he argued, relieved us of military obligations to France. Jefferson's most important difference with Hamilton was that he proposed to withhold assurance of neutrality from Great Britain until some compensatory concession had been won from her. Washington compromised. On the central issue he followed Hamilton's course: he simply proclaimed neutrality without trying to extract any promises from England in return. But in deference to Jefferson's views, he avoided the use of the word "neutrality," saying instead that the intention of the United States was to "pursue a conduct friendly and impartial toward the belligerent Powers," and he did not repudiate the treaty of 1778. Moreover, in accordance with Jefferson's wishes, he received the French minister, Edmond Genêt, without any conditions or warnings. But Genêt's abuse of his position which even Jefferson could not condone, weakened America's sympathy toward France.

It was difficult to steer a neutral course. Britain, counting on complaisance from the Federalist administration, was seizing American cargoes headed for France or the French colonies and was impressing seamen on the high seas. The British still occupied garrisons on the American frontier, and encouraged the Indians to resist American land claims.

John Jay, sent to London to arrange a settlement of these differences, returned with a most controversial treaty. Though it contained a renewed promise by the British to evacuate the western posts which they had promised to surrender in 1783, it capitulated on substantially every other count. Many problems, including impressment of seamen, English influence among the Indians, and compensation to Americans for slaves carried off during the Revolutionary War, were not settled. Most outrageous of all was the treaty's acceptance of the British demand that cargoes of provisions for France might be confiscated so long as the British paid for them. Not only did this violate the spirit of the Treaty of 1778, but, because of American acceptance of other British violations of neutrality, it made the French feel that the United States had entered, however reluctantly, into alliance with France's enemies.

The unpalatable treaty caused an uproar (Document 1) when its terms were made public in March 1795. Jay was accused of selling out his country, and was burned in effigy; the treaty was denounced throughout the country. There was, however, one persuasive argument in favor of the treaty: it did avoid war with Britain—a war which the country could not afford. While the treaty was being passionately argued, Hamilton, now retired to private life, wrote the "Camillus" letters (Document 2) in which he defended the treaty, clause by clause. The treaty was ratified by the Senate in June 1795, but appropriations necessary to carry it out were not voted by the House until the following April.

Washington was much alarmed at the heat of partisan discussion and at the emotional commitments to foreign countries that Americans had become involved in since the outbreak of the French Revolution. Accordingly, in his valedictory to the American people, the famous Farewell Address of September 1796 (Document 3), he warned against the dangers of partisanship, sectionalism, and passionate involvement with the affairs of foreign countries. But his successor, John Adams, found it more difficult than ever to maintain true neutrality. By 1798 the impertinences of French diplomacy pushed America almost to the point of declaring war. An undeclared naval war actually was fought for two years, chiefly in West Indian waters, but Adams bravely resisted the pressure of men in his own party who wanted a full-scale war with France. In 1800 he was able to arrive at an understanding with Napoleon by which the treaty of 1778 was terminated. By this time, Adams had alienated his party, and Jefferson defeated him in the election of 1800.

Jefferson's accession to the Presidency meant a reversal of America's policy as it had been made by the pro-English and anti-French Federalists. But, above all, it brought to the helm an administration sensitive to the interests of the people of the West and South for whom New Orleans was of decisive importance as an entrepôt for their trade. That Jefferson was more concerned with fostering American interests in this area than with involving himself in any commitment to England or France was shown by his famous letter to Robert R. Livingston (Document 4). In this letter he stressed the importance of New Orleans to the United States and said that if necessary he was willing to "marry ourselves to the British fleet and nation" in order to oppose any obstructive French occupation. Much to his surprise, his effort to buy New Orleans and Florida was answered by Napoleon's proposal that the whole great territory of Louisiana, retroceded by Spain to France in 1800, be bought by the United States. The Louisiana Purchase of 1803 was an immense coup for the nation and for the Jeffersonians, and was no less a blow to the Federalists of New England. Timothy Pickering, once one of the most ardently anti-French members of Adams's cabinet, fought the purchase in the Senate on constitutional grounds, and warned that the Union might now fly asunder. The correspondence of Pickering and his school of arch-Federalists (Document 5) shows how the most intransigent New Englanders saw that the immense expansion of the western (and hence Jeffersonian) areas of the Union might mean the complete and permanent submergence of their section. In 1804 some of these men were scheming to help Aaron Burr win the governorship of New York, which they hoped would be followed by the secession of New York and New England to form a sep-

arate confederation. Burr was stopped in New York—
Hamilton was killed because of his efforts to stop him—
and secession was dropped for the time. But after 1807,
Jefferson's attempt to win concessions for American interests from the warring powers through his embargo
policy proved immensely costly to the country, and again
the intense hostility of New England was brought down
upon him (Document 5).

Under Jefferson's successor, James Madison, a coalition of "War Hawks" formed, who were eager for war with
England in order to push expansion northward into Canada and southward into Florida, as well as to defend
American maritime rights. War Hawk expansionism was
opposed by men both in and out of New England (Document 6). When President Madison sent his message to
Congress calling for war with England (Document 7), he
emphasized maritime rights and impressment, not expansionist goals. But whatever the real or professed aims
of the war party, the War of 1812 was unpopular and ill-
supported in New England. Long-festering discontents now
came to a head, and delegates from the New England
states met late in 1814 and early in 1815 to draw up a
statement of their grievances, together with some proposals to protect their interests and their power within the
Union (Document 8). The immediate conclusion of the
war and, the striking victory of Jackson at New Orleans
threw the New Englanders into confusion. After the war's
end, the Federalist party rapidly disappeared.

Restoration of peace in Europe and the collapse of
Federalism put an end to domestic strife over foreign
policy. Diplomacy during the second administration of
James Monroe became newly self-confident and had un-
precedented united support. In September 1821, the Czar
issued a ukase, extending Russian claims along the Pacific Coast downward to the 51st parallel. This, together
with the fear that the Holy Alliance (Russia, Prussia,
France, and Austria) might act to restore to Spain her
recently revolted colonies in South America, called for
some display of firm American opposition. The British
Foreign Secretary, George Canning, proposed a joint
Anglo-American statement against action by the Holy
Alliance in the New World, but the United States, largely

at the urging of Secretary of State John Quincy Adams, decided to act independently (Document 9). Adams proposed that the United States send separate diplomatic communications to the various governments involved. Monroe decided instead to include an announcement of American policy in his annual message to Congress. The Monroe Doctrine (Document 10) sent to Congress on December 2, 1823, was in part written by Adams; it enunciated principles which he had been striving to establish: first, that the American continents were no longer to be considered open for future colonization by the European powers; second, that the political system of the Americas was different from that of Europe; third, that the United States would consider any attempt on the part of the European powers to extend their system to the Western Hemisphere as dangerous to its peace and safety; and finally, that the United States would not interfere with existing colonies or dependencies in the New World nor in the internal affairs of European countries, and that she would take no part in European wars of interest solely to European powers. Although the United States lacked the power to make good immediately on its every aspect, this declaration was received with enthusiasm at home. The young Republic entered the second quarter of the nineteenth century with an established foreign policy behind which public opinion was united.

DOCUMENT 1

ROBERT R. LIVINGSTON, *EXAMINATION OF THE TREATY . . . BETWEEN THE UNITED STATES AND GREAT BRITAIN,*

1795

Robert R. Livingston of New York had been in charge of the department of foreign affairs set up by Congress during the last few years of the Revolution, and he was one of the outstanding jurists of his state. He became a leader of the opposition to Jay's treaty and, in 1795, under the pen name of "Cato," published his Examination of the Treaty of Amity, Commerce and Navigation Between the United States and Great Britain. *Jefferson later appointed him minister to France* (*Document 4*).

Britain, on the day of the signature of the treaty, was involved in a war with the bravest people in Europe: in the whole course of this war, she had experienced continued defeats and disgraces; her treasures were wasted upon allies that either deserted or were too feeble to afford her effectual aid; her debt had grown to the enormous sum of three hundred millions; her navy could only be manned by the most destructive burthens upon her commerce; her manufactures were languishing; her fleets were unable to protect her trade, which had suffered unexampled losses. And while she was sinking under her burdens, her antagonist was consolidating her government, and growing so rapidly in strength, reputation, and vigour, as to threaten her existence as a nation. The United States were, on the other hand, in the highest prosperity; their numbers had doubled since they had successfully measured swords with Britain; they possessed men, arms, military stores, and an ally, who was alone too powerful for her enemies. Sweden and Denmark who had received insults from Britain, were ready to make a common cause with her; as the marine of England and France were nearly balanced, the weight of America, had she been forced into the war, would have turned the scale, and compleated the ruin of the British commerce, without any other effort than that of granting letters of marque. Independent of which, without a violation of their neutrality by those acts of sovereignty which no one would dispute their right to exercise, they could involve the British trade in the utmost distress, by an additional duty on British tonnage, by granting advantages to rival manufactures, by retaining debts due to her merchants, until the injuries ours had sustained were compensated. By following her example, both in the present and in the late American war, and suffering no part of the public debt to be paid to her citizens until justice was done us, we could have forced her into any measure that it was just or proper for us to ask. And, indeed, so fully satisfied were the Americans, of every party, of the superiority of our situation, that no doubt was entertained of a favorable issue to Mr. Jay's negociation, and all that his friends lamented, and his enemies rejoiced in, was, that the principal credit of them would be ascribed rather to the victories of France, than to the address of our minister. Under these happy auspices the negociation began. . . .

By the 2d article of the treaty, the British promise to evacuate the western posts by the 1st of June, 1796. By the treaty of Paris, in 1782, they promised to evacuate with all convenient speed; which, if we may judge by the speed with which they have found it convenient to evacuate all their posts in France, Flanders, Germany, Holland, and Brabant, one would have supposed must have meant a much shorter time than eighteen months, so that all that the treaty acquires with respect to the posts, is less than we were entitled to by the treaty of Paris. Surely we might expect better security than a mere promise, from a nation which has already shewn, in their violation of the past, the little reliance that can be placed on their future engagements. By June, 1796, it is not improbable that our situation, or that of Britain, may be changed; what security shall we then have for the performance of the treaty? It is said (by those shameless apologists who are determined to find every ministerial measure right) that every treaty is a promise, and that if we are not to rely upon a promise, there can be no treaties, I answer, that it is the practice of negociators, where the character of the nation, or other circumstances, give reason to suspect a violation of their engagements, *not to rely* upon a naked promise, but to expect some guarantee or surety for the performance; that in the present case, as the promise was evidently extorted by the pressure of existing circumstances, we should see to the performance while those circumstances continue to exist. It is evident, before Mr. Jay left this country, that the British were so far from intending to evacuate the posts, that they had determined to extend their limits; this may not only be inferred from the encouragement they gave to the depredations of the Indians, but undeniably proved by Lord Dorchester's speech, which, though disavowed by Dundas, is now admitted to have been made in consequence of express instructions. The promise, then to evacuate, has been extorted by French victories, by the humiliation of the British nation, and by their apprehension that we might at last be provoked to do ourselves justice while they were embarrassed with France. Surely then the evacuation should have been insisted upon, while these circumstances operated with full force. . . . Are we not at this moment at war with the savages? Is not this war attended with much expence to the nation, and much private distress? Is not the blood of our citizens daily shed? These evils must continue as long as the posts are in the hands of the British, or a peace, if practicable, must be purchased by the United States at very considerable expence. Were we to estimate the difference on this point of view, between an immediate evacuation, and one that is to take place in June 1796, it would certainly not fall short of one million of dollars, independent of the price. If to this we add the annual profits of the Indian trade, amounting to 800,000, it will appear, that the United States loose above a million of dollars by retention of the posts, supposing (which is at least problematical) that they will be surrendered at the period proposed. Those who think with me, that decision of the part of our government, and firmness in our minister, could not have failed to effect an immediate restitution of our territory, will know to what account to charge this heavy loss of blood and treasure.

Would to God, my fellow citizens, I could here find some source of consolation, some ray of light, to eradicate the sullen gloom!—But alas! every step we take plunges us into thicker darkness. We might, perhaps, have submitted to past losses; have seen our commerce given away without an equivalent; our navigation ruined; our seamen (I blush with shame and indignation while I say it) our citizen seamen delivered over to the insolence of brutal tyrants, could our national honour have been preserved in future—could alliances, formed by interest and gratitude, have been left unimpaired—could peace have been established upon firm and honorable terms; could the private rights of our citizens, the public ones of our government, have remained unviolated—but, the indiscriminate ruin of all these is too much to be borne in silence. Even the coward advocates for peace, feel their spirits rise on the unexampled indignities which this treaty imposes. And for what? Are we nearer peace (if by peace is meant the security of our persons and property, from foreign depredations) than when Mr. Jay left this country? Is there a single outrage which we suffered before which is not continued to this moment? And yet the advocates for the treaty are continually ringing in our ears, the blessings of peace, the horrors of war; and they have the effrontery to assure us, that we enjoy the first and have escaped the last, merely (to borrow a ministerial term) through the instrumentality of the treaty. Does any body believe, that if we had continued to suffer the British to plunder our trade, to man their ships with our seamen, to possess our frontiers in quiet, that they would have declared war upon us, at least till they had conquered France? . . . In a political view, the treaty is bad, as it detaches us from engagements which our interest and honour equally invite us to maintain; as it sacrifices our friends to our enemies, and holds forth to the world, that those nations who treat us worst, will share the greatest portion or our attachment, and that, like fawning spaniels, we can be beaten into love and submission. . . .

I trust, however, that enough has been said to shew, that the treaty has obtained no adequate compensation for the injuries we have suffered; that it has relinquished important claims that we had upon British government, that it has given no protection to our seamen, that it is injurious to our commerce, and ruinous to our navigation, that it takes from us the means we possessed of retaliating injuries without the hazard of a war, that it pledged the country for immense sums of money, which it does not owe, while it curtails our demands upon Britain; that it gives the British subjects a variety of privileges in our country, which are but partially returned to us, that it counteracts the existing laws, and violates the federal constitution, and that it infringes the rights of individual states. . . .

DOCUMENT 2

ALEXANDER HAMILTON, CAMILLUS, NUMBERS I AND II,

1795

The Camillus letters were recognized, even by Hamilton's foes, to be an effective defense of a treaty that needed much defending. As Jefferson wrote to Madison: "Hamilton is really a colossus to the anti-republican party. Without numbers, he is a host within himself. . . . We have had only middling performances to oppose him. In truth, when he comes forward, there is nobody but yourself who can meet him. . . . For God's sake take up your pen, and give a fundamental reply to . . . Camillus."

No. I

It was to have been foreseen, that the treaty which Mr. Jay was charged to negotiate with Great Britain, whenever it should appear, would have to contend with many perverse dispositions and some honest prejudices; that there was no measure in which the government could engage, so little likely to be viewed according to its intrinsic merits—so very likely to encounter misconception, jealousy, and unreasonable dislike. For this, many reasons may be assigned.

It is only to know the vanity and vindictiveness of human nature, to be convinced, that while this generation lasts there will always exist among us men irreconcilable to our present national Constitution; embittered in their animosity in proportion to the success of its operations, and the disappointment of their inauspicious predictions. It is a material inference from this, that such men will watch, with lynx's eyes, for opportunities of discrediting the proceedings of the government, and will display a hostile and malignant zeal upon every occasion, where they think there are any prepossessions of the community to favor their enterprises. A treaty with Great Britain was too fruitful an occasion not to call forth all their activity.

It was known, that the resentment produced by our revolution war with Great Britain had never been entirely extinguished, and that recent injuries had rekindled the flame with additional violence. It was a natural consequence of this, that many should be disinclined to any amicable arrangement with Great Britain, and that many others should be prepared to acquiesce only in a treaty which should present advantages of so striking and preponderant a kind as it was not reasonable to expect could be obtained, unless the United States were in a condition to give the law to Great Britain, and as, if obtained under the coercion of such a situation, could only have been the short–lived prelude of a speedy rupture to get rid of them. . . .

It was not to be mistaken, that an enthusiasm for France and her revolution, throughout all its wonderful vicissitudes, has continued to possess the minds of the great body of the people of this country; and it was to be inferred, that this sentiment would predispose to a jealousy of any agreement or treaty with her most persevering competitor,—a jealousy so excessive, as would give the fullest scope to insidious arts to perplex and mislead the public opinion. It was well understood, that a numerous party among us, though disavowing the design, because the avowal would defeat it, have been steadily endeavoring to make the United States a party in the present European war, by advocating all those measures which would widen the breach between us and Great Britain, and by resisting all those which would tend to close it; and it was morally certain, that this party would eagerly improve every circumstance which would serve to render the treaty odious, and to frustrate it, as the most effectual road of their favorite goal. . . .

To every man who is not an enemy to the national government, who is not a prejudiced partisan, who is capable of comprehending the argument, and dispassionate enough to attend to it with impartiality, I flatter myself I shall be able to demonstrate satisfactorily in the course of some succeeding papers:

1. That the treaty adjusts, in a reasonable manner, the points in controversy between the United States and

Great Britain, as well those depending on the inexecution of the treaty of peace, as those growing out of the present European war.

2. That it makes no improper concessions to Great Britain, no sacrifices on the part of the United States.

3. That it secures to the United States equivalents for what they grant.

4. That it lays upon them no restrictions which are incompatible with their honor or their interest.

5. That in the articles which respect war, it conforms to the laws of nations.

6. That it violates no treaty with, nor duty towards, any foreign power.

7. That, compared with our other commercial treaties, it is, upon the whole entitled to a preference.

8. That it contains concessions of advantages by Great Britain to the United States, which no other nation has obtained from the same power.

9. That it gives to her no superiority of advantages over other nations with whom we have treaties.

10. That the interests of primary importance to our general welfare are promoted by it.

11. That the too probable result of a refusal to ratify is war, or, what would be still worse, a disgraceful passiveness under violations of our rights, unredressed, and unadjusted; and consequently that it is the true interest of the United States that the treaty should go into effect. . . .

No. II

If we can avoid a war for ten or twelve years more, we shall then have acquired a maturity, which will make it no more than a common calamity, and will authorize us, in our national discussions, to take a higher and more imposing tone.

This is a consideration of the greatest weight to determine us to exert all our prudence and address to keep out of war as long as it shall be possible; to defer, to a state of manhood, a struggle to which infancy is ill adapted. This is the most effectual way to disappoint the enemies of our welfare; to pursue a contrary conduct may be to play into their hands, and to gratify their wishes. If there be a foreign power which sees with envy or ill–will our growing prosperity, that power must discern that our infancy is the time for clipping our wings. We ought to be wise enough to see that this is not a time for trying our strength.

Should we be able to escape the storm which at this juncture agitates Europe, our disputes with Great Britain terminated, we may hope to postpone war to a distant period. This, at least, will greatly diminish the chances of it. For then there will remain only one power with whom we have any embarrassing discussions. I allude to Spain, and the question of the Mississippi; and there is reason to hope that this question, by the natural progress of things, and perseverance in an amicable course, will finally be arranged to our satisfaction without the necessity of the *dernier ressort*. . . .

I proceed now to observe summarily that the objects of the mission, contrary to what has been asserted, have been substantially obtained. What were these? They were principally:

1. To adjust the matters of controversy concerning the inexecution of the treaty of peace, and especially to obtain restitution of our Western posts.

2. To obtain reparation for the captures and spoliations of our property in the course of the existing war.

Both these objects have been provided for, and it will be shown, when we come to comment upon the articles which make the provisions in each case, that it is a reasonable one, as good a one as ought to have been expected; as good a one as there is any prospect of obtaining hereafter; one which it is consistent with our honor to accept, and which our interest bids us to close with.

DOCUMENT 3

GEORGE WASHINGTON, FAREWELL ADDRESS,
SEPTEMBER 17, 1796

The immediate purpose of this message, which was not delivered by Washington but was published in the newspapers, was to announce that Washington would not permit himself to be considered for a third term. But he took this occasion to issue a warning against sectional and party spirit and against excessive involvement with foreign nations. When Washington urged that the ·nation "steer clear of permanent alliances with any portion of the foreign world," what he undoubtedly had in mind were the difficulties created by the French treaty of 1778. In the pursuit of national interest, however, Washington also said that "we may safely trust to temporary alliances for extraordinary emergencies." The address was actually drafted by Hamilton on Washington's instructions.

While, then, every part of our country thus feels an immediate and particular interest in union, all the parts combined can not fail to find in the united mass of means and efforts greater strength, greater resource, proportionably greater security from external danger, a less frequent interruption of their peace by foreign nations, and what is of inestimable value, they must derive from union an exemption from those broils and wars between themselves which so frequently afflict neighboring countries not tied together by the same governments, which their own rivalships alone would be sufficient to produce, but which opposite foreign alliances, attachments, and intrigues would stimulate and imbitter. Hence, likewise, they will avoid the necessity of those overgrown military establishments which, under any form of government, are inauspicious to liberty, and which are to be regarded as particularly hostile to republican liberty. In this sense it is that your union ought to be considered as a main prop of your liberty, and that the love of the one ought to endear to you the preservation of the other. . . .

In contemplating the causes which may disturb our union it occurs as matter of serious concern that any ground should have been furnished for characterizing parties by *geographical* discriminations—*Northern* and *Southern, Atlantic* and *Western*—whence designing men may endeavor to excite a belief that there is a real difference of local interests and views. One of the expedients of party to acquire influence within particular districts is to misrepresent the opinions and aims of other districts. You can not shield yourselves too much against the jealousies and heartburnings which spring from these misrepresentations; they tend to render alien to each other those who ought to be bound together by fraternal affection. . . .

To the efficacy and permanency of your union a government for the whole is indispensable. . . . This Government, the offspring of our own choice, uninfluenced and unawed, adopted upon full investigation and mature deliberation, completely free in its principles, in the distribution of its powers, uniting security with energy, and containing within itself a provision for its own amendment, has a just claim to your confidence and your support. Respect for its authority, compliance with its laws, acquiescence in its measures, are duties enjoined by the fundamental maxims of true liberty. The basis of our political systems is the right of the people to make and to alter their constitutions of government. But the constitution which at any time exists till changed by an explicit and authentic act of the whole people is sacredly obligatory upon all. The very idea of the power and the right of the people to establish government presupposes the duty of every individual to obey the established government.

I have already intimated to you the danger of parties in the State, with particular reference to the founding of them on geographical discriminations. Let me now take a more comprehensive view, and warn you in the most solemn manner against the baneful effects of the spirit of party generally.

This spirit, unfortunately, is inseparable from our nature, having its root in the strongest passions of the human mind. It exists under different shapes in all governments, more or less stifled, controlled, or repressed; but in those of the popular form it is seen in its greatest rankness and is truly their worst enemy. . . .

It serves always to distract the public councils and enfeeble the public administration. It agitates the community with ill-founded jealousies and false alarms; kindles the animosity of one part against another; foments occasionally riot and insurrection. It opens the door to foreign influence and corruption, which find a facilitated access to the government itself through the channels of party passion. Thus the policy and the will of one country are subjected to the policy and will of another.

There is an opinion that parties in free countries are useful checks upon the administration of the government, and serve to keep alive the spirit of liberty. This within certain limits is probably true; and in governments of a monarchical cast patriotism may look with indulgence, if not with favor, upon the spirit of party. But in those of the popular character, in governments purely elective, it is a spirit not to be encouraged. From their natural tendency it is certain there will always be enough of that spirit for every salutary purpose; and there being constant danger of excess, the effort ought to be by force of public opinion to mitigate and assuage it. A fire not to be quenched, it demands a uniform vigilance to prevent its bursting into a flame, lest, instead of warming, it should consume. . . .

Observe good faith and justice toward all nations. Cultivate peace and harmony with all. Religion and morality enjoin this conduct. And can it be that good policy does not equally enjoin it? It will be worthy of a free, enlightened, and at no distant period a great nation to give to mankind the magnanimous and too novel example of a people always guided by an exalted justice and benevolence. Who can doubt that in the course of time and things the fruits of such a plan would richly repay any temporary advantages which might be lost by a steady adherence to it? Can it be that Providence has not connected the permanent felicity of a nation with its virtue? The experiment, at least, is recommended by every sentiment which ennobles human nature. Alas! is it rendered impossible by its vices?

In the execution of such a plan nothing is more essential than that permanent, inveterate antipathies against particular nations and passionate attachments for others should be excluded, and that in place of them just and amicable feelings toward all should be cultivated. The nation which indulges toward another an habitual hatred or an habitual fondness is in some degree a slave. It is a slave to its animosity or to its affection, either of which is sufficient to lead it astray from its duty and its interest. Antipathy in one nation against another disposes each more readily to offer insult and injury, to lay hold of slight causes of umbrage, and to be haughty and intractable when accidental or trifling occasions of dispute occur. . . .

So, likewise, a passionate attachment of one nation for another produces a variety of evils. Sympathy for the favorite nation, facilitating the illusion of an imaginary common interest in cases where no real common interest exists, and infusing into one the enmities of the other, betrays the former into a participation in the quarrels and wars of the latter without adequate inducement or justification. It leads also to concessions to the favorite nation of privileges denied to others, which is apt doubly to injure the nation making the concessions by unnecessarily parting with what ought to have been retained, and by exciting jealousy, ill will, and a disposition to retaliate in the parties from whom equal privileges are withheld; and it gives to ambitious, corrupted, or deluded citizens (who devote themselves to the favorite nation) facility to betray or sacrifice the interests of their own country without odium, sometimes even with popularity, gilding with the appearances of a virtuous sense of obligation, a commendable deference for public opinion, or a laudable zeal for public good the base or foolish compliances of ambition, corruption, or infatuation. . . .

Against the insidious wiles of foreign influence (I conjure you to believe me, fellow-citizens) the jealousy of a free people ought to be *constantly* awake, since history and experience prove that foreign influence is one of the most baneful foes of republican government. But that jealousy, to be useful, must be impartial, else it becomes the instrument of the very influence to be avoided, instead of a defense against it. Excessive partiality for one foreign nation and excessive dislike of another cause those whom they actuate to see danger only on one side, and serve to veil and even second the arts of influence on the other. Real patriots who may resist the intrigues of the favorite are liable to become suspected and odious, while its tools and dupes usurp the applause and confidence of the people to surrender their interests.

The great rule of conduct for us in regard to foreign nations is, in extending our commercial relations to have with them as little *political* connection as possible. So far as we have already formed engagements let them be fulfilled with perfect good faith. Here let us stop.

Europe has a set of primary interests which to us have

none or a very remote relation. Hence she must be engaged in frequent controversies, the causes of which are essentially foreign to our concerns. Hence, therefore, it must be unwise in us to implicate ourselves by artificial ties in the ordinary vicissitudes of her politics or the ordinary combinations and collisions of her friendships or enmities.

Our detached and distant situation invites and enables us to pursue a different course. If we remain one people, under an efficient government, the period is not far off when we may defy material injury from external annoyance; when we may take such an attitude as will cause the neutrality we may at any time resolve upon to be scrupulously respected; when belligerent nations, under the impossibility of making acquisitions upon us, will not lightly hazard the giving us provocation; when we may choose peace or war, as our interest, guided by justice, shall counsel.

Why forego the advantages of so peculiar a situation? Why quit our own to stand upon foreign ground? Why, by interweaving our destiny with that of any part of Europe, entangle our peace and prosperity in the toils of European ambition, rivalship, interest, humor, or caprice?

It is our true policy to steer clear of permanent alliances with any portion of the foreign world, so far, I mean, as we are now at liberty to do it; for let me not be understood as capable of patronizing infidelity to existing engagements. I hold the maxim no less applicable to public than to private affairs that honesty is always the best policy. I repeat, therefore, let those engagements be observed in their genuine sense. But in my opinion it is unnecessary and would be unwise to extend them.

Taking care always to keep ourselves by suitable establishments on a respectable defensive posture, we may safely trust to temporary alliances for extraordinary emergencies.

Harmony, liberal intercourse with all nations are recommended by policy, humanity, and interest. But even our commercial policy should hold an equal and impartial hand, neither seeking nor granting exclusive favors or preferences; consulting the natural course of things; diffusing and diversifying by gentle means the streams of commerce, but forcing nothing; establishing with powers so disposed, in order to give trade a stable course, to define the rights of our merchants, and to enable the Government to support them, conventional rules of intercourse, the best that present circumstances and mutual opinion will permit, but temporary and liable to be from time to time abandoned or varied as experience and circumstances shall dictate; constantly keeping in view that it is folly in one nation to look for disinterested favors from another; that it must pay with a portion of its independence for whatever it may accept under that character; that by such acceptance it may place itself in the condition of having given equivalents for nominal favors, and yet of being reproached with ingratitude for not giving more. There can be no greater error than to expect or calculate upon real favors from nation to nation. It is an illusion which experience must cure, which a just pride ought to discard.

DOCUMENT 4

THOMAS JEFFERSON TO ROBERT R. LIVINGSTON,
APRIL 18, 1802

At the end of 1801, Jefferson learned that a year earlier Spain had secretly retroceded the Louisiana Territory to the French government. The prospect of the French holding New Orleans frightened Jefferson. But it delighted many Federalists who felt that even a Republican administration would now be driven to war with France—or, if it continued in its pacifism, would lose support in strong Republican territory. Jefferson sent this letter to Livingston through his friend DuPont de Nemours; he may have hoped its threatening contents would reach Napoleon, for he sent it unsealed. Napoleon, when his plans for the New World collapsed, offered Livingston, and James Monroe who had joined him, the chance to buy the entire Louisiana Territory. The purchase was an immense diplomatic success, which not only set aside the danger of war with France but opened up an immense area which Republicans and Federalists alike expected yeomen farmers of the Jeffersonian persuasion to occupy.

Thomas Jefferson to Robert R. Livingston, Washington, April 18, 1802.

The cession of Louisiana and the Floridas by Spain to France, works most sorely on the United States. . . . It completely reverses all the political relations of the United States, and will form a new epoch in our political course. Of all nations of any consideration, France is the one which, hitherto, has offered the fewest points on which we could have any conflict of right, and the most points of a communion of interests. From these causes, we have ever looked to her as our *natural friend,* as one with which we never could have an occasion of difference. Her growth, therefore, we viewed as our own, her misfortunes ours. There is on the globe one single spot, the possessor of which is our natural and habitual enemy. It is New Orleans, through which the produce of three-eighths of our territory must pass to market, and from its fertility it will ere long yield more than half of our whole produce, and contain more than half of our inhabitants. France, placing herself in that door, assumes to us the attitude of defiance. Spain might have retained it quietly for years. Her pacific dispositions, her feeble state, would induce her to increase our facilities there, so that her possession of the place would be hardly felt by us, and it would not, perhaps, be very long before some circumstance might arise, which might make the cession of it to us the price of something of more worth to her. Not so can it ever be in the hands of France: the impetuosity of her temper, the energy and restlessness of her character, placed in a point of eternal friction with us, and our character, which, though quiet and loving peace and the pursuit of wealth, is high-minded, despising wealth in competition with insult or injury, enterprising and energetic as any nation on earth; these circumstances render it impossible that France and the United States can continue long friends, when they meet in so irritable a position. They, as well as we, must be blind if they do not see this; and we must be very improvident if we do not begin to make arrangements on that hypothesis. The day that France takes possession of New Orleans, fixes the sentence which is to restrain her forever within her low-water mark. It seals the union of two nations, who, in conjunction, can maintain exclusive possession of the ocean. From that moment, we must marry ourselves to the British fleet and nation. We must turn all our attention to a maritime force, for which our resources place us on very high ground; and having formed and connected together a power which may render reinforcement of her settlements here impossible to France, make the first cannon which shall be fired in Europe the signal for the tearing up any settlement she may have made, and for holding the two continents of America in sequestration for the common purposes of the United British and American nations. This is not a state of things we seek or desire. It is one which this measure, if adopted by France, forces on us as necessarily, as any other cause, by the laws of nature, brings on its necessary effect. . . .

If France considers Louisiana, however, as indispensable for her views, she might perhaps be willing to look about for arrangements which might reconcile it to our interests. If anything could do this, it would be the ceding to us the island of New Orleans and the Floridas. This would certainly, in a great degree, remove the causes of jarring and irritation between us, and perhaps for such a length of time, as might produce other means of making the measure permanently conciliatory to our interests and friendships. . . .

DOCUMENT 5

LETTERS OF TIMOTHY PICKERING,
JANUARY 29, MARCH 4, 1804, AND JANUARY 8, 1809

By 1804 extreme Federalists in New England were desperate. The Jeffersonian attack on the judiciary, then in full swing, convinced them that their opponents were without principle, while the purchase of Louisiana threatened them with permanent minority status in a Union dominated by a grand coalition of South and West. Even in their own bailiwick, New England, democracy was gaining. The correspondence of Timothy Pickering to George Cabot and Rufus

*King of New York illustrates how these men hated
Jefferson and how their desperation tempted their
clique of Federalist Senators and Representatives to
think of secession as the only remedy. Pickering, who
had become Secretary of State in 1795 and had remained in that post under John Adams until dismissed
in 1800, was an old hand at intrigue, for he had tried
hard, from within the administration, to undermine
Adams's policies toward France. In 1803, Pickering
returned to Washington as a Senator from Massachusetts and was soon engaged in a plan to disrupt the
Union. However, men like George Cabot and Rufus
King, whose support Pickering hoped to enlist, were
more circumspect than he. Cabot replied to the first
of these letters that secession would be no remedy
because the real enemy, democracy, was too strong
even within New England itself. He believed nothing
could be done until still greater evils brought the
people to their senses. In early 1809, after Jefferson's
embargo had been in effect for more than a year,
Pickering was still urging the united action of New
England, though the plan for secession had been
tabled since the New England secessionists had failed
to secure Aaron Burr's election to the governorship of
New York.*

Pickering to George Cabot, January 29, 1804.

The Federalists are dissatisfied, because they see the
public morals debased by the corrupt and corrupting system of our rulers. Men are tempted to become apostates,
not to Federalism merely, but to virtue and to religion and
to good government. Apostasy and original depravity are
the qualifications for official honors and emoluments, while
men of sterling worth are displaced, and held up to popular contempt and scorn. And shall we sit still, until this
system shall universally triumph? until even in the Eastern
States the principles of genuine Federalism shall be over-
whelmed? Mr. Jefferson's plan of destruction has been
gradually advancing. If at once he had removed from
office all the Federalists, and given to the people such sub-
stitutes as we generally see, even his followers (I mean
the mass) would have been shocked. He is still making

progress in the same course; and he has the credit of being the real source of all the innovations which threaten the subversion of the Constitution, and the prostration of every barrier erected by it for the protection of the *best,* and therefore to him the most obnoxious, part of the community. His instruments manifest tempers so malignant, so inexorable, as convince observing Federalists that the mild manners and habits of our countrymen are the only security against their extreme vengeance. How long we shall enjoy even this security, God only knows. And must we with folded hands wait the result, or timely think of other protection? This is a delicate subject. The principles of our Revolution point to the remedy,—a separation. . . .

I do not believe in the practicability of a long-continued union. A Northern confederacy would unite congenial characters, and present a fairer prospect of public happiness; while the Southern States, having a similarity of habits, might be left "to manage their own affairs in their own way." If a separation were to take place, our mutual wants would render a friendly and commercial intercourse inevitable. The Southern States would require the naval protection of the Northern Union, and the products of the former would be important to the navigation and commerce of the latter. I believe, indeed, that, if a Northern confederacy were forming, our Southern brethren would be seriously alarmed, and probably abandon their virulent measures. But I greatly doubt whether prudence should suffer the connection to continue much longer. They are so devoted to their chief, and he is so necessary to accomplish their plans of misrule and oppression, that as they have projected an alteration of the Constitution to secure his next election, with a continued preponderance of their party, so it would not surprise me, were they, soon after his next election, to choose him President for life. I am assured that some of his blind worshippers in South Carolina have started the idea. . . .

Pickering to Rufus King, March 4, 1804.

I am disgusted with the men who now rule, and with their measures. At some manifestations of their malignancy, I am shocked. The cowardly wretch at their head, while, like a Parisian revolutionary monster, prating about humanity, would feel an infernal pleasure in the utter destruction of his opponents. We have too long witnessed his general turpitude, his cruel removals of faithful officers, and the substitution of corruption and looseness for integrity and worth. . . . I am therefore ready to say, "Come out from among them, and be ye separate." Corruption is the object and instrument of the chief, and the tendency of his administration, for the purpose of maintaining himself in power and the accomplishment of his infidel and visionary schemes. The corrupt portion of the people are the agents of his misrule. Corruption is the recommendation to office; and many of some pretensions to character, but too feeble to resist temptation, become apostates. Virtue and worth are his enemies, and therefore he would overwhelm them. The collision of Democrats in your State promises some amendment: the administration of your government cannot well be worse.

The Federalists here in general anxiously desire the election of Mr. Burr to the chair of New York; for they despair of a present ascendancy of the Federal party. Mr. Burr alone, we think, can break your Democratic phalanx; and we anticipate much good from his success. Were New York detached (as under his administration it would be) from the Virginian influence, the whole Union would be benefited. Jefferson would then be forced to observe some caution and forbearance in his measures. And, if a separation should be deemed proper, the five New England States, New York, and New Jersey would naturally be united. Among those seven States, there is a sufficient congeniality of character to authorize the expectation of practicable harmony and a permanent union, New York the centre. Without a separation, can those States ever rid themselves of negro Presidents and negro Congresses, and regain their just weight in the political balance? At this moment, the slaves of the Middle and Southern States have fifteen representatives in Congress, and they will appoint that number of electors of the next President and Vice–President; and the number of slaves is continually increasing. You notice this evil. But will the slave States ever renounce the advantage? As population is in *fact* no rule of taxation, the negro representation ought to be given up. If refused, it would be a strong ground for separation, though perhaps an earlier occasion may present to declare it. How many Indian wars, excited by the avidity of the Western and Southern States for Indian lands, shall we have to encounter, and who will pay the millions to support them? The Atlantic States. Yet the first moment we ourselves need assistance, and call on the Western States for taxes, they will declare off, or at any rate refuse to obey the call. Kentucky effectually resisted the collection of the excise; and of the thirty–seven thousand dollars' direct tax assessed upon her so many years ago, she has paid only four thousand dollars, and probably will never pay the residue. In the mean time, we are maintaining their representatives in Congress for governing us, who surely can much better govern ourselves. Whenever the Western States detach themselves, they will take Louisiana with them. In thirty years, the white population on the Western waters will equal that of the thirteen States when they declared themselves independent of Great Britain. On the census of 1790, Kentucky was entitled to two representatives; under that of 1800, she sends *six!* . . .

Pickering to Christopher Gore, January 8, 1809.

It is scarcely conceivable that Mr. Jefferson should so obstinately persevere in the odious measure of the embargo, which he cannot but see has impaired his popularity and hazards its destruction, if he were not under secret engagements to the French emperor; unless you can suppose that he would run that hazard and the ruin of his country, rather than that a measure which he explicitly recommended should be pronounced unwise. . . . When we advert to the real character of Mr. Jefferson, there is no nefarious act of which we may not suppose him capable. *He would rather the United States should sink than change the present system of measures.* This is not opinion, but history. . . .

New England must be united in whatever great measure shall be adopted. During the approaching session of our legislature, there may be such farther advances in mischief as may distinctly point out the course proper to be adopted. A convention of delegates from those States, including Vermont, seems obviously proper and necessary. . . . A strong and solemn address, stating as concisely as will consist with perspicuity the evil conduct of our administration as manifested in their measures, ought to be prepared to be laid before our legislature when they meet, to be sent forth by their authority to the people. . . .

Pray look into the Constitution, and particularly to the 10th article of the amendments. How are the powers reserved to the States respectively, or to the people, to be maintained, *but by the respective States judging for themselves and putting their negative on the usurpations of the general government?*

The unceasing cry of war among the President's pack is a gross artifice, so gross that I wonder men of understanding here are alarmed by it. Its sole object is to make them and the people at large acquiesce in the embargo; for the administration believe that the alternative of war is not terrible to mothers only, but to the men of the United States.

DOCUMENT 6

DEBATE IN THE HOUSE OF REPRESENTATIVES,
DECEMBER 1811

The War Hawks in Congress had been pressing for war with Britain for many months when, in November 1811, President Madison recommended a stepping-up of military preparation. In the following month, Peter B. Porter, chairman of a select committee to deal with the message, and a leading proponent of the acquisition of Canada, introduced measures providing for an increase in the army and in military matériel. During the House debate on these resolutions, the war party candidly revealed their expansionist aims, which were challenged by some of their more outspoken opponents. In these excerpts from the Annals of Congress, *two expansionists, Felix Grundy of Tennessee and Richard M. Johnson of Kentucky, argue their case, while that of the opposition is presented by John Randolph of Virginia.*

MR. GRUNDY, December 9

What, Mr. Speaker, are we now called on to decide? It is, whether we will resist by force the attempt, made by that Government, to subject our maritime rights to the arbitrary and capricious rule of her will; for my part I am not prepared to say that this country shall submit to have her commerce interdicted or regulated, by any foreign nation. Sir, I prefer war to submission.

Over and above these unjust pretensions of the British Government, for many years past they have been in the practice of impressing our seamen, from merchant vessels; this unjust and lawless invasion of personal liberty, calls loudly for the interposition of this Government. To those better acquainted with the facts in relation to it, I leave it to fill up the picture. My mind is irresistibly drawn to the West.

Although others may not strongly feel the bearing which the late transactions in that quarter have on this subject, upon my mind they have great influence. It cannot be believed by any man who will reflect, that the savage tribes, uninfluenced by other Powers, would think of making war on the United States. They understand too well their own weakness, and our strength. They have already felt the weight of our arms; they know they hold the very soil on which they live as tenants at sufferance. How, then, sir, are we to account for their late conduct? In one way only; some powerful nation must have intrigued with them, and turned their peaceful disposition towards us into hostilities. Great Britain alone has intercourse with those Northern tribes; I therefore infer, that if British gold has not been employed, their baubles and trinkets, and the promise of support and a place of refuge if necessary, have had their effect. . . .

This war, if carried on successfully, will have its advantages. We shall drive the British from our Continent —they will no longer have an opportunity of intriguing with our Indian neighbors, and setting on the ruthless savage to tomahawk our women and children. That nation will lose her Canadian trade, and, by having no resting place in this country, her means of annoying us will be diminished. The idea I am now about to advance is at war,

I know, with sentiments of the gentleman from Virginia: I am willing to receive the Canadians as adopted brethren; it will have beneficial political effects; it will preserve the equilibrium of the Government. When Louisiana shall be fully peopled, the Northern States will lose their power; they will be at the discretion of others; they can be depressed at pleasure, and then this Union might be endangered—I therefore feel anxious not only to add the Floridas to the South, but the Canadas to the North of this empire . . .

MR. RANDOLPH, December 10

An insinuation had fallen from the gentleman from Tennessee, (Mr. Grundy) that the late massacre of our brethren on the Wabash had been instigated by the British Government. Has the President given any such information? has the gentleman received any such, even informally, from any officer of this Government? Is it so believed by the Administration? He had cause to think the contrary to be the fact; that such was not their opinion. This insinuation was of the grossest kind—a presumption the most rash, the most unjustifiable. Show but good ground for it, he would give up the question at the threshold—he was ready to march to Canada. It was indeed well calculated to excite the feelings of the Western people particularly, who were not quite so tenderly attached to our red brethren as some modern philosophers; but it was destitute of any foundation, beyond mere surmise and suspicion. . . . There was an easy and natural solution of the late transaction on the Wabash, in the well known character of the aboriginal savage of North America, without resorting to any such mere conjectural estimate. He was sorry to say that for this signal calamity and disgrace the House was, in part, at least, answerable. Session after session, their table had been piled up with Indian treaties, for which the appropriations had been voted as a matter of course, without examination. Advantage had been taken of the spirit of the Indians, broken by the war which ended in the Treaty of Greenville. Under the ascendency then acquired over them, they had been pent up by subsequent treaties into nooks, straightened in their quarters by a blind cupidity, seeking to extinguish their title to immense wildernesses, for which, (possessing, as we do already, more land than we can sell or use) we shall not have occasion, for half a century to come. It was our own thirst for territory, our own want of moderation, that had driven these sons of nature to desperation, of which we felt the effects. . . .

He [Randolph] could but smile at the liberality of the gentleman, in giving Canada to New York, in order to strengthen the Northern balance of power, while at the same time he forwarned her that the Western scale must preponderate. Mr. R. said he could almost fancy that he saw the Capitol in motion towards the falls of Ohio—after a short sojourn taking its flight to the Mississippi, and finally alighting on Darien; which, when the gentleman's dreams are realized, will be a most eligible seat of Government for the new Republic (or Empire) of the two Americas! . . .

Mr. R. then proceeded to notice the unjust and illiberal imputation of British attachments, against certain characters in this country, sometimes insinuated in that House but openly avowed out of it. Against whom were these charges brought? Against men, who in the war of the Revolution were in the councils of the nation, or fighting the battles of your country. And by whom were they made? By runaways, chiefly from the British dominions, since the breaking out of the French troubles. He indignantly said—it is insufferable. It cannot be borne. It must, and ought, with severity, be put down in this House, and, out of it, to meet the lie direct. . . . Name, however, but England, and all our antipathies are up in arms against her. Against whom? Against those whose blood runs in our veins; in common with whom we claim Shakespeare, and Newton, and Chatham, for our countrymen; whose form of government is the freest on earth, our own only excepted; from whom every valuable principle of our own institutions has been borrowed—representation, jury trial, voting the supplies, writ of habeas corpus—our whole civil and criminal jurisprudence—against our fellow Protestants identified in blood, in language, in religion with ourselves. In what school did the worthies of our land, the Washingtons, Henrys, Hancocks, Franklins, Rutledges of America learn those princi-

ples of civil liberty which were so nobly asserted by their
wisdom and valor? And American resistance to British
usurpation had not been more warmly cherished by these
great men and their compatriots; not more by Washington,
Hancock, and Henry, than by Chatham and his illustrious
associates in the British Parliament. It ought to be remembered, too, that the heart of the English people was with
us. It was a selfish and corrupt Ministry, and their servile
tools, to whom we were not more opposed than they were.
He trusted that none such might ever exist among us—for
tools will never be wanting to subserve the purposes, however ruinous or wicked, of Kings and Ministers of
State. . . .

He called upon those professing to be Republicans
to make good the promises held out by their Republican
predecessors when they came into power—promises, which
for years afterwards they had honestly, faithfully fulfilled.
We had vaunted of paying off the national debt, of re-
trenching useless establishments; and yet had now become
as infatuated with standing armies, loans, taxes, navies,
and war, as ever were the Essex Junto. What Republicanism
is this? . . .

MR. RANDOLPH, December 16

Sir, if you go to war it will not be for the protection of, or defence of your maritime rights. Gentlemen from the North have been taken up to some high
mountain and shown all the kingdoms of the earth; and
Canada seems tempting in their sight. That rich vein of
Gennesee land, which is said to be even better on the other
side of the lake than on this. Agrarian cupidity, not maritime right, urges the war. Ever since the report of the Committee on Foreign Relations came into the House, we have
heard but one word—like the whip-poor-will, but one
eternal monotonous tone—Canada! Canada! Canada! Not
a syllable about Halifax, which unquestionably should be
our great object in a war for maritime security. It is to
acquire a prepondering northern influence, that you are
to launch into war. For purposes of maritime safety, the
barren rocks of Bermuda were worth more to us than all
the deserts through which Hearne and McKenzie had
pushed their adventurous researches. . . .

MR. JOHNSON, December 11

. . . Mr. J. said we must now oppose the farther encroachments of Great Britain by war, or formally annul the Declaration of our Independence, and acknowledge ourselves her devoted colonies. The people whom I represent will not hesitate which of the two courses to choose; and, if we are involved in war, to maintain our dearest rights, and to preserve our independence, I pledge myself to this House, and my constituents to this nation, that they will not be wanting in valor, nor in their proportion of men and money to prosecute the war with effect. Before we relinquish the conflict, I wish to see Great Britain renounce the piratical system of paper blockade; to liberate our captured seamen on board her ships of war; relinquish the practice of impressment on board our merchant vessels; to repeal her Orders in Council; and cease, in every other respect, to violate our neutral rights; to treat us as an independent people. The gentleman from Virginia (Mr. Randolph) has objected to the destination of this auxiliary force—the occupation of the Canadas, and the other British possessions upon our borders where our laws are violated, the Indians stimulated to murder our citizens, and where there is a British monopoly of the peltry and fur trade. I should not wish to extend the boundary of the United States by war if Great Britain would leave us to the quiet enjoyment of independence; but, considering her deadly and implacable enmity, and her continued hostility, I shall never die contented until I see her expulsion from North America, and her territories incorporated with the United States. It is strange that the gentleman would pause before refusing this force, if destined to keep the negroes in subordination—who are not in a state of insurrection as I understand—and he will absolutely refuse to vote this force to defend us against the lawless aggressions of Great Britain—a nation in whose favor he had said so much. . . .

But it has been denied that British influence had any agency in the late dreadful conflict and massacre upon the Wabash; and this is said to vindicate the British nation from so foul a charge. Sir, look to the book of the Revolution. See the Indian savages in Burgoyne's army urged on

every occasion to use the scalping-knife and tomahawk—
not in battle, but against old men, women, and children;
in the night, when they were taught to believe an Omnis-
cient eye could not see their guilty deeds; and thus
hardened to iniquity, they perpetrated the same deeds by
the light of the sun, when no arm was found to oppose or
protect. And when this crying sin was opposed by Lord
Chatham, in the House of Lords, the employment of these
Indians was justified by a speech from one of the Ministry.
Thus we see how the principles of honor, of humanity, of
christianity, were violated and justified in the face of the
world. Therefore, I can have no doubt of the influence of
British agents in keeping up Indian hostility to the people
of the United States, independent of the strong proofs on
this occasion; and, I hope it will not be pretended that
these agents are too moral or too religious to do the infamous deed. So much for the expulsion of Great Britain
from her dominions in North America, and their incorporation into the United States of America.

The gentleman from Virginia says we are identified
with the British in religion, in blood, in language, and
deeply laments our hatred to that country, who can boast
of so many illustrious characters. This deep rooted enmity
to Great Britain arises from her insidious policy, the
offspring of her perfidious conduct towards the United
States. Her disposition is unfriendly; her enmity is implacable; she sickens at our prosperity and happiness. If
obligations of friendship do exist, why does Great Britain
rend those ties asunder, and open the bleeding wounds of
former conflicts? Or does the obligation of friendship
exist on the part of the United States alone? I have never
thought that the ties of religion, of blood, of language, and
of commerce, would justify or sanctify insult and injury
—on the contrary, that a premeditated wrong from the
hand of a friend created more sensibility, and deserved the
greater chastisement and the higher execration. . . . For
God's sake let us not again be told of the ties of religion,
of laws, of blood, and of customs, which bind the two
nations together, with a view to extort our love for the
English Government, and more especially, when the same
gentleman has acknowledged that we have ample cause of
war against that nation—let us not be told of the freedom

of that corrupt Government whose hands are washed alike in the blood of her own illustrious statesmen, for a manly opposition to tyranny, and the citizens of every other clime. . . . It has been said that Great Britain was fighting the battles of the world—that she stands against universal dominion, threatened by the arch–fiend of mankind. I should be sorry if our independence depended upon the power of Great Britain. If, however, she would act the part of a friendly Power towards the United States, I should never wish to deprive her of power, of wealth, of honor, of prosperity. But if her energies are to be directed against the liberties of this free and happy people, against my native country, I should not drop a tear if the fast–anchored isle would sink into the waves, provided the innocent inhabitants could escape the deluge and find an asylum in a more favorable soil. And as to the power of France, I fear it as little as any other power; I would oppose her aggressions, under any circumstances, as soon as I would British outrages. . .

DOCUMENT 7

JAMES MADISON, WAR MESSAGE TO CONGRESS, JUNE 1, 1812

Madison here urges a declaration of war against Great Britain because of her impressment of American seamen, interference with American trade, and incitement of the Indians on the frontier. The message was debated in secret session in both houses of Congress. The House voted for war by 79 to 49, June 4, 1812; the Senate followed, 19 to 13, on June 18.

Without going back beyond the renewal in 1803 of the war in which Great Britain is engaged, and omitting unrepaired wrongs of inferior magnitude, the conduct of her Government presents a series of acts hostile to the United States as an independent and neutral nation.

British cruisers have been in the continued practice of violating the American flag on the great highway of nations, and of seizing and carrying off persons sailing under it, not in the exercise of a belligerent right founded on the law of nations against an enemy, but of a municipal prerogative over British subjects. British jurisdiction is thus extended to neutral vessels in a situation where no laws can operate but the law of nations and the laws of the country to which the vessels belong, and a self-redress is assumed which, if British subjects were wrongfully detained and alone concerned, is that substitution of force for a resort to the responsible sovereign which falls within the definition of war. . . .

The practice, hence, is so far from affecting British subjects alone that, under the pretext of searching for these, thousands of American citizens, under the safeguard of public law and of their national flag, have been torn from their country and from everything dear to them; have been dragged on board ships of war of a foreign nation and exposed, under the severities of their discipline, to be exiled to the most distant and deadly climes, to risk their lives in the battles of their oppressors, and to be the melancholy instruments of taking away those of their own brethren.

Against this crying enormity, which Great Britain would be so prompt to avenge if committed against herself, the United States have in vain exhausted remonstrances and expostulations, and that no proof might be wanting of their conciliatory dispositions, and no pretext left for a continuance of the practice, the British Government was formally assured of the readiness of the United States to enter into arrangements such as could not be rejected if the recovery of British subjects were the real and the sole object. The communication passed without effect.

British cruisers have been in the practice also of violating the rights and the peace of our coasts. They hover over and harass our entering and departing commerce. To the most insulting pretensions they have added the most lawless proceedings in our very harbors, and have wantonly spilt American blood within the sanctuary of our territorial jurisdiction. : . .

Under pretended blockades, without the presence of an adequate force and sometimes without the practicability of applying one, our commerce has been plundered in every sea, the great staples of our country have been cut off from their legitimate markets, and a destructive blow aimed at our agricultural and maritime interests. . . .

Not content with these occasional expedients for laying waste our neutral trade, the cabinet of Britain resorted at length to the sweeping system of blockades, under the name of orders in council, which has been molded and managed as might best suit its political views, its commercial jealousies, or the avidity of British cruisers. . . .

It has become, indeed, sufficiently certain that the commerce of the United States is to be sacrificed, not as interfering with the belligerent rights of Great Britain; not as supplying the wants of her enemies, which she herself supplies; but as interfering with the monopoly which she covets for her own commerce and navigation. She carries on a war against the lawful commerce of a friend that she may the better carry on a commerce with an enemy—a commerce polluted by the forgeries and perjuries which are for the most part the only passports by which it can succeed. . . .

In reviewing the conduct of Great Britain toward the United States our attention is necessarily drawn to the warfare just renewed by the savages on one of our extensive frontiers—a warfare which is known to spare neither age nor sex and to be distinguished by features peculiarly shocking to humanity. It is difficult to account for the activity and combinations which have for some time been developing themselves among tribes in constant intercourse with British traders and garrisons without connecting their hostility with that influence and without recollecting the authenticated examples of such interpositions heretofore furnished by the officers and agents of that Government.

Such is the spectacle of injuries and indignities which have been heaped on our country, and such the crisis which its unexampled forbearance and conciliatory efforts have not been able to avert. . . .

Our moderation and conciliation have had no other effect than to encourage perseverance and to enlarge pretensions. We behold our seafaring citizens still the daily victims of lawless violence, committed on the great common and highway of nations, even within sight of the country which owes them protection. We behold our vessels, freighted with the products of our soil and industry, or returning with the honest proceeds of them, wrested from their lawful destinations, confiscated by prize courts no longer the organs of public law but the instruments of arbitrary edicts, and their unfortunate crews dispersed and lost, or forced or inveigled in British ports into British fleets. . . .

We behold, in fine, on the side of Great Britain a state of war against the United States, and on the side of the United States a state of peace toward Great Britain.

Whether the United States shall continue passive under these progressive usurpations and these accumulating wrongs, or, opposing force to force in defense of their national rights, shall commit a just cause into the hands of the Almighty Disposer of Events, avoiding all connections which might entangle it in the contest or views of other powers, and preserving a constant readiness to concur in an honorable reëstablishment of peace and friendship, is a solemn question which the Constitution wisely confides to the legislative department of the Government. In recommending it to their early deliberations I am happy in the assurance that the decision will be worthy the enlightened and patriotic councils of a virtuous, a free, and a powerful nation. . . .

DOCUMENT 8

REPORT AND RESOLUTIONS OF THE HARTFORD CONVENTION,

JANUARY 4, 1815

Invitations for the Hartford Convention were issued by the Massachusetts legislature on October 14, 1814. Delegates were appointed by the legislatures of Connecticut, Massachusetts, and Rhode Island, and by local conventions in New Hampshire and Vermont; the sessions were held in secret from December 15 to

January 5, 1815. From the beginning the Convention was controlled by the moderates, who did not want to force an open break with the federal government. Among the moderates was Harrison Gray Otis, then a member of the Massachusetts Senate, who wrote the final report of the Convention.

It will be recollected, that the immediate influence of the Federal Constitution, upon its first adoption, and for twelve succeeding years, upon the prosperity and happiness of the nation, seemed to countenance a belief in the transcendency of its perfection over all other human institutions. In the catalogue of blessings which have fallen to the lot of the most favoured nations, none could be enumerated from which our country was excluded. . . .

But no sooner was a new administration established in the hands of the party opposed to the Washington policy, than a fixed determination was perceived and avowed of changing a system which had already produced these substantial fruits. . . . Under the withering influence of this new system, the declension of the nation has been uniform and rapid. . . .

To investigate and explain the means whereby this fatal reverse has been effected, would require a voluminous discussion. Nothing more can be attempted in this report than a general allusion to the principal outlines of the policy which has produced this vicissitude. Among these may be enumerated—

First.—A deliberate and extensive system for effecting a combination among certain states, by exciting local jealousies and ambition, so as to secure to popular leaders in one section of the Union, the control of public affairs in perpetual succession. To which primary object most other characteristics of the system may be reconciled.

Secondly.—The political intolerance displayed and avowed in excluding from office men of unexceptionable merit, for want of adherence to the executive creed.

Thirdly.—The infraction of the judiciary authority and rights, by depriving judges of their offices in violation of the constitution.

Fourthly.—The abolition of existing taxes, requisite

to prepare the country for those changes to which nations are always exposed, with a view to the acquisition of popular favour.

Fifthly.—The influence of patronage in the distribution of offices, which in these states has been almost invariably made among men the least entitled to such distinction, and who have sold themselves as ready instruments for distracting public opinion, and encouraging administration to hold in contempt the wishes and remonstrances of a people thus apparently divided.

Sixthly.—The admission of new states into the Union formed at pleasure in the western region, has destroyed the balance of power which existed among the original states, and deeply affected their interest.

Seventhly.—The easy admission of naturalized foreigners to places of trust, honour or profit, operating as an inducement to the malcontent subjects of the old world to come to these states, in quest of executive patronage, and to repay it by an abject devotion to executive measures.

Eighthly.—Hostility to Great Britain, and partiality to the late government of France, adopted as coincident with popular prejudice, and subservient to the main object, party power. Connected with these must be ranked erroneous and distorted estimates of the power and resources of those nations, of the probable results of their controversies, and of our political relations to them respectively.

Lastly and principally.—A visionary and superficial theory in regard to commerce, accompanied by a real hatred but a feigned regard to its interests, and a ruinous perseverance in efforts to render it an instrument of coercion and war.

But it is not conceivable that the obliquity of any administration could, in so short a period, have so nearly consummated the work of national ruin, unless favoured by defects in the constitution.

To enumerate all the improvements of which that instrument is susceptible, and to propose such amendments as might render it in all respects perfect, would be a task which this convention has not thought proper to assume. They have confined their attention to such as experience has demonstrated to be essential, and even among these, some are considered entitled to a more serious attention than others. They are suggested without any intentional disrespect to other states, and are meant to be such as all shall find an interest in promoting. Their object is to strengthen, and if possible to perpetuate, the union of the states, by removing the grounds of existing jealousies, and providing for a fair and equal representation, and a limitation of powers which have been misused. . . .

THEREFORE RESOLVED—

That it be and hereby is recommended to the legislatures of the several states represented in this Convention, to adopt all such measures as may be necessary effectually to protect the citizens of said states from the operation and effects of all acts which have been or may be passed by the Congress of the United States, which shall contain provisions, subjecting the militia or other citizens to forcible drafts, conscriptions, or impressments, not authorised by the constitution of the United States.

Resolved, That it be and hereby is recommended to the said Legislatures, to authorize an immediate and earnest application to be made to the government of the United States, requesting their consent to some arrangement, whereby the said states may, separately or in concert, be empowered to assume upon themselves the defence of their territory against the enemy; and a reasonable portion of the taxes, collected within said states, may be paid into the respective treasuries thereof, and appropriated to the payment of the balance due said states, and to the future defence of the same. The amount so paid into the said treasuries to be credited, and the disbursements made as aforesaid to be charged to the United States.

Resolved, That it be, and hereby is, recommended to the legislatures of the aforesaid states, to pass laws (where it has not already been done) authorizing the governors or commanders-in-chief of their militia to make detachments from the same, or to form voluntary corps, as shall be most convenient and conformable to their constitutions, and to cause the same to be well armed, equipped and disciplined, and held in readiness for service; and upon the request of the governor of either of the other states to employ the whole of such detachment or corps, as well as the regular forces of the state, or such part thereof as may be required and can be spared consistently with the safety of the state, in assisting the state, making such request to repel any invasion thereof which shall be made or attempted by the public enemy.

Resolved, That the following amendments of the constitution of the United States be recommended to the states represented as aforesaid, to be proposed by them for adoption by the state legislatures, and in such cases as may be deemed expedient by a convention chosen by the people of each state. . . .

First. Representatives and direct taxes shall be apportioned among the several states which may be included within this Union, according to their respective numbers of free persons, including those bound to serve for a term of years, and excluding Indians not taxed, and all other persons.

Second. No new state shall be admitted into the Union by Congress, in virtue of the power granted by the constitution, without the concurrence of two thirds of both houses.

Third. Congress shall not have power to lay any embargo on the ships or vessels of the citizens of the United States, in the ports or harbours thereof, for more than sixty days.

Fourth. Congress shall not have power, without the concurrence of two thirds of both houses, to interdict the commercial intercourse between the United States and any foreign nation or the dependencies thereof.

Fifth. Congress shall not make or declare war, or authorize acts of hostility against any foreign nation, without the concurrence of two thirds of both houses, except such acts of hostility be in defence of the territories of the United States when actually invaded.

Sixth. No person who shall hereafter be naturalized, shall be eligible as a member of the senate or house of representatives of the United States, nor capable of holding any civil office under the authority of the United States.

Seventh. The same person shall not be elected president of the United States a second time; nor shall the President be elected from the same state two terms in succession.

Resolved, That if the application of these states to the

government of the United States, recommended in a foregoing resolution, should be unsuccessful and peace should not be concluded, and the defence of these states should be neglected, as it has been since the commencement of the war, it will, in the opinion of this convention, be expedient for the legislatures of the several states to appoint delegates to another convention, to meet at Boston . . . with such powers and instructions as the exigency of a crisis so momentous may require.

DOCUMENT 9

JOHN QUINCY ADAMS, DIARY,
NOVEMBER 7, 1823

One of the main issues that eventually led to the promulgation of the Monroe Doctrine was the question of whether to act in concert with Great Britain, as British Foreign Secretary Canning had proposed, or to issue an independent American statement. In his Diary John Quincy Adams reported the discussions that took place in President Monroe's Cabinet.

Diary of John Quincy Adams, November 7, 1823
—Cabinet meeting at the President's from half–past one till four. Mr. Calhoun, Secretary of War, and Mr. Southard, Secretary of the Navy, present. The subject for consideration was, the confidential proposals of the British Secretary of State, George Canning, to R. Rush, and the correspondence between them relating to the projects of the Holy Alliance upon South America. There was much conversation, without coming to any definite point. The object of Canning appears to have been to obtain some public pledge from the Government of the United States, ostensibly against the forcible interference of the Holy Alliance between Spain and South America; but really or especially against the acquisition to the United States themselves of any part of the Spanish-American possessions.

Mr. Calhoun inclined to giving a discretionary power

to Mr. Rush to join in a declaration against the interference of the Holy Allies, if necessary, even if it should
pledge us not to take Cuba or the province of Texas; because the power of Great Britain being greater than ours
to seize upon them, we should get the advantage of obtaining from her the same declaration we should make
ourselves.

I thought the case not parallel. We have no intention
of seizing either Texas or Cuba. But the inhabitants of
either or both may exercise their primitive rights, and solicit a union with us. They will certainly do no such thing
to Great Britain. By joining with her, therefore, in her
proposed declaration, we give her a substantial and perhaps inconvenient pledge against ourselves, and really
obtain nothing in return. Without entering now into the
enquiry of the expediency of our annexing Texas or Cuba
to our Union, we should at least keep ourselves free to act
as emergencies may arise, and not tie ourselves down to
any principle which might immediately afterwards be
brought to bear against ourselves.

Mr. Southard inclined much to the same opinion.

The President was averse to any course which should
have the appearance of taking a position subordinate to
that of Great Britain, and suggested the idea of sending
a special Minister to protest against the interposition of the
Holy Alliance. . . .

I remarked that the communications recently received
from the Russian Minister, Baron Tuyl, afforded, as I
thought, a very suitable and convenient opportunity for
us to take our stand against the Holy Alliance, and at the
same time to decline the overture of Great Britain. It
would be more candid, as well as more dignified, to avow
our principles explicitly to Russia and France, than to
come in as a cockboat in the wake of the British man-of-
war.

This idea was acquiesced in on all sides. . . .

DOCUMENT 10

JAMES MONROE, MESSAGE TO CONGRESS, DECEMBER 2, 1823

These now-famous words were not referred to as the "Monroe Doctrine" until 1852. Secretary of State John Quincy Adams, who had been most active in formulating the principles in the Monroe Doctrine, wrote the passage on the "non-colonization principle" at the close of the first paragraph. President Monroe himself wrote the rest of the message. Although the doctrine did not have much immediate influence in the world, it satisfactorily represented American opinion. The British chargé, H. U. Addington, reported to his superiors in the Foreign Office: "The message seems to have been received with acclamation throughout the United States. The explicit and manly tone . . . has evidently found in every bosom a chord which vibrates in strict unison with the sentiments so conveyed. They have been echoed from one end of the union to the other."

At the proposal of the Russian Imperial Government, made through the minister of the Emperor residing here, a full power and instructions have been transmitted to the minister of the United States at St. Petersburg to arrange by amicable negotiations the respective rights and interests of the two nations on the northwest coast of this continent. A similar proposal had been made by His Imperial Majesty to the Government of Great Britain, which has likewise been acceded to. The Government of the United States has been desirous by this friendly proceeding of manifesting the great value which they have invariably attached to the friendship of the Emperor and their solicitude to cultivate the best understanding with his Government. In the discussions to which this interest has given rise and in the arrangements by which they may terminate the occasion has been judged proper for asserting, as a principle in which the rights and interests of the United States are involved, that the American continents, by the free and independent condition which they have assumed and maintain, are henceforth not to be considered as subjects for future colonization by any European powers. . . .

It was stated at the commencement of the last session that a great effort was then making in Spain and Portugal to improve the condition of the people of those countries, and that it appeared to be conducted with extraordinary moderation. It need scarcely be remarked that the result has been so far very different from what was then anticipated. Of events in that quarter of the globe, with which we have so much intercourse and from which we derive our origin, we have always been anxious and interested spectators. The citizens of the United States cherish sentiments the most friendly in favor of the liberty and happiness of their fellow-men on that side of the Atlantic. In the wars of the European powers in matters relating to themselves we have never taken any part, nor does it comport with our policy so to do. It is only when our rights are invaded or seriously menaced that we resent injuries or make preparation for our defense. With the movements in this hemisphere we are of necessity more immediately connected, and by causes which must be obvious to all enlightened and impartial observers. The political system of the allied powers is essentially different in this respect from that of America. This difference proceeds from that which exists in their respective Governments; and to the defense of our own, which has been achieved by the loss of so much blood and treasure, and matured by the wisdom of their most enlightened citizens, and under which we have enjoyed unexampled felicity, this whole nation is devoted. We owe it, therefore, to candor and to the amicable relations existing between the United States and those powers to declare that we should consider any attempt on their part to extend their system to any portion of this hemisphere as dangerous to our peace and safety. With the existing colonies or dependencies of any European power we have not interfered and shall not interfere. But with the Governments who have declared their independence and maintained it, and whose independence we have, on great consideration and on just principles, acknowledged, we could not view any interposition for the purpose of oppressing them, or controlling in any other manner their destiny, by any European power in any other light than as the manifestation of an unfriendly disposition toward the United States. In the war between those new Governments and Spain we declared our neutrality at the time of their recognition, and to this we have adhered, and shall continue to adhere, provided no change shall occur which, in the judgment of the competent authorities of this Government, shall make a corresponding change on the part of the United States indispensable to their security.

The late events in Spain and Portugal shew that Europe is still unsettled. Of this important fact no stronger proof can be adduced than that the allied powers should have thought it proper, on any principle satisfactory to themselves, to have interposed by force in the internal concerns of Spain. To what extent such interposition may be carried, on the same principle, is a question in which all independent powers whose governments differ from theirs are interested, even those most remote, and surely none more so than the United States. Our policy in regard to Europe, which was adopted at an early stage of the wars which have so long agitated that quarter of the globe, nevertheless remains the same, which is, not to interfere in the internal concerns of any of its powers; to consider the government *de facto* as the legitimate government for us; to cultivate friendly relations with it, and to preserve those relations by a frank, firm, and manly policy, meeting in all instances the just claims of every power, submitting to injuries from none. But in regard to those continents circumstances are eminently and conspicuously different. It is impossible that the allied powers should extend their political system to any portion of either continent without endangering our peace and happiness; nor can anyone believe that our southern brethren, if left to themselves, would adopt it of their own accord. It is equally impossible, therefore, that we should behold such interposition in any form with indifference. If we look to the comparative strength and resources of Spain and those new Governments, and their distance from each other, it must be obvious that she can never subdue them. It is still the true policy of the United States to leave the parties to themselves, in the hope that other powers will pursue the same course.

✳ PART V ✳

The Jacksonian Era

THE period in American history which was dominated by the powerful figure of Andrew Jackson was a time of rapid change, constant conflict, and shifting alliances. The economy was expanding and changing at an erratic pace; the political system of the country was still being formed. Restless social interests, economic interests, sectional interests jostled each other, made alliances, fell out, argued furiously on one issue, then mercurially turned to something else. While all this was going on, the common man was constantly demanding with an increasingly powerful voice a full place in the political order. The old way of nominating presidential candidates by Congressional caucus was displaced by the theoretically more democratic method of national party conventions. The states that were still choosing presidential electors through their legislatures changed to the system of election by popular vote. Older conceptions of office-holding and a settled body of public officials were challenged by the increasingly widespread idea that rotation of office-holders was more democratic. Perhaps most important of all, states that were now coming into the Union put no encumbrances on the right to vote, and the older states—among them New York—abandoned, after extensive and revealing debate (Document 1), the last restrictions that still stood in the way of universal manhood suffrage.

A major issue during this period was the question of the proper role of the federal government in economic development. Most Americans seemed to prefer that such enterprises as the development of manufacturing and the building of a national network of roads and canals should be launched without central direction from the federal government. But political leaders such as Henry Clay and John Quincy Adams believed in a national plan that Clay called "the American System." They proposed to arrange sectional interests in a national harmony—the East should receive high tariffs to aid its manufacturers; the interior should get federally aided transportation to improve its access to market; and the agricultural sections should benefit from good roads and canals and the presence of domestic urban markets. John Quincy Adams went beyond these proposals. He hoped to enlist the federal government to also support science and education. His first annual message (Document 2), which proposed a national university and astronomical observatories, courageously expressed his belief that federal resources should be used in some general plan, but his views were received with obloquy and ridicule, and had much to do with his defeat in 1828. His successor, Andrew Jackson, checked but by no means stopped the movement for federal aid to internal improvements in his veto of the Maysville Road Bill (Document 3) in 1830. Since Jackson sometimes accepted and sometimes opposed such proposals, Henry Clay, whose project the bill was, twitted him for his inconsistency. Clay stated the general case for a system of internal improvements in a speech on the "American System" (Document 4) which he gave in answer to Jackson's veto.

Fighting nearly broke out during one controversy precipitated by the tariff. Henry Clay spoke eloquently (Document 5) for the high tariff of 1824, which was passed to meet the demand from the nation's emergent manufacturing interests. But Clay's insistence that the development of a home market would fully compensate agricultural producers, even cotton planters, for the partial loss of their overseas markets did not succeed in persuading the South. The more prosperous planters of the inland South, who were developing new lands with remarkable rapidity and making fat profits, could afford for the time being to accept the tariff. But the cotton planters of South Carolina could not. Working long-cultivated, depleted soil, and hard pressed by competition from the interior, they were too severely pinched to receive the tariffs quietly. A group of

militants, taking a constitutional cue from the opposition
to the Alien and Sedition Acts in 1798 (Part III, Document 8), worked out the doctrine of nullification as a ra-
tionale for resistance. This doctrine asserted that a state
could refuse to allow laws it deemed unconstitutional to be
executed within its borders. Nullification was stated as a
formal doctrine in the South Carolina Exposition and
Protest of 1828 (Document 6), drafted anonymously by
Vice President Calhoun; it commanded nationwide attention when Calhoun later decided to take the risk of espous-
ing it openly, as he did in his Fort Hill Address (Document
7). In 1832, when South Carolina attempted to nullify a
new tariff, President Jackson rushed into action. In his
Nullification Proclamation (Document 8) he elaborately
and forcefully stated the nationalist view that nullification
was anarchical and constitutionally absurd. South Carolina
at first defied him (Document 9); but the failure of the
other Southern states to rally behind nullification, together
with Jackson's obvious determination to call out the militia
against South Carolina, made the nullifiers back down.
Retreat was softened for them by the passage of the compromise tariff of 1833, which provided for a gradual reduction of duties.

The struggle over the Second Bank of the United
States was less violent than the nullification controversy,
but it aroused the passions of a much larger part of the
country. The Bank of the United States had been successfully fulfilling its functions as a central banking institution
under the direction of Nicholas Biddle. But its power to
check inflation and its monopoly of the government's de-
posits were widely resented, not only by the public at large,
but by various state banking interests and the politicians
connected with them. Powerful enemies, some of them
Jackson's close advisors, were able to make the bank sym-
bolize all privileged business, indeed all privilege, in a nation that was rampant against any ideas or institutions that
stood in the way of human equality. In 1832, Biddle, urged
on by Clay and Webster, secured a Congressional vote to
renew the Bank's charter, but Jackson returned the recharter bill with a resounding veto (Document 10). Jackson brandished the spectres of foreign influence and special
privilege, and argued lengthily against the Bank's constitu-

tionality. Men of brilliant talents were arrayed on the side of the Bank; and Webster's surgical dissection of Jackson's veto (Document 11) was a devastating performance. But the Bank's friends could not muster enough support to pass the recharter over Jackson's veto; and the Bank as a federal agency was finished. Its destruction satisfied the popular American desire to check centralized power and overturn privilege, but left the nation deprived of a valuable financial balance wheel. A more constructive aspect of the Jacksonian impulse against economic privilege was the movement to destroy the chartered privileges of old corporations in the various states, which stood in the way of competitive businesses and hampered the diffusion of economic opportunity. Chief Justice Roger B. Taney's statesmanlike decision in the Charles River Bridge case of 1837 (Document 12) gave a forceful exposition of the philosophy of this movement; and the lamentations of such spokesmen of Federalist legal principles as James Kent and Joseph Story (Document 13) merely underlined the passing of the old order.

DOCUMENT 1

DEBATE IN THE NEW YORK CONSTITUTIONAL CONVENTION,
1821

In 1821 the New York Constitutional Convention dropped substantially all property qualifications for voting, but not before some formidable old-school opponents of the change had protested it. The leader of the opposition was James Kent, an outstanding jurist and a member of the New York Supreme Court. The proposal to drop property qualifications was defended by Nathan Sandford, a farmer.

CHANCELLOR KENT . . . Let us recall our attention, for a moment, to our past history.

This state has existed for forty-four years under our present constitution, which was formed by those illustrious sages and patriots who adorned the revolution. It has wonderfully fulfilled all the great ends of civil government. During that long period, we have enjoyed in an eminent degree, the blessings of civil and religious liberty. We have had our lives, our privileges, and our property protected. . . .

We have trebled our numbers within the last twenty-five years, have displayed mighty resources, and have made unexampled progress in the career of prosperity and greatness. . . .

These are some of the fruits of our present government; and yet we seem to be dissatisfied with our condition, and we are engaged in the bold and hazardous experiment of remodeling the constitution. Is it not fit and discreet—I speak as to wise men—is it not fit and proper that we should pause in our career and reflect well on the immensity of the innovation in contemplation? Discontent in the midst of so much prosperity, and with such abundant means of happiness, looks like ingratitude and as if we were disposed to arraign the goodness of Providence. Do we not expose ourselves to the danger of being deprived of the blessings we have enjoyed? . . .

The senate has hitherto been elected by the farmers of the state—by the free and independent lords of the soil, worth at least $250 in freehold estate, over and above all debts charged thereon. The governor has been chosen by the same electors, and we have hitherto elected citizens of elevated rank and character. Our assembly has been chosen by freeholders, possessing a freehold of the value of $50, or by persons renting a tenement of the yearly value of $5, and who have been rated and actually paid taxes to the state. By the report before us, we propose to annihilate, at one stroke, all those property distinctions and to bow before the idol of universal suffrage. That extreme democratic principle, when applied to the legislative and executive departments of government, has been regarded with terror by the wise men of every age because, in every European republic, ancient and modern, in which it has been tried, it has terminated disastrously and been productive of corruption, injustice, violence, and tyranny. And dare we flatter ourselves that we are a peculiar people who can run the career of history, exempted from the passions which have disturbed and corrupted the rest of mankind? If we are like other races of men, with similar follies and vices, then I greatly fear that our posterity will have reason to deplore, in sackcloth and ashes, the delusion of the day.

It is not my purpose at present to interfere with the report of the committee, so far as respects the qualifications of electors for governor and members of assembly. I shall feel grateful if we may be permitted to retain the stability and security of a senate, bottomed upon the freehold property of the state. Such a body, so constituted, may prove a sheet anchor amidst the future factions and storms of the republic. The great leading and governing interest of this state is, at present, the agricultural; and what madness would it be to commit that interest to the winds. The great body of the people are now the owners and actual cultivators of the soil. With that wholesome population we always expect to find moderation, frugality, order, honesty, and a due sense of independence, liberty, and justice. It is impossible that any people can lose their liberties by internal fraud or violence, so long as the country is parceled out among freeholders of moderate possessions, and those freeholders have a sure and efficient control in the affairs of the government. Their habits, sympathies, and employments necessarily inspire them with a correct spirit of freedom and justice; they are the safest guardians of property and the laws. We certainly cannot too highly appreciate the value of the agricultural interest. It is the foundation of national wealth and power. According to the opinion of her ablest political economists, it is the surplus produce of the agriculture of England that enables her to support her vast body of manufacturers, her formidable fleets and armies, and the crowds of persons engaged in the liberal professions and the cultivation of the various arts.

Now, sir, I wish to preserve our senate as the representative of the landed interest. I wish those who have an interest in the soil to retain the exclusive possession of a branch in the legislature as a stronghold in which they may find safety through all the vicissitudes which the state may be destined, in the course of Providence, to experience. I wish them to be always enabled to say that their freeholds cannot be taxed without their consent. The men of no property, together with the crowds of dependents connected with great manufacturing and commercial establishments, and the motley and undefinable population of crowded ports, may, perhaps, at some future day, under skilful management, predominate in the assembly, and yet we should be perfectly safe if no laws could pass without the free consent of the owners of the soil. That security we at present enjoy; and it is that security which I wish to retain.

The apprehended danger from the experiment of universal suffrage applied to the whole legislative department is no dream of the imagination. It is too mighty an excitement for the moral constitution of men to endure. The tendency of universal suffrage is to jeopardize the rights of property and the principles of liberty. There is a constant tendency in human society, and the history of every age proves it; there is a tendency in the poor to covet and to share the plunder of the rich; in the debtor to relax or avoid the obligation of contracts; in the majority to tyrannize over the minority and trample down their rights; in the indolent and the profligate to cast the whole burthens of society upon the industrious and the virtuous; and *there is a tendency in ambitious and wicked men to inflame these combustible materials*. It requires a vigilant government, and a firm administration of justice, to counteract that tendency. Thou shalt not covet; Thou shalt not steal, are divine injunctions induced by this miserable depravity of our nature. Who can undertake to calculate with any precision how many millions of people this great state will contain in the course of this and the next century, and who can estimate the future extent and magnitude of our commercial ports? The disproportion between the men of property and the men of no property will be in every society in a ratio to its commerce, wealth, and population. We are no longer to remain plain and simple republics of farmers like the New England colonists or the Dutch settlements on the Hudson. We are fast becoming a great nation, with great commerce, manufactures, population, wealth, luxuries, and with the vices and miseries that they engender. One-seventh of the population of the city of Paris at this day subsists on charity, and one-third of the inhabitants of that city die in the hospitals; what would become of such a city with universal suffrage? France has upward of four, and England upward of five millions of manufacturing and commercial laborers without property. Could these kingdoms sustain the weight of universal suffrage? The radicals in England, with the force of that mighty engine, would at once sweep away the property, the laws, and the liberties of that island like a deluge.

The growth of the city of New York is enough to startle and awaken those who are pursuing the *ignis fatuus* of universal suffrage.

> In 1773 it had 21,000 souls.
> In 1801 it had 60,000 do.
> In 1806 it had 76,000 do.
> In 1820 it had 123,000 do.

It is rapidly swelling into the unwieldy population, and with the burdensome pauperism, of a European metropolis. New York is destined to become the future London of America; and in less than a century that city, with the operation of universal suffrage and under skilful direction, will govern this state.

The notion that every man that works a day on the road, or serves an idle hour in the militia, is entitled as of right to an equal participation in the whole power of the government is most unreasonable and has no foundation in justice. We had better at once discard from the report such a nominal test of merit. If such persons have an equal share in one branch of the legislature, it is surely as much as they can in justice or policy demand. Society is an association for the protection of property as well as of life, and the individual who contributes only one cent to the common stock ought not to have the same power and influence in directing the property concerns of the partnership, as he who contributes his thousands. He will not have the same inducements to care, and diligence, and fidelity. His inducements and his temptation would be to divide the whole capital upon the principles of an agrarian law.

Liberty, rightly understood, is an inestimable blessing, but liberty without wisdom, and without justice, is no better than wild and savage licentiousness. The danger which we have hereafter to apprehend is not the want, but the abuse, of liberty. We have to apprehend the oppression of minorities and a disposition to encroach on private right—to disturb chartered privileges—and to weaken, degrade, and overawe the administration of justice; we have to apprehend the establishment of unequal and, consequently, unjust systems of taxation and all the mischiefs of a crude and mutable legislation. A stable senate, exempted from the influence of universal suffrage, will powerfully check these dangerous propensities, and such a check becomes the more necessary, since this Convention has already determined to withdraw the watchful eye of the judicial department from the passage of laws.

We are destined to become a great manufacturing as well as commercial state. We have already numerous and prosperous factories of one kind or another, and one master capitalist with his one hundred apprentices, and journeymen, and agents, and dependents will bear down at the polls an equal number of farmers of small estates in his vicinity who cannot safely unite for their common defense. Large manufacturing and mechanical establishments can act in an instant with the unity and efficacy of disciplined troops. It is against such combinations, among others, that I think we ought to give to the freeholders, or those who have interest in land, one branch of the legislature for their asylum and their comfort. Universal suffrage once granted, is granted forever and never can be recalled. There is no retrograde step in the rear of democracy. However mischievous the precedent may be in its consequences, or however fatal in its effects, universal suffrage never can be recalled or checked but by the strength of the bayonet. We stand, therefore, this moment, on the brink of fate, on the very edge of the precipice. If we let go our present hold on the senate, we commit our proudest hopes and our most precious interests to the waves. . . .

Mr. N. SANDFORD took the floor. The question before us is the right of suffrage—who shall, or who shall not, have the right to vote. The committee have presented the scheme they thought best; to abolish all existing distinctions and make the right of voting uniform. Is this not right? Where did these distinctions arise? They arose from British precedents. In England they have their three estates, which must always have their separate interests represented. Here there is but one estate—the people. To me the only qualifications seem to be the virtue and morality of the people; and if they may be safely intrusted to vote for one class of our rulers, why not for all? In my opinion, these distinctions are fallacious. We have the experience of almost all the other states against them. The principle of the scheme now proposed is that those who bear the burthens of the state should choose those that rule it. There is no privilege given to property as such; but those who contribute to the public support we consider as entitled to a share in the election of rulers. The burthens are annual, and the elections are annual, and this appears proper. To me, and the majority of the committee, it appeared the only reasonable scheme that those who are to be affected by the acts of the government should be annually entitled to vote for those who administer it. Our taxes are of two sorts, on real and personal property. The payment of a tax on either, we thought, equally entitled a man to a vote, and thus we intended to destroy the odious distinctions of property which now exist. But we have considered personal service, in some cases, equivalent to a tax on personal property, as in work on the high roads. This is a burthen and should entitle those subject to it to equivalent privileges. The road duty is equal to a poll tax on every male citizen, of twenty–one years, of 62½ cents per annum, which is about the value of each individual's work on the road. This work is a burden imposed by the legislature—a duty required by rulers, and which should entitle those subject to it to a choice of those rulers. Then, sir, the militia next presents itself; the idea of personal service, as applicable to the road duty, is, in like manner, applicable here; and this criterion has been adopted in other states. In Mississippi mere enrolment gives a vote. In Connecticut, as is proposed here, actual service, and that without the right of commutation, is required. The duty in the militia is obligatory and onerous. The militia man must find his arms and accoutrements and lose his time. But, after admitting all these persons, what restrictions, it will be said, are left on the right of suffrage? 1st. The voter must be a citizen. 2d. The service required must be performed within the year, on the principle that taxation is annual, and election annual; so that when the person ceases to contribute or serve, he ceases to vote.

A residence is also required. We propose the term of six months, because we find it already in the constitution; but we propose this residence in the state and not in the county or town, so that, wherever a voter may be at the time of election, he may vote there, if he has been a resident of the state for six months. The object of this was to enable those who move, as very many do, in the six months preceding an election, out of the town or ward in which they have resided, to retain the right of voting in their new habitations. The term of six months is deemed long enough to qualify those who come into our state from abroad to understand and exercise the privileges of a citizen here. Now, sir, this scheme will embrace almost the whole male population of the state. There is perhaps no subject so purely matter of opinion as the question how far the right of suffrage may be safely carried. We propose to carry it almost as far as the male population of the state. The Convention may perhaps think this too broad. On this subject we have much experience; yet there are respectable citizens who think this extension of suffrage unfavorable to the rights of property. Certainly this would be a fatal objection, if well founded; for any government, however constituted, which does not secure property to its rightful owners is a bad government. But how is the extension of the right of suffrage unfavorable to property? Will not our laws continue the same? Will not the administration of justice continue the same? And if so, how is private property to suffer? Unless these are changed, and upon them rest the rights and security of property, I am unable to perceive how property is to suffer by the extension of the right of suffrage. But we have abundant experience on this point in other states. Now, sir, in many of the states the right of suffrage has no restriction; every male inhabitant votes. Yet what harm has been done in those states? What evil has resulted to them from this cause? The course of things in this country is for the extension and not the restriction of popular rights. I do not know that in Ohio or Pennsylvania, where the right of suffrage is universal, there is not the same security for private rights and private happiness as elsewhere. Every gentleman is aware that the scheme now proposed is derived from the law calling this Convention, and in the constitution of this body we have the first fruits of the operation of the principle of extensive suffrage—and will anyone say that this example is not one evincing the discretion with which our people exercise this right? In our town meetings too, throughout the state, we have the same principle. In our town elections we have the highest proof of the virtue and intelligence of our people; they assemble in town meetings as a pure democracy and choose their officers and local legislatures, if I may so call them; and if there is any part of our public business well done, it is that done in town meetings. Is not this a strong practical lesson of the beneficial operation of this principle? This scheme has been proposed by a majority of the committee; they think it safe and beneficial, founded in just and rational principles, and in the experience of this and neighboring states. The committee have no attachment, however, to this particular scheme and are willing to see it amended or altered if it shall be judged for the interest of the people.

DOCUMENT 2

JOHN QUINCY ADAMS, FIRST ANNUAL MESSAGE TO CONGRESS,
DECEMBER 6, 1825

With its wide range of novel proposals, this message not only revealed John Quincy Adams as the most far-sighted exponent of internal improvements and centralized government, but it went so far that it frightened his entire Cabinet. It surpassed anything Secretary of State Clay would have advised. Clay urged that a reference to a national university be discarded. "Let us not recommend anything so unpopular as not likely to succeed," he suggested. When Secretary of War James Barbour mischievously added: "Let us not propose anything so popular as to be carried without recommendation," Adams commented: "It's like the man with two wives. One is plucking out his white hairs, the other the black, until none are left." In the end Adams paid dearly for what he

called the "perilous experiment" of this speech. His
proposal for astronomical observatories—"lighthouses
of the skies"—was laughed at; his tactless suggestion
that members of Congress not be "palsied by the will
of our constituents" was taken as proof that he did
not trust American democracy.

. . . In inviting the attention of Congress to the subject of internal improvements upon a view thus enlarged it is not my design to recommend the equipment of an expedition for circumnavigating the globe for purposes of scientific research and inquiry. We have objects of useful investigation nearer home, and to which our cares may be more beneficially applied. The interior of our own territories has yet been very imperfectly explored. Our coasts along many degrees of latitude upon the shores of the Pacific Ocean, though much frequented by our spirited commercial navigators, have been barely visited by our public ships. The River of the West, first fully discovered and navigated by a countryman of our own, still bears the name of the ship in which he ascended its waters, and claims the protection of our armed national flag at its mouth. With the establishment of a military post there or at some other point of that coast, recommended by my predecessor and already matured in the deliberations of the last Congress, I would suggest the expediency of connecting the equipment of a public ship for the exploration of the whole northwest coast of this continent.

The establishment of an uniform standard of weights and measures was one of the specific objects contemplated in the formation of our Constitution, and to fix that standard was one of the powers delegated by express terms in that instrument to Congress. The Governments of Great Britain and France have scarcely ceased to be occupied with inquiries and speculations on the same subject since the existence of our Constitution, and with them it has expanded into profound, laborious, and expensive researches into the figure of the earth and the comparative length of the pendulum vibrating seconds in various latitudes from the equator to the pole. These researches have resulted in the composition and publication of several works highly interesting to the cause of science. The experiments are yet in the process of performance. Some of them have recently been made on our own shores, within the walls of one of our own colleges, and partly by one of our own fellow-citizens. It would be honorable to our country if the sequel of the same experiments should be countenanced by the patronage of our Government, as they have hitherto been by those of France and Britain.

Connected with the establishment of an university, or separate from it, might be undertaken the erection of an astronomical observatory, with provision for the support of an astronomer, to be in constant attendance of observation upon the phenomena of the heavens, and for the periodical publication of his observations. It is with no feeling of pride as an American that the remark may be made that on the comparatively small territorial surface of Europe there are existing upward of 130 of these light-houses of the skies, while throughout the whole American hemisphere there is not one. If we reflect a moment upon the discoveries which in the last four centuries have been made in the physical constitution of the universe by the means of these buildings and of observers stationed in them, shall we doubt of their usefulness to every nation? And while scarcely a year passes over our heads without bringing some new astronomical discovery to light, which we must fain receive at second hand from Europe, are we not cutting ourselves off from the means of returning light for light while we have neither observatory nor observer upon our half of the globe and the earth revolves in perpetual darkness to our unsearching eyes? . . .

The Constitution under which you are assembled is a charter of limited powers. After full and solemn deliberation upon all or any of the objects which, urged by an irresistible sense of my own duty, I have recommended to your attention should you come to the conclusion that, however desirable in themselves, the enactment of laws for effecting them would transcend the powers committed to you by that venerable instrument which we are all bound to support, let no consideration induce you to assume the exercise of powers not granted to you by the people. But if the power to exercise exclusive legislation in all cases whatsoever over the District of Columbia; if the power to lay and collect taxes, duties, imposts, and excises, to pay the debts and provide for the common defense and general welfare of the United States; if the power to regulate commerce with foreign nations and among the several States and with the Indian tribes, to fix the standard of weights and measures, to establish post-offices and post-roads, to declare war, to raise and support armies, to provide and maintain a navy, to dispose of and make all needful rules and regulations respecting the territory or other property belonging to the United States, and to make all laws which shall be necessary and proper for carrying these powers into execution—if these powers and others enumerated in the Constitution may be effectually brought into action by laws promoting the improvement of agriculture, commerce, and manufactures, the cultivation and encouragement of the mechanic and of the elegant arts, the advancement of literature, and the progress of the sciences, ornamental and profound, to refrain from exercising them for the benefit of the people themselves would be to hide in the earth the talent committed to our charge—would be treachery to the most sacred of trusts.

The spirit of improvement is abroad upon the earth. It stimulates the hearts and sharpens the faculties not of our fellow-citizens alone, but of the nations of Europe and of their rulers. While dwelling with pleasing satisfaction upon the superior excellence of our political institutions, let us not be unmindful that liberty is power; that the nation blessed with the largest portion of liberty must in proportion to its numbers be the most powerful nation upon earth, and that the tenure of power by man is, in the moral purposes of his Creator, upon condition that it shall be exercised to ends of beneficence, to improve the condition of himself and his fellow-men. While foreign nations less blessed with that freedom which is power than ourselves are advancing with gigantic strides in the career of public improvement, were we to slumber in indolence or fold up our arms and proclaim to the world that we are palsied by the will of our constituents, would it not be to cast away the bounties of Providence and doom ourselves to perpetual inferiority? In the course of the year now drawing to its close we have beheld, under the auspices and at the expense of one State of this Union, a new university unfolding its portals to the sons of science and holding up the torch of human improvement to eyes that seek the light. We have seen under persevering and enlightened enterprise [Erie Canal] of another State the waters of our Western lakes mingle with those of the ocean. If undertakings like these have been accomplished in the compass of a few years by the authority of single members of our Confederation, can we, the representative authorities of the whole Union, fall behind our fellow–servants in the exercise of the trust committed to us for the benefit of our common sovereign by the accomplishment of works important to the whole and to which neither the authority nor the resources of any one State can be adequate? . . .

DOCUMENT 3

ANDREW JACKSON, VETO OF MAYSVILLE ROAD BILL,
MAY 27, 1830

The man behind this message was Martin Van Buren, who influenced Jackson's decision and almost certainly put the message into its final form. In his Autobiography Van Buren fully and candidly reports the background of the veto message. On the morning the message was sent to Congress Van Buren and Jackson had breakfast at the White House, along with a number of Jackson's friends whose anxious faces revealed their concern that the veto would damage the Democratic party. Van Buren, assisting the sick and enfeebled President upstairs, observed that the others seemed alarmed. "Yes, but don't mind that," said Jackson. "The thing is here [touching his breast pocket] and shall be sent up as soon as Congress convenes." Advocates of states rights and opponents of internal improvements celebrated the veto. At one party in Virginia a toast was drunk which ran: "The rejection of the Maysville Road Bill—it falls upon the ear like the music of other days." The veto was not, however, the final blow against internal improvement that it is sometimes judged to be. Annual appropriations

for internal improvements under Jackson averaged
$1,323,000; under his predecessor, John Quincy
Adams, the great advocate of internal improvements,
they had averaged only $702,000.

Gentlemen: I have maturely considered the bill proposing to authorize "a subscription of stock in the Maysville, Washington, Paris, and Lexington Turnpike Road Company," and now return the same to the House of Representatives, in which it originated, with my objections to its passage. . . .

The constitutional power of the Federal Government to construct or promote works of internal improvement presents itself in two points of view—the first as bearing upon the sovereignty of the States within whose limits their execution is contemplated, if jurisdiction of the territory which they may occupy be claimed as necessary to their preservation and use; the second as asserting the simple right to appropriate money from the National Treasury in aid of such works when undertaken by State authority, surrendering the claim of jurisdiction. In the first view the question of power is an open one, and can be decided without the embarrassments attending the other, arising from the practice of the Government. Although frequently and strenuously attempted, the power to this extent has never been exercised by the Government in a single instance. It does not, in my opinion, possess it; and no bill, therefore, which admits it can receive my official sanction.

But in the other view of the power the question is differently situated. The ground taken at an early period of the Government was "that whenever money has been raised by the general authority and is to be applied to a particular measure, a question arises whether the particular measure be within the enumerated authorities vested in Congress. If it be, the money requisite for it may be applied to it; if not, no such application can be made."

The bill before me does not call for a more definite opinion upon the particular circumstances which will warrant appropriations of money by Congress to aid works of internal improvement, for although the extension of the power to apply money beyond that of carrying into effect the object for which it is appropriated has . . . been long claimed and exercised by the Federal Government, yet such grants have always been professedly under the control of the general principle that the works which might be thus aided should be "of a general, not local, national, not State," character. A disregard of this distinction would of necessity lead to the subversion of the federal system. That even this is an unsafe one, arbitrary in its nature, and liable, consequently, to great abuses, is too obvious to require the confirmation of experience. It is, however, sufficiently definite and imperative to my mind to forbid my approbation of any bill having the character of the one under consideration. I have given to its provisions all the reflection demanded by a just regard for the interests of those of our fellow-citizens who have desired its passage, and by the respect which is due to a coördinate branch of the Government, but I am not able to view it in any other light than as a measure of purely local character; or, if it can be considered national, that no further distinction between the appropriate duties of the General and State Governments need be attempted, for there can be no local interest that may not with equal propriety be denominated national. It has no connection with any established system of improvements; is exclusively within the limits of a State, starting at a point on the Ohio River and running out 60 miles to an interior town, and even as far as the State is interested conferring partial instead of general advantages.

Considering the magnitude and importance of the power, and the embarrassments to which, from the very nature of the thing, its exercise must necessarily be subjected, the real friends of internal improvement ought not to be willing to confide it to accident and chance. . . .

In the other view of the subject, and the only remaining one which it is my intention to present at this time, is involved the expediency of embarking in a system of internal improvement without a previous amendment of the Constitution explaining and defining the precise powers of the Federal Government over it. Assuming the right to appropriate money to aid in the construction of national works to be warranted by the contemporaneous and continued exposition of the Constitution, its insufficiency for the successful prosecution of them must be admitted by all candid minds. If we look to usage to define the extent of the right, that will be found so variant and embracing so much that has been overruled as to involve the whole subject in great uncertainty and to render the execution of our respective duties in relation to it replete with difficulty and embarrassment. It is in regard to such works and the acquisition of additional territory that the practice obtained its first footing. In most, if not all, other disputed questions of appropriation the construction of the Constitution may be regarded as unsettled if the right to apply money in the enumerated cases is placed on the ground of usage. . . .

If it be the wish of the people that the construction of roads and canals should be conducted by the Federal Government, it is not only highly expedient, but indispensably necessary, that a previous amendment of the Constitution, delegating the necessary power and defining and restricting its exercise with reference to the sovereignty of the States, should be made. Without it nothing extensively useful can be effected.

DOCUMENT 4

HENRY CLAY, SPEECH ON THE MAYSVILLE ROAD VETO,

AUGUST 3, 1830

The Maysville Road had been one of Clay's favorite projects, a main link in his plans for improving the transportation system of Kentucky. Jackson's veto seemed to put Clay's whole "American System" on trial, and Clay launched a veritable campaign to answer Jackson's arguments. This speech, delivered in Cincinnati, attacks the President for his inconsistencies.

If I could believe that the executive message, which was communicated to Congress upon the application of the veto to the Maysville road, really expressed the opinion of the President of the United States, in consequence of the unfortunate relations which have existed between us, I would forbear to make any observation upon it. . . . It is impossible that the veto message should express the opinions of the President, and I prove it by evidence derived from himself. Not forty days before that message was sent to Congress, he approved a bill embracing appropriations to various objects of internal improvement, and, among others, to improve the navigation of Conneaut creek. Although somewhat acquainted with the geography of our country, I declare I did not know of the existence of such a stream until I read the bill. I have since made it an object of inquiry and have been told that it rises in one corner of Pennsylvania and is discharged into Lake Erie, in a corner of the state of Ohio; and that the utmost extent to which its navigation is susceptible of improvement is about seven miles. Is it possible that the President could conceive *that a national* object, and that the improvement of a great thoroughfare, on which the mail is transported for some eight or ten states and territories, is not a national consideration? The power to improve the navigation of watercourses, nowhere expressly recognized in the Constitution, is infinitely more doubtful than the establishment of mail roads, which is explicitly authorized in that instrument! Did not the President, during the canvass which preceded his election, in his answer to a letter from Governor Ray, of Indiana, written at the instance of the senate of that respectable state, expressly refer to his votes given in the Senate of the United States, for his opinion as to the power of the general government and inform him that his opinion remained unaltered? And do we not find, upon consulting the journals of the Senate, that, among other votes affirming the existence of the power, he voted for an appropriation to the Chesapeake and Delaware Canal, which is only about fourteen miles in extent? And do we not know that it was at that time, like the Maysville road now, in progress of execution under the direction of a company incorporated by a state? And that, whilst the Maysville road had a connection with roads east of Maysville and southwest of Lexington, the turnpiking of which was contemplated, that canal had no connection with any other existing canal.

The veto message is perfectly irreconcilable with the previous acts, votes, and opinions of General Jackson. It does not express *his* opinions, but those of his advisers and counselors, and especially those of his cabinet. . . .

Let us glance at a few only of the reasons, if reasons they can be called, of this piebald message. The first is that the exercise of the power has produced discord, and to restore harmony to the national councils, it should be abandoned, or, which is tantamount, the Constitution must be amended. The President is therefore advised to throw himself into the minority. Well—did that revive harmony? When the question was taken in the House of the people's Representatives, an obstinate majority still voted for the bill, the objections in the message notwithstanding. And in the Senate the representatives of the states, a refractory majority, stood unmoved. But does the message mean to assert that no great measure, about which public sentiment is much divided, ought to be adopted in consequence of that division? Then none can ever be adopted. . . . What would have become of the settlement of the Missouri question, the tariff, the Indian bill of the last session, if the existence of a strong and almost equal division in the public councils ought to have prevented their adoption? The principle is nothing more nor less than a declaration that the right of the majority to govern must yield to the perseverance, respectability, and numbers of the minority. It is in keeping with the nullifying doctrines of South Carolina and is such a principle as might be expected to be put forth by such a cabinet. The government of the United States, at this juncture, exhibits a most remarkable spectacle. *It is that of a majority of the nation having put the powers of government into the hands of the minority.* . . .

Another reason assigned in the Maysville message is the desire of paying the national debt. By an act passed in the year 1817, an annual appropriation was made of ten millions of dollars, which were vested in the commissioners of the sinking fund, to pay the principal and interest of the public debt. . . .

As much of the public debt as can be paid will be discharged in four years by the operation of the sinking fund. I have seen, in some late paper, a calculation of the delay which would have resulted, in its payment, from the appropriation to the Maysville road, and it was less than one week! How has it happened that, under the administration of Mr. Adams, and during every year of it, such large and liberal appropriations could be made for internal improvements without touching the fund devoted to the public debt and that this administration should find itself balked in its first year?

The veto message proceeds to insist that the Maysville and Lexington road is not a national but a local road, of sixty miles in length, and confined within the limits of a particular state. If, as that document also asserts, the power can, in *no case,* be exercised until it shall have been explained and defined by an amendment of the Constitution, the discrimination of national and local roads would seem to be altogether unnecessary. What is or is not a national road, the message supposes, may admit of controversy and is not susceptible of precise definition. The difficulty which its authors imagine grows out of their attempt to substitute a rule founded upon the extent and locality of the road, instead of the *use* and *purposes* to which it is applicable. If the road facilitates, in a considerable degree, the transportation of the mail to a considerable portion of the Union, and at the same time promotes internal commerce among several states and may tend to accelerate the movement of armies and the distribution of the munitions of war, it is of national consideration. Tested by this, the true rule, the Maysville road was undoubtedly national. It connects the largest body, perhaps, of fertile land in the Union, with the navigation of the Ohio and Mississippi rivers and with the canals of the states of Ohio, Pennsylvania, and New York. It begins on the line which divides the state of Ohio and Kentucky, and, of course, quickens trade and intercourse between them. Tested by the character of other works, for which the President, as a senator, voted, or which were approved by him only about a month before he rejected the Maysville bill, the road was undoubtedly national. . . .

The same scheme which has been devised and practiced to defeat the tariff has been adopted to undermine internal improvements. They are to be attacked in detail. Hence the rejection of the Maysville road, the Fredericktown road, and the Louisville Canal. But is this fair? Ought each proposed road to be viewed separately and detached? Ought it not to be considered in connection with other great works which are in progress of execution or are projected? The policy of the foes indicates what ought to be the policy of the friends of the power.

The blow aimed at internal improvements has fallen within unmerited severity upon the state of Kentucky. No state in the union has ever shown more generous devotion to its preservation and to the support of its honor and its interest than she has. During the late war, her sons fought gallantly by the side of the President, on the glorious eighth of January, when he covered himself with unfading laurels. Wherever the war raged, they were to be found among the foremost in battle, freely bleeding in the service of their country. They have never threatened nor calculated the value of this happy union. Their representatives in Congress have constantly and almost unanimously supported the power, cheerfully voting for large appropriations to works of internal improvements in other states. Not one cent of the common treasure has been expended on any public road in that state. They contributed to the elevation of the President, under a firm conviction, produced by his deliberate acts, and his solemn assertions, that he was friendly to the power. Under such circumstances, have they not just and abundant cause of surprise, regret, and mortification at the late unexpected decision? . . .

DOCUMENT 5

HENRY CLAY, SPEECH ON THE TARIFF, MARCH 31, 1824

Although a protective tariff policy had been launched in 1816, a new and considerably higher tariff bill that was before Congress in 1824 drew formidable opposition from both the commercial and the planting states. Webster of Massachusetts and Robert Y. Hayne of South Carolina led the attack. Clay was the tariff's outstanding spokesman. These selections from his long and able speech show his emphasis on the economic distress from which the country had been suffering for five years and the need for a home market, for which the tariff was essential.

In casting our eyes around us, the most prominent circumstance which fixes our attention, and challenges our deepest regret, is the general distress which pervades the whole country. . . . This distress pervades every part of the Union, every class of society; all feel it, though it may be felt, at different places, in different degrees. It is like the atmosphere which surrounds us—all must inhale it, and none can escape it. . . .

What, . . . I would ask, is the cause of the unhappy condition of our country, which I have faintly depicted? It is to be found in the fact that, during almost the whole existence of this Government, we have shaped our industry, our navigation, and our commerce, in reference to an extraordinary war in Europe, and to foreign markets, which no longer exist; in the fact that we have depended too much upon foreign sources of supply, and excited too little the native; in the fact that, whilst we have cultivated, with assiduous care, our foreign resources, we have suffered those at home to wither, in a state of neglect and abandonment. . . .

The greatest want of civilized society is a market for the sale and exchange of the surplus of the produce of the labor of its members. This market may exist at home or abroad, or both, but it must exist somewhere, if society prospers, and wherever it does exist, it should be competent to the absorption of the entire surplus of production. It is most desirable that there should be both a home and a foreign market. But, with respect to their relative superiority, I cannot entertain a doubt. The home market is first in order, and paramount in importance. The object of the bill under consideration is to create this home market, and to lay the foundations of a genuine American policy. It is opposed; and it is incumbent upon the partisans of the foreign policy (terms which I shall use without any invidious intent) to demonstrate that the foreign market is an adequate vent for the surplus produce of our labor. But is it so? 1. Foreign nations cannot, if they would, take our surplus produce. . . .

But, secondly; if they could, they will not. The policy of all Europe is adverse to the reception of our agricultural produce, so far as it comes into collision with its own; and, under that limitation, we are absolutely forbid to enter their ports, except under circumstances which deprive them of all value as a steady market. . . .

Our agricultural is our greatest interest. It ought ever to be predominant. All others should bend to it. And, in considering what is for its advantage, we should contemplate it in all its varieties, of planting, farming, and grazing. Can we do nothing to invigorate it? . . . We must then change somewhat our course. We must give a new direction to some portion of our industry. We must speedily adopt a genuine American policy. Still cherishing a foreign market, let us create also a home market, to give further scope to the consumption of the produce of American industry. Let us counteract the policy of foreigners, and withdraw the support which we now give to their industry, and stimulate that of our own country. It should be a prominent object with wise legislators, to multiply the vocations and extend the business of society, as far as it can be done by the protection of our interests at home, against the injurious effects of foreign legislation. . . .

The creation of a home market is not only necessary to procure for our agriculture a just reward of its labors, but it is indispensable to obtain a supply of our necessary wants. If we cannot sell, we cannot buy. That portion of our population (and we have seen that it is not less than four-fifths) which makes comparatively nothing that foreigners will buy, has nothing to make purchases with from foreigners. It is in vain that we are told of the amount of our exports supplied by the planting interest. They may enable the planting interest to supply all its wants; but they bring no ability to the interests not planting, unless, which cannot be pretended, the planting interest was an adequate vent for the surplus produce of the labor of all other interests. . . . The superiority of the home market results, 1st, from its steadiness and comparative certainty at all times; 2d, from the creation of reciprocal interest; 3d, from its greater security; and, lastly, from an ultimate and not distant augmentation of consumption, and, consequently, of comfort from increased quantity and reduced prices. But this home market, highly desirable as it is, can only be created and cherished by the PROTECTION of our own legislation against the inevitable prostration of our industry, which must ensue from the action of foreign policy and legislation. . . .

This is only to be accomplished by the establishment of a tariff, to the consideration of which I am now brought.

And what is this tariff? It seems to have been regarded as a sort of monster, huge and deformed; a wild beast, endowed with tremendous powers of destruction, about to be let loose among our people, if not to devour them, at least to consume their substance. But let us calm our passions, and deliberately survey this alarming, this terrific being. The sole object of the tariff is to tax the produce of foreign industry, with the view of promoting American industry. The tax is exclusively levelled at foreign industry. That is the avowed and the direct purpose of the tariff. If it subjects any part of American industry to burdens, that is an effect not intended, but is altogether incidental, and perfectly voluntary.

It had been treated as an imposition of burdens upon one part of the community by design for the benefit of another; as if, in fact, money were taken from the pockets of one portion of the people and put into the pockets of another. But, is that a fair representation of it? No man pays the duty assessed on the foreign article by compulsion, but voluntarily; and this voluntary duty, if paid, goes into the common exchequer, for the common benefit of all. . . .

We perceive that the proposed measure [Tariff Act of 1824], instead of sacrificing the South to the other parts of the Union, seeks only to preserve them from being absolutely sacrificed under the operation of the tacit compact which I have described. Supposing the South to be actually incompetent, or disinclined to embark at all in the business of manufacturing, is not its interest, nevertheless, likely to be promoted by creating a new and an American source of supply for its consumption? Now foreign Powers, and Great Britain principally, have the monopoly of the supply of Southern consumption. If this bill should pass, an American competitor in the supply of the South would be raised up, and ultimately, I cannot doubt, that it will be supplied more cheaply and better. . . .

The second objection to the proposed bill is, that it will diminish the amount of our exports. It can have no effect upon our exports, except those which are sent to Europe. Except tobacco and rice, we send there nothing but the raw materials. The argument is, that Europe will not buy of us if we do not buy of her. The first objection to it is, that it calls upon us to look to the question, and to take care of European ability in legislating for American interests. Now, if, in legislating for their interests, they would consider and provide for our ability, the principle of reciprocity would enjoin us so to regulate our intercourse with them, as to leave their ability unimpaired. But I have shown that, in the adoption of their own policy, their inquiry is strictly limited to a consideration of their peculiar interests, without any regard to that of ours. . . .

DOCUMENT 6

THE SOUTH CAROLINA PROTEST AGAINST THE TARIFF OF 1828,
DECEMBER 19, 1828

After the passage of the tariff of 1828—the so-called "Tariff of Abominations"—Vice President Calhoun was asked by a committee of the South Carolina legislature to prepare an attack on the protective tariff. The result was the "South Carolina Exposition and Protest," which was accepted with some changes by the committee. The Exposition was widely circulated, though not formally adopted, by the legislature. It contained a sharp statement of the theory of nullification. This theory had been anticipated by others, notably by Robert J. Turnbull, but Calhoun brought his own dialectical skill to its final formulation. Only later, however, in his Fort Hill Address (Document 7) did Calhoun openly identify himself with the nullification movement. The Protest, which followed

Calhoun's Exposition, and which was adopted by the legislature, is reprinted here. It does not discuss nullification, but succinctly states the economic and constitutional objections of the state to the protective tariff.

The Senate and House of Representatives of South Carolina, now met, and sitting in General Assembly, through the Hon. William Smith and the Hon. Robert Y. Hayne, their representatives in the Senate of the United States, do, in the name and on behalf of the good people of the said commonwealth, solemnly PROTEST against the system of protecting duties, lately adopted by the federal government, for the following reasons:—

1st. *Because* the good people of this commonwealth believe that the powers of Congress were delegated to it in trust for the accomplishment of certain specified objects which limit and control them, and that every exercise of them for any other purposes, is a violation of the Constitution as unwarrantable as the undisguised assumption of substantive, independent powers not granted or expressly withheld.

2d. *Because* the power to lay duties on imports is, and in its very nature can be, only a means of effecting objects specified by the Constitution; since no free government, and least of all a government of enumerated powers, can of right impose any tax, any more than a penalty, which is not at once justified by public necessity, and clearly within the scope and purview of the social compact; and since the right of confining appropriations of the public money to such legitimate and constitutional objects is as essential to the liberties of the people as their unquestionable privilege to be taxed only by their consent.

3d. *Because* they believe that the tariff law passed by Congress at its last session, and all other acts of which the principal object is the protection of manufactures, or any other branch of domestic industry, if they be considered as the exercise of a power in Congress to tax the people at its own good will and pleasure, and to apply the money raised to objects not specified in the Constitution, is a violation of these fundamental principles, a breach of a well-defined trust, and a perversion of the high powers vested in the federal government for federal purposes only.

4th. *Because* such acts, considered in the light of a regulation of commerce, are equally liable to objection; since, although the power to regulate commerce may, like other powers, be exercised so as to protect domestic manufactures, yet it is clearly distinguishable from a power to do so *eo nomine*, both in the nature of the thing and in the common acception of the terms; and because the confounding of them would lead to the most extravagant results, since the encouragement of domestic industry implies an absolute control over all the interests, resources, and pursuits of a people, and is inconsistent with the idea of any other than a simple, consolidated government.

5th. *Because,* from the contemporaneous exposition of the Constitution in the numbers of the *Federalist,* (which is cited only because the Supreme Court has recognized its authority), it is clear that the power to regulate commerce was considered by the Convention as only incidentally connected with the encouragement of agriculture and manufactures; and because the power of laying imposts and duties on imports was not understood to justify in any case, a prohibition of foreign commodities, except as a means of extending commerce, by coercing foreign nations to a fair reciprocity in their intercourse with us, or for some other *bona fide* commercial purpose.

6th. *Because,* whilst the power to protect manufactures is nowhere expressly granted to Congress, nor can be considered as necessary and proper to carry into effect any specified power, it seems to be expressly reserved to the states, by the 10th section of the 1st article of the Constitution.

7th. *Because* even admitting Congress to have a constitutional right to protect manufactures by the imposition of duties, or by regulations of commerce, designed principally for that purpose, yet a tariff of which the operation is grossly unequal and oppressive, is such an abuse of power as is incompatible with the principles of a free government and the great ends of civil society, justice, and equality of rights and protection.

8th. *Finally,* because South Carolina, from her climate, situation, and peculiar institutions, is, and must ever continue to be, wholly dependent upon agriculture and commerce, not only for her prosperity, but for her very existence as a state; because the valuable products of her soil—the blessings by which Divine Providence seems to have designed to compensate for the great disadvantages under which she suffers in other respects—are among the very few that can be cultivated with any profit by slave labor; and if, by the loss of her foreign commerce, these products should be confined to an inadequate market, the fate of this fertile state would be poverty and utter desolation; her citizens, in despair, would emigrate to more fortunate regions, and the whole frame and constitution of her civil polity be impaired and deranged, if not dissolved entirely.

Deeply impressed with these considerations, the representatives of the good people of this commonwealth, anxiously desiring to live in peace with their fellow-citizens, and to do all that in them lies to preserve and perpetuate the union of the states, and liberties of which it is the surest pledge, but feeling it to be their bounden duty to expose and resist all encroachments upon the true spirit of the Constitution, lest an apparant acquiescence in the system of protecting duties should be drawn into precedent —do, in the name of the commonwealth of South Carolina, claim to enter upon the Journal of the Senate their *protest* against it as unconstitutional, oppressive, and unjust.

DOCUMENT 7

JOHN C. CALHOUN, FORT HILL ADDRESS,
JULY 26, 1831

Though Calhoun for some time had embraced the idea of nullification, he had done so privately. This address made public the fact that the Vice President of the United States now stood with the nullifiers. Three thousand copies were printed for use as campaign literature within South Carolina, and everywhere throughout the Union men were forced to take it seriously. To a friend, Virgil Maxcy, Calhoun wrote concerning it: "My first and great object was to state my opinions clearly, and with critical regard to

truth. . . . We have much to learn in political science.
The rule of the majority and the right of suffrage are
good things, but they alone are not sufficient to
guard liberty, as experience will teach us."

The great and leading principle is, that the General Government emanated from the people of the several States, forming distinct political communities, and acting in their separate and sovereign capacity, and not from all of the people forming one aggregate political community; that the Constitution of the United States is, in fact, a compact, to which each State is a party, in the character already described; and that the several States, or parties, have a right to judge of its infractions; and in case of a deliberate, palpable, and dangerous exercise of power not delegated, they have the right, in the last resort, to use the language of the Virginia Resolutions, *"to interpose for arresting the progress of the evil, and for maintaining, within their respective limits, the authorities, rights, and liberties appertaining to them."* This right of interposition, thus solemnly asserted by the State of Virginia, be it called what it may,—State-right, veto, nullification, or by any other name,—I conceive to be the fundamental principle of our system, resting on facts historically as certain as our revolution itself, and deductions as simple and demonstrative as that of any political or moral truth whatever; and I firmly believe that on its recognition depend the stability and safety of our political institutions.

I am not ignorant that those opposed to the doctrine have always, now and formerly, regarded it in a very different light, as anarchial and revolutionary. . . . I have examined, with the utmost care, the bearing of the doctrine in question; and, so far from anarchial or revolutionary, I solemnly believe it to be the only solid foundation of our system, and of the Union itself; and that the opposite doctrine, which denies to the States the right of protecting their reserved powers, and which would vest in the General Government (it matters not through what department) the right of determining, exclusively and finally, the powers delegated to it, is incompatible with the sovereignty of the States, and of the Constitution itself, considered as the basis of a Federal Union. As strong as this language is, it is not stronger than that used by the illustrious Jefferson, who said, to give to the General Government the final and exclusive right to judge of its powers, is to make *"its discretion, and not the Constitution, the measure of its powers;"* and that, *"in all cases of compact between parties having no common judge, each party has an equal right to judge for itself, as well of the infraction as of the mode and measure of redress."* Language cannot be more explicit, nor can higher authority be adduced. . . .

To realize its perfection, we must view the General Government and those of the States as a whole, each in its proper sphere independent; each perfectly adapted to its respective objects; the States acting separately, representing and protecting the local and peculiar interests; and acting jointly through one General Government, with the weight respectively assigned to each by the Constitution, representing and protecting the interest of the whole; and thus perfecting, by an admirable but simple arrangement, the great principle of representation and responsibility, without which no government can be free or just. To preserve this sacred distribution as originally settled, by coercing each to move in its prescribed orbit, is the great and difficult problem, on the solution of which the duration of our Constitution, of our Union, and, in all probability, our liberty depends. How is this to be effected?

The question is new, when applied to our peculiar political organization, where the separate and conflicting interests of society are represented by distinct but connected governments; but it is, in reality, an old question under a new form, long since perfectly solved. Whenever separate and dissimilar interests have been separately represented in any government; whenever the sovereign power has been divided in its exercise, the experience and wisdom of ages have devised but one mode by which such political organization can be preserved,—the mode adopted in England, and by all governments, ancient and modern, blessed with constitutions deserving to be called free,—to give to each co-estate the right to judge of its powers, with a negative or veto on the acts of the others, in order to protect against encroachments the interests it particularly represents: a principle which all of our constitutions recognize in the distribution of power among their respective departments, as essential to maintain the independence of each; but which, to all who will duly reflect on the subject, must appear far more essential, for the same object, in that great and fundamental distribution of powers between the General and State Governments. So essential is the principle, that, to withhold the right from either, where the sovereign power is divided, is, in fact, to *annul the division* itself, and to *consolidate,* in the one left in the exclusive possession of the right, *all* powers of government; for it is not possible to distinguish, practically, between a government having all power, and one having the right to take what powers it pleases. . . .

So far from extreme danger, I hold that there never was a free State in which this great conservative principle, indispensable to all, was ever so safely lodged. In others, when the co-estates representing the dissimilar and conflicting interests of the community came into contact, the only alternative was compromise, submission, or force. Not so in ours. Should the General Government and a State come into conflict, we have a higher remedy: the power which called the General Government into existence, which gave it all its authority, and can enlarge, contract, or abolish its powers at its pleasure, may be invoked. The States themselves may be appealed to,—three fourths of which, in fact, form a power, whose decrees are the Constitution itself, and whose voice can silence all discontent. The utmost extent, then, of the power is, that a State, acting in its sovereign capacity as one of the parties to the constitutional compact, may compel the Government, created by that compact, to submit a question touching its infraction, to the parties who created it; to avoid the supposed dangers of which, it is proposed to resort to the novel, the hazardous, and, I must add, fatal project of giving to the General Government the sole and final right of interpreting the Constitution;—thereby reversing the whole system, making that instrument the creature of its will, instead of a rule of action impressed on it at its creation, and annihilating, in fact, the authority which imposed it, and from which the Government itself derives its existence.

DOCUMENT 8

ANDREW JACKSON, PROCLAMATION TO THE PEOPLE OF SOUTH CAROLINA,
DECEMBER 10, 1832

This was Andrew Jackson's reply to the South Carolina Ordinance of Nullification. In this Proclamation Jackson first committed himself to forceful nationalism. Previously he had been so sympathetic to states' rights that the powerfully nationalistic constitutional theory expressed here caused considerable surprise. It is significant, however, that Jackson asked his Secretary of State, Edward Livingston, whose nationalistic views were well known, to prepare this document. The wording of the Proclamation reflects Livington's legal training and his long years of concern with constitutional issues, though the closing paragraphs strongly suggest Jackson's temperament. Jackson's own mode of expression can be seen in a letter he wrote to General John Coffee, December 14: "Can any one of common sense believe the absurdity that a faction of any state, or a state, has a right to secede and destroy this union and the liberty of our country with it; or nullify the laws of the union; then indeed is our constitution a rope of sand; under such I would not live. . . . The union must be preserved, and it will now be tested, by the support I get by the people. I will die for the union."

The ordinance is founded, not on the indefeasible right of resisting acts which are plainly unconstitutional and too oppressive to be endured, but on the strange position that any one State may not only declare an act of Congress void, but prohibit its execution; that they may do this consistently with the Constitution; that the true construction of that instrument permits a State to retain its place in the Union and yet be bound by no other of its laws than those it may choose to consider as constitutional. It is true, they add, that to justify this abrogation of a law it must be palpably contrary to the Constitution; but it is evident that to give the right of resisting laws of that description, coupled with the uncontrolled right to decide what laws deserve that character, is to give the power of resisting all laws; for as by the theory there is no appeal, the reasons alleged by the State, good or bad, must prevail. If it should be said that public opinion is a sufficient check against the abuse of this power, it may be asked why it is not deemed a sufficient guard against the passage of an unconstitutional act by Congress? There is, however, a restraint in this last case which makes the assumed power of a State more indefensible, and which does not exist in the other. There are two appeals from an unconstitutional act passed by Congress—one to the judiciary, the other to the people and the States. There is no appeal from the State decision in theory, and the practical illustration shows that the courts are closed against an application to review it, both judges and jurors being sworn to decide in its favor. But reasoning on this subject is superfluous when our social compact, in express terms, declares that the laws of the United States, its Constitution, and treaties made under it are the supreme law of the land, and, for greater caution, adds "that the judges in every State shall be bound thereby, anything in the constitution or laws of any State to the contrary not-withstanding." And it may be asserted without fear of refutation that no federative government could exist without a similar provision. Look for a moment to the consequence. If South Carolina considers the revenue laws unconstitutional and has a right to prevent their execution in the port of Charleston, there would be a clear constitutional objection to their collection in every other port; and no revenue could be collected anywhere, for all imposts must be equal. . . .

If this doctrine had been established at an earlier day, the Union would have been dissolved in its infancy. . . .

If the doctrine of a State veto upon the laws of the Union carries with it internal evidence of its impracticable absurdity, our constitutional history will also afford abundant proof that it would have been repudiated with indignation had it been proposed to form a feature in our Government. . . .

I consider, then, the power to annul a law of the United States, assumed by one State, *incompatible with the existence of the Union, contradicted expressly by the letter of the Constitution, unauthorized by its spirit, inconsistent with every principle on which it was founded, and destructive of the great object for which it was formed.*

After this general view of the leading principle, we must examine the particular application of it which is made in the ordinance.

The preamble rests its justification on these grounds: It assumes as a fact that the obnoxious laws, although they purport to be laws for raising revenue, were in reality intended for the protection of manufactures, which purpose it asserts to be unconstitutional; that the operation of these laws is unequal; that the amount raised by them is greater than is required by the wants of the Government; and, finally, that the proceeds are to be applied to objects unauthorized by the Constitution. These are the only causes alleged to justify an open opposition to the laws of the country and a threat of seceding from the Union if any attempt should be made to enforce them. The first virtually acknowledges that the law in question was passed under a power expressly given by the Constitution to lay and collect impósts; but its constitutionality is drawn in question from the *motives* of those who passed it. However apparent this purpose may be in the present case, nothing can be more dangerous than to admit the position that an unconstitutional purpose entertained by the members who assent to a law enacted under a constitutional power shall make that law void. For how is that purpose to be ascertained? Who is to make the scrutiny? How often may bad purposes be falsely imputed, in how many cases are they concealed by false professions, in how many is no declaration of motive made? Admit this doctrine, and you give to the States an uncontrolled right to decide, and every law may be annulled under this pretext. If, therefore, the absurd and dangerous doctrine should be admitted that a State may annul an unconstitutional law, or one that it deems such, it will not apply to the present case.

The next objection is that the laws in question operate unequally. This objection may be made with truth to every law that has been or can be passed. The wisdom of man never yet contrived a system of taxation that would operate with perfect equality. If the unequal operation of a law makes it unconstitutional, and if all laws of that description may be abrogated by any State for that cause, then, indeed, is the Federal Constitution unworthy of the slightest effort for its preservation. . . .

In vain have these sages [the framers of the Constitution] declared that Congress shall have power to lay and collect taxes, duties, imposts, and excises; in vain have they provided that they shall have power to pass laws which shall be necessary and proper to carry those powers into execution, that those laws and that Constitution shall be the "supreme law of the land, and that the judges in every State shall be bound thereby, anything in the constitution or laws of any State to the contrary notwithstanding;" . . . Vain provisions! ineffectual restrictions! vile profanation of oaths! miserable mockery of legislation! if a bare majority of the voters in any one State may, on a real or supposed knowledge of the intent with which a law has been passed, declare themselves free from its operation; . . .

The Constitution declares that the judicial powers of the United States extend to cases arising under the laws of the United States, and that such laws, the Constitution, and treaties shall be paramount to the State constitutions and laws. The judiciary act prescribes the mode by which the case may be brought before a court of the United States by appeal when a State tribunal shall decide against this provision of the Constitution. The ordinance declares there shall be no appeal—makes the State law paramount to the Constitution and laws of the United States, forces judges and jurors to swear that they will disregard their provisions, and even makes it penal in a suitor to attempt relief by appeal. It further declares that it shall not be lawful for the authorities of the United States or of that State to enforce the payment of duties imposed by the revenue laws within its limits.

Here is a law of the United States, not even pretended to be unconstitutional, repealed by the authority of a small majority of the voters of a single State. Here is a provision of the Constitution which is solemnly abrogated by the same authority.

On such expositions and reasonings the ordinance grounds not only an assertion of the right to annul the laws of which it complains, but to enforce it by a threat of seceding from the Union if any attempt is made to execute them.

This right to secede is deduced from the nature of the Constitution, which, they say, is a compact between sovereign States who have preserved their whole sovereignty and therefore are subject to no superior; that because they made the compact they can break it when in their opinion it has been departed from by the other States. Fallacious as this course of reasoning is, it enlists State pride and finds advocates in the honest prejudices of those who have not studied the nature of our Government sufficiently to see the radical error on which it rests. . . .

The Constitution of the United States, then, forms a *government,* not a league; and whether it be formed by compact between the States or in any other manner, its character is the same. It is a Government in which all the people are represented, which operates directly on the people individually, not upon the States; they retained all the power they did not grant. But each State, having expressly parted with so many powers as to constitute, jointly with the other States, a single nation, can not, from that period, possess any right to secede, because such secession does not break a league, but destroys the unity of a nation; and any injury to that unity is not only a breach which would result from the contravention of a compact, but it is an offense against the whole Union. To say that any State may at pleasure secede from the Union is to say that the United States are not a nation, because it would be a solecism to contend that any part of a nation might dissolve its connection with the other parts, to their injury or ruin, without committing any offense. Secession, like any other revolutionary act, may be morally justified by the extremity of oppression; but to call it a constitutional right is confounding the meaning of terms, and can only be done through gross error or to deceive those who are willing to assert a right, but would pause before they made a revolution or incur the penalties consequent on a failure.

Because the Union was formed by a compact, it is said the parties to that compact may, when they feel them-

selves aggrieved, depart from it; but it is precisely because
it is a compact that they can not. A compact is an agreement or binding obligation. . . . An attempt, by force of
arms, to destroy a government is an offense, by whatever
means the constitutional compact may have been formed:
and such government has the right by the law of self-
defense to pass acts for punishing the offender, unless that
right is modified, restrained, or resumed by the constitutional act. In our system, although it is modified in the
case of treason, yet authority is expressly given to pass all
laws necessary to carry its powers into effect, and under
this grant provision has been made for punishing acts
which obstruct the due administration of the laws. . . .

This, then, is the position in which we stand: A small
majority of the citizens of one State in the Union have
elected delegates to a State convention; that convention
has ordained that all the revenue laws of the United States
must be repealed, or that they are no longer a member of
the Union. The governor of that State has recommended
to the legislature the raising of an army to carry the secession into effect, and that he may be empowered to give
clearances to vessels in the name of the State. No act of
violent opposition to the laws has yet been committed, but
such a state of things is hourly apprehended. And it is the
intent of this instrument to *proclaim,* not only that the
duty imposed on me by the Constitution "to take care that
the laws be faithfully executed" shall be performed to the
extent of the powers already vested in me by law, or of
such others as the wisdom of Congress shall devise and
intrust to me for that purpose, but to warn the citizens of
South Carolina who have been deluded into an opposition
to the laws of the danger they will incur by obedience to
the illegal and disorganizing ordinance of the convention;
to exhort those who have refused to support it to persevere
in their determination to uphold the Constitution and laws
of their country; and to point out to all the perilous situation into which the good people of that State have been
led, and that the course they are urged to pursue is one of
ruin and disgrace to the very State whose rights they affect
to support. . . .

If your leaders could succeed in establishing a separation, what would be your situation? Are you united at

home? Are you free from the apprehension of civil discord, with all its fearful consequences? Do our neighboring republics, every day suffering some new revolution or contending with some new insurrection, do they excite your envy? But the dictates of a high duty oblige me solemnly to announce that you can not succeed. The laws of the United States must be executed. I have no discretionary power on the subject; my duty is emphatically pronounced in the Constitution. Those who told you that you might peaceably prevent their execution deceived you; they could not have been deceived themselves. They know that a forcible opposition could alone prevent the execution of the laws, and they know that such opposition must be repelled. Their object is disunion. But be not deceived by names. Disunion by armed force is *treason*. Are you really ready to incur its guilt? If you are, on the heads of the instigators of the act be the dreadful consequences; on their heads be the dishonor, but on yours may fall the punishment. On your unhappy State will inevitably fall all the evils of the conflict you force upon the Government of your country. . . .

Having the fullest confidence in the justness of the legal and constitutional opinion of my duties which has been expressed, I rely with equal confidence on your undivided support in my determination to execute the laws, to preserve the Union by all constitutional means, to arrest, if possible, by moderate and firm measures the necessity of a recourse to force; and if it be the will of Heaven that the recurrence of its primeval curse on man for the shedding of a brother's blood should fall upon our land, that it be not called down by any offensive act on the part of the United States.

Fellow-citizens, the momentous case is before you. On your undivided support of your Government depends the decision of the great question it involves—whether your sacred Union will be preserved and the blessing it secures to us as one people shall be perpetuated. . . .

May the Great Ruler of Nations grant that the signal blessings with which He has favored ours may not, by the madness of party or personal ambition, be disregarded and lost; and may His wise providence bring those who have produced this crisis to see the folly before they feel the misery of civil strife, and inspire a returning veneration for that Union which, if we may dare to penetrate His designs, He has chosen as the only means of attaining the high destinies to which we may reasonably aspire.

DOCUMENT 9

RESOLUTIONS OF SOUTH CAROLINA ON JACKSON'S NULLIFICATION PROCLAMATION,
DECEMBER 20, 1832

Governor Hayne and the South Carolina legislature gave defiant answers to Jackson, Hayne in a counter-proclamation and a call for 10,000 citizens to repel an invasion, the legislature in this admirably succinct set of resolutions.

The Committee on federal relations, to which was referred the proclamation of the President of the United States, has had it under consideration, and recommend the adoption of the following resolutions:

Resolved, That the power vested by the Constitution and laws in the President of the United States, to issue his proclamation, does not authorize him in that mode, to interfere whenever he may think fit, in the affairs of the respective states, or that he should use it as a means of promulgating executive expositions of the Constitution, with the sanction of force thus superseding the action of other departments of the general government.

Resolved, That it is not competent to the President of the United States, to order by proclamation the constituted authorities of a state to repeal their legislation, and that the late attempt of the President to do so is unconstitutional, and manifests a disposition to arrogate and exercise a power utterly destructive of liberty.

Resolved, That the opinions of the President, in regard to the rights of the States, are erroneous and dangerous, leading not only to the establishment of a consolidated government in the stead of our free confederacy, but to the concentration of all powers in the chief executive.

Resolved, That the proclamation of the President is the more extraordinary, that he had silently, and as it is supposed, with entire approbation, witnessed our sister state of Georgia avow, act upon, and carry into effect, even to the taking of life, principles identical with those now denounced by him in South Carolina.

Resolved, That each state of the Union has the right, whenever it may deem such a course necessary for the preservation of its liberties or vital interests, to secede peaceably from the Union, and that there is no constitutional power in the general government, much less in the executive department, of that government, to retain by force such state in the Union.

Resolved, That the primary and paramount allegiance of the citizens of this state, native or adopted, is of right due to this state.

Resolved, That the declaration of the President of the United States in his said proclamation, of his personal feelings and relations towards the State of South Carolina, is rather an appeal to the loyalty of subjects, than to the patriotism of citizens, and is a blending of official and individual character, heretofore unknown in our state papers, and revolting to our conception of political propriety.

Resolved, That the undisguised indulgence of personal hostility in the said proclamation would be unworthy of the animadversion of this legislature, but for the seldom and official form of the instrument which is made its vehicle.

Resolved, That the principles, doctrines and purposes, contained in the said proclamation are inconsistent with any just idea of a limited government, and subversive of the rights of the states and liberties of the people, and if submitted to in silence would lay a broad foundation for the establishment of monarchy.

Resolved, That while this legislature has witnessed with sorrow such a relaxation of the spirit of our institutions, that a President of the United States dare venture upon this high handed measure, it regards with indignation the menaces which are directed against it, and the concentration of a standing army on our borders—that the state will repel force by force, and relying upon the blessings of God, will maintain its liberty at all hazards.

Resolved, That copies of these resolutions be sent to our members in Congress, to be laid before that body. . . .

DOCUMENT 10

ANDREW JACKSON, BANK VETO MESSAGE, JULY 10, 1832

This famous message was first drafted for Jackson by Amos Kendall, a "Kitchen Cabinet" crony and an old foe of the Bank. A second draft was reworked by Attorney General Roger B. Taney, though Jackson's nephew Andrew Jackson Donelson and Secretary of the Navy Levi Woodbury also had a hand in it. The Bank advocates, considering the message so palpably unreasonable that it would help their side rather than Jackson's, ordered 30,000 copies printed for distribution. The Bank's President, Nicholas Biddle, said of the message: "It has all the fury of a chained panther biting the bars of his cage. It is really a manifesto of anarchy."

The present corporate body, denominated the president, directors, and company of the Bank of the United States, will have existed at the time this act is intended to take effect twenty years. It enjoys an exclusive privilege of banking under the authority of the General Government, a monopoly of its favor and support, and, as a necessary consequence, almost a monopoly of the foreign and domestic exchange. The powers, privileges, and favors bestowed upon it in the original charter, by increasing the value of the stock far above its par value, operated as a gratuity of many millions to the stockholders. . . .

The act before me proposes another gratuity to the holders of the same stock, and in many cases to the same men, of at least seven millions more. . . . It is not our own citizens only who are to receive the bounty of our Government. More than eight millions of the stock of this bank are held by foreigners. By this act the American Republic proposes virtually to make them a present of some millions of dollars. For these gratuities to foreigners and to some of our own opulent citizens the act secures no equivalent whatever. They are the certain gains of the present stockholders under the operation of this act, after making full allowance for the payment of the bonus.

Every monopoly and all exclusive privileges are granted at the expense of the public, which ought to receive a fair equivalent. The many millions which this act proposes to bestow on the stockholders of the existing bank must come directly or indirectly out of the earnings of the American people. . . .

It is not conceivable how the present stockholders can have any claim to the special favor of the Government. The present corporation has enjoyed its monopoly during the period stipulated in the original contract. If we must have such a corporation, why should not the Government sell out the whole stock and thus secure to the people the full market value of the privileges granted? Why should not Congress create and sell twenty-eight millions of stock, incorporating the purchasers with all the powers and privileges secured in this act and putting the premium upon the sales into the Treasury?

But this act does not permit competition in the purchase of this monopoly. It seems to be predicated on the erroneous idea that the present stockholders have a prescriptive right not only to the favor but to the bounty of Government. It appears that more than a fourth part of the stock is held by foreigners and the residue is held by a few hundred of our own citizens, chiefly of the richest class. For their benefit does this act exclude the whole American people from competition in the purchase of this monopoly and dispose of it for many millions less than it is worth. This seems the less excusable because some of our citizens not now stockholders petitioned that the door of competition might be opened, and offered to take a charter on terms much more favorable to the Government and country.

But this proposition, although made by men whose aggregate wealth is believed to be equal to all the private stock in the existing bank, has been set aside, and the bounty of our Government is proposed to be again bestowed on the few who have been fortunate enough to secure the stock and at this moment wield the power of the existing institution. I can not perceive the justice or policy of this course. If our Government must sell monopolies, it would seem to be its duty to take nothing less than their full value, and if gratuities must be made once in fifteen or twenty years let them not be bestowed on the subjects of a foreign government nor upon a designated and favored class of men in our own country. It is but justice and good policy, as far as the nature of the case will admit, to confine our favors to our own fellow–citizens, and let each in his turn enjoy an opportunity to profit by our bounty. In the bearings of the act before me upon these points I find ample reasons why it should not become a law. . . .

Is there no danger to our liberty and independence in a bank that in its nature has so little to bind it to our country? The president of the bank has told us that most of the State banks exist by its forbearance. Should its influence become concentered, as it may under the operation of such an act as this, in the hands of a self-elected directory whose interests are identified with those of the foreign stockholders, will there not be cause to tremble for the purity of our elections in peace and for the independence of our country in war? Their power would be great whenever they might choose to exert it; but if this monopoly were regularly renewed every fifteen or twenty years on terms proposed by themselves, they might seldom in peace put forth their strength to influence elections or control the affairs of the nation. But if any private citizen or public functionary should interpose to curtail its powers or prevent a renewal of its privileges, it can not be doubted that he would be made to feel its influence.

Should the stock of the bank principally pass into the hands of the subjects of a foreign country, and we should unfortunately become involved in a war with that country, what would be our condition? Of the course which would be pursued by a bank almost wholly owned by the subjects of a foreign power, and managed by those whose interests, if not affections, would run in the same direction there can be no doubt. All its operations within would be in aid of the hostile fleets and armies without. Controlling our currency, receiving our public moneys, and holding thousands of our citizens in dependence, it would be more formidable and dangerous than the naval and military power of the enemy.

If we must have a bank with private stockholders, every consideration of sound policy and every impulse of American feeling admonishes that it should be *purely American.* Its stockholders should be composed exclusively of our own citizens, who at least ought to be friendly to our Government and willing to support it in times of difficulty and danger. . . .

The bank is professedly established as an agent of the executive branch of the Government, and its constitutionality is maintained on that ground. Neither upon the propriety of present action nor upon the provisions of this act was the Executive consulted. It has had no opportunity to say that it neither needs nor wants an agent clothed with such powers and favored by such exemptions. There is nothing in its legitimate functions which makes it necessary or proper. Whatever interest or influence, whether public or private, has given birth to this act, it can not be found either in the wishes or necessities of the executive department, by which present action is deemed premature, and the powers conferred upon its agent not only unnecessary, but dangerous to the Government and country.

It is to be regretted that the rich and powerful too often bend the acts of government to their selfish purposes. Distinctions in society will always exist under every just government. Equality of talents, of education, or of wealth can not be produced by human institutions. In the full enjoyment of the gifts of Heaven and the fruits of superior industry, economy, and virtue, every man is equally entitled to protection by law; but when the laws undertake to add to these natural and just advantages artificial distinctions, to grant titles, gratuities, and exclusive privileges, to make the rich richer and the potent more powerful, the humble members of society—the farmers, mechanics, and laborers—who have neither the time nor the means of securing like favors to themselves, have a right to complain of the injustice of their Government. There are no necessary evils in government. Its evils exist only in its abuses. If it would confine itself to equal protection, and, as Heaven does its rains, shower its favors alike on the high and the low, the rich and the poor, it would be an unqualified blessing. In the act before me there seems to be a wide and unnecessary departure from these just principles.

Nor is our Government to be maintained or our Union preserved by invasions of the rights and powers of the several States. In thus attempting to make our General Government strong we make it weak. Its true strength consists in leaving individuals and States as much as possible to themselves—in making itself felt, not in its power, but in its beneficence; not in its control, but in its protection; not in binding the States more closely to the center, but leaving each to move unobstructed in its proper orbit.

Experience should teach us wisdom. Most of the difficulties our Government now encounters and most of the dangers which impend over our Union have sprung from an abandonment of the legitimate objects of Government by our national legislation, and the adoption of such principles as are embodied in this act. Many of our rich men have not been content with equal protection and equal benefits, but have besought us to make them richer by act of Congress. By attempting to gratify their desires we have in the results of our legislation arrayed section against section, interest against interest, and man against man, in a fearful commotion which threatens to shake the foundations of our Union. It is time to pause in our career to review our principles, and if possible revive that devoted patriotism and spirit of compromise which distinguished the sages of the Revolution and the fathers of our Union. If we can not at once, in justice to interests vested under improvident legislation, make our Government what it ought to be, we can at least take a stand against all new grants of monopolies and exclusive privileges, against any prostitution of our Government to the advancement of the few at the expense of the many, and in favor of compromise and gradual reform in our code of laws and system of political economy. . . .

DOCUMENT 11

DANIEL WEBSTER, SPEECH ON JACKSON'S VETO OF THE UNITED STATES BANK BILL,
JULY 11, 1832

This penetrating critique of Jackson's veto message is the more remarkable because Webster had so little time to prepare it. It was delivered in the Senate on the day after the veto message was sent to Congress, and at a time when Webster was tired and ill.

Mr. President, I will not conceal my opinion that the affairs of the country are approaching an important and dangerous crisis. At the very moment of almost unparalleled general prosperity, there appears an unaccountable disposition to destroy the most useful and most approved institutions of the government. Indeed, it seems to be in the midst of all this national happiness that some are found openly to question the advantages of the Constitution itself; and many more ready to embarrass the exercise of its just power, weaken its authority, and undermine its foundations. How far these notions may be carried it is impossible yet to say. We have before us the practical result of one of them. The bank has fallen, or is to fall. . . .

Before proceeding to the constitutional question, there are some other topics, treated in the message, which ought to be noticed. It commences by an inflamed statement of what it calls the "favor" bestowed upon the original bank by the government, or, indeed, as it is phrased, the "monopoly of its favor and support"; and through the whole message all possible changes are rung on the "gratuity," the "exclusive privileges," and "monopoly," of the bank charter. Now, Sir, the truth is, that the powers conferred on the bank are such, and no others, as are usually conferred on similar institutions. They constitute no monopoly, although some of them are of necessity, and with propriety, exclusive privileges. "The original act," says the message, "operated as a gratuity of many millions to the stockholders." What fair foundation is there for this remark? The stockholders received their charter, not gratuitously, but for a valuable consideration in money, prescribed by Congress, and actually paid. At some times the stock has been above *par,* at other times below *par,* according to prudence in management, or according to commercial occurrences. But if, by a judicious administration of its affairs, it had kept its stock always above *par,* what pretence would there be, nevertheless, for saying that such augmentation of its value was a "gratuity" from government? The message proceeds to declare, that the present act proposes another donation, another gratuity, to the same men, of at least seven millions more. It seems to me that this is an extraordinary statement, and an extraordinary style of argument, for such a subject and on such an occasion. In the first place, the facts are all assumed; they are taken for true without evidence. There are no proofs that any benefit to that amount will accrue to the stockholders, nor any experience to justify the expectation of it. It rests on random estimates, or mere conjecture. But suppose the continuance of the charter should prove beneficial to the stockholders; do they not pay for it? They give twice as much for a charter of fifteen years, as was given before for one of twenty. And if the proposed *bonus,* or premium, be not, in the President's judgment, large enough, would he, nevertheless, on such a mere matter of opinion as that, negative the whole bill? May not Congress be trusted to decide even on such a subject as the amount of the money premium to be received by government for a charter of this kind?

But, Sir, there is a larger and a much more just view of this subject. The bill was not passed for the purpose of benefiting the present stockholders. Their benefit, if any, is incidental and collateral. Nor was it passed on any idea that they had a right to a renewed charter, although the message argues against such right, as if it had been somewhere set up and asserted. No such right has been asserted by any body. Congress passed the bill, not as a bounty or a favor to the present stockholders, nor to comply with any demand of right on their part; but to promote great public interests, for great public objects. Every bank must have some stockholders, unless it be such a bank as the President has recommended, and in regard to which he seems not likely to find much concurrence of other men's opinions; and if the stockholders, whoever they may be, conduct the affairs of the bank prudently, the expectation is always, of course, that they will make it profitable to themselves, as well as useful to the public. If a bank charter is not to be granted, because, to some extent, it may be profitable to the stockholders, no charter can be granted. The objection lies against all banks.

Sir, the object aimed at by such institutions is to connect the public safety and convenience with private interests. It has been found by experience, that banks are safest under private management, and that government banks are among the most dangerous of all inventions. Now, Sir, the whole drift of the message is to reverse the settled judgment of all the civilized world, and to set up government banks, independent of private interest or private control. For this purpose the message labors, even beyond the measure of all its other labors, to create jealousies and prejudices, on the ground of the alleged benefit which individuals will derive from the renewal of this charter. Much less effort is made to show that government, or the public, will be injured by the bill, than that individuals will profit by it. Following up the impulses of the same spirit, the message goes on gravely to allege, that the act, as passed by Congress, proposes to make a *present* of some millions of dollars to foreigners, because a portion of the stock is held by foreigners. Sir, how would this sort of argument apply to other cases? The President has shown himself not only willing, but anxious, to pay off the three per cent. stock of the United States at *par,* notwithstanding that it is notorious that foreigners are owners of the greater part of it. Why should he not call that a donation to foreigners of many millions? . . .

From the commencement of the government, it has been thought desirable to invite, rather than to repel, the introduction of foreign capital. Our stocks have all been open to foreign subscriptions; and the State banks, in like manner, are free to foreign ownership. Whatever State has created a debt has been willing that foreigners should become purchasers, and desirous of it. How long is it, Sir, since Congress itself passed a law vesting new powers in the President of the United States over the cities in this District, for the very purpose of increasing their credit abroad, the better to enable them to borrow money to pay their subscriptions to the Chesapeake and Ohio Canal? It is easy to say that there is danger to liberty, danger to independence, in a bank open to foreign stockholders, because it is easy to say any thing. But neither reason nor experience proves any such danger. The foreign stockholder cannot be a director. He has no voice even in the choice of directors. His money is placed entirely in the management of the directors appointed by the President and Senate and by the American stockholders. So far as there is dependence or influence either way, it is to the disadvantage of the foreign stockholder. He has parted with the control over his own property, instead of exercising control over the property or over the actions of others. . . .

In order to justify its alarm for the security of our independence, the message supposes a case. It supposes that the bank should pass principally into the hands of the subjects of a foreign country, and that we should be involved in war with that country, and then it exclaims, "What would be our condition?" Why, Sir, it is plain that all the advantages would be on our side. The bank would still be our institution, subject to our own laws, and all its directors elected by ourselves; and our means would be enhanced, not by the confiscation and plunder, but by the proper use, of the foreign capital in our hands. And, Sir, it is singular enough, that this very state of war, from which this argument against a bank is drawn, is the very thing which, more than all others, convinced the country and the government of the necessity of a national bank. So much was the want of such an institution felt in the late war, that the subject engaged the attention of Congress, constantly, from the declaration of that war down to the time when the existing bank was actually established; so that in this respect, as well as in others, the argument of the message is directly opposed to the whole experience of the government, and to the general and long-settled convictions of the country. . . .

Mr. President, we have arrived at a new epoch. We are entering on experiments, with the government and the

Constitution of the country, hitherto untried, and of fearful and appalling aspect. This message calls us to the contemplation of a future which little resembles the past. Its principles are at war with all that public opinion has sustained, and all which the experience of the government has sanctioned. It denies first principles; it contradicts truths, heretofore received as indisputable. It denies to the judiciary the interpretation of law, and claims to divide with Congress the power of originating statutes. It extends the grasp of executive pretension over every power of the government. But this is not all. It presents the chief magistrate of the Union in the attitude of arguing away the powers of that government over which he has been chosen to preside; and adopting for this purpose modes of reasoning which, even under the influence of all proper feeling towards high official station, it is difficult to regard as respectable. It appeals to every prejudice which may betray men into a mistaken view of their own interests, and to every passion which may lead them to disobey the impulses of their understanding. It urges all the specious topics of State rights and national encroachment against that which a great majority of the States have affirmed to be rightful, and in which all of them have acquiesced. It sows, in an unsparing manner, the seeds of jealousy and ill-will against that government of which its author is the official head. It raises a cry, that liberty is in danger, at the very moment when it puts forth claims to powers heretofore unknown and unheard of. It effects alarm for the public freedom, when nothing endangers that freedom so much as its own unparalleled pretences. This, even, is not all. It manifestly seeks to inflame the poor against the rich; it wantonly attacks whole classes of the people, for the purpose of turning against them the prejudices and the resentments of other classes. It is a state paper which finds no topic too exciting for its use, no passion too inflammable for it address and its solicitation.

Such is this message. It remains now for the people of the United States to choose between the principles here avowed and their government. These cannot subsist together. The one or the other must be rejected. If the sentiments of the message shall receive general approbation, the Constitution will have perished even earlier than the moment which its enemies originally allowed for the termination of its existence. It will not have survived to its fiftieth year.

DOCUMENT 12

CHARLES RIVER BRIDGE v. WARREN BRIDGE, 1837

Just as John Marshall's great decisions expressed Federalist respect for property rights and the sanctity of contract, so did this opinion express Jacksonian support of competitive enterprise and the rights of the community against vested business interests. In 1785 a charter had been issued by Massachusetts to the Charles River Bridge Company. As the years passed, traffic over the river increased enormously. Massachusetts then chartered the Warren Bridge Company and authorized it to build another toll bridge not far from the first. The Charles River Bridge brought suit on the ground that the contract in the first charter had been violated by the grant of the second. But the Court, speaking through Chief Justice Taney, held that the first grant was not an exclusive one; that state grants are always to be strictly construed; and that in the absence of a specific grant of exclusive rights, none could be inferred. Taney's closing remarks about the devastating effect that any contrary conclusion would have upon technical progress and business enterprise are characteristic of the Jacksonians' concern for new business and their distaste for chartered privileges.

TANEY, C. J. . . . Borrowing, as we have done, our system of jurisprudence from the English law . . . it would present a singular spectacle, if, while the courts in England are restraining, within the strictest limits, the spirit of monopoly, and exclusive privileges in nature of monopolies, and confining corporations to the privileges plainly given to them in their charter, the courts of this country should be found enlarging these privileges by implication; and construing a statute more unfavorably to the public, and to the rights of the community, than would be done in a like case in an English court of justice. . . .

The case now before the court is, in principle, precisely the same [as that of *Providence Bank* v. *Billings* (1830)]. It is a charter from a state; the act of incorporation is silent in relation to the contested power. The argument in favor of the proprietors of the Charles River bridge, is the same, almost in words, with that used by the Providence Bank; that is, that the power claimed by the state, if it exists, may be so used as to destroy the value of the franchise they have granted to the corporation. The argument must receive the same answer; and the fact that the power has been already exercised, so as to destroy the value of the franchise, cannot in any degree affect the principle. The existence of the power does not, and cannot, depend upon the circumstance of its having been exercised or not.

It may, perhaps, be said, that in the case of the Providence Bank, this court were speaking of the taxing power; which is of vital importance to the very existence of every government. But the object and end of all government is to promote the happiness and prosperity of the community by which it is established; and it can never be assumed, that the government intended to diminish its power of accomplishing the end for which it was created. And in a country like ours, free, active and enterprising, continually advancing in numbers and wealth, new channels of communication are daily found necessary, both for travel and trade, and are essential to the comfort, convenience and prosperity of the people. A state ought never to be presumed to surrender this power, because, like the taxing power, the whole community have an interest in preserving it undiminished. And when a corporation alleges, that a state has surrendered, for seventy years, its power of improvement and public accommodation, in a great and important line of travel, along which a vast number of its citizens must daily pass, the community have a right to insist, in the language of this court, above quoted, "that its abandonment ought not to be presumed, in a case, in which the deliberate purpose of the state to abandon it does not appear." The continued existence of a government would be of no great value, if, by implications and presumptions, it was disarmed of the powers necessary to accomplish the ends of its creation, and the functions it was designed to perform, transferred to the hands of privileged corporations. The rule of construction announced by the court, was not confined to the taxing power, nor is it so limited, in the opinion delivered. On the contrary, it was distinctly placed on the ground, that the interests of the community were concerned in preserving, undiminished, the power then in question; and whenever any power of the state is said to be surrendered or diminished, whether it be the taxing power, or any other affecting the public interest, the same principle applies, and the rule of construction must be the same. No one will question, that the interests of the great body of the people of the state, would, in this instance, be affected by the surrender of this great line of travel to a single corporation, with the right to exact toll, and exclude competition, for seventy years. While the rights of private property are sacredly guarded, we must not forget, that the community also have rights, and that the happiness and well-being of every citizen depends on their faithful preservation.

Adopting the rule of construction above stated as the settled one, we proceed to apply it to the charter of 1785 to the proprietors of the Charles River bridge. This act of incorporation is in the usual form, and the privileges such as are commonly given to corporations of that kind. It confers on them the ordinary faculties of a corporation, for the purpose of building the bridge; and establishes certain rates of toll, which the company are authorized to take. This is the whole grant. There is no exclusive privilege given to them over the waters of Charles river, above or below their bridge; no right to erect another bridge themselves, nor to prevent other persons from erecting one, no engagement from the State, that another shall not be erected; and no undertaking not to sanction competition, nor to make improvements that may diminish the amount of its income. Upon all these subjects the charter is silent; and nothing is said in it about a line of travel, so much insisted on in the argument, in which they are to have exclusive privileges. No words are used from which an intention to grant any of these rights can be inferred. If the plaintiff is entitled to them, it must be implied, simply from the nature of the grant, and cannot be inferred from the words by which the grant is made. . . .

The inquiry then is, does the charter contain such a contract on the part of the State? Is there any such stipulation to be found in that instrument? It must be admitted on all hands, that there is none—no words that even relate to another bridge, or to the diminution of their tolls, or to the line of travel. If a contract on that subject can be gathered from the charter, it must be by implication, and cannot be found in the words used. Can such an agreement be implied? The rule of construction before stated is an answer to the question. In charters of this description, no rights are taken from the public, or given to the corporation, beyond those which the words of the charter, by their natural and proper construction, purport to convey. There are no words which import such a contract as the plaintiffs in error contend for, and none can be implied. . . . The whole community are interested in this inquiry, and they have a right to require that the power of promoting their comfort and convenience, and of advancing the public prosperity, by providing safe, convenient, and cheap ways for the transportation of produce and the purposes of travel, shall not be construed to have been surrendered or diminished by the State, unless it shall appear by plain words that it was intended to be done. . . .

Indeed, the practice and usage of almost every State in the Union old enough to have commenced the work of internal improvement, is opposed to the doctrine contended for on the part of the plaintiffs in error. Turnpike roads have been made in succession, on the same line of travel; the later ones interfering materially with the profits of the first. These corporations have, in some instances, been utterly ruined by the introduction of newer and better modes of transportation and travelling. In some cases, railroads have rendered the turnpike roads on the same line of travel so entirely useless, that the franchise of the turnpike corporation is not worth preserving. Yet in none of these cases have the corporations supposed that their privileges were invaded, or any contract violated on the part of the State. . . .

And what would be the fruits of this doctrine of implied contracts on the part of the States, and of property in a line of travel by a corporation, if it should now be sanctioned by this court? To what results would it lead us? If it is to be found in the charter to this bridge, the same process of reasoning must discover it, in the various acts which have been passed, within the last forty years, for turnpike companies. . . . If this court should establish the principles now contended for, what is to become of the numerous railroads established on the same line of travel with turnpike companies, and which have rendered the franchises of the turnpike corporations of no value? Let it once be understood that such charters carry with them these implied contracts, and give this unknown and undefined property in a line of travelling, and you will soon find the old turnpike corporations awakening from their sleep and calling upon this court to put down the improvements which have taken their place. The millions of property which have been invested in railroads and canals upon lines of travel which had been before occupied by turnpike corporations will be put in jeopardy. We shall be thrown back to the improvements of the last century, and obliged to stand still until the claims of the old turnpike corporations shall be satisfied, and they shall consent to permit these States to avail themselves of the lights of modern science, and to partake of the benefit of those improvements which are now adding to the wealth and prosperity, and the convenience and comfort, of every other part of the civilized world. Nor is this all. This court will find itself impelled to fix, by some arbitrary rule, the width of this new kind of property in a line of travel. . . . This court are not prepared to sanction the principles which must lead to such results.

DOCUMENT 13

JOSEPH STORY, DISSENTING OPINION IN CHARLES RIVER BRIDGE v. WARREN BRIDGE, 1837

Older and more severe conceptions of the sanctity of contract were still represented on the Supreme Court by Justice Joseph Story of Massachusetts, who wrote a long and learned dissent, which, in Daniel Webster's opinion, left the majority view "not a foot, nor an inch, of ground to stand on." Its essential argument is excerpted here. The moderate language of judicial utterance gives little sense of the real feelings of men like Story and his friend James Kent, toward the Court's decision. Story wrote his wife: "A case of grosser injustice, or more oppressive legislation, never existed." To Story, Kent wrote on June 23, 1837 that he had just reread the Charles River Bridge case "with increased disgust." He saw in it an end to all commercial morality, for if the legislature were free to "whittle away its contracts with impunity, the people will be free to follow." "Now we feel with a pang the loss of Marshall," he lamented. "Now we sadly realize that we are to be under the reign of little men—a pigmy race, and that the sages of the last age are extinguished."

Mr. Justice Story, dissenting. . . .

I admit, that, where the terms of a grant are to impose burthens upon the public, or to create restraint injurious to the public interest, there is sound reason for interpreting the terms, if ambiguous, in favour of the public. But at the same time, I insist, that there is not the slightest reason for saying, even in such a case, that the grant is not to be construed favourably to the grantee, so as to secure him in the enjoyment of what is actually granted. . . .

Parliamentary grants never enjoyed any such privileges [as had been enjoyed by the kings]. They were always con-

strued according to common sense and common reason,
upon their language and their intent. What reason is there,
that our legislative acts should not receive a similar interpretation? Is it not at least as important in our free governments, that a citizen should have as much security for his
rights and estate derived from the grants of the legislature,
as he would have in England? What solid ground is there
to say, that the words of a grant in the mouth of a citizen,
shall mean one thing, and in the mouth of a legislature
shall mean another thing? That in regard to the grant of a
citizen, every word shall in case of any question of interpretation or implication be construed against him, and in
regard to the grant of the government, every word shall be
construed in its favour? . . .

But it has been argued, and the argument has been
pressed in every form which ingenuity could suggest, that if
grants of this nature are to be construed liberally, as conferring any exclusive rights on the grantees, it will interpose an effectual barrier against all general improvements
of the country. For myself, I profess not to feel the cogency
of this argument; either in its general application to the
grant of franchises, or in its special application to the
present grant. This is a subject upon which different minds
may well arrive at different conclusions, both as to policy
and principle. Men may, and will, complexionally differ
upon topics of this sort, according to their natural and acquired habits of speculation and opinion. For my own
part, I can conceive of no surer plan to arrest all public
improvements, founded on private capital and enterprise,
than to make the outlay of that capital uncertain, and questionable both as to security, and as to productiveness. . . .
If the government means to invite its citizens to enlarge
the public comforts and conveniences, to establish bridges,
or turnpikes, or canals, or railroads, there must be some
pledge, that the property will be safe; that the enjoyment
will be co-extensive with the grant: and that success will
not be the sign of a general combination to overthrow its
rights and to take away its profits. The very agitation of a
question of this sort, is sufficient to alarm every stockholder in every public enterprise of this sort, throughout
the whole country. . . .

To sum up, then . . . I maintain, that, upon the prin-

ciples of common reason and legal interpretation; the
present grant carries with it a necessary implication that
the legislature shall do no act to destroy or essentially to
impair the franchise; that . . . there is an implied agreement that the state will not grant another bridge between
Boston and Charlestown, so near as to draw the custom
away from the old one; and . . . that there is an implied
agreement of the state to grant the undisturbed use of the
bridge and its tolls, so far as respects any acts of its own,
or of any persons acting under its authority. In other words,
the state, impliedly, contracts not to resume its grant, or to
do any act to the prejudice and destruction of its grant.
. . . I maintain, that under the principles of the common
law, there exists no more right in the legislature of Massachusetts, to erect the Warren bridge, to the ruin of the
franchise of the Charles river bridge, than exists to transfer
the latter to the former, or to authorize the former to de-
molish the latter. If the legislature does not mean in its
grant to give any exclusive rights, let it say so, expressly;
directly; and in terms admitting of no misconstruction. The
grantees will then take of their peril, and must abide the results of their overweening confidence, indiscretion, and
zeal. . . .

✳ PART VI ✳

Slavery and Expansion

✳ ✳ ✳ ✳ ✳ ✳ ✳ ✳

AMONG Jefferson's generation of Southern planters there were many who thought, as he did, that slavery was evil and who hoped it would eventually disappear from the South. But Jefferson's death in 1826 coincided with the demise of Southern anti-slavery feeling. The invention of the cotton gin had made slavery profitable in the inland South, and even in the last decade of Jefferson's lifetime the cotton-slave economy was spreading with fantastic rapidity. In Jefferson's own Virginia, where slavery had a weaker hold than in the deep South, public opinion was faced with a crisis in 1831, after a slave uprising led by Nat Turner. The question of abandoning slavery was earnestly debated in the Virginia legislative session of 1831–2, but in the end emancipation was rejected. After that date emancipation was not seriously proposed anywhere in the South. Professor Thomas R. Dew of the College of William and Mary wrote an elaborate defense of slavery in his review of the Virginia debates (Document 1), in which he gave a new formulation to pro-slavery opinion: that slavery was not an evil but a positive good, and that it had come to stay. At the same time, William Lloyd Garrison's *Liberator* (Document 2) launched a militant abolitionist movement in the North. In the South, Garrison's abolitionism only had the effect of confirming the planters' resistance to outside interference with their institutions and their conviction that those who proposed to abolish slavery were merely wild and irresponsible agitators. But the anti-slavery movement spread westward from Boston, Garrison's stronghold. Recent scholarship has shown that Garrison's influence in the North was extremely limited, but there were others who spoke to the people farther West with greater effectiveness. Among these was the preacher Theodore Weld, whose *Slavery As It Is* (Document 3) was one of the most effective attacks on the system. In the 1840's and 1850's, the passionate moral dialogue between anti-slavery advocates and the South was beginning to occupy the center of national attention. Harriet Beecher Stowe's *Uncle Tom's Cabin* (1852) (Document 4) made the anti-slavery protest a part of the folklore not only of America but of the Western world. The South answered her with many essays, stories, and poems (Document 5), but none of them had anything like the same impact.

The struggle over slavery, at once a profound moral issue and a conflict between economic and social interests, became a still more serious threat to American union when it became entangled with problems raised by westward expansion. The delicate balance of power between the sections, which it was now more vital than ever to maintain, was again threatened. In 1820 the Missouri Compromise provided a method for keeping the balance of Northern and Southern voting power in the Senate; and the policy of barring slavery from large areas of the West, dating back to the Northwest Ordinance of 1787, was extended by the establishment of the line 36° 30′ as the northernmost limit of slavery in the lands acquired by the Louisiana Purchase. But the balance became precarious again in the early 1840's, when factions in the South and Southwest began to demand the annexation of Texas, which had become an independent republic after its revolt from Mexico in 1835. The failure of Henry Clay's presidential aspirations became a warning to politicians not to stand in the way of the expansionist drive. In Clay's Raleigh letter (Document 6), written when his chances for election to the presidency seemed good, he had warned that annexation would bring war with Mexico, that the acquisition of Texas for the purpose of strengthening the South would "menace the existence, if it did not certainly sow the seeds of a dissolution of the Union." Clay's remarks were prophetic, but they were also unpopular. Later he tried to modify his position, but in doing so gave offense to the anti-slavery men. Neither the ardent expansionists nor their anti-slavery opponents were appeased by his moderate stand; and the expansion issue may have contributed to Clay's defeat in 1844. He lost to the warm expansionist James K. Polk; and the incorporation of Texas into the Union, rejected in 1837, was accomplished under Polk's predecessor, John Tyler, three days before Polk took office. But the United States and Mexico were far from agreement on the extent of Texas's boundaries. Further expansion at the expense of Mexico, compensated by Northern expansion in the Oregon country, became the primary goals of Polk's administration. By pushing an aggressive policy in the Texas-Mexico border region (Document 7), Polk succeeded in precipitating a war which won not only a favorable boundary for Texas, but the vast territory of New Mexico and California as well. Northern Whigs and anti-slavery men violently criticized the Mexican War (Document 8); they could reconcile themselves neither to the way in which it had been brought about, nor to the prospect that huge new territories might now be opened up for the expansion of the slave system. The North found an answer to the anticipated gains of the slave system when Polk requested $2 million to facilitate territorial negotiations with Mexico. David Wilmot, a free-soil Democrat from Pennsylvania, introduced a proviso to the effect that slavery should never exist in the territory to be acquired from Mexico, and that acceptance of this ban should be a condition of the acquisition of any of Mexico's territory. The Wilmot Proviso was rejected by the Senate, and the new territory was acquired without it. But the basic principle of the Proviso kept turning up in Congressional debates and ultimately became the central plank in the new Republican party's platform.

The question of the terms upon which the acquired territories should be admitted into the Union as states precipitated another crisis early in 1850. California, having adopted a constitution that prohibited slavery, applied for admission as a free state in March. Even before her application was received, a debate began which raged in the Senate for weeks (Document 9). By early September a set of compromise measures devised by Clay was enacted:

California was admitted as a free state; New Mexico was organized as a territory without restriction on slavery but on the principle of popular sovereignty—that is, its inhabitants were to decide the question at the time of their admission as a state; Utah was organized with the same provisions; a stronger Fugitive Slave Act was passed to please the South, which in turn was balanced by the abolition of the slave trade in the District of Columbia.

Though moderate men hoped the Compromise of 1850 would finally solve the vexing question of slavery in the territories, too many interests were still unsatisfied. Abolitionists gagged on the Fugitive Slave Act, and Northern free-soil men refused to accept the popular-sovereignty principle. Four years later a still more violent argument broke out over a proposal made by Stephen A. Douglas to organize the territories of Kansas and Nebraska on the popular sovereignty principle. The Kansas-Nebraska Act (May 30, 1854) explicitly repealed the Missouri Compromise and thus seemingly committed Congress to the principle of non-intervention in the territories. Anti-slavery men were outraged by this part of the Act. Leading free-soilers responded with a fierce blast of criticism, the "Appeal of the Independent Democrats" (Document 10), which accused Douglas of having joined an alleged slaveholders' "plot" to undermine freedom in the territories. Though answered by Douglas in a formidable and exceptionally bitter speech (Document 11), the "Appeal" did much to spur the formation of the Republican party, dedicated to Congressional exclusion of slavery from the territories.

From 1855 on, the violent struggle in Kansas between pro-slavery men and free-soilers kept both North and South stirred up. Then, in 1857, the Supreme Court dealt the Republican party a heavy blow. It found, in the Dred Scott decision (Document 12), that the Missouri Compromise was unconstitutional because by depriving persons of their property in slaves without due process of law it violated the Fifth Amendment of the Constitution. In effect this meant that the proposal to which the Republican party was firmly dedicated—Congressional exclusion of slavery from the territories—demanded measures that were now adjudicated unconstitutional. The Republicans raised an outcry, and many of them, including Lincoln, swore they would somehow get the decision reversed. Frequently they charged that the decision was the result of a conspiracy to carry slavery not merely into the new territories but even into the old free states—in short, to make it a nationwide institution. In the Lincoln-Douglas debates of 1858 (Document 13) the implications of the Dred Scott decision for both the principle of Congressional exclusion and that of popular sovereignty were argued. Douglas taunted Lincoln with the inconsistency between his position and the Dred Scott decision; but Lincoln replied that popular sovereignty was equally inconsistent, for if Congress had no constitutional power to exclude slavery from territories, then the territorial legislatures, which were merely the creations of Congress, had no such power either. This Douglas answered with his "Freeport Doctrine," in which he argued that the people of a territory could lawfully exclude slavery prior to the writing of a state constitution simply by neglecting to pass those local ordinances without which slavery could not exist. Douglas, not his challenger, was returned to the Senate. But Lincoln had shown himself to be a formidable debater. By getting Douglas to declare that he did not care whether slavery was voted in or out, he succeeded in destroying the prestige Douglas had enjoyed among moderate anti-slavery men who believed that popular sovereignty would be sufficient to keep slavery out of the West. Lincoln further undermined Douglas by making it painfully clear that the "Freeport Doctrine" was at odds with the strategy of the Southern wing of the Democratic party. The breech between the Douglas Democrats, who adhered to popular sovereignty, and the militant Southern Democrats now widened, and the split helped elect Lincoln President in 1860.

DOCUMENT 1

THOMAS R. DEW, REVIEW OF THE DEBATE IN THE VIRGINIA LEGISLATURE OF 1831 AND 1832, 1832

In the year 1831 slavery in Virginia passed through a major crisis. The Nat Turner insurrection, in which at least 57 whites were killed, shocked people into questioning the very safety of slavery. At that time, too, the prices of slaves were low, and it was known that some states of the deeper South, the market for Virginia's surplus slaves, were thinking of closing the domestic slave trade. A full-scale debate began in the legislative session of 1831–2 between critics and proponents of slavery. Shortly after the debate ended, Thomas R. Dew, Professor of Political Economy at the College of William and Mary, wrote a critique of it in which he presented a clear and systematic defense of the institution. The views he expressed already dominated the deeper South, but his essay did much to crystallize Virginia opinion in favor of the status quo. The South as a whole was now united in defense of slavery, and Dew's essay became a major source for pro-slavery argument.

III. *Injustice and Evils of Slavery.*—1st. It is said slavery is wrong, in the *abstract* at least, and contrary to the spirit of Christianity. . . . With regard to the assertion that slavery is against the spirit of Christianity, we are ready to admit the general assertion, but deny most positively, that there is any thing in the Old or New Testament, which would go to show that slavery, when once introduced, ought at all events to be abrogated, or that the master commits any offence in holding slaves. The children of Israel themselves were slaveholders, and were not condemned for it. All the patriarchs themselves were slaveholders; Abraham had more than three hundred; Isaac had a "great store" of them; and even the patient and meek Job

himself had *"a very great household."* When the children
of Israel conquered the land of Canaan, they made one
whole tribe "hewers of wood and drawers of water," and
they were at that very time under the special guidance of
Jehovah; they were permitted expressly to purchase slaves
of the heathen, and keep them as an inheritance for their
posterity; and even the children of Israel might be enslaved
for six years. When we turn to the New Testament, we
find not one single passage at all calculated to disturb the
conscience of an honest slaveholder. No one can read it
without seeing and admiring that the meek and humble
Saviour of the world in no instance meddled with the
established institutions of mankind; he came to save a
fallen world, and not to excite the black passions of men,
and array them in deadly hostility against each other.
From no one did he turn away; his plan was offered alike
to all—to the monarch and the subject, the rich and the
poor, the master and the slave. He was born in the Roman
world—a world in which the most galling slavery existed, a
thousand times more cruel than the slavery in our own
country; and yet he no where encourages insurrection;
he no where fosters discontent; but exhorts *always* to implicit obedience and fidelity. What a rebuke does the practice of the Redeemer of mankind imply upon the conduct
of some of his nominal disciples of the day, who seek to
destroy the contentment of the slaves, to rouse their most
deadly passions, to break up the deep foundations of society, and to lead on to a night of darkness and confusion!
"Let every man (says Paul) abide in the same calling
wherein he is called. Art thou called *being* a servant? care
not for it; but if thou mayest be made free, use *it* rather."
—(1 *Corinth.* vii. 20,21.) Again: "Let as many servants
as are under the yoke, count their own masters worthy of
all honor, that the name of God and his doctrines be not
blasphemed; and they that have believing masters, let
them not despise *them,* because they are brethren, but
rather do them service, because they are faithful and beloved partakers of the benefit. These things teach and exhort."—(1 *Tim.* vi. 1,2.) Servants are even commanded
in Scripture to be faithful and obedient to unkind masters.
"Servants," (says Peter,) "be subject to your masters with
all fear; not only to the good and gentle, but to the froward.

For what glory is it if when ye shall be buffeted for your faults ye take it patiently; but if when ye do well and suffer for it, ye take it patiently, this is acceptable with God."—(1 *Peter,* ii. 18,20.) These and many other passages in the New Testament, most convincingly prove, that slavery in the Roman world was no where charged as a fault or crime upon the holder, and every where is the most implicit obedience enjoined. . . .

2dly. *But it further said that the moral effects of slavery are of the most deleterious and hurtful kind;* and as Mr. Jefferson has given the sanction of his great name to this charge, we shall proceed to examine it with all that respectful deference to which every sentiment of so pure and philanthropic a heart is justly entitled.

"The whole commerce between master and slave," says he, "is a perpetual exercise of the most boisterous passions; the most unremitting despotism on the one part, and degrading submission on the other. Our children see this, and learn to imitate it, for man is an imitative animal —this quality is the germ of education in him. From his cradle to his grave, he is learning what he sees others do. If a parent had no other motive, either in his own philanthropy or self–love, for restraining the intemperance of passion towards his slave, it should always be a sufficient one that his child is present. But generally it is not sufficient. The parent storms, the child looks on, catches the lineaments of wrath, puts on the same airs in the circle of smaller slaves, gives a loose to his worst of passions, and thus nursed, educated, and daily exercised in the worst of tyranny, cannot but be stamped by it with odious peculiarities." Now we boldly assert that the fact does not bear Mr. Jefferson out in his conclusions. He has supposed the master in a continual passion—in the constant exercise of the most odious tyranny, and the child, a creature of imitation, looking on and learning. But is not this master sometimes kind and indulgent to his slaves? Does he not mete out to them, for faithful service, the reward of his cordial approbation? Is it not his interest to do it? and when thus acting humanely, and speaking kindly, where is the child, the creature of imitation, that he does not look on and learn? We may rest assured, in this intercourse between a good master and his servant, more good than evil *may* be taught the child; the exalted principles of morality and religion may thereby be sometimes indelibly inculcated upon his mind, and instead of being reared a selfish contracted being, with nought but self to look to—he acquires a more exalted benevolence, a greater generosity and elevation of soul, and embraces for the sphere of his generous actions a much wider field. Look to the slaveholding population of our country, and you every where find them characterized by noble and elevated sentiments, by humane and virtuous feelings. We do not find among them that cold, contracted, calculating *selfishness,* which withers and repels every thing around it, and lessens or destroys all the multiplied enjoyments of social intercourse. Go into our national councils, and ask for the most generous, the most disinterested, the most conscientious, and the least unjust and oppressive in their principles, and see whether the slaveholder will be past by in the selection. . . .

Is it not a fact, known to every man in the south, that the most cruel masters are those who have been unaccustomed to slavery. It is well known that northern gentlemen who marry southern heiresses, are much severer masters than southern gentlemen. And yet, if Mr. Jefferson's reasoning were correct, they ought to be milder: in fact, it follows from his reasoning, that the authority which the father is called on to exercise over his children, must be seriously detrimental; and yet we know that this is not the case; that on the contrary, there is nothing which so much humanizes and softens the heart, as this *very authority;* and there are none, even among those who have no children themselves, so disposed to pardon the follies and indiscretion of youth, as those who have seen most of them, and suffered greatest annoyance. There may be many cruel masters, and there are unkind and cruel fathers too; but both the one and the other make all those around them shudder with horror. We are disposed to think that their example in society tends rather to strengthen than weaken the principle of benevolence and humanity.

Let us now look a moment to the slave, and contemplate his position. Mr. Jefferson has described him as hating, rather than loving his master, and as losing, too, all that *amor patriae* which characterizes the true patriot. We assert again, that Mr. Jefferson is not borne out by the fact. We are well convinced that there is nothing but the mere relations of husband and wife, parent and child, brother and sister, which produce a closer tie, than the relation of master and servant. We have no hesitation in affirming, that throughout the whole slaveholding country, the slaves of a good master are his warmest, most constant, and most devoted friends; they have been accustomed to look up to him as their supporter, director and defender. Every one acquainted with southern slaves, knows that the slave rejoices in the elevation and prosperity of his master; and the heart of no one is more gladdened at the successful debut of young master or miss on the great theatre of the world, than that of either the young slave who has grown up with them, and shared in all their sports, and even partaken of all their delicacies—or the aged one who has looked on and watched them from birth to manhood, with the kindest and most affectionate solicitude, and has ever met from them all the kind treatment and generous sympathies of feeling, tender hearts. Judge Smith, in his able speech on Foote's Resolutions, in the Senate, said, in an emergency, he would rely upon his own slaves for his defence—he would put arms into their hands, and he had no doubt they would defend him faithfully. In the late Southampton insurrection, we know that many actually convened their slaves and armed them for defence, although slaves were here the cause of the evil which was to be repelled. . . .

In the debate in the Virginia Legislature, no speaker *insinuated even,* we believe, that the slaves in Virginia were not treated kindly; and all, too, agree that they were most abundantly fed; and we have no doubt but that they form the happiest portion of our society. A merrier being does not exist on the face of the globe, than the negro slave of the U. States. Even Captain Hall himself, with his thick "crust of prejudice," is obliged to allow that they are happy and contented, and the master much less cruel than is generally imagined. Why, then, since the slave is happy, and happiness is the great object of all animated creation, should we endeavor to disturb his contentment by infusing into his mind a vain and indefinite desire for liberty—a something which he cannot comprehend, and which must inevitably dry up the very sources of his happiness.

The fact is that all of us, and the great author of the Declaration of Independence is like us in this respect, are too prone to judge of the happiness of others by ourselves —we make *self* the standard, and endeavor to draw down every one to its dimensions—not recollecting that the benevolence of the Omnipotent has made the mind of man pliant and susceptible of happiness in almost every situation and employment. We might rather die than be the obscure slave that waits at our back—our education and our habits generate an ambition that makes us aspire at something loftier—and disposes us to look upon the slave as unsusceptible of happiness in his humble sphere, when he may indeed be much happier than we are, and have his ambition too; but his ambition is to excel all his other slaves in the performance of his servile duties—to please and to gratify his master—and to command the praise of all who witness his exertions. Let the wily philanthropist but come and whisper into the ears of such a slave that his situation is degrading and his lot a miserable one—let him but light up the dungeon in which he persuades the slave that he is caged—and that moment, like the serpent that entered the garden of Eden, he destroys his happiness and his usefulness. We cannot, therefore, agree with Mr. Jefferson, in the opinion that slavery makes the unfeeling tyrant and ungrateful dependent; and in regard to Virginia especially, we are almost disposed, judging from the official returns of crimes and convictions, to assert, with a statesman who has descended to his tomb, (Mr. Giles,) "that the whole population of Virginia, consisting of three *castes*—of free white, free colored, and slave colored population, is the soundest and most moral of any other, according to numbers, in the whole world, as far as is known to me."

3dly. *It has been contended that slavery is unfavorable to a republican spirit;* but the whole history of the world proves that this is far from being the case. In the ancient republics of Greece and Rome, where the spirit of liberty glowed with most intensity, the slaves were more numerous than the freemen, Aristotle, and the great men of antiquity, believed slavery necessary to keep alive the spirit of freedom. In Sparta, the freemen were even forbidden to perform the offices of slaves, lest he might lose the spirit of independence. In modern times, too, liberty has always been more ardently desired by slaveholding communities. "Such" says Burke, "were our Gothic ancestors; such, in our days, were the Poles; and such will be all masters of slaves who are not slaves themselves." "These people of the southern (American) colonies are much more strongly, and with a higher and more stubborn spirit, attached to liberty, than those of the northward." And from the time of Burke down to the present day, the Southern States have always borne the same honorable distinction. Burke says, "it is because freedom is to them not only an enjoyment, but a kind of rank and privilege." Another, and perhaps more efficient cause of this, is the perfect spirit of equality so prevalent among the whites of all the slaveholding States. Jack Cade, the English reformer, wished all mankind to be brought to one common level. We believe slavery in the U. States has accomplished this, in regard to the whites, as nearly as can be expected or even desired in this world. The menial and low offices being all performed by the blacks, there is at once taken away the greatest cause of distinction and separation of the ranks of society. The man to the north will not shake hands familiarly with his servant, and converse, and laugh and dine with him, no matter how honest and respectable he may be. But go to the south, and you will find that no white man feels such inferiority of rank as to be unworthy of association with those around him. Color alone is here the badge of distinction, the true mark of aristocracy, and all who are white are equal in spite of the variety of occupation. . . .

DOCUMENT 2

WILLIAM LLOYD GARRISON, *THE LIBERATOR,*
JANUARY 1, 1831

On the first page of his new paper, Garrison stated his mission to the public. The editor was 26, dedicated, and absolutely intransigent. A minister who often visited his office later recalled: "He slept in the office with a table for a bed, a book for a pillow, and a self-

prepared scanty meal for his rations in the office, while he set up his articles in the Liberator *with his own hand, and without previous committal to paper."*

In the month of August, I issued proposals for publishing *The Liberator* in Washington city; but the enterprise, though hailed in different sections of the country, was palsied by public indifference. Since that time, the removal of the *Genius of Universal Emancipation* to the Seat of Government has rendered less imperious the establishment of a similar periodical in that quarter.

During my recent tour for the purpose of exciting the minds of the people by a series of discourses on the subject of slavery, every place that I visited gave fresh evidence of the fact, that a greater revolution in public sentiment was to be effected in the free states—*and particularly in New England*—than at the south. I found contempt more bitter, opposition more active, detraction more relentless, prejudice more stubborn, and apathy more frozen, than among slave owners themselves. Of course, there were individual exceptions to the contrary. This state of things afflicted, but did not dishearten me. I determined, at every hazard, to lift up the standard of emancipation in the eyes of the nation, *within sight of Bunker Hill and in the birth place of liberty*. That standard is now unfurled; and long may it float, unhurt by the spoliations of time or the missiles of a desperate foe—yea, till every chain be broken, and every bondman set free! Let southern oppressors tremble—let their secret abettors tremble—let their Northern apologists tremble—let all the enemies of the persecuted blacks tremble.

I deem the publication of my original Prospectus unnecessary, as it has obtained a wide circulation. The principles therein inculcated will be steadily pursued in this paper, excepting that I shall not array myself as the political partisan of any man. In defending the great cause of human rights, I wish to derive the assistance of all religions and of all parties.

Assenting to the "self-evident truth" maintained in the American Declaration of Independence, "that all men are created equal, and endowed by their Creator with certain inalienable rights—among which are life, liberty and the pursuit of happiness," I shall strenuously contend for the immediate enfranchisement of our slave population. In Park–street Church, on the Fourth of July, 1829, in an address on slavery, I unreflectingly assented to the popular but pernicious doctrine of *gradual* abolition. I seize this opportunity to make a full and unequivocal recantation, and thus publicly to ask pardon of my God, of my country, and of my brethren the poor slaves, for having uttered a sentiment so full of timidity, injustice and absurdity. A similar recantation, from my pen, was published in the *Genius of Universal Emancipation* at Baltimore, in September, 1829. My conscience is now satisfied.

I am aware, that many object to the severity of my language; but is there not cause for severity? I *will be* as harsh as truth, and as uncompromising as justice. On this subject, I do not wish to think, or speak, or write, with moderation. No! no! Tell a man whose house is on fire to give a moderate alarm; tell him to moderately rescue his wife from the hands of the ravisher; tell the mother to gradually extricate her babe from the fire into which it has fallen;—but urge me not to use moderation in a cause like the present. I am in earnest—I will not equivocate—I will not excuse—I will not retreat a single inch—AND I WILL BE HEARD. The apathy of the people is enough to make every statue leap from its pedestal, and to hasten the resurrection of the dead.

It is pretended, that I am retarding the cause of emancipation, by the coarseness of my invective, and the precipitancy of my measures. *The charge is not true.* On this question my influence,—humble as it is,—is felt at this moment to a considerable extent, and shall be felt in coming years—not perniciously, but beneficially—not as a curse, but as a blessing; and posterity will bear testimony that I was right. I desire to thank God, that he enables me to disregard "the fear of man which bringeth a snare" and to speak his truth in its simplicity and power. . . .

DOCUMENT 3

THEODORE DWIGHT WELD, *SLAVERY AS IT IS*, 1839

*Weld's Slavery As It Is: Testimony of a Thousand
Witnesses was probably the most important anti-
slavery work published before Uncle Tom's Cabin.
While it was a picture only of the excesses of slavery
rather than of its characteristic operation, Weld carefully tried to exclude from the work everything that
was not authentic. This selection illustrates Weld's
general argument and the materials he used to indict
slavery. In gathering the material he was assisted by
his wife, Angelina, and her sister, Sarah Grimké.
"Those dear souls," he wrote, "spent six months,
averaging more than six hours a day, in searching
through thousands upon thousands of Southern newspapers, marking and cutting out the facts of slaveholding disclosures. . . . After the work was finished
we were curious to know how many newspapers had
been examined. So we went up to our attic and took
an inventory of bundles, as they were packed heap
upon heap. When our count had reached twenty
thousand newspapers, we said: 'There, let that
suffice.'" The work, which appeared without Weld's
name upon it (though it was immediately understood
to be his), was priced at 37½ cents a copy; it sold
over 100,000 within a year. The chapter on slavery
in Charles Dickens's American Notes was taken largely
from Weld's book, without acknowledgment.*

Reader, you are empannelled as a juror to try a plain
case and bring in an honest verdict. The question at issue
is not one of law, but of fact—"What is the actual condition of the slaves in the United States?" A plainer case
never went to a jury. Look at it. TWENTY–SEVEN HUNDRED
THOUSAND PERSONS in this country, men, women, and
children, are in SLAVERY. Is slavery, as a condition for hu-

man beings, good, bad, or indifferent? We submit the question without argument. You have common sense, and conscience, and a human heart;—pronounce upon it. You have a wife, or a husband, a child, a father, a mother, a brother or a sister—make the case your own, make it theirs, and bring in your verdict. The case of Human Rights against Slavery has been adjudicated in the court of conscience times innumerable. The same verdict has always been rendered—"guilty;" the same sentence has always been pronounced, "Let it be accursed;" . . . His heart is false to human nature, who will not say "Amen." There is not a man on earth who does not believe that slavery is a curse. Human beings may be inconsistent, but human *nature* is true to herself. She has uttered her testimony against slavery with a shriek ever since the monster was begotten; and till it perishes amidst the execrations of the universe, she will traverse the world on its track, dealing her bolts upon its head, and dashing against it her condemning brand. . . .

Two millions seven hundred thousand persons in these States are in this condition. They were made slaves and are held such by force, and by being put in fear, and this for no crime! Reader, what have you to say of such treatment? Is it right, just, benevolent? Suppose I should seize you, rob you of your liberty, drive you into the field, and make you work without pay as long as you live, would that be justice and kindness, or monstrous injustice and cruelty? Now, every body knows that the slaveholders do these things to the slaves every day, and yet it is stoutly affirmed that they treat them well and kindly, and that their tender regard for their slaves restrains the masters from inflicting cruelties upon them. We shall go into no metaphysics to show the absurdity of this pretence. The man who *robs* you every day, is, forsooth, quite too tender-hearted ever to cuff or kick you! True, he can snatch your money, but he does it gently lest he should hurt you. He can empty your pockets without qualms, but if your *stomach* is empty, it cuts him to the quick. He can make you work a life time without pay, but loves you too well to let you go hungry. He fleeces you of your *rights* with a relish, but is shocked if you work bareheaded in summer, or in winter without warm stockings. He can make you go without your *liberty*, but never without a shirt. He can crush, in you, all hope of bettering your condition, by vowing that you shall die his slave, but though he can coolly torture your feelings, he is too compassionate to lacerate your back—he can break your heart, but he is very tender of your skin. He can strip you of all protection and thus expose you to all outrages, but if you are exposed to the *weather,* half clad and half sheltered, how yearn his tender bowels! What! slaveholders talk of treating men well, and yet not only rob them of all they get, and as fast as they get it, but rob them of *themselves,* also; their very hands and feet, all their muscles, and limbs, and senses, their bodies and minds, their time and liberty and earnings, their free speech and rights of conscience, their right to acquire knowledge, and property, and reputation;—and yet they, who plunder them of all these, would fain make us believe that their soft hearts ooze out so lovingly toward their slaves that they always keep them well housed and well clad, never push them too hard in the field, never make their dear backs smart, nor let their dear stomachs get empty.

But there is no end to these absurdities. Are slaveholders dunces, or do they take all the rest of the world to be, that they think to bandage our eyes with such thin gauzes? Protesting their kind regard for those whom they hourly plunder of all they have and all they get! What! when they have seized their victims, and annihilated all their *rights,* still claim to be the special guardians of their *happiness!* Plunderers of their liberty, yet the careful suppliers of their wants? Robbers of their earnings, yet watchful sentinels round their interests, and kind providers of their comforts? Filching all their time, yet granting generous donations for rest and sleep? Stealing the use of their muscles, yet thoughtful of their ease? Putting them under *drivers,* yet careful that they are not hard-pushed? Too humane forsooth to stint the stomachs of their slaves, yet force their *minds* to starve, and brandish over them pains and penalties, if they dare to reach forth for the smallest crumb of knowledge, even a letter of the alphabet!

It is no marvel that slaveholders are always talking of their *kind treatment* of their slaves. The only marvel is, that men of sense can be gulled by such professions. Despots always insist that they are merciful. . . .

Slaveholders, the world over, have sung the praises of their tender mercies towards their slaves. Even the wretches that plied the African slave trade, tried to rebut Clarkson's proofs of their cruelties, by speeches, affidavits, and published pamphlets, setting forth the accommodations of the "middle passage," and their kind attentions to the comfort of those whom they had stolen from their homes, and kept stowed away under hatches, during a voyage of four thousand miles. . . .

As slaveholders and their apologists are volunteer witnesses in their own cause, and are flooding the world with testimony that their slaves are kindly treated; that they are well fed, well clothed, well housed, well lodged, moderately worked, and bountifully provided with all things needful for their comfort, we propose—first, to disprove their assertions by the testimony of a multitude of impartial witnesses, and then to put slaveholders themselves through a course of cross–questioning which shall draw their condemnation out of their own mouths. We will prove that the slaves in the United States are treated with barbarous inhumanity; that they are overworked, underfed, wretchedly clad and lodged, and have insufficient sleep; that they are often made to wear round their necks iron collars armed with prongs, to drag heavy chains and weights at their feet while working in the field, and to wear yokes, and bells, and iron horns; that they are often kept confined in the stocks day and night for weeks together, made to wear gags in their mouths for hours or days, have some of their front teeth torn out or broken off, that they may be easily detected when they run away; that they are frequently flogged with terrible severity, have red pepper rubbed into their lacerated flesh, and hot brine, spirits of turpentine, &c., poured over the gashes to increase the torture; that they are often stripped naked, their backs and limbs cut with knives, bruised and mangled by scores and hundreds of blows with the paddle, and terribly torn by the claws of cats, drawn over them by their tormentors; that they are often hunted with bloodhounds and shot down like beasts, or torn in pieces by dogs; that they are often suspended by the arms and whipped and beaten till they faint, and when revived by restoratives, beaten again till they faint, and sometimes till they die; that their ears are often cut off, their eyes knocked out, their bones broken, their flesh branded with red hot irons; that they are maimed, mutilated and burned to death over slow fires. All these things, and more, and worse, we shall *prove*. Reader, we know whereof we affirm, we have weighed it well; *more and worse* WE WILL PROVE. Mark these words, and read on; we will establish all these facts by the testimony of scores and hundreds of eye witnesses, by the testimony of *slaveholders* in all parts of the slave states, by slaveholding members of Congress and of state legislatures, by ambassadors to foreign courts, by judges, by doctors of divinity, and clergymen of all denominations, by merchants, mechanics, lawyers and physicians, by presidents and professors in colleges and *professional* seminaries, by planters, overseers and drivers. We shall show, not merely that such deeds are committed, but that they are frequent; not done in corners, but before the sun; not in one of the slave states, but in all of them; not perpetrated by brutal overseers and drivers merely, but by magistrates, by legislators, by professors of religion, by preachers of the gospel, by governors of states, by "gentlemen of property and standing," and by delicate females moving in the "highest circles of society.". . .

THE PROTECTION OF "PUBLIC OPINION" TO DOMESTIC TIES.

The barbarous indifference with which slaveholders regard the forcible sundering of husbands and wives, parents and children, brothers and sisters, and the unfeeling brutality indicated by the language in which they describe the efforts made by the slaves, in their yearnings after those from whom they have been torn away, reveals a 'public opinion' towards them as dead to their agony as if they were cattle. It is well nigh impossible to open a southern paper without finding evidence of this. Though the truth of this assertion can hardly be called in question, we subjoin a few illustrations, and could easily give hundreds.

[The following are selected from the advertisements Weld used.]

From the "Savannah Georgian," Jan. 17, 1839.

$100 reward will be given for my two fellows, Abram and Frank. Abram has a *wife* at Colonel Stewart's, in

Liberty county, and a *sister* in Savannah, at Capt. Groven-stine's. Frank has a *wife* at Mr. Le Cont's, Liberty county; a *mother* at Thunderbolt, and a *sister* in Savannah.

WM. ROBARTS.

Walhourville, 5th Jan. 1839.

From the "Lexington (Ky.) Intelligencer." July 7, 1838.

$160 Reward.—Ranaway from the subscribers, living in this city, on Saturday 16th inst. a negro man, named Dick, about 37 years of age. It is highly probable said boy will make for New Orleans, as *he has a wife* living in that city, and he has been heard to say frequently that *he was determined to go to New Orleans.*

DRAKE & THOMPSON.

Lexington, June 17, 1838.

From the "Southern Argus," Oct. 31, 1837.

Runaway—my negro man, Frederick, about 20 years of age. He is no doubt near the plantation of G. W. Cor-prew, Esq. of Noxubbee county, Mississippi, as *his wife belongs to that gentleman, and he followed her from my residence.* The above reward will be paid to any one who will confine him in jail and inform me of it at Athens, Ala.

KERKMAN LEWIS.

Athens, Alabama.

From the "Savannah Georgian," July 8, 1837.

Ran away from the subscriber, his man Joe. He visits the city occasionally, where he has been harbored by his *mother* and *sister.* I will give one hundred dollars for proof sufficient to *convict his harborers.*

R. P. T. MONGIN.

From the "Savannah (Ga.) Republican," Sept. 3, 1838.

$20 Reward for my negro man Jim.—Jim is about 50 or 55 years of age. It is probable that he will aim for Savannah, as he said *he had children* in that vicinity.

J. G. OWENS.

Barnwell District, S.C.

From the "Richmond (Va.) Compiler," Sept. 8, 1837.

Ranaway from the subscriber, Ben. He ran off without any known cause, and *I suppose he is aiming to go to his wife, who was carried from the neighborhood last winter.*

JOHN HUNT.

From the "Jackson (Tenn.) Telegraph," Sept. 14, 1838.

Committed to the jail of Madison county, a negro woman, who calls her name Fanny, and says she belongs to William Miller, of Mobile. She formerly belonged to John Givins, of this county, who now owns *several of her children.*

DAVID SHROPSHIRE, Jailor.

From the "Richmond (Va.) Enquirer," Feb. 20, 1838.

Stop the Runaway! ! !—$25 Reward. Ranaway from the Eagle Tavern, a negro fellow, named Nat. He is no doubt attempting to *follow his wife, who was lately sold to a speculator named Redmond.* The above reward will be paid by Mrs. Lucy M. Downman, of Sussex county, Va.

Multitudes of advertisements like the above appear annually in the southern papers. Reader, look at the preceding list—mark the unfeeling barbarity with which their masters and *mistresses* describe the struggles and perils of sundered husbands and wives, parents and children, in their weary midnight travels through forests and rivers, with torn limbs and breaking hearts, seeking the embraces of each other's love. In one instance, a mother torn from all her children and taken to a remote part of another state, presses her way back through the wilderness, hundreds of miles, to clasp once more her children to her heart; but, when she has arrived within a few miles of them, in the same county, is discovered, seized, dragged to jail, and her purchaser told, through an advertisement, that she awaits his order. But we need not trace out the harrowing details already before the reader. . . .

DOCUMENT 4

HARRIET BEECHER STOWE,
UNCLE TOM'S CABIN,
1852

This novel, under its full title, Uncle Tom's Cabin, or
Life Among the Lowly, *was first published serially
in the* National Era *beginning on May 8, 1851. Mrs.
Stowe wrote with the most intense personal involvement; the installment dealing with the death of Little
Eva put her in bed for forty-eight hours. Like Theodore Weld, whose work had much influence on her
(Document 3), she thought her book would be taken
more seriously if it were proved to be based on fact,
and published in 1853* A Key to Uncle Tom's Cabin,
in which she documented all her characters and ideas.
Uncle Tom's Cabin *was an instantaneous success.
Brought out in book form in March 1852, it sold
astonishingly in England and America, and was trans-
lated into several languages within the year. Frank
Luther Mott, in his study of American best-sellers,
estimates that it has sold almost 3,000,000 copies. A
drama based on it opened in 1852, and from that year
until 1931 it was never off the American stage. The
impact of the book upon its contemporaries can hardly
be overestimated. Family legend, based upon the
recollection of Mrs. Stowe's son Charles, has it that
during the Civil War when she called on Lincoln he
said: "So this is the little lady who made this big
war?" In the chapter excerpted here, Uncle Tom de-
fies the cruel slaveowner, Simon Legree.*

Slowly the weary, dispirited creatures wound their way
into the room, and with crouching reluctance, presented
their baskets to be weighed.

Legree noted on a slate, on the side of which was
pasted a list of names, the amount.

Tom's basket was weighed and approved; and he looked, with an anxious glance, for the success of the woman he had befriended.

Tottering with weakness, she came forward, and delivered her basket. It was of full weight, as Legree well perceived; but, affecting anger, he said,

"What, you lazy beast! short again! stand aside, you'll catch it, pretty soon!"

The woman gave a groan of utter despair, and sat down on a board.

The person who had been called Misse Cassy now came forward, and, with a haughty, negligent air, delivered her basket. As she delivered it, Legree looked in her eyes with a sneering yet inquiring glance.

She fixed her black eyes steadily on him, her lips moved slightly, and she said something in French. What it was, no one knew; but Legree's face became perfectly demoniacal in its expression, as she spoke; he half raised his hand, as if to strike,—a gesture which she regarded with fierce disdain, as she turned and walked away.

"And now," said Legree, "come here, you Tom. You see, I telled ye I didn't buy ye jest for the common work; I mean to promote ye, and make a driver of ye; and to-night ye may jest as well begin to get yer hand in. Now, ye jest take this yer gal and flog her; ye've seen enough on't to know how."

"I beg Mas'r's pardon," said Tom; "hopes Mas'r won't set me at that. It's what I an't used to,—never did,—and can't do, no way possible."

"Ye'll larn a pretty smart chance of things ye never did know, before I've done with ye!" said Legree, taking up a cow-hide, and striking Tom a heavy blow across the cheek, and following up the infliction by a shower of blows.

"There!" he said, as he stopped to rest; "now, will ye tell me ye can't do it?"

"Yes, Mas'r," said Tom, putting up his hand, to wipe the blood that trickled down his face. "I'm willin' to work night and day, and work while there's life and breath in me; but this yer thing I can't feel it right to do;—and, Mas'r, I *never* shall do it,—*never!*"

Tom had a remarkably smooth, soft voice, and a habitually respectful manner, that had given Legree an idea that he would be cowardly, and easily subdued. When he spoke these last words, a thrill of amazement went through every one; the poor woman clasped her hands, and said, "O Lord!" and every one involuntarily looked at each other and drew in their breath, as if to prepare for the storm that was about to burst.

Legree looked stupefied and confounded; but at last burst forth,—

"What! ye blasted black beast! tell *me* ye don't think it *right* to do what I tell ye! What have any of you cussed cattle to do with thinking what's right? I'll put a stop to it! Why, what do ye think ye are? May be ye think ye'r a gentleman, master Tom, to be a telling your master what's right, and what an't! So you pretend it's wrong to flog the gal!"

"I think so, Mas'r," said Tom; "the poor crittur's sick and feeble; 'twould be downright cruel, and it's what I never will do, nor begin to. Mas'r, if you mean to kill me, kill me; but, as to my raising my hand agin any one here, I never shall,—I'll die first!"

Tom spoke in a mild voice, but with a decision that could not be mistaken. Legree shook with anger; his greenish eyes glared fiercely, and his very whiskers seemed to curl with passion; but, like some ferocious beast, that plays with its victim before he devours it, he kept back his strong impulse to proceed to immediate violence, and broke out into bitter raillery.

"Well, here's a pious dog, at last, let down among us sinners!—a saint, a gentleman, and no less, to talk to us sinners about our sins! Powerful holy crittur, he must be! Here, you rascal, you make believe to be so pious,—didn't you never hear, out of yer Bible, "Servants, obey yer masters"? An't I yer master? Didn't I pay down twelve hundred dollars cash, for all there is inside yer old cussed black shell? An't yer mine, now, body and soul?" he said, giving Tom a violent kick with his heavy boot; "tell me!"

In the very depth of physical suffering, bowed by brutal oppression, this question shot a gleam of joy and triumph through Tom's soul. He suddenly stretched himself up, and, looking earnestly to heaven, while the tears and blood that flowed down his face mingled, he ex-claimed,—

"No! no! no! my soul an't yours, Mas'r! You haven't bought it,—ye can't buy it! It's been bought and paid for, by one that is able to keep it;—no matter, no matter, you can't harm me!"

"I can't!" said Legree, with a sneer; "we'll see,—we'll see! Here, Sambo, Quimbo, give this dog such a breakin' in as he won't get over, this month!"

The two gigantic Negroes that now laid hold of Tom, with fiendish exultation in their faces, might have formed no unapt personification of the powers of darkness. The poor woman screamed with apprehension, and all rose, as by a general impulse, while they dragged him unresisting from the place.

DOCUMENT 5

WILLIAM J. GRAYSON, "THE HIRELING AND THE SLAVE,"
1854

William J. Grayson was a cultivated South Carolinian who was for many years Collector of the Port of Charleston. During the Nullification controversy, he had been a strong Unionist; but he was also an ardent defender of slavery, and had already written a tract in favor of the institution before he published this long poem in heroic couplets, displaying, in one part, a seamy picture of the terrible conditions endured by wage labor, and in another an idyllic version of the slave's condition. Grayson thought very ill of Harriet Beecher Stowe, and wrote the following lines about her:

Not such with Stowe, the wish or power to please,
She finds no joy in gentle deeds like these;
A moral scavenger, with greedy eye,
In social ills her coarser labors lie;
On fields where vice eludes the light of day,
She hunts up crimes as beagles hunt their prey; . . .

With hatred's ardor gathers Newgate spoils,
And trades for gold the garbage of her toils.

And yet the Master's lighter rule ensures
More order than the sternest code secures;
No mobs of factious workmen gather here,
No strikes we dread, no lawless riots fear;
Nuns, from their convent driven, at midnight fly,
Churches, in flames, ask vengeance from the sky,
Seditious schemes in bloody tumults end,
Parsons incite, and Senators defend,
But not where Slaves their easy labours ply,
Safe from the snare, beneath a Master's eye;
In useful tasks engaged, employed their time,
Untempted by the demagogue to crime,
Secure they toil, uncursed their peaceful life,
With freedom's hungry broils and wasteful strife,
No want to goad, no faction to deplore,
The Slave escapes the perils of the poor. . . .
And yet the life, so unassailed by care,
So blest with moderate work, with ample fare,
With all the good the pauper Hireling needs,
The happier Slave on each plantation leads;
Safe from harassing doubts and annual fears,
He dreads no famine, in unfruitful years;
If harvest fail from inauspicious skies,
The Master's providence his food supplies;
No paupers perish here for want of bread,
Or lingering live, by foreign bounty fed;
No exiled trains of homeless peasants go,
In distant climes, to tell their tales of woe;
Far other fortune, free from care and strife,
For work, or bread, attends the Negro's life,
And Christian Slaves may challenge as their own,
The blessings claimed in fabled states alone—
The cabin home, not comfortless, though rude,
Light daily labour, and abundant food,
The sturdy health, that temperate habits yield,
The cheerful song, that rings in every field,
The long, loud laugh, that freemen seldom share,
Heaven's boon to bosoms unapproached by care,

And boisterous jest and humour unrefined,
That leave, though rough, no painful sting behind;
While, nestling near, to bless their humble lot,
Warm social joys surround the Negro's cot,
The evening dance its merriment imparts,
Love, with his rapture, fills their youthful hearts,
And placid age, the task of labour done,
Enjoys the summer shade, the winter's sun,
And, as through life no pauper want he knows,
Laments no poorhouse penance at its close. . . .

DOCUMENT 6

HENRY CLAY, RALEIGH LETTER,
APRIL 17, 1844

In April 1844, when Henry Clay was in Raleigh, North Carolina during his campaign for the Whig presidential nomination, he sent this letter to the editors of the National Intelligencer *expressing his views on the annexation of Texas. The letter is a classic and remarkably foresighted statement of the position of those who saw serious dangers to the Union in hasty annexation. Clay thought it safe to take the stand he did because he confidently expected that Martin Van Buren would be the Democratic candidate, and the two men had agreed that they would both come out against immediate annexation. Van Buren, however, lost the Democratic nomination, in part because of his position on annexation, so that Clay had to run against James K. Polk, a vigorous annexationist. Clay was now out on a limb, and to retrieve his position wrote two "Alabama Letters" in July 1844, in which he emphasized that he would be glad to see Texas annexed, if it could be done without dishonor or war, with the common consent of the Union, and upon just and fair terms. These letters, in turn, offended strong anti-slavery men, and may have lost Clay the decisive state of New York.*

Gentlemen: Subsequent to my departure from Ashland, in December last, I received various communications from popular assemblages and private individuals, requesting an expression of my opinion upon the question of the annexation of Texas to the United States. . . . The rejection of the overture of Texas, some years ago, to become annexed to the United States, had met with general acquiescence. Nothing had since occurred materially to vary the question. I had seen no evidence of a desire being entertained, on the part of any considerable portion of the American people, that Texas should become an integral part of the United States. . . . To the astonishment of the whole nation, we are now informed that a treaty of annexation has been actually concluded, and is to be submitted to the senate for its consideration. . . .

I regret that I have not the advantage of a view of the treaty itself, so as to enable me to adapt an expression of my opinion to the actual conditions and stipulations which it contains. Not possessing that opportunity, I am constrained to treat the question according to what I presume to be the terms of the treaty. If, without the loss of national character, without the hazard of foreign war, with the general concurrence of the nation, without any danger to the integrity of the Union, and without giving an unreasonable price for Texas, the question of annexation were presented, it would appear in quite a different light from that in which, I apprehend, it is now to be regarded. . . .

Annexation and war with Mexico are identical. Now, for one, I certainly am not willing to involve this country in a foreign war for the object of acquiring Texas. I know there are those who regard such a war with indifference and as a trifling affair, on account of the weakness of Mexico, and her inability to inflict serious injury upon this country. But I do not look upon it thus lightly. I regard all wars as great calamities, to be avoided, if possible, and honorable peace as the wisest and truest policy of this country. What the United States most need are union, peace, and patience. Nor do I think that the weakness of a power should form a motive, in any case, for inducing us to engage in or to depreciate the evils of war.—Honor and good faith and justice are equally due from this country towards the weak as towards the strong. And, if an act of injustice were to be perpetrated towards any power, it would be more compatible with the dignity of the nation, and, in my judgment, less dishonorable, to inflict it upon a powerful instead of a weak foreign nation. But are we perfectly sure that we should be free from injury in a state of war with Mexico? Have we any security that countless numbers of foreign vessels, under the authority and flag of Mexico, would not prey upon our defenceless commerce in the Mexican gulf, on the Pacific ocean, and on every other sea and ocean? What commerce, on the other hand, does Mexico offer, as an indemnity for our losses, to the gallantry and enterprise of our countrymen? This view of the subject supposes that the war would be confined to the United States and Mexico as the only belligerents. But have we any certain guaranty that Mexico would obtain no allies among the great European powers? . . .

Assuming that the annexation of Texas is war with Mexico, is it competent to the treaty-making power to plunge this country into war, not only without the concurrence of, but without deigning to consult congress, to which, by the constitution, belongs exclusively the power of declaring war?

I have hitherto considered the question upon the supposition that the annexation is attempted without the assent of Mexico. If she yields her consent, that would materially affect the foreign aspect of the question, if it did not remove all foreign difficulties. On the assumption of that assent, the question would be confined to the domestic considerations which belong to it, embracing the terms and conditions upon which annexation is proposed. I do not think that Texas ought to be received into the Union, as an integral part of it, in decided opposition to the wishes of a considerable and respectable portion of the confederacy. I think it far more wise and important to compose and harmonize the present confederacy, as it now exists, than to introduce a new element of discord and distraction into it. . . . Mr. Jefferson expressed the opinion, and others believed, that it never was in the contemplation of the framers of the constitution to add foreign territory to the confederacy, out of which new states were to be formed. The acquisitions of Louisiana and Florida may be defended upon the peculiar ground of the relation in which they stood to the states of the Union. After they were admitted, we might well pause a while, people our vast wastes, develop our resources, prepare the means of defending what we possess, and augment our strength, power, and greatness. If hereafter further territory should be wanted for an increased population, we need entertain no apprehensions but that it will be acquired by means, it is to be hoped, fair, honorable, and constitutional.

It is useless to disguise that there are those who espouse and those who oppose the annexation of Texas upon the ground of the influence which it would exert, in the balance of political power, between two great sections of the Union. I conceive that no motive for the acquisition of foreign territory would be more unfortunate, or pregnant with more fatal consequences, than that of obtaining it for the purpose of strengthening one part against another part of the common confederacy. Such a principle, put into practical operation, would menace the existence, if it did not certainly sow the seeds of a dissolution of the Union. It would be to proclaim to the world an insatiable and unquenchable thirst for foreign conquest or acquisition of territory. For if today Texas be acquired to strengthen one part of the confederacy, tomorrow Canada may be required to add strength to another. And, after that might have been obtained, still other and further acquisitions would become necessary to equalize and adjust the balance of political power. Finally, in the progress of this spirit of universal dominion, the part of the confederacy which is now weakest, would find itself still weaker from the impossibility of securing new theatres for those peculiar institutions which it is charged with being desirous to extend.

But would Texas, ultimately, really add strength to that which is now considered the weakest part of the confederacy? If my information be correct, it would not. According to that, the territory of Texas is susceptible of a division into five states of convenient size and form. Of these, two only would be adapted to those peculiar institutions to which I have referred, and the other three, lying west and north of San Antonio, being only adapted to farming and grazing purposes, from the nature of their soil, climate, and productions, would not admit of those institutions. In the end, therefore, there would be two slave and three free states probably added to the Union. If this view of the soil and geography of Texas be correct, it might serve to diminish the zeal both of those who oppose and those who are urging annexation. . . .

In the future progress of events, it is probable that there will be a voluntary or forcible separation of the British North American possessions from the parent country. I am strongly inclined to think that it will be best for the happiness of all parties that, in that event, they should be erected into a separate and independent republic. With the Canadian republic on one side, that of Texas on the other, and the United States, the friend of both, between them, each could advance its own happiness by such constitutions, laws, and measures, as were best adapted to its peculiar condition. They would be natural allies, ready, by co-operation, to repel any European or foreign attack upon either. Each would afford a secure refuge to the persecuted and oppressed driven into exile by either of the others. They would emulate each other in improvements, in free institutions, and in the science of self-government. Whilst Texas has adopted our constitution as the model of hers, she has, in several important particulars, greatly improved upon it.

Although I have felt compelled, from the nature of the inquiries addressed to me, to extend this communication to a much greater length than I could have wished, I could not do justice to the subject, and fairly and fully expose my own opinions in a shorter space. In conclusion, they may be stated in a few words to be, that I consider the annexation of Texas, at this time, without the assent of Mexico, as a measure compromising the national character, involving us certainly in war with Mexico, probably with other foreign powers, dangerous to the integrity of the Union, inexpedient in the present financial condition of the country, and not called for by any general expression of public opinion.

DOCUMENT 7

JAMES K. POLK, WAR MESSAGE TO CONGRESS,
MAY 11, 1846

*President Polk was determined to have California,
and the disputed area between Texas and Mexico—
peacefully and on generous terms if he could; by war
if he must. When his attempt to negotiate a purchase
failed in January 1846, he ordered General Zachary
Taylor to proceed to the Rio Grande. This order
brought American forces well within the disputed
area. On April 24 and 25 a skirmish took place at
Matamoros. Upon learning of the failure of negotiations, Polk recommended to his Cabinet on May 9,
1846, that war be declared because of Mexico's un-
willingness to negotiate. The Cabinet agreed, except
for the Secretary of the Navy, the historian George
Bancroft, who suggested that it would be better to
wait for some Mexican act of aggression. That evening
a message arrived from Taylor reporting the action at
Matamoros. Now the Cabinet was unanimous. The
following day, a Sunday, Polk, Bancroft, and James
Buchanan drafted a war message, which was sent to
Congress on Tuesday, May 11. Though the action at
Matamoros had taken place in disputed territory, Polk
claimed that Mexico "has invaded our territory and
shed American blood upon the American soil." War
was voted by the House, 174–14; by the Senate,
40–2.*

To the Senate and House of Representatives:

The existing state of the relations between the United
States and Mexico renders it proper that I should bring
the subject to the consideration of Congress. . . .

In my message at the commencement of the present
session I informed you that upon the earnest appeal both
of the Congress and convention of Texas I had ordered an
efficient military force to take a position "between the
Nueces and the Del Norte." This had become necessary

to meet a threatened invasion of Texas by the Mexican forces, for which extensive military preparations had been made. The invasion was threatened solely because Texas had determined, in accordance with a solemn resolution of the Congress of the United States, to annex herself to our Union, and under these circumstances it was plainly our duty to extend our protection over her citizens and soil.

This force was concentrated at Corpus Christi, and remained there until after I had received such information from Mexico as rendered it probable, if not certain, that the Mexican Government would refuse to receive our envoy.

Meantime Texas, by the final action of our Congress, had become an integral part of our Union. The Congress of Texas, by its act of December 19, 1836, had declared the Rio del Norte to be the boundary of that Republic. Its jurisdiction had been extended and exercised beyond the Nueces. The country between that river and the Del Norte had been represented in the Congress and in the convention of Texas, had thus taken part in the act of annexation itself, and is now included within one of our Congressional districts. Our own Congress had, moreover, with great unanimity, by the act approved December 31, 1845, recognized the country beyond the Nueces as a part of our territory by including it within our own revenue system, and a revenue officer to reside within that district has been appointed by and with the advice and consent of the Senate. It became, therefore, of urgent necessity to provide for the defense of that portion of our country. Accordingly, on the 13th of January last instructions were issued to the general in command of these troops to occupy the left bank of the Del Norte. This river, which is the southwestern boundary of the State of Texas, is an exposed frontier. . . .

The movement of the troops to the Del Norte was made by the commanding general under positive instructions to abstain from all aggressive acts toward Mexico or Mexican citizens and to regard the relations between that Republic and the United States as peaceful unless she should declare war or commit acts of hostility indicative of a state of war. . . .

The Mexican forces at Matamoras assumed a belligerent attitude, and on the 12th of April General Ampudia, then in command, notified General Taylor to break up his camp within twenty-four hours and to retire beyond the Nueces River, and in the event of his failure to comply with these demands announced that arms, and arms alone, must decide the question. But no open act of hostility was committed until the 24th of April. On that day General Arista, who had succeeded to the command of the Mexican forces, communicated to General Taylor that "he considered hostilities commenced and should prosecute them." A party of dragoons of 63 men and officers were on the same day dispatched from the American camp up the Rio del Norte, on its left bank, to ascertain whether the Mexican troops had crossed or were preparing to cross the river, "became engaged with a large body of these troops, and after a short affair, in which some 16 were killed and wounded, appear to have been surrounded and compelled to surrender.". . .

The cup of forbearance had been exhausted even before the recent information from the frontier of the Del Norte. But now, after reiterated menaces, Mexico has passed the boundary of the United States, has invaded our territory and shed American blood upon the American soil. She has proclaimed that hostilities have commenced, and that the two nations are now at war.

As war exists, and, notwithstanding all our efforts to avoid it, exists by the act of Mexico herself, we are called upon by every consideration of duty and patriotism to vindicate with decision the honor, the rights, and the interests of our country. . . .

In further vindication of our rights and defense of our territory, I invoke the prompt action of Congress to recognize the existence of the war, and to place at the disposition of the Executive the means of prosecuting the war with vigor, and thus hastening the restoration of peace. . . .

DOCUMENT 8

MASSACHUSETTS LEGISLATURE, RESOLUTIONS ON THE WAR WITH MEXICO,
1847

This fervid expression of the case against the war was written by Charles Sumner and adopted by the legislature of his state. It argues the anti–slavery view that the war was the result of a concerted plan for expansion and domination by the "Slave Power."

It is a War to Strengthen the "Slave Power." But it is not merely proposed to open new markets for slavery: it is also designed to confirm and fortify the "Slave Power." . . . Slavery is odious as an institution, if viewed in the light of morals and Christianity. On this account alone we should refrain from rendering it any voluntary support. But it has been made the basis of a political combination, to which has not inaptly been applied the designation of the "Slave Power." The slaveholders of the country—who are not supposed to exceed 200,000 or at most 300,000 in numbers—by the spirit of union which animates them, by the strong sense of a common interest, and by the audacity of their leaders, have erected themselves into a new "estate," as it were, under the Constitution. Disregarding the sentiments of many of the great framers of that instrument, who notoriously considered slavery as *temporary,* they proclaim it a *permanent* institution; and, with a strange inconsistency, at once press its title to a paramount influence in the general government, while they deny the right of that government to interfere, in any way, with its existence. According to them, it may never be restrained or abolished by the general government, though it may be indefinitely extended. And it is urged that, as new free States are admitted into the Union, other slave States should be admitted, in order to preserve, in the Senate, what is called the "balance of power"; in other words, the equipoise between slavery and freedom, though it might, with more propriety, be termed the preponderance of slavery. . . .

The object of the bold measure of annexation was not only to extend slavery, but to strengthen the "Slave Power." The same object is now proposed by the Mexican war. This is another link in the gigantic chain by which our country and the Constitution are to be bound to the "Slave Power." This has been proclaimed in public journals. The following passage from the *Charleston* (S. C.) *Courier* avows it: "Every battle fought in Mexico, and every dollar spent there, but insures the acquisition of territory which must widen the field of Southern enterprise and power in future. And the final result will be to readjust the balance of power in the confederacy, so as to give us control over the operations of government in all time to come."

It is a War Against the Free States. Regarding it as a war to strengthen the "Slave Power," we are conducted to a natural conclusion, that it is virtually, and in its consequences, a war against the free States of the Union. Conquest and robbery are attempted in order to obtain a political control at home; and distant battles are fought, less with a special view of subjugating Mexico than with the design of overcoming the power of the free States, under the Constitution. The lives of Mexicans are sacrificed in this cause; and a domestic question, which should be reserved for bloodless debate in our own country, is transferred to fields of battle in a foreign land. . . .

Criminality of the War. And it is also a violation of the fundamental law of Heaven, of that great law of Right which is written by God's own finger on the heart of man. . . . An unjust and unnecessary war is the dismal offspring of national insensibility, steeping the conscience in forgetfulness, and unkennelling the foul brood of murder, rapine, and rape. How, then, must we regard the acts in the present war? Have they any extenuation beyond the sanction of mortals, like ourselves, who have rashly undertaken to direct them? The war is a crime, and all who have partaken in the blood of its well-fought fields have aided in its perpetration. . . .

Resolves. Concerning the Mexican War, and the Institution of Slavery.

Resolved, That the present war with Mexico has its

primary origin in the unconstitutional annexation to the United States of the foreign State of Texas, while the same was still at war with Mexico; that it was unconstitutionally commenced by the order of the President, to General Taylor, to take military possession of territory in dispute between the United States and Mexico, and in the occupation of Mexico; and that it is now waged ingloriously,—by a powerful nation against a weak neighbor,—unnecessarily and without just cause, at immense cost of treasure and life, for the dismemberment of Mexico, and for the conquest of a portion of her territory, from which slavery has already been excluded, with the triple object of extending slavery, of strengthening the "Slave Power," and of obtaining the control of the Free States, under the Constitution of the United States.

Resolved, That such a war of conquest, so hateful in its objects, so wanton, unjust, and unconstitutional in its origin and character, must be regarded as a war against freedom, against humanity, against justice, against the Union, against the Constitution, and against the Free States; and that a regard for the true interests and the highest honor of the country, not less than the impulses of Christian duty, should arouse all good citizens to join in efforts to arrest this gigantic crime, by withholding supplies, or other voluntary contributions, for its further prosecution, by calling for the withdrawal of our army within the established limits of the United States, and in every just way aiding the country to retreat from the disgraceful position of aggression which it now occupies towards a weak, distracted neighbor and sister republic.

Resolved, That our attention is directed anew to the wrong and "enormity" of slavery, and to the tyranny and usurpation of the "Slave Power," as displayed in the history of our country, particularly in the annexation of Texas, and the present war with Mexico; and that we are impressed with the unalterable conviction that a regard for the fair fame of our country, for the principles of morals, and for that righteousness which exalteth a nation, sanctions and requires all constitutional efforts for the abolition of slavery within the limits of the United States, while loyalty to the Constitution, and a just self–defence, make it specially incumbent on the people of the free

States to co-operate in strenuous exertions to restrain and overthrow the "Slave Power."

DOCUMENT 9

HENRY CLAY, JOHN C. CALHOUN, AND DANIEL WEBSTER, DEBATE ON THE COMPROMISE OF 1850,

FEBRUARY 5—MARCH 7, 1850

In the weeks of Senatorial debate which preceded the enactment of the Compromise of 1850 a wide range of attitudes was expressed. Clay took the lead early in speaking for the resolutions he had introduced. "The Great Compromiser" advised the North against insisting on the terms of the Wilmot Proviso and the South against thinking seriously of disunion. Calhoun, who was dying, asked Senator James M. Mason of Virginia to read his gloomy speech for him. After explaining why the bonds of sentiment between North and South had been progressively weakened, Calhoun goes on, in the section printed here, to say how he thought the Union could be saved. Three days later, he was followed by Daniel Webster, who agreed with Clay that there could be no peaceable secession. Webster's attempt to restrain Northern extremists brought him abuse from anti-slavery men in his own section where formerly he had been so admired. Extreme views were expressed on both sides, but the passage of the compromise measures showed that the moderate spirit of Clay and Webster was still dominant.

HENRY CLAY, Feb. 5 and 6, 1850.

Sir, I have said that I never could vote for it, and I repeat that I never can, and never will vote for it; and no earthly power shall ever make me vote to plant slavery where slavery does not exist. Still, if there be a majority —and there ought to be such a majority—for interdicting slavery north of the line, there ought to be an equal majority—if equality and justice be done to the South—to admit slavery south of the line. And if there be a majority ready to accomplish both of these purposes, though I can not concur in the action, yet I would be one of the last to create any disturbance, I would be one of the first to acquiesce in such legislation, though it is contrary to my own judgment and my own conscience. I think, then, it would be better to keep the whole of these territories untouched by any legislation by Congress on the subject of slavery, leaving it open, undecided, without any action of Congress in relation to it; that it would be best for the South, and best for all the views which the South has, from time to time, disclosed to us as correspondent with her wishes. . . .

And, sir, I must take occasion here to say that in my opinion there is no right on the part of any one or more of the States to secede from the Union. War and dissolution of the Union are identical and inevitable, in my opinion. There can be a dissolution of the Union only by consent or by war. Consent no one can anticipate, from any existing state of things, is likely to be given; and war is the only alternative by which a dissolution could be accomplished. If consent were given—if it were possible that we were to be separated by one great line—in less than sixty days after such consent was given war would break out between the slaveholding and non-slaveholding portions of this Union—between the two independent parts into which it would be erected in virtue of the act of separation. In less than sixty days, I believe, our slaves from Kentucky, flocking over in numbers to the other side of the river, would be pursued by their owners. Our hot and ardent spirits would be restrained by no sense of the right which appertains to the independence of the other side of the river, should that be the line of separation. They would pursue their slaves into the adjacent free States; they would be repelled; and the consequence would be that, in less than sixty days, war would be blazing in every part of this now happy and peaceful land.

And, sir, how are you going to separate the States of this confederacy? In my humble opinion, Mr. President, we should begin with at least three separate confederacies. There would be a confederacy of the North, a confederacy of the Southern Atlantic slaveholding States, and a confederacy of the valley of the Mississippi. My life upon it, that the vast population which has already concentrated and will concentrate on the head-waters and the tributaries of the Mississippi will never give their consent that the mouth of that river shall be held subject to the power of any foreign State or community whatever. Such, I believe, would be the consequences of a dissolution of the Union, immediately ensuing; but other confederacies would spring up from time to time, as dissatisfaction and discontent were disseminated throughout the country—the confederacy of the lakes, perhaps the confederacy of New England, or of the middle States. Ah, sir, the veil which covers these sad and disastrous events that lie beyond it, is too thick to be penetrated or lifted by any mortal eye or hand. . . .

Mr. President, I have said, what I solemnly believe, that dissolution of the Union and war are identical and inevitable; and they are convertible terms; and such a war as it would be, following a dissolution of the Union! Sir, we may search the pages of history, and none so ferocious, so bloody, so implacable, so exterminating—not even the wars of Greece, including those of the Commoners of England and the revolutions of France—none, none of them all would rage with such violence, or be characterized with such bloodshed and enormities as would the war which must succeed, if that ever happens, the dissolution of the Union. And what would be its termination? Standing armies, and navies, to an extent stretching the revenues of each portion of the dissevered members, would take place. An exterminating war would follow—not sir, a war of two or three years' duration, but a war of interminable duration—and exterminating wars would ensue, until, after the struggles and exhaustion of both parties, some Philip or Alexander, some Caesar or Napoleon, would arise and cut the Gordian knot, and solve the problem of the capacity of man for self-government, and crush the liberties of both the severed portions of this common empire. Can you doubt it?

Sir, I implore gentlemen, . . . to pause, solemnly to pause at the edge of the precipice, before the fearful and dangerous leap be taken into the yawning abyss below, from which none who ever take it shall return in safety.

Finally, Mr. President, and in conclusion, I implore,

as the best blessing which Heaven can bestow upon me upon earth, that if the direful event of the dissolution of this Union is to happen, I shall not survive to behold the sad and heart-rending spectacle.

JOHN C. CALHOUN, March 4, 1850.

Having now, Senators, explained what it is that endangers the Union, and traced it to its cause, and explained its nature and character, the question again recurs, How can the Union be saved? To this I answer, there is but one way by which it can be, and that is, by adopting such measures as will satisfy the States belonging to the southern section that they can remain in the Union consistently with their honor and their safety. There is, again, only one way by which this can be effected, and that is, by removing the causes by which this belief has been produced. Do *that* and discontent will cease, harmony and kind feelings between the sections be restored, and every apprehension of danger to the Union removed. The question, then, is, By what can this be done? But, before I undertake to answer this question, I propose to show by what the Union cannot be saved.

It cannot, then, be saved by eulogies on the Union, however splendid or numerous. The cry of "Union, Union, the glorious Union!" can no more prevent disunion than the cry of "Health, health, glorious health!" on the part of the physician, can save a patient lying dangerously ill. So long as the Union, instead of being regarded as a protector, is regarded in the opposite character, by not much less than a majority of the States, it will be in vain to attempt to conciliate them by pronouncing eulogies on it.

Besides, this cry of Union comes commonly from those whom we cannot believe to be sincere. It usually comes from our assailants. But we cannot believe them to be sincere; for, if they loved the Union, they would necessarily be devoted to the constitution. It made the Union, and to destroy the constitution would be to destroy the Union. But the only reliable and certain evidence of devotion to the Constitution is, to abstain, on the one hand, from violating it, and to repel, on the other, all attempts to violate it. It is only by faithfully performing these high duties that the Constitution can be preserved, and with it the Union. . . .

Having now shown what cannot save the Union, I return to the question with which I commenced, How can the Union be saved? There is but one way by which it can with any certainty; and that is, by a full and final settlement, on the principle of justice, of all the questions at issue between the two sections. The South asks for justice, simple justice, and less she ought not to take. She has no compromise to offer, but the Constitution; and no concession or surrender to make. She has already surrendered so much that she has little left to surrender. Such a settlement would go to the root of the evil, and remove all cause of discontent, by satisfying the South she could remain honorably and safely in the Union, and thereby restore the harmony and fraternal feelings between the sections which existed anterior to the Missouri agitation. Nothing else can, with any certainty, finally and forever settle the questions at issue, terminate agitation, and save the Union.

But can this be done? Yes, easily; not by the weaker party, for it can of itself do nothing—not even protect itself—but by the stronger. The North has only to will it to accomplish it—to do justice by conceding to the South an equal right in the acquired territory, and to do her duty by causing the stipulations relative to fugitive slaves to be faithfully fulfilled—to cease the agitation of the slave question, and to provide for the insertion of a provision in the Constitution, by an amendment, which will restore to the South, in substance, the power she possessed of protecting herself, before the equilibrium between the sections was destroyed by the action of this Government. There will be no difficulty in devising such a provision—one that will protect the South, and which, at the same time, will improve and strengthen the Government, instead of impairing and weakening it.

But will the north agree to this? It is for her to answer the question. But, I will say, she cannot refuse, if she has half the love of the Union which she professes to have, or without justly exposing herself to the charge that her love of power and aggrandizement is far greater than her love of the Union. At all events, the responsibility of saving the Union rests on the North, and not the South. The South cannot save it by any act of hers, and the North may save it without any sacrifice whatever, unless to do justice, and to perform her duties under the Constitution, should be regarded by her as a sacrifice.

It is time, Senators, that there should be an open and manly avowal on all sides, as to what is intended to be done. If the question is not now settled, it is uncertain whether it ever can hereafter be; and we, as the representatives of the States of this Union, regarded as governments, should come to a distinct understanding as to our respective views, in order to ascertain whether the great questions at issue can be settled or not. If you, who represent the stronger portion, cannot agree to settle them on the broad principle of justice and duty, say so; and let the States we both represent agree to separate and part in peace. If you are unwilling we should part in peace, tell us so; and we shall know what to do, when you reduce the question to submission or resistance. If you remain silent, you will compel us to infer by your acts what you intend. In that case, California will become the test question. If you admit her, under all the difficulties that oppose her admission, you compel us to infer that you intend to exclude us from the whole of the acquired territories, with the intention of destroying, irretrievably, the equilibrium between the two sections. We would be blind not to perceive, in that case, that your real objects are power and aggrandizement, and infatuated not to act accordingly.

I have now, Senators, done my duty in expressing my opinions fully, freely, and candidly, on this solemn occasion. In doing so, I have been governed by the motives which have governed me in all the stages of the agitation of the slavery question since its commencement. I have exerted myself, during the whole period, to arrest it, with the intention of saving the Union, if it could be done; and if it could not, to save the section where it has pleased Providence to cast my lot, and which I sincerely believe has justice and the Constitution on its side. Having faithfully done my duty to the best of my ability, both to the Union and my section, throughout this agitation, I shall have the consolation, let what will come, that I am free from all responsibility.

DANIEL WEBSTER, March 7, 1850.

Mr. President, I should much prefer to have heard, from every member on this floor, declarations of opinion that this Union could never be dissolved, than the declaration of opinion that in any case, under the pressure of circumstances, such a dissolution was possible. I hear with pain, and anguish, and distress, the word secession, especially when it falls from the lips of those who are eminently patriotic, and known to the country, and known all over the world, for their political services. Secession! Peaceable secession! Sir, your eyes and mine are never destined to see that miracle. The dismemberment of this vast country without convulsion! The breaking up of the fountains of the great deep without ruffling the surface! Who is so foolish—I beg everybody's pardon—as to expect to see any such thing? . . . There can be no such thing as a peaceable secession. Peaceable secession is an utter impossibility. Is the great Constitution under which we live—covering this whole country—is it to be thawed and melted away by secession, as the snows on the mountain melt under the influence of a vernal sun—disappear almost unobserved, and die off? No, sir! No, sir! I will not state what might produce the disruption of the States; but, sir, I see it as plainly as I see the sun in heaven—I see that disruption must produce such a war as I will not describe, in its twofold characters!

Peaceable secession! peaceable secession! The concurrent agreement of all the members of this great Republic to separate! A voluntary separation, with alimony on one side and on the other! Why, what would be the result? Where is the line to be drawn? What states are to secede? —What is to remain American? What am I to be?—an American no longer? Where is the flag of the republic to remain? Where is the eagle still to tower? or is he to cower, and shrink, and fall to the ground? Why, Sir, our ancestors —our fathers and our grandfathers, those of them that are yet living amongst us with prolonged lives—would rebuke and reproach us; and our children and our grandchildren would cry out, Shame on us! if we of this generation, should dishonor those ensigns of the power of the Government, and the harmony of the Union, which is every day felt among us with so much joy and gratitude. What is to become of the navy? What is to become of the army? What is to become of the public lands? How is each of the thirty States to defend itself? I know, although the idea has not been stated distinctly, there is to be a southern Confederacy. I do not mean, when I allude to this statement, that any one seriously contemplates such a state of things. I do not mean to say that it is true, but I have heard it suggested elsewhere, that that idea has originated in a design to separate, I am sorry, sir, that it has ever been thought of, talked of, or dreamed of, in the wildest flights of human imagination. But the idea must be of a separation, including the slave States upon one side and the free States on the other. Sir, there is not—I may express myself too strongly, perhaps—but some things, some moral things, are almost as impossible, as other natural or physical things; and I hold the idea of a separation of these States—those that are free to form one government, and those that are slaveholding to form another—as a moral impossibility. We could not separate the States by any such line, if we were to draw it. We could not sit down here today and draw a line of separation, that would satisfy any five men in the country. There are natural causes that would keep and tie us together, and there are social and domestic relations which we could not break if we would, and which we should not, if we could. Sir, nobody can look over the face of this country at the present moment —nobody can see where its population is the most dense and growing—without being ready to admit, and compelled to admit, that, ere long, America will be in the valley of the Mississippi. . . .

And now, Mr. President, instead of speaking of the possibility or utility of secession, instead of dwelling in these caverns of darkness, instead of groping with those ideas so full of all that is horrid and horrible, let us come out into the light of day; let us enjoy the fresh air of liberty and union; let us cherish those hopes which belong to us; let us devote ourselves to those great objects that are fit for our consideration and our action; let us raise our conceptions to the magnitude and the importance of the duties that devolve upon us; let our comprehension be as broad as the country for which we act, our aspirations as high as its certain destiny; let us not be pigmies in a case that calls for men. Never did there devolve, on any generation of men, higher trusts than now devolve upon us for the preservation of this Constitution and the harmony and peace of all who are destined to live under it. Let us make our generation one of the strongest and brightest links in that golden chain which is destined, I fully believe, to grapple the people of all the States to this Constitution, for ages to come. It is a great popular Constitutional Government, guarded by legislation, law, and by judicature, and defended by the affections of the whole people. No monarchical throne presses the States together; no iron chain of despotic power encircles them; they live and stand upon a Government popular in its form, representative in its character, founded upon principles of equality, and calculated, we hope, as to last forever. In all its history, it has been beneficent; it has trodden down no man's liberty; it has crushed no State. Its daily respiration is liberty and patriotism; its yet youthful veins are full of enterprise, courage, and honorable love of glory and renown. Large before, the country has now, by recent events, become vastly larger. This Republic now extends, with a vast breadth, across the whole continent. The two great seas of the world wash the one and the other shore. We realize on a mighty scale, the beautiful description of the ornamental edging of the buckler of Achilles—

"Now the broad shield complete the artist crowned,
  With his last band, and poured the ocean round;
  In living silver seemed the waves to roll,
  And beat the buckler's verge, and bound the whole."

DOCUMENT 10

APPEAL OF THE INDEPENDENT DEMOCRATS,
JANUARY 19, 1854

This expression of outrage over the Kansas-Nebraska Bill was written by Senator Salmon P. Chase of Ohio, in part from a draft prepared by Representative Joshua Giddings. Chase was attempting to capture segments of the Democratic party for the anti-slavery cause. As it turned out, this appeal, which was widely circulated in the newspapers of the free states, did a great deal to marshal sentiment for the organization of the Republican party. Although it may have delayed, it did not prevent the passage of the Kansas-Nebraska Bill on May 30, 1854.

As Senators and Representatives in the Congress of the United States it is our duty to warn our constituents, whenever imminent danger menaces the freedom of our institutions or the permanency of the Union.

Such danger, as we firmly believe, now impends, and we earnestly solicit your prompt attention to it.

At the last session of Congress a bill for the organization of the Territory of Nebraska passed the House of Representatives by an overwhelming majority. That bill was based on the principle of excluding slavery from the new Territory. It was not taken up for consideration in the Senate and consequently failed to become a law.

At the present session a new Nebraska bill has been reported by the Senate Committee on Territories, which, should it unhappily receive the sanction of Congress, will open all the unorganized Territories of the Union to the ingress of slavery.

We arraign this bill as a gross violation of a sacred pledge; as a criminal betrayal of precious rights; as part and parcel of an atrocious plot to exclude from a vast unoccupied region immigrants from the Old World and free laborers from our own States, and convert it into a dreary region of despotism, inhabited by masters and slaves.

Take your maps, fellow citizens, we entreat you, and see what country it is which this bill gratuitously and recklessly proposes to open to slavery. . . .

This immense region, occupying the very heart of the North American Continent, and larger, by thirty-three thousand square miles, than all the existing free States—including California . . . this immense region the bill now before the Senate, without reason and without excuse, but in flagrant disregard of sound policy and sacred faith, purposes to open to slavery.

We beg your attention, fellow-citizens, to a few historical facts:

The original settled policy of the United States, clearly indicated by the Jefferson proviso of 1784 and the Ordinance of 1787, was non-extension of slavery.

In 1803 Louisiana was acquired by purchase from France. . . .

In 1818, six years later, the inhabitants of the Territory of Missouri applied to Congress for authority to form a State constitution, and for admission into the Union. There were, at that time, in the whole territory acquired from France, outside of the State of Louisiana, not three thousand slaves.

There was no apology, in the circumstances of the country, for the continuance of slavery. The original national policy was against it, and not less the plain language of the treaty under which the territory had been acquired from France.

It was proposed, therefore, to incorporate in the bill authorizing the formation of a State government, a provision requiring that the constitution of the new State should contain an article providing for the abolition of existing slavery, and prohibiting the further introduction of slaves.

This provision was vehemently and pertinaciously opposed, but finally prevailed in the House of Representatives by a decided vote. In the Senate it was rejected, and —in consequence of the disagreement between the two Houses—the bill was lost.

At the next session of Congress, the controversy was renewed with increased violence. It was terminated at length by a compromise. Missouri was allowed to come into the Union with slavery; but a section was inserted in the act authorizing her admission, excluding slavery forever from all the territory acquired from France, not included in the new State, lying north of 36° 30'. . . .

Nothing is more certain in history than the fact that Missouri could not have been admitted as a slave State had not certain members from the free States been reconciled to the measure by the incorporation of this prohibition into the act of admission. Nothing is more certain than that this prohibition has been regarded and accepted by the whole country as a solemn compact against the extension of slavery into any part of the territory acquired from France lying north of 36° 30', and not included in the new State of Missouri. The same act—let it be ever remembered—which authorized the formation of a constitution by the State, without a clause forbidding slavery, consecrated, beyond question and beyond honest recall, the whole remainder of the Territory to freedom and free institutions forever. For more than thirty years—during more than half our national existence under our present Constitution—this compact has been universally regarded and acted upon as inviolable American law. In conformity with it, Iowa was admitted as a free State and Minnesota has been organized as a free Territory.

It is a strange and ominous fact, well calculated to awaken the worst apprehensions and the most fearful forebodings of future calamities, that it is now deliberately proposed to repeal this prohibition, by implication or directly —the latter certanly the manlier way—and thus to subvert the compact, and allow slavery in all the yet unorganized territory.

We cannot, in this address, review the various pretenses under which it is attempted to cloak this monstrous wrong, but we must not altogether omit to notice one.

It is said that Nebraska sustains the same relations to slavery as did the territory acquired from Mexico prior to 1850, and that the pro-slavery clauses of the bill are necessary to carry into effect the compromise of that year.

No assertion could be more groundless. . . .

The statesmen whose powerful support carried the Utah and New Mexico acts never dreamed that their provisions would be ever applied to Nebraska. . . .

Here is proof beyond controversy that the principle of the Missouri act prohibiting slavery north of 36° 30′, far from being abrogated by the Compromise Acts, is expressly affirmed; and that the proposed repeal of this prohibition, instead of being an affirmation of the Compromise Acts, is a repeal of a very prominent provision of the most important act of the series. It is solemnly declared in the very Compromise Acts *"that nothing herein contained shall be construed to impair or qualify"* the prohibition of slavery north of 36° 30′; and yet in the face of this declaration, that sacred prohibition is said to be overthrown. Can presumption further go? To all who, in any way, lean upon these compromises, we commend this exposition.

The pretenses, therefore, that the territory covered by the positive prohibition of 1820, sustains a similar relation to slavery with that acquired from Mexico, covered by no prohibition except that of disputed constitutional or Mexican law, and that the Compromises of 1850 require the incorporation of the pro-slavery clauses of the Utah and New Mexico Bill in the Nebraska act, are mere inventions, designed to cover up from public reprehension meditated bad faith. Were he living now, no one would be more forward, more eloquent, or more indignant in his denunciation of that bad faith, than Henry Clay, the foremost champion of both compromises. . . .

We appeal to the people. We warn you that the dearest interests of freedom and the Union are in imminent peril. Demagogues may tell you that the Union can be maintained only by submitting to the demands of slavery. We tell you that the Union can only be maintained by the full recognition of the just claims of freedom and man. The Union was formed to establish justice and secure the blessings of liberty. When it fails to accomplish these ends it will be worthless, and when it becomes worthless it cannot long endure.

We entreat you to be mindful of that fundamental maxim of Democracy—EQUAL RIGHTS AND EXACT JUSTICE FOR ALL MEN. Do not submit to become agents in extending legalized oppression and systematized injustice over a vast territory yet exempt from these terrible evils.

We implore Christians and Christian ministers to interpose. Their divine religion requires them to behold in every man a brother, and to labor for the advancement and regeneration of the human race.

Whatever apologies may be offered for the toleration of slavery in the States, none can be offered for its extension into Territories where it does not exist, and where that extension involves the repeal of ancient law and the violation of solemn compact. Let all protest, earnestly and emphatically, by correspondence, through the press, by memorials, by resolutions of public meetings and legislative bodies, and in whatever other mode may seem expedient, against this enormous crime.

For ourselves, we shall resist it by speech and vote, and with all the abilities which God has given us. Even if overcome in the impending struggle, we shall not submit. We shall go home to our constituents, erect anew the standard of freedom, and call on the people to come to the rescue of the country from the domination of slavery. We will not despair; for the cause of human freedom is the cause of God.

> S. P. Chase
> Charles Sumner
> J. R. Giddings
> Edward Wade
> Gerritt Smith
> Alexander De Witt.

DOCUMENT 11

STEPHEN A. DOUGLAS, SPEECH IN THE SENATE,
JANUARY 30, 1854

After the introduction of the Kansas-Nebraska Bill, Douglas was so violently criticized that one Washington newspaper declared: "Never before has a public man been so hunted and hounded." He was particularly stung by Chase's "Appeal of the Independent Democrats," and his answer, given in this speech, was one of the major efforts of his life. After a contemptuous interchange with Chase, Douglas goes on to chide the anti-slavery men for their inconsistency. It was they, he argues, who had always opposed compromise; and he charges them with bad grace in saying it was he who betrayed the Missouri Compromise.

The argument of this manifesto is predicated upon the assumption that the policy of the fathers of the republic was to prohibit slavery in all the territory ceded by the old States to the Union, and made United States territory, for the purpose of being organized into new States. I take issue upon that statement. Such was not the practice in the early history of the government. It is true that in the territory northwest of the Ohio river slavery was prohibited by the ordinance of 1787; but it is also true that in the territory south of the Ohio river, slavery was permitted and protected. . . . The only conclusion that can be fairly and honestly drawn from that legislation is, that it was the policy of the fathers of the republic to prescribe a line of demarkation between free territories and slaveholding territories by a natural or a geographical line, being sure to make that line correspond, as near as might be, to the laws of climate, of production, and all those other causes that would control the institution and make it either desirable or undesirable to the people inhabiting the respective territories.

Sir, I wish you to bear in mind, too, that this geographical line, established by the founders of the republic between free territories and slave territories, extended as far westward as our territory then reached; the object being to avoid all agitation on the slavery question by settling that question forever, as far as our territory extended, which was then to the Mississippi river. . . .

Then, sir, in 1848 we acquired from Mexico the country between the Rio del Norte and the Pacific Ocean. Immediately after that acquisition, the Senate, on my own motion, voted into a bill a provision to extend the Missouri compromise indefinitely westward to the Pacific ocean, in the same sense and with the same understanding with which it was originally adopted. That provision passed this body by a decided majority, I think by ten at least, and went to the House of Representatives, and was defeated there by northern votes.

Now, sir, let us pause and consider for a moment. The first time that the principles of the Missouri compromise were ever abandoned, the first time they were ever rejected by Congress, was by the defeat of that provision in the House of Representatives in 1848. By whom was that defeat effected? By northern votes with freesoil proclivities. It was the defeat of that Missouri compromise that reopened the slavery agitation with all its fury. It was the defeat of that Missouri compromise that created the tremendous struggle of 1850. It was the defeat of that Missouri compromise that created the necessity for making a new compromise in 1850. Had we been faithful to the principles of the Missouri compromise in 1848, this question would not have arisen. Who was it that was faithless? I undertake to say it was the very men who now insist that the Missouri compromise was a solemn compact and should never be violated or departed from. Every man who is now assailing the principle of the bill under consideration, so far as I am advised, was opposed to the Missouri compromise in 1848. The very men who now arraign me for a departure from the Missouri compromise are the men who successfully violated it, repudiated it, and caused it to be superseded by the compromise measures of 1850. Sir, it is with rather bad grace that the men who proved faithless themselves should charge upon me and others, who were ever faithful, the responsibilities and consequences of their own treachery.

Then, sir, as I before remarked, the defeat of the Missouri compromise in 1848 having created the necessity for the establishment of a new one in 1850, let us see what that compromise was.

The leading feature of the compromise of 1850 was congressional non–intervention as to slavery in the Territories; that the people of the Territories, and of all the States, were to be allowed to do as they pleased upon the subject of slavery, subject only to the provisions of the Constitution of the United States.

That, sir, was the leading feature of the compromise measures of 1850. Those measures, therefore, abandoned the idea of a geographical line as the boundary between free States and slave States; abandoned it because compelled to do it from an inability to maintain it: and in lieu of that, substituted a great principle of self–government which would allow the people to do as they thought proper. Now the question is, when that new compromise, resting upon that great fundamental principle of freedom, was established, was it not an abandonment of the old one —the geographical line? . . . They say my bill annuls the Missouri compromise. If it does, it had already been done before by the act of 1850; for these words [on the Missouri compromise in the Kansas–Nebraska bill] were copied from the act of 1850. . . .

Let me ask you, where have you succeeded in excluding slavery by an act of Congress from one inch of the American soil? You may tell me that you did it in the Northwest Territory by the ordinance of 1787. I will show you by the history of the country that you did not accomplish any such thing. You prohibited slavery there by law, but you did not exclude it in fact. Illinois was a part of the northwest territory. With the exception of a few French and white settlements, it was a vast wilderness, filled with hostile savages, when the ordinance of 1787 was adopted. Yet, sir, when Illinois was organized with a territorial government, it established and protected slavery, and maintained it in spite of your ordinance and in defiance of its express prohibition. It is a curious fact, that, so long as Congress said the territory of Illinois should not have slavery, she actually had it; and on the very day when you withdrew your Congressional prohibition the people of Illinois, of their own free will and accord, provided for a system of emancipation.

Thus you did not succeed in Illinois Territory with your ordinance or your Wilmot Proviso, because the people there regarded it as an invasion of their rights; they regarded it as an usurpation on the part of the federal government. They regarded it as violative of the great principles of self-government, and they determined that they would never submit even to have freedom so long as you forced it upon them. . . .

I know of but one territory of the United States where slavery does exist, and that one is where you have prohibited it by law; and it is this very Nebraska country. In defiance of the eighth section of the act of 1820, in defiance of congressional dictation, there have been, not many, but a few slaves introduced. I heard a minister of the Gospel the other day conversing with a member of the Committee on Territories upon this subject. The preacher was from the country, and a member put this question to him: "Have you any negroes out there?" He said there were a few held by the Indians. I asked him if there were not some held by white men? He said there were a few under *peculiar circumstances,* and he gave an instance. An abolition missionary, a very good man, had gone there from Boston, and he took his wife with him.

He got out into the country but could not get any help; hence he, being a kind-hearted man, went down to Missouri and gave $1,000 for a negro, and took him up there as "help." [Laughter]. So, under peculiar circumstances, when these freesoil and abolition preachers and missionaries go into the country, they can buy a negro for their own use, but they do not like to allow any one else to do the same thing. [Renewed laughter]. I suppose the fact of the matter is simply this: there the people can get no servants—no "help," as they are called in the section of country where I was born—and from the necessity of the case, they must do the best they can, and for this reason a few slaves have been taken there. I have no doubt that whether you organize the territory of Nebraska or not, this will continue for some little time to come. It certainly does exist, and it will increase as long as the Missouri compromise applies to the territory; and I suppose it will continue for a little while during their territorial condition, whether a prohibition is imposed or not. But when settlers rush in—when labor becomes plenty, and therefore cheap, in that climate, with its productions—it is worse than folly to think of its being a slaveholding country. I do not believe there is a man in Congress who thinks it could be permanently a slaveholding country. I have no idea that it could. All I have to say on that subject is, that, when you create them into a territory, you thereby acknowledge that they ought to be considered a distinct political organization. And when you give them in addition a legislature, you thereby confess that they are competent to exercise the powers of legislation. If they wish slavery, they have a right to it. If they do not want it, they will not have it, and you should not attempt to force it upon them.

I do not like, I never did like, the system of legislation on our part, by which a geographical line, in violation of the laws of nature, and climate, and soil, and of the laws of God, should be run to establish institutions for a people contrary to their wishes; yet, out of a regard for the peace and quiet of the country, out of respect for past pledges, and out of a desire to adhere faithfully to all compromises, I sustained the Missouri compromise so long as it was in force, and advocated its extension to the Pacific ocean. Now, when that has been abandoned, when it has been superseded, when a great principle of self-government has been substituted for it, I choose to cling to that principle, and abide in good faith, not only by the letter, but by the spirit of the last compromise. . . .

Did not every abolitionist and freesoiler in America

denounce the Missouri compromise in 1820? Did they not for years hunt down ravenously, for his blood, every man who assisted in making that compromise? Did they not in 1845, when Texas was annexed, denounce all of us who went for the annexation of Texas and the continuation of the Missouri compromise line through it? Did they not, in 1848, denounce me as a slavery propagandist for standing by the principles of the Missouri compromise, and proposing to continue it to the Pacific ocean? Did they not themselves violate and repudiate it then? Is not the charge of bad faith true as to every abolitionist in America, instead of being true as to me and the committee, and those who advocate this bill?

They talk about the bill being a violation of the compromise measures of 1850. Who can show me a man in either house of Congress who was in favor of those compromise measures in 1850, and who is not now in favor of leaving the people of Nebraska and Kansas to do as they please upon the subject of slavery, according to the principle of my bill? Is there one? If so, I have not heard of him. This tornado has been raised by abolitionists, and abolitionists alone. They have made an impression upon the public mind, in the way in which I have mentioned, by a falsification of the law and the facts; and this whole organization against the compromise measures of 1850 is an abolition movement. I presume they had some hope of getting a few tender-footed democrats into their plot; and, acting on what they supposed they might do, they sent forth publicly to the world the falsehood that their address was signed by the senators and a majority of the representatives from the State of Ohio; but when we come to examine signatures, we find no one whig there, no one democrat there; none but pure, unmitigated, unadulterated abolitionists. . . .

DOCUMENT 12

DRED SCOTT v. SANDFORD,
1857

These are the facts of the case: a Negro slave, Dred Scott, owned in Missouri, was taken by his owner to reside for a time in two free territories—the first was Illinois, a free state, once part of the territory from which the Ordinance of 1787 had barred slavery; and the second was a place in what is now Minnesota, from which slavery had been barred by the Missouri Compromise. Finally, the owner brought Dred Scott back to Missouri. There, after a change of ownership, Dred Scott sued for his freedom in a Missouri court, arguing that his periods of residence in free territory had in effect emancipated him. Though he won in the lower court, his present owner appealed to the state Supreme Court, which reversed the earlier decision. At this point, sympathizers of Scott arranged to bring the case to the federal courts by devising a "sale" of the Negro to a citizen of New York. They hoped that Scott, as a citizen of Missouri bringing suit against a citizen of New York, could be heard by the federal courts under the constitutional provision giving them jurisdiction over suits between citizens of different states. The case was first argued before the Supreme Court in February 1856, and then, because of complex differences among the justices, was reargued a year later. Finally, on March 6, 1857, the aged Chief Justice Taney read this opinion, which shook the entire country. This selection from the case omits Taney's long argument to show that Scott was not a citizen of Missouri, and hence not entitled to bring suit. It includes only that part in which the Missouri Compromise was declared unconstitutional.

TANEY, C. J. . . .

And upon a full and careful consideration of the subject, the court is of opinion that, upon the facts stated in the plea in abatement, Dred Scott was not a citizen of Missouri within the meaning of the Constitution of the United States, and not entitled as such to sue in its courts; and, consequently, that the Circuit Court had no jurisdiction of the case, and that the judgment on the plea in abatement is erroneous. . . .

We proceed, therefore, to inquire whether the facts relied on by the plaintiff entitled him to his freedom. . . .

In considering this part of the controversy, two questions arise: 1st. Was he, together with his family, free in Missouri by reason of the stay in the territory of the United States hereinbefore mentioned? And 2d, If they were not, is Scott himself free by reason of his removal to Rock Island, in the State of Illinois, as stated in the above admissions?

We proceed to examine the first question.

The Act of Congress, upon which the plaintiff relies, [the Missouri compromise] declares that slavery and involuntary servitude, except as a punishment for crime, shall be forever prohibited in all that part of the territory ceded by France, under the name of Louisiana, which lies north of thirty-six degrees thirty minutes north latitude, and not included within the limits of Missouri. And the difficulty which meets us at the threshold of this part of the inquiry is, whether Congress was authorized to pass this law under any of the powers granted to it by the Constitution; for if the authority is not given by that instrument, it is the duty of this court to declare it void and inoperative, and incapable of conferring freedom upon any one who is held as a slave under the laws of any one of the States.

The counsel for the plaintiff has laid much stress upon that article in the Constitution which confers on Congress the power "to dispose of and make all needful rules and regulations respecting the territory or other property belonging to the United States;" but, in the judgment of the court, that provision has no bearing on the present controversy, and the power there given, whatever it may be, is confined, and was intended to be confined, to the territory which at that time belonged to, or was claimed by, the United States, and was within their boundaries as settled by the treaty with Great Britain, and can have no influence upon a territory afterwards acquired from a foreign

Government. It was a special provision for a known and particular territory, and to meet a present emergency, and nothing more. . . .

If this clause is construed to extend to territory acquired by the present Government from a foreign nation, outside of the limits of any charter from the British Government to a colony, it would be difficult to say, why it was deemed necessary to give the Government the power to sell any vacant lands belonging to the sovereignty which might be found within it; and if this was necessary, why the grant of this power should precede the power to legislate over it and establish a Government there; and still more difficult to say, why it was deemed necessary so specially and particularly to grant the power to make needful rules and regulations in relation to any personal or movable property it might acquire there. For the words, *other property* necessarily, by every known rule of interpretation, must mean property of a different description from territory or land. And the difficulty would perhaps be insurmountable in endeavoring to account for the last member of the sentence, which provides that "nothing in this Constitution shall be so construed as to prejudice any claims of the United States or any particular State," or to say how any particular State could have claims in or to a territory ceded by a foreign Government, or to account for associating this provision with the preceding provisions of the clause, with which it would appear to have no connection. . . .

But the power of Congress over the person or property of a citizen can never be a mere discretionary power under our Constitution and form of Government. The powers of the Government and the rights and privileges of the citizen are regulated and plainly defined by the Constitution itself. And when the Territory becomes a part of the United States, the Federal Government enters into possession in the character impressed upon it by those who created it. It enters upon it with its powers over the citizen strictly defined, and limited by the Constitution, from which it derives its own existence, and by virtue of which alone it continues to exist and act as a Government and sovereignty. It has no power of any kind beyond it; and it cannot, when it enters a Territory of the United States, put off its character, and assume discretionary or despotic powers which the Constitution has denied to it. It cannot create for itself a new character separated from the citizens of the United States, and the duties it owes them under the provisions of the Constitution. The Territory being a part of the United States, the Government and the citizen both enter it under the authority of the Constitution, with their respective rights defined and marked out; and the Federal Government can exercise no power over his person or property, beyond what that instrument confers, nor lawfully deny any right which it has reserved. . . .

The rights of private property have been guarded with equal care. Thus the rights of property are united with the rights of person, and placed on the same ground by the fifth amendment to the Constitution. . . . An Act of Congress which deprives a person of the United States of his liberty or property merely because he came himself or brought his property into a particular Territory of the United States, and who had committed no offense against the laws, could hardly be dignified with the name of due process of law. . . .

And this prohibition is not confined to the States, but the words are general, and extend to the whole territory over which the Constitution gives it power to legislate, including those portions of it remaining under territorial government, as well as that covered by States. It is a total absence of power everywhere within the dominion of the United States, and places the citizens of a territory, so far as these rights are concerned, on the same footing with citizens of the States, and guards them as firmly and plainly against any inroads which the general government might attempt, under the plea of implied or incidental powers. And if Congress itself cannot do this—if it is beyond the powers conferred on the Federal Government—it will be admitted, we presume, that it could not authorize a territorial government to exercise them. It could confer no power on any local government, established by its authority, to violate the provisions of the Constitution.

It seems, however, to be supposed, that there is a difference between property in a slave and other property, and that different rules may be applied to it in expounding the Constitution of the United States. And the laws and usages of nations, and the writings of eminent jurists upon the relation of master and slave and their mutual rights and duties, and the powers which governments may exercise over it, have been dwelt upon in the argument.

But . . . if the Constitution recognizes the right of property of the master in a slave, and makes no distinction between that description of property and other property owned by a citizen, no tribunal, acting under the authority of the United States, whether it be legislative, executive, or judicial, has a right to draw such a distinction, or deny to it the benefit of the provisions and guarantees which have been provided for the protection of private property against the encroachments of the Government.

Now . . . the right of property in a slave is distinctly and expressly affirmed in the Constitution. The right to traffic in it, like an ordinary article of merchandise and property, was guaranteed to the citizens of the United States, in every State that might desire it, for twenty years. And the Government in express terms is pledged to protect it in all future time, if the slave escapes from his owner. . . . And no word can be found in the Constitution which gives Congress a greater power over slave property, or which entitles property of that kind to less protection than property of any other description. The only power conferred is the power coupled with the duty of guarding and protecting the owner in his rights.

Upon these considerations, it is the opinion of the court that the Act of Congress [the Missouri compromise] which prohibited a citizen from holding and owning property of this kind in the territory of the United States north of the line therein mentioned, is not warranted by the Constitution, and is therefore void; and that neither Dred Scott himself, nor any of his family, were made free by being carried into this territory; even if they had been carried there by the owner, with the intention of becoming a permanent resident. . . .

Upon the whole, therefore, it is the judgment of this court, that it appears by the record before us that the plaintiff in error is not a citizen of Missouri, in the sense in which that word is used in the Constitution; and that the Circuit Court of the United States, for that reason, had no jurisdiction in the case, and could give no judgment in it.

Its judgment for the defendant must, consequently, be reversed, and a mandate issued directing the suit to be dismissed for want of jurisdiction.

DOCUMENT 13

THE LINCOLN-DOUGLAS DEBATES, 1858

These debates were held when Lincoln challenged Douglas for his seat in the Senate. Douglas's strategy was to portray Lincoln as a radical, an advocate of racial equality, and a promoter of sectional war, who was defying the Supreme Court's decision in the Dred Scott case. Lincoln tried in his answers to make it clear that he was a conservative on race relations but that he believed in the principles enunciated in the Declaration of Independence; that he did not advocate or threaten violence; and that he expected the Dred Scott decision to be reversed in time through entirely peaceful means, as many other Supreme Court decisions had been reversed. Something must be done, he insisted, to reassure the people of the North that the spread of slavery would be stopped. Lincoln also made the most of the fact that the Supreme Court's decision was as troublesome for advocates of popular sovereignty as it was for advocates of Congressional exclusion of slavery from the territories. This was the significance of his clever second question to Douglas at Freeport: Could the people of a territory lawfully exclude slavery before the formation of a state constitution? If Douglas answered No, he would disappoint his followers throughout the North. If he answered Yes, he would offend the South. The "Freeport Doctrine," which Douglas formulated in answer to this question, although consistent with his long-standing advocacy of popular sovereignty, hurt him in the South and added to the pressures that split the Democratic party in 1860. By professing moral indifference to slavery, Douglas also lost ground in the eyes of those Northerners who had supported him because they believed that popular sovereignty would be an effective way of keeping slavery out of the territories and would avoid the controversy involved in the idea of Congressional exclusion. Although Lincoln did not go to the Senate, he attracted nationwide attention for his debating skill and laid the foundations for his presidential nomination two years later. These selections illustrate some of the main issues.

Lincoln's question at the second debate, Freeport, August 27, 1858

I now proceed to propound to the Judge [Douglas] the interrogatories, so far as I have framed them. I will bring forward a new instalment when I get them ready. I will bring them forward now, only reaching to number four.

The first one is:

Question 1. If the people of Kansas shall, by means entirely unobjectionable in all other respects, adopt a state constitution, and ask admission into the Union under it, *before* they have the requisite number of inhabitants according to the English Bill—some ninety-three thousand—will you vote to admit them?

Q. 2. Can the people of a United States territory, in any lawful way, against the wish of any citizen of the United States, exclude slavery from its limits prior to the formation of a state constitution?

Q. 3. If the Supreme Court of the United States shall decide that states cannot exclude slavery from their limits, are you in favor of acquiescing in, adopting, and following such decision as a rule of political action?

Q. 4. Are you in favor of acquiring additional territory, in disregard of how such acquisition may affect the nation on the slavery question? . . .

Douglas' reply, Freeport, August 27, 1858

First. . . . in reference to Kansas, it is my opinion that as she has population enough to constitute a slave State, she has people enough for a free State. I will not make Kansas an exceptional case to the other States of the Union. . . . Either Kansas must come in as a free State, with whatever population she may have, or the rule must be applied to all the other Territories alike. . . .

The next question propounded to me by Mr. Lincoln is: Can the people of a territory in any lawful way, against the wishes of any citizen of the United States, exclude slavery from their limits prior to the formation of a state constitution? I answer emphatically, as Mr. Lincoln has heard me answer a hundred times from every stump in Illinois, that in my opinion the people of a territory can, by lawful means, exclude slavery from their limits prior to the formation of a state constitution. Mr. Lincoln knew that I had answered that question over and over again. He heard me argue the Nebraska Bill on that principle all over the state in 1854, in 1855, and in 1856, and he has no excuse for pretending to be in doubt as to my position on that question. It matters not what way the Supreme Court may hereafter decide as to the abstract question whether slavery may or may not go into a territory under the Constitution, the people have the lawful means to introduce it or exclude it as they please, for the reason that slavery cannot exist a day or an hour anywhere unless it is supported by local police regulations. Those police regulations can only be established by the local legislature, and, if the people are opposed to slavery, they will elect representatives to that body who will by unfriendly legislation effectually prevent the introduction of it into their midst. If, on the contrary, they are for it, their legislation will favor its extension. Hence, no matter what the decision of the Supreme Court may be on that abstract question, still the right of the people to make a slave territory or a free territory is perfect and complete under the Nebraska Bill. I hope Mr. Lincoln deems my answer satisfactory on that point. . . .

The third question which Mr. Lincoln presented is, if the Supreme Court of the United States shall decide that a state of this Union cannot exclude slavery from its own limits, will I submit to it? I am amazed that Lincoln should ask such a question. ["A schoolboy knows better."] Yes, a schoolboy does know better. Mr. Lincoln's object is to cast an imputation upon the Supreme Court. He knows that there never was but one man in America, claiming any degree of intelligence or decency, who ever for a moment pretended such a thing. . . . He casts an imputation upon the Supreme Court of the United States, by supposing that they would violate the Constitution of the United States. I tell him that such a thing is not possible. It would be an act of moral treason that no man on the bench could ever descend to. Mr. Lincoln himself would never in his partisan feelings so far forget what was right as to be guilty of such an act.

The fourth question of Mr. Lincoln is: Are you in favor of acquiring additional territory, in disregard as to how such acquisition may affect the Union on the slavery questions? This question is very ingeniously and cunningly put.

The Black Republican creed lays it down expressly, that under no circumstances shall we acquire any more territory unless slavery is first prohibited in the country. I ask Mr. Lincoln whether he is in favor of that proposition. Are you [addressing Mr. Lincoln] opposed to the acquisition of any more territory, under any circumstances, unless slavery is prohibited in it? That he does not like to answer. When I ask him whether he stands up to that article in the platform of his party, he turns, Yankee-fashion, and without answering it, asks me whether I am in favor of acquiring territory without regard to how it may affect the Union on the slavery question. I answer that whenever it becomes necessary, in our growth and progress, to acquire more territory, that I am in favor of it, without reference to the question of slavery, and, when we have acquired it, I will leave the people free to do as they please, either to make it slave or free territory, as they prefer. . . .

Lincoln's Speech, Jonesboro, September 15, 1858

The second interrogatory that I propounded to him, was this:

"Question 2. Can the people of a United States territory, in any lawful way, against the wish of any citizen of the United States, exclude slavery from its limits prior to the formation of a state constitution?"

To this Judge Douglas answered that they can lawfully exclude slavery from the territory prior to the formation of a constitution. He goes on to tell us how it can be done. As I understand him, he holds that it can be done by the territorial legislature refusing to make any enactments for the protection of slavery in the territory, and especially by adopting unfriendly legislation to it. For the sake of clearness I state it again: that they can exclude slavery from the territory, first, by withholding what he assumes to be an indispensable assistance to it in the way of legislation and, second, by unfriendly legislation. If I rightfully understand him, I wish to ask your attention for a while to his position.

In the first place, the Supreme Court of the United States has decided that any congressional prohibition of slavery in the territories is unconstitutional—that they have reached this proposition as a conclusion from their former proposition, that the Constitution of the United States expressly recognizes property in slaves, and from that other constitutional provision that no person shall be deprived of property without due process of law. Hence they reach the conclusion that as the Constitution of the United States expressly recognizes property in slaves, and prohibits any person from being deprived of property without due process of law, to pass an act of Congress by which a man who owned a slave on one side of a line would be deprived of him if he took him on the other side, is depriving him of that property without due process of law. That I understand to be the decision of the Supreme Court. I understand also that Judge Douglas adheres most firmly to that decision; and the difficulty is: How is it possible for any power to exclude slavery from the territory unless in violation of that decision? That is the difficulty. . . .

I hold that the proposition that slavery cannot enter a new country without police regulations is historically false. It is not true at all. I hold that the history of this country shows that the institution of slavery was originally planted upon this continent *without* these "police regulations" which the Judge now thinks necessary for the actual establishment of it. Not only so, but is there not another fact—how came this Dred Scott decision to be made? It was made upon the case of a Negro being taken and actually held in slavery in Minnesota Territory, claiming his freedom because the act of Congress prohibited his being so held there. *Will the Judge pretend that Dred Scott was not held there without police regulations?* There is at least one matter of record as to his having been held in slavery in the territory, not only without police regulations, but in the teeth of congressional legislation supposed to be valid at the time. This shows that there is vigor enough in slavery to plant itself in a new country even against unfriendly legislation. It takes not only law but the *enforcement* of law to keep it out. That is the history of this country upon the subject. . . .

Douglas' Opening Speech, Alton, October 15, 1858

Ladies and Gentlemen:

It is now nearly four months since the canvass between Mr. Lincoln and myself commenced. On the sixteenth of June the Republican Convention assembled at Springfield and nominated Mr. Lincoln as their candidate for the United States Senate, and he, on that occasion, delivered a speech in which he laid down what he understood to be the Republican creed, and the platform on which he proposed to stand during the contest.

The principal points in that speech of Mr. Lincoln's were: First, that this government could not endure permanently divided into free and slave States, as our fathers made it; that they must all become free or all become slave; all become one thing or all become the other,— otherwise this Union could not continue to exist. I give you his opinions almost in the identical language he used. His second proposition was a crusade against the Supreme Court of the United States because of the Dred Scott decision, urging as an especial reason for his opposition to that decision that it deprived the negroes of the rights and benefits of that clause in the Constitution of the United States which guarantees to the citizens of each State all the rights, privileges, and immunities of the citizens of the several States.

On the tenth of July I returned home, and delivered a speech to the people of Chicago, in which I announced it to be my purpose to appeal to the people of Illinois to sustain the course I had pursued in Congress. In that speech I joined issue with Mr. Lincoln on the points which he had presented. Thus there was an issue clear and distinct made up between us on these two propositions laid down in the speech of Mr. Lincoln at Springfield, and controverted by me in my reply to him at Chicago. On the next day, the eleventh of July, Mr. Lincoln replied to me at Chicago, explaining at some length, and reaffirming the positions which he had taken in his Springfield speech. In that Chicago speech he even went further than he had before, and uttered sentiments in regard to the negro being on an equality with the white man. He adopted in support of this position the argument which Lovejoy and Codding and other Abolition lecturers had made familiar in the northern and central portions of the State: to wit, that the Declaration of Independence having declared all men free and equal, by divine law, also that negro equality was an inalienable right, of which they could not be deprived. He insisted, in that speech, that the Declaration of Independence included the negro in the clause asserting that all men were created equal, and went so far as to say that if one man was allowed to take the position that it did not include the negro, others might take the position that it did not include other men. He said that all these distinctions between this man and that man, this race and the other race, must be discarded, and we must all stand by the Declaration of Independence, declaring that all men were created equal.

The issue thus being made up between Mr. Lincoln and myself on three points, we went before the people of the State. During the following seven weeks, between the Chicago speeches and our first meeting at Ottawa, he and I addressed large assemblages of the people in many of the central counties. In my speeches I confined myself closely to those three positions which he had taken, controverting his proposition that this Union could not exist as our fathers made it, divided into free and slave States, controverting his proposition of a crusade against the Supreme Court because of the Dred Scott decision, and controverting his proposition that the Declaration of Independence included and meant the negroes as well as the white men, when it declared all men to be created equal. . . . I took up Mr. Lincoln's three propositions in my several speeches, analyzed them, and pointed out what I believed to be the radical errors contained in them. First, in regard to his doctrine that this government was in violation of the law of God, which says that a house divided against itself cannot stand, I repudiated it as slander upon the immortal framers of our Constitution. I then said, I have often repeated, and now again assert, that in my opinion our government can endure forever, divided into free and slave States as our fathers made it,—each State having the right to prohibit, abolish, or sustain slavery, just as it pleases. This government was made upon the great basis of the sovereignty of the States, the right of each State to regulate its own domestic institutions to suit itself; and that right was conferred with the understanding and expectation that, inasmuch as each locality had separate interests, each locality must have different and distinct local and domestic institutions, corresponding to its wants and interests. Our fathers knew when they made the government that the laws and institutions which were well adapted to the Green Mountains of Vermont were unsuited to the rice plantations of South Carolina. They knew then, as well as we know now, that the laws and institutions which would be well adapted to the beautiful prairies of Illinois would not be suited to the mining regions of California. They knew that in a republic as broad as this, having such a variety of soil, climate, and interest, there must necessarily be a corresponding variety of local laws,—the policy and institutions of each State adapted to its condition and wants. For this reason this Union was established on the right of each State to do as it pleased on the question of slavery, and every other question; and the various states were not allowed to complain of, much less interfere with, the policy of their neighbors.

Lincoln's Reply, Alton, October 15, 1858

It is not true that our fathers, as Judge Douglas assumes, made this government part slave and part free. Understand the sense in which he puts it. He assumes that slavery is a rightful thing within itself,—was introduced by the framers of the Constitution. The exact truth is, that they found the institution existing among us, and they left it as they found it. But in making the government they left this institution with many clear marks of disapprobation upon it. They found slavery among them, and they left it among them because of the difficulty—the absolute impossibility—of its immediate removal. And when Judge Douglas asks me why we cannot let it remain part slave and part free, as the fathers of the government made it, he asks a question based upon an assumption which is itself a falsehood; and I turn upon him and ask him the question, when the policy that the fathers of the government had adopted in relation to this element among us was the best policy in the world, the only wise policy the only policy that we can ever safely continue upon, that will ever give us peace, unless this dangerous element masters us all and becomes a national institution,—*I turn upon him and ask him why he could not leave it alone.* I turn and ask him why he was driven to the necessity of introducing a *new policy* in regard to it. He has himself said he introduced a new policy. He said so in his speech on the twenty-second of March of the present year, 1858. I ask him why he could not let it remain where our fathers placed it. I ask, too, of Judge Douglas and his friends why we shall not again place this institution upon the basis on which the fathers left it. I ask you, when he infers that I am in favor of setting the free and slave States at war, when the institution was placed in that attitude by those who made the Constitution, *did they make any war?* If we had no war out of it, when thus placed, wherein is the ground of belief that we shall have war out of it if we return to that policy? Have we had any peace upon this matter springing from any other basis? I maintain that we have not. I have proposed nothing more than a return to the policy of the fathers.

Now, irrespective of the moral aspect of this question as to whether there is a right or wrong in enslaving a negro, I am still in favor of our new Territories being in such a condition that white men may find a home,—may find some spot where they can better their condition; where they can settle upon new soil and better their condition in life. I am in favor of this, not merely (I must say it here as I have elsewhere) for our own people who are born amongst us, but as an outlet for *free white people everywhere*—the world over—in which Hans, and Baptiste, and Patrick, and all other men from all the world, may find new homes and better their conditions in life.

I have stated upon former occasions, and I may as well state again, what I understand to be the real issue in this controversy between Judge Douglas and myself. On the point of my wanting to make war between the free and the slave States, there has been no issue between us. So, too, when he assumes that I am in favor of introducing a perfect social and political equality between the white and black races. These are false issues, upon which Judge Douglas has tried to force the controversy. There is no foundation in truth for the charge that I maintain either of these propositions. The real issue in this controversy—the one pressing upon every mind—is the sentiment on the part of one class that looks upon the institution of slavery *as a wrong,* and of another class that *does not* look upon it as a wrong. The sentiment that contemplates the institution of slavery in this country as a wrong is the sentiment of the Republican party. It is the sentiment around which all their actions, all their arguments, circle, from which all their propositions radiate. They look upon it as being a moral, social, and political wrong; and, while they contemplate it as such, they nevertheless have due regard for its actual existence among us, and the difficulties of getting rid of it in any satisfactory way, and to all the constitutional obligations thrown about it. Yet, having a due regard for these, they desire a policy in regard to it that looks to its not creating any more danger. They insist that it should, as far as may be, *be treated* as a wrong; and one of the methods of treating it as a wrong is to *make provision that it shall grow no larger.* They also desire a policy that looks to a peaceful end of slavery at sometime, as being wrong. These are the views they entertain in regard to it as I understand them; and all their sentiments, all their arguments and propositions, are brought within this range. I have said, and I repeat it here, that if there be a man amongst us who does not think that the institution of slavery is wrong in any one of the aspects of which I have spoken, he is misplaced and ought not to be with us. And if there be a man amongst us who is so impatient of it as a wrong as to disregard its actual presence among us and the difficulty of getting rid of it suddenly in a satisfactory way, and to disregard the constitutional obligations thrown about it, that man is misplaced if he is on our platform. We disclaim sympathy with him in practical action. He is not placed properly with us.

On this subject of treating it as a wrong, and limiting its spread, let me say a word. Has anything ever threatened the existence of this Union save and except this very insti-

tution of slavery? What is it that we hold most dear
amongst us? Our own liberty and prosperity. What has ever
threatened our liberty and prosperity, save and except this
institution of slavery? If this is true, how do you propose
to improve the condition of things by enlarging slavery—
by spreading it out and making it bigger? You may have a
wen or cancer upon your person, and not be able to cut it
out, lest you bleed to death; but surely it is no way to cure
it, to engraft it and spread it over your whole body. That
is no proper way of treating what you regard a wrong. You
see this peaceful way of dealing with it as a wrong,—restricting the spread of it, and not allowing it to go into
new countries where it has not already existed. That is
the peaceful way, the old-fashioned way, the way in which
the fathers themselves set us the example.

On the other hand, I have said there is a sentiment
which treats it as *not* being wrong. This is the Democratic
sentiment of this day. I do not mean to say that every man
who stands within that range positively asserts that it is
right. That class will include all who positively assert that
it is right, and all who, like Judge Douglas, treat it as indifferent and do not say it is either right or wrong. These
two classes of men fall within the general class of those
who do not look upon it as a wrong. . . .

The Democratic policy in regard to that institution
will not tolerate the merest breath, the slightest hint, of
the least degree of wrong about it. Try it by some of Judge
Douglas' arguments. He says he "don't care whether it is
voted up or voted down" in the Territories. I do not care
myself, in dealing with that expression, whether it is intended to be expressive of his individual sentiments on the
subject or only of the national policy he desires to have
established. It is alike valuable for my purpose. Any man
can say that who does not see anything wrong in slavery;
but no man can logically say it who does see a wrong in it,
because no man can logically say he does not care whether
a wrong is voted up or voted down. He may say he does
not care whether an indifferent thing is voted up or down,
but he must logically have a choice between a right thing
and a wrong thing. He contends that whatever community
wants slaves has a right to have them. So they have, if it
is not a wrong. But if it is a wrong, he cannot say people

have a right to do wrong. He says that upon the score of equality slaves should be allowed to go in a new Territory, like other property. This is strictly logical if there is no difference between it and other property. If it and other property are equal, this argument is entirely logical. But if you insist that one is wrong and the other right, there is no use to institute a comparison between right and wrong. You may turn over everything in the Democratic policy from beginning to end, whether in the shape it takes on the statute book, in the shape it takes in the Dred Scott decision, in the shape it takes in conversation, or the shape it takes in short maxim–like arguments,—it everywhere carefully excludes the idea that there is anything wrong in it.

That is the real issue. That is the issue that will continue in this country when these poor tongues of Judge Douglas and myself shall be silent. It is the eternal struggle between these two principles—right and wrong—throughout the world. They are the two principles that have stood face to face from the beginning of time and will ever continue to struggle. The one is the common right of humanity, and the other the divine right of kings. It is the same principle in whatever shape it develops itself. It is the same spirit that says, "You work and toil and earn bread, and I'll eat it." No matter in what shape it comes, whether from the mouth of a king who seeks to bestride the people of his own nation and live by the fruit of their labor, or from one race of men as an apology for enslaving another race, it is the same tyrannical principle. . . .

✳ PART VII ✳

Secession, Civil War, and Emancipation

DURING the winter and spring of 1860 the political leaders and state legislatures of the deep South warned that if the Republicans won the coming presidential election, the South would secede. Promptly after Lincoln's election in November, on a platform which denied the authority of either Congress or any territorial legislature to legalize slavery in any territory, the South acted. The South Carolina legislature unanimously called a state convention, which met on December 17 and three days later passed an ordinance of secession, again by a unanimous vote. In her "Declaration of Causes," December 24, 1860 (Document 1), South Carolina referred to herself as a "nation," and briefly reviewed the events that had led to her action. No hope was expressed for her rejoining the Union, and no terms of reunion were suggested.

So rapid was the pace of events that seven Southern states had seceded and adopted the Confederate Constitution before Lincoln delivered his First Inaugural Address on March 4, 1861 (Document 2). In that address, Lincoln restated his conviction that secession was illegal, and reaffirmed his intention to hold federal property and to deliver mails in the Southern states. But in a conciliatory spirit he appealed to old bonds of friendship, promised that force would not be used, reassured the South that he would not interfere with slavery where it already existed, and offered to support an amendment to the Constitution specifically providing that the federal government would never interfere with slavery in the states.

But the South was in no mood to listen to conciliatory words. After the fighting at Fort Sumter in April, four border states went over to the Confederacy. In his proclamation of April 15, Lincoln declared that an "insurrection" existed and called for 75,000 volunteers; in answer, Jefferson Davis prepared a message to the Confederate Congress (Document 3) which included a forceful legal and historical justification of secession. A little over two months later, Lincoln, in a message to a special session of Congress (Document 4), set forth the interpretation of the war he continued to express throughout its course and which he restated with immortal simplicity and eloquence in the Gettysburg Address (Document 7). He maintained that the war was, in essence, defensive; that it was being waged to defend the great American experiment in constitutional democracy; and that if this defense should fail, the result would be fatal to "free government upon the earth." The war had forced upon the world a fundamental question: "Is there in all republics this inherent weakness? Must a government, of necessity, be too strong for the liberties of its own people, or too weak to maintain its own existence?" Thus, while Southern spokesmen argued that the Confederacy was upholding the principle of self-determination and self-government, Lincoln refused to state the case for the Union negatively by admitting that the Union was merely trying to prevent the departure of dissatisfied states. Instead, he gave the Union cause a positive formulation, more attractive to both Americans and foreign peoples, by suggesting that it was the very workability of republican institutions that was at stake.

At no time in the first years of the war did Lincoln say it was being waged to abolish slavery: the purpose of the war was to preserve the Union, not to destroy the institutions of the Southern states. Though he consistently argued for a plan of compensated emancipation, he opposed with equal consistency the efforts of some of his generals to use local emancipation as a war weapon against the Confederacy. But as month after month went by and casualties rose, Northern anti-slavery men began to demand that emancipation be espoused as a war aim. They insisted that slavery was the real cause of the war, and that to win the war and reconstitute the Union without destroying slavery would only be asking for further trouble with "the slave power." The most notable assertion of this point of view was Horace Greeley's "Prayer of Twenty Millions," an open letter to Lincoln dated August 19, 1862 (Document 5). Lincoln's answer was another instance of his capacity for memorably succinct expression: he was fighting only to save the Union; if he did anything about slavery he would do it only because it contributed to this end. But even while this interchange was going on, Lincoln was, in fact, changing his mind about the value of emancipation to the Union cause. Exactly a month after his answer to Greeley, he issued a proclamation giving notice that on January 1, 1863, he would declare free the slaves in those states still rebelling. On the day designated, he issued the Emancipation Proclamation (Document 6). Since the Proclamation did not free slaves under Union jurisdiction, but only those under Confederate jurisdiction whom the Union could not actually liberate, it was much criticized as having no force. But by committing the Union to emancipation, it made emancipation inevitable, and paved the way for the Thirteenth Amendment (Part II, Document 4).

Lincoln wrote his Second Inaugural Address (Document 8) after the victory of the Union cause was secure, and showed that by then he had accepted the conception of the war urged upon him in 1862 by the emancipationists. Concerning slavery he declared: "All knew that this interest was somehow the cause of the war." But neither the South nor the North, he added, "anticipated that the *cause* of the conflict might cease with or even before the conflict itself should cease." There followed a remarkable passage which expressed the conflict in his own feelings. He suggested that the war was a providential scourge inflicted on America for the wrongs of slavery. But having thus invoked the wrath of God, he closed with an appeal to human mercy, in one of the great passages in American literature.

DOCUMENT 1

SOUTH CAROLINA DECLARATION OF CAUSES OF SECESSION,

DECEMBER 24, 1860

To justify secession, the Convention of South Carolina adopted two manifestoes. The first was an Address to the People of the Slaveholding States, drawn up by Robert Barnwell Rhett; the second, this declaration, was prepared by a recent convert to secession, Christopher G. Memminger, who later became Secretary of the Treasury under the Confederacy.

The people of the State of South Carolina in Convention assembled, on the 2d day of April, A.D. 1852, declared that the frequent violations of the Constitution of the United States by the Federal Government, and its encroachments upon the reserved rights of the States, fully justified this State in their withdrawal from the Federal Union; but in deference to the opinions and wishes of the other Slaveholding States, she forbore at that time to exercise this right. Since that time these encroachments have continued to increase, and further forbearance ceases to be a virtue.

And now the State of South Carolina having resumed her separate and equal place among nations, deems it due to herself, to the remaining United States of America, and to the nations of the world, that she should declare the immediate causes which have led to this act. . . .

In 1787, Deputies were appointed by the States to revise the articles of Confederation; and on 17th September, 1787, these Deputies recommended, for the adoption of the States, the Articles of Union, known as the Constitution of the United States.

Thus was established, by compact between the States, a Government with defined objects and powers, limited to the express words of the grant. . . . We hold that the Government thus established is subject to the two great principles asserted in the Declaration of Independence; and we hold further, that the mode of its formation subjects it to a third fundamental principle, namely, the law of compact. We maintain that in every compact between two or more parties, the obligation is mutual; that the failure of one of the contracting parties to perform a material part of the agreement, entirely releases the obligation of the other; and that, where no arbiter is provided, each party is remitted to his own judgment to determine the fact of failure, with all its consequences.

In the present case, that fact is established with certainty. We assert that fourteen of the States have deliberately refused for years past to fulfil their constitutional obligations, and we refer to their own statutes for the proof.

The Constitution of the United States, in its fourth Article, provides as follows:

"No person held to service or labor in one State under the laws thereof, escaping into another, shall, in consequence of any law or regulation therein, be discharged from such service or labor, but shall be delivered up, on claim of the party to whom such service or labor may be due."

This stipulation was so material to the compact that without it that compact would not have been made. The greater number of the contracting parties held slaves, and they had previously evinced their estimate of the value of such a stipulation by making it a condition in the Ordinance for the government of the territory ceded by Virginia, which obligations, and the laws of the General Government, have ceased to effect the objects of the Constitution. The States of Maine, New Hampshire, Vermont, Massachusetts, Connecticut, Rhode Island, New York, Pennsylvania, Illinois, Indiana, Michigan, Wisconsin and Iowa, have enacted laws which either nullify the acts of Congress, or render useless any attempt to execute them. . . . Thus the constitutional compact has been deliberately broken and disregarded by the non-slaveholding States; and the consequence follows that South Carolina is released from her obligation. . . .

We affirm that these ends for which this Government was instituted have been defeated, and the Government itself has been destructive of them by the action of the non-slaveholding States. Those States have assumed the right of deciding upon the propriety of our domestic institutions; and have denied the rights of property established in fifteen of the States and recognized by the Constitution; they have denounced as sinful the institution of Slavery; they have permitted the open establishment among them of societies, whose avowed object is to disturb the peace of and eloin the property of the citizens of other States. They have encouraged and assisted thousands of our slaves to leave their homes; and those who remain, have been incited by emissaries, books, and pictures, to servile insurrection.

For twenty-five years this agitation has been steadily increasing, until it has now secured to its aid the power of the common Government. Observing the *forms* of the Constitution, a sectional party has found within that article establishing the Executive Department, the means of subverting the Constitution itself. A geographical line has been drawn across the Union, and all the States north of that line have united in the election of a man to the high office of President of the United States whose opinions and purposes are hostile to Slavery. He is to be intrusted with the administration of the common Government, because he has declared that "Government cannot endure permanently half slave, half free," and that the public mind must rest in the belief that Slavery is in the course of ultimate extinction.

This sectional combination for the subversion of the Constitution has been aided, in some of the States, by elevating to citizenship persons who, by the supreme law of the land, are incapable of becoming citizens; and their votes have been used to inaugurate a new policy, hostile to the South, and destructive of its peace and safety.

On the 4th of March next this party will take possession of the Government. It has announced that the South shall be excluded from the common territory, that the Judicial tribunal shall be made sectional, and that a war must be waged against Slavery until it shall cease throughout the United States.

The guarantees of the Constitution will then no longer exist; the equal rights of the States will be lost. The Slaveholding States will no longer have the power of self-government, or self-protection, and the Federal Government will have become their enemy.

Sectional interest and animosity will deepen the irritation; and all hope of remedy is rendered vain, by the fact that the public opinion at the North has invested a great political error with the sanctions of a more erroneous religious belief.

We, therefore, the people of South Carolina, by our delegates in Convention assembled, appealing to the Supreme Judge of the world for the rectitude of our intentions, have solemnly declared that the Union heretofore existing between this State and the other States of North America is dissolved, and that the State of South Carolina has resumed her position among the nations of the world, as a separate and independent state, with full power to levy war, conclude peace, contract alliances, establish commerce, and to do all other acts and things which independent States may of right do.

DOCUMENT 2

ABRAHAM LINCOLN, FIRST INAUGURAL ADDRESS,

MARCH 4, 1861

This address was awaited anxiously, for at the time of its delivery several states had already seceded, the crisis was acute, and thus far Lincoln had not revealed what his political strategy would be. He wrote his speech with four references before him: the Constitution, Jackson's Nullification Proclamation, Clay's speech in the Senate in February 1850, and Webster's reply to Hayne. Although Lincoln had had a copy printed before he left Springfield for Washington, only a few persons saw the draft before its delivery. One of them was Seward, the designated Secretary of State. He did not want Lincoln to keep the paragraph which announced that the new administration intended to "hold, occupy, and possess" federal property in the South Lincoln would not change this, but Seward did per-

suade him to soften an abrupt and rather harsh end-
ing, and to add the appealing final paragraph. The
contents of this last paragraph were outlined by
Seward; the words were Lincoln's.

It is seventy-two years since the first inauguration of
a President under our national Constitution. During that
period fifteen different and greatly distinguished citizens
have in succession administered the executive branch of
the government. They have conducted it through many
perils, and generally with great success. Yet, with all this
scope for precedent, I now enter upon the same task for
the brief constitutional term of four years under great and
peculiar difficulty. A disruption of the federal Union, heretofore only menaced, is now formidably attempted.

I hold that in contemplation of universal law and of
the Constitution the union of these states is perpetual.
Perpetuity is implied, if not expressed, in the fundamental
law of all national governments. It is safe to assert that no
government proper ever had a provision in its organic law
for its own termination. Continue to execute all the express
provisions of our national Constitution, and the Union
will endure forever, it being impossible to destroy it except
by some action not provided for in the instrument itself.

Again: *If* the United States be not a government
proper, but an association of states in the nature of contract merely, can it, as a contract, be peaceably unmade by
less than all the parties who made it? One party to a contract may violate it—break it, so to speak—but does it
not require all to lawfully rescind it?

Descending from these general principles, we find the
proposition that in legal contemplation the Union is perpetual confirmed by the history of the Union itself. The
Union is much older than the Constitution. It was formed,
in fact, by the Articles of Association in 1774. It was matured and continued by the Declaration of Independence
in 1776. It was further matured, and the faith of all the
then thirteen states expressly plighted and engaged that it
should be perpetual, by the Articles of Confederation in
1778. And finally, in 1787, one of the declared objects for
ordaining and establishing the Constitution was *"to form a*
more perfect Union."

But if destruction of the Union by one or by a part only of the states be lawfully possible, the Union is *less* perfect than before the Constitution, having lost the vital element of perpetuity.

It follows from these views that no state upon its own mere motion can lawfully get out of the Union; that *resolves* and *ordinances* to that effect are legally void, and that acts of violence within any state or states against the authority of the United States are insurrectionary or revolutionary, according to circumstances.

I therefore consider that in view of the Constitution and the laws the Union is unbroken, and to the extent of my ability I shall take care, as the Constitution itself expressly enjoins upon me, that the laws of the Union be faithfully executed in all the states. Doing this I deem to be only a simple duty on my part; and I shall perform it so far as practicable unless my rightful masters, the American people, shall withhold the requisite means or in some authoritative manner direct the contrary. I trust this will not be regarded as a menace, but only as the declared purpose of the Union that it *will* constitutionally defend and maintain itself.

In doing this, there needs to be no bloodshed or violence, and there shall be none unless it be forced upon the national authority. The power confided to me will be used to hold, occupy, and possess the property and places belonging to the government and to collect the duties and imposts; but, beyond what may be necessary for these objects, there will be no invasion, no using of force against or among the people anywhere. Where hostility to the United States in any interior locality, shall be so great and so universal as to prevent competent resident citizens from holding the federal offices, there will be no attempt to force obnoxious strangers among the people for that object. While the strict legal right may exist in the government to enforce the exercise of these offices, the attempt to do so would be so irritating and so nearly impracticable withal, that I deem it better to forego for the time the uses of such offices.

The mails, unless repelled, will continue to be furnished in all parts of the Union. So far as possible the people everywhere shall have that sense of perfect security which is most favorable to calm thought and reflection. The course here indicated will be followed unless current events and experience shall show a modification or change to be proper, and in every case and exigency my best discretion will be exercised, according to circumstances actually existing and with a view and a hope of a peaceful solution of the national troubles and the restoration of fraternal sympathies and affections.

That there are persons in one section or another who seek to destroy the Union at all events and are glad of any pretext to do it I will neither affirm nor deny; but if there be such, I need address no word to them. To those, however, who really love the Union may I not speak?

Before entering upon so grave a matter as the destruction of our national fabric, with all its benefits, its memories, and its hopes, would it not be wise to ascertain precisely why we do it? Will you hazard so desperate a step while there is any possibility that any portion of the ills you fly from have no real existence? Will you, while the certain ills you fly to are greater than all the real ones you fly from, will you risk the commission of so fearful a mistake?

All profess to be content in the Union if all constitutional rights can be maintained. Is it true, then, that any right plainly written in the Constitution has been denied? I think not. Happily, the human mind is so constituted that no party can reach to the audacity of doing this. Think, if you can, of a single instance in which a plainly written provision of the Constitution has ever been denied. If by the mere force of numbers a majority should deprive a minority of any clearly written constitutional right, it might in a moral point of view justify revolution; certainly would if such right were a vital one. But such is not our case. All the vital rights of minorities and of individuals are so plainly assured to them by affirmations and negations, guaranties and prohibitions, in the Constitution that controversies never arise concerning them. But no organic law can ever be framed with a provision specifically applicable to every question which may occur in practical administration. No foresight can anticipate nor any document of reasonable length contain express provisions for all possible questions. Shall fugitives from labor be surrendered by national or by state authority? The Constitution does not expressly say. *May* Congress prohibit slavery in the territories? The Constitution does not expressly say. *Must* Congress protect slavery in the territories? The Constitution does not expressly say.

From questions of this class spring all our constitutional controversies, and we divide upon them into majorities and minorities. If the minority will not acquiesce, the majority must, or the government must cease. There is no other alternative, for continuing the government is acquiescence on one side or the other. If a minority in such case will secede rather than acquiesce, they make a precedent which in turn will divide and ruin them, for a minority of their own will secede from them whenever a majority refuses to be controlled by such minority. For instance, why may not any portion of a new confederacy a year or two hence arbitrarily secede again, precisely as portions of the present Union now claim to secede from it? All who cherish disunion sentiments are now being educated to the exact temper of doing this.

Is there such perfect identity of interests among the states to compose a new union as to produce harmony only and prevent renewed secession?

Plainly the central idea of secession is the essence of anarchy. A majority held in restraint by constitutional checks and limitations, and always changing easily with deliberate changes of popular opinions and sentiments, is the only true sovereign of a free people. Whoever rejects it does of necessity fly to anarchy or to despotism. Unanimity is impossible. The rule of a minority, as a permanent arrangement, is wholly inadmissible; so that, rejecting the majority principle, anarchy, or despotism in some form is all that is left.

I do not forget the position assumed by some that constitutional questions are to be decided by the Supreme Court, nor do I deny that such decisions must be binding in any case upon the parties to a suit as to the object of that suit, while they are also entitled to very high respect and consideration in all parallel cases by all other departments of the government. And while it is obviously possible that such decision may be erroneous in any given case, still the evil effect following it, being limited to that particular case, with the chance that it may be overruled and never become a precedent for other cases, can better be borne than could the evils of a different practice. At the same time, the candid citizen must confess that if the policy of the government upon vital questions affecting the whole people is to be irrevocably fixed by decisions of the Supreme Court, the instant they are made in ordinary litigation between parties in personal actions the people will have ceased to be their own rulers, having to that extent practically resigned their government into the hands of that eminent tribunal. Nor is there in this view any assault upon the Court or the judges. It is a duty from which they may not shrink to decide cases properly brought before them, and it is no fault of theirs if others seek to turn their decisions to political purposes.

One section of our country believes slavery is *right* and ought to be extended, while the other believes it is *wrong* and ought not to be extended. This is the only substantial dispute. The fugitive-slave clause of the Constitution and the law for the suppression of the foreign slave trade are each as well enforced, perhaps, as any law can ever be in a community where the moral sense of the people imperfectly supports the law itself. The great body of the people abide by the dry legal obligation in both cases, and a few break over in each. This, I think, cannot be perfectly cured, and it would be worse in both cases *after* the separation of the sections than before. The foreign slave trade, now imperfectly suppressed, would be ultimately revived without restriction in one section, while fugitive slaves, now only partially surrendered, would not be surrendered at all by the other.

Physically speaking, we cannot separate. We cannot remove our respective sections from each other nor build an impassable wall between them. A husband and wife may be divorced and go out of the presence and beyond the reach of each other, but the different parts of our country cannot do this. They cannot but remain face to face, and intercourse, either amicable or hostile, must continue between them. Is it possible, then, to make that intercourse more advantageous or more satisfactory *after* separation than *before*? Can aliens make treaties easier than friends can make laws? Can treaties be more faithfully enforced between aliens than laws can among friends? Suppose you go to war, you cannot fight always; and when, after much loss on both sides and no gain on either, you cease fighting, the identical old questions, as to terms of intercourse, are again upon you.

This country, with its institutions, belongs to the people who inhabit it. Whenever they shall grow weary of the existing government, they can exercise their *constitutional* right of amending it or their *revolutionary* right to dismember or overthrow it. I cannot be ignorant of the fact that many worthy and patriotic citizens are desirous of having the national Constitution amended. While I make no recommendation of amendments, I fully recognize the rightful authority of the people over the whole subject, to be exercised in either of the modes prescribed in the instrument itself; and I should, under existing circumstances, favor rather than oppose a fair opportunity being afforded the people to act upon it. I will venture to add that to me the convention mode seems preferable, in that it allows amendments to originate with the people themselves, instead of only permitting them to take or reject propositions originated by others, not especially chosen for the purpose, and which might not be precisely such as they would wish to either accept or refuse. I understand a proposed amendment to the Constitution—which amendment, however, I have not seen—has passed Congress, to the effect that the federal government shall never interfere with the domestic institutions of the states, including that of persons held to service. To avoid misconstruction of what I have said, I depart from my purpose not to speak of particular amendments so far as to say that, holding such a provision to now be implied constitutional law, I have no objection to its being made express and irrevocable.

The Chief Magistrate derives all his authority from the people, and they have conferred none upon him to fix terms for the separation of the states. The people themselves can do this also if they choose, but the Executive as such has nothing to do with it. His duty is to administer the present government as it came to his hands and to transmit it unimpaired by him to his successor.

Why should there not be a patient confidence in the ultimate justice of the people? Is there any better or equal hope in the world? In our present differences, is either party without faith of being in the right? If the Almighty Ruler of Nations, with His eternal truth and justice, be on your side of the North, or on yours of the South, that truth and that justice will surely prevail by the judgment of this great tribunal of the American people.

By the frame of the government under which we live this same people have wisely given their public servants but little power for mischief and have with equal wisdom provided for the return of that little to their own hands at very short intervals. While the people retain their virtue and vigilance no administration by any extreme of wickedness or folly can very seriously injure the government in the short space of four years.

My countrymen, one and all, think calmly and *well* upon this whole subject. Nothing valuable can be lost by taking time. If there be an object to *hurry* any of you in hot haste to a step which you would never take *deliberately*, that object will be frustrated by taking time; but no good object can be frustrated by it. Such of you as are now dissatisfied still have the old Constitution unimpaired, and, on the sensitive point, the laws of your own framing under it; while the new administration will have no immediate power, if it would, to change either. If it were admitted that you who are dissatisfied hold the right side in the dispute, there still is no single good reason for precipitate action. Intelligence, patriotism, Christianity, and a firm reliance on Him who has never yet forsaken this favored land are still competent to adjust in the best way all our present difficulty.

In *your* hands, my dissatisfied fellow-countrymen, and not in *mine*, is the momentous issue of civil war. The government will not assail *you*. You can have no conflict without being yourselves the aggressors. *You* have no oath registered in heaven to destroy the government, while *I* shall have the most solemn one to "preserve, protect, and defend it."

I am loath to close. We are not enemies, but friends. We must not be enemies. Though passion may have strained, it must not break our bonds of affection. The mystic chords of memory, stretching from every battlefield and patriot grave to every living heart and hearthstone all over this broad land, will yet swell the chorus of the Union, when again touched, as surely they will be, by the better angels of our nature.

DOCUMENT 3

JEFFERSON DAVIS, MESSAGE TO THE CONFEDERATE CONGRESS,
APRIL 29, 1861

Regular elections were not held in the Confederacy until November 1861. Jefferson Davis was provisionally elected President February 1861, and the Montgomery Convention that formed the Confederate Constitution acted as a provisional Congress. Soon after Lincoln's call for Northern volunteers, Davis sent this well-argued statement of the Southern case to the provisional Congress of the Confederacy.

Gentlemen of the Congress. . . .

The declaration of war made against this Confederacy by Abraham Lincoln, the President of the United States, in his proclamation issued on the 15th day of the present month, rendered it necessary, in my judgment, that you should convene at the earliest practicable moment to devise the measures necessary for the defense of the country. The occasion is indeed an extraordinary one. It justifies me in a brief review of the relations heretofore existing between us and the States which now unite in warfare against us and in a succinct statement of the events which have resulted in this warfare, to the end that mankind may pass intelligent and impartial judgment on its motives and objects. . . . [Davis here surveyed those clauses in the Articles of Confederation and the Constitution which indicated that they were compacts in which the states retained sovereignty.]

Strange, indeed, must it appear to the impartial observer, but it is none the less true that all these carefully worded clauses proved unavailing to prevent the rise and growth in the Northern States of a political school which has persistently claimed that the government thus formed was not a compact *between* States, but was in effect a national government, set up *above* and *over* the States. An organization created by the States to secure the blessings of liberty and independence against *foreign* aggression, has been gradually perverted into a machine for their control in their *domestic* affairs. The *creature* has been exalted above its *creators*; the *principals* have been made subordinate to the *agent* appointed by themselves. The people of the Southern States, whose almost exclusive occupation was agriculture, early perceived a tendency in the Northern States to render the common government subservient to their own purposes by imposing burdens on commerce as a protection to their manufacturing and shipping interests. . . . By degrees, as the Northern States gained preponderance in the National Congress, self-interest taught their people to yield ready assent to any plausible advocacy of their right as a majority to govern the minority without control. They learned to listen with impatience to the suggestion of any constitutional impediment to the exercise of their will, and so utterly have the principles of the Constitution been corrupted in the Northern mind that, in the inaugural address delivered by President Lincoln in March last, he asserts as an axiom, which he plainly deems to be undeniable, that the theory of the Constitution requires that in all cases the majority shall govern; . . . This is the lamentable and fundamental error on which rests the policy that has culminated in his declaration of war against these Confederate States. In addition to the long-continued and deep-seated resentment felt by the Southern States at the persistent abuse of the powers they had delegated to the Congress, for the purpose of enriching the manufacturing and shipping classes of the North at the expense of the South, there has existed for nearly half a century another subject of discord, involving interests, of such transcendent magnitude as at all times to create the apprehension in the minds of many devoted lovers of the Union that its permanence was impossible. When the several States delegated certain powers to the United States Congress, a large portion of the laboring population consisted of African slaves imported into the colonies by the mother country. In twelve out of the thirteen States negro slavery existed, and the right of property in slaves was protected by law. This property was recognized in the Constitution, and provision was made against its loss by the escape of the slave. The increase in the number of slaves by further importation from Africa was also secured by a clause forbidding Congress to prohibit the slave trade anterior to a certain date, and in no clause can there be found any delegation of power to the Congress authorizing it in any manner to legislate to the prejudice, detriment, or discouragement of the owners of that species of property, or excluding it from the protection of the Government.

The climate and soil of the Northern States soon proved unpropitious to the continuance of slave labor, whilst the converse was the case at the South. Under the unrestricted free intercourse between the two sections, the Northern States consulted their own interest by selling their slaves to the South and prohibiting slavery within their limits. The South were willing purchasers of property suitable to their wants, and paid the price of the acquisition without harboring a suspicion that their quiet possession was to be disturbed by those who were inhibited not only by want of constitutional authority, but by good faith as vendors, from disquieting a title emanating from themselves. As soon, however, as the Northern States that prohibited African slavery within their limits had reached a number sufficient to give their representation a controlling voice in the Congress, a persistent and organized system of hostile measures against the rights of the owners of slaves in the Southern States was inaugurated and gradually extended. A continuous series of measures was devised and prosecuted for the purpose of rendering insecure the tenure of property in slaves. . . . Emboldened by success, the theatre of agitation and aggression against the clearly expressed constitutional rights of the Southern States was transferred to the Congress; Senators and Representatives were sent to the common councils of the nation, whose chief title to this distinction consisted in the display of a spirit of ultra-fanaticism, and whose business was not "to promote the general welfare or insure domestic tranquillity," but to awaken the bitterest hatred against the citizens of sister States, by violent denunciation of their institutions; the transaction of public affairs was impeded by repeated effort to usurp powers not delegated by the Constitution, for the purpose of impairing the security of property in slaves, and reducing those States which held slaves to a condition of inferiority. Finally a great party was organized for the purpose of obtaining the administration of the Government, with the avowed object of using its power for the total exclusion of the slave States from all participation in the benefits of the public domain acquired by all the States in common, whether by conquest or purchase; of surrounding them entirely by States in which slavery should be prohibited; of thus rendering the property in slaves so insecure as to be comparatively worthless, and thereby annihilating in effect property worth thousands of millions of dollars. This party, thus organized, succeeded in the month of November last in the election of its candidate for the Presidency of the United States.

In the meantime, under the mild and genial climate of the Southern States and the increasing care and attention for the well-being and comfort of the laboring classes, dictated alike by interest and humanity, the African slaves had augmented in number from about 600,000, at the date of the adoption of the constitutional compact, to upward of 4,000,000. In moral and social condition they had been elevated from brutal savages into docile, intelligent, and civilized agricultural laborers, and supplied not only with bodily comforts but with careful religious instruction. Under the supervision of a superior race their labor had been so directed as not only to allow a gradual and marked amelioration of their own condition, but to convert hundreds of thousands of square miles of the wilderness into cultivated lands covered with a prosperous people; towns and cities had sprung into existence, and had rapidly increased in wealth and population under the social system of the South; the white population of the Southern slaveholding States had augmented from about 1,250,000 at the date of the adoption of the Constitution to more than 8,500,000, in 1860; and the productions in the South of cotton, rice, sugar, and tobacco, for the full development and continuance of which the labor of African slaves was and is indispensable, had swollen to an amount which formed nearly three-fourths of the exports of the whole United States and had become absolutely necessary to the wants of civilized man. With interests of such overwhelming magnitude imperiled, the people of the Southern States were driven by the conduct of the North to the adoption of some course of action to avert the danger with which they were openly menaced. With this view the Legislatures of the several States invited the people to select delegates to conventions to be held for the purpose of determining for themselves what measures were best adapted to meet so alarming a crisis in their history. Here it may be proper to observe that from a period as early as 1798 there had existed in *all* of the States of the Union a party almost uninterruptedly in the majority based upon the creed that each State was, in the last resort, the sole judge as well of its wrongs as of the mode and measure of redress. . . .

In the exercise of a right so ancient, so well-established, and so necessary for self-preservation, the people of the Confederate States, in their conventions, determined that the wrongs which they had suffered and the evils with which they were menaced required that they should revoke the delegation of powers to the Federal Government which they had ratified in their several conventions. They consequently passed ordinances resuming all their rights as sovereign and independent States and dissolved their connection with the other States of the Union.

Having done this, they proceeded to form a new compact amongst themselves by new articles of confederation, which have been also ratified by the conventions of the several States with an approach to unanimity far exceeding that of the conventions which adopted the Constitution of 1787. They have organized their new Government in all its departments; the functions of the executive, legislative, and judicial magistrates are performed in accordance with the will of the people, as displayed not merely in a cheerful acquiescence, but in the enthusiastic support of the Government thus established by themselves; and but for the interference of the Government of the United States in this legitimate exercise of the right of a people to self-government, peace, happiness, and prosperity would now smile on our land. . . .

DOCUMENT 4

ABRAHAM LINCOLN, MESSAGE TO CONGRESS, JULY 4, 1861

This message to a special session of Congress was a major statement of Lincoln's policies and views, and he revised it with great care, accepting some changes suggested by Secretary of State Seward.

At the beginning of the present Presidential term, four months ago, the functions of the Federal Government were found to be generally suspended within the several States of South Carolina, Georgia, Alabama, Mississippi, Louisiana, and Florida, excepting only those of the Post-office Department. . . .

The purpose to sever the Federal Union was openly avowed. In accordance with this purpose, an ordinance had been adopted in each of these States, declaring the States respectively to be separated from the national Union. A formula for instituting a combined government of these States had been promulgated; and this illegal organization, in the character of confederate States, was already invoking recognition, aid, and intervention from foreign powers. . . .

And this issue embraces more than the fate of these United States. It presents to the whole family of man the question whether a constitutional republic or democracy—a government of the people by the same people—can or cannot maintain its territorial integrity against its own domestic foes. It presents the question whether discontented individuals, too few in number to control administration according to organic law in any case, can always, upon the pretenses made in this case, or on any other pretenses, or arbitrarily without any pretense, break up their government, and thus practically put an end to free government upon the earth. It forces us to ask: Is there in all republics this inherent and fatal weakness? Must a government, of necessity, be too *strong* for the liberties of its own people, or too *weak* to maintain its own existence?

So viewing the issue, no choice was left but to call out the war power of the government, and so to resist force employed for its destruction by force for its preservation. . . .

The forbearance of this government had been so extraordinary and so long continued as to lead some foreign nations to shape their action as if they supposed the early destruction of our national Union was probable. While this, on discovery, gave the executive some concern, he is now happy to say that the sovereignty and rights of the United States are now everywhere practically respected by foreign powers; and a general sympathy with the country is manifested throughout the world. . . .

It might seem, at first thought, to be of little difference whether the present movement at the South be called "secession" or "rebellion." The movers, however, well understand the difference. At the beginning they knew they could never raise their treason to any respectable magnitude by any name which implies *violation* of law. They knew their people possessed as much of moral sense, as much of devotion to law and order, and as much pride in and reverence for the history and government of their common country as any other civilized and patriotic people. They knew they could make no advancement directly in the teeth of these strong and noble sentiments. Accordingly, they commenced by an insidious debauching of the public mind. They invented an ingenious sophism which, if conceeded, was followed by perfectly logical steps, through all the incidents, to the complete destruction of the Union. The sophism itself is that any State of the Union may *consistently* with the national Constitution, and therefore lawfully and peacefully, withdraw from the Union without the consent of the Union or of any other State. . . .

This sophism derives much, perhaps the whole, of its currency from the assumption that there is some omnipotent and sacred supremacy pertaining to a State—to each State of our Federal Union. Our States have neither more nor less power than that reserved to them in the Union by the Constitution—no one of them ever having been a State out of the Union. The original ones passed into the Union even before they cast off their British colonial dependence; and the new ones each came into the Union directly from a condition of dependence, excepting Texas. And even Texas in its temporary independence was never designated a State. The new ones only took the designation of States on coming into the Union, while that name was first adopted for the old ones in and by the Declaration of Independence. . . . Having never been States either in substance or in name outside of the Union, whence this magical omnipotence of "State rights," asserting a claim of power to lawfully destroy the Union itself? Much is said about the "sovereignty" of the States; but the word even is not in the national Constitution, nor, as is believed, in any of the State constitutions. What is "sovereignty" in the political sense of the term? Would it be far wrong to define it as "a political community without a political superior"? Tested by this, no one of our States except Texas ever was a sovereignty. . . . The States have their status in the Union, and they have no other legal status. If they break from this, they can only do so against law and by revolution. The Union, and not themselves separately, procured their independence and their liberty. By conquest or purchase the Union gave each of them whatever of independence or liberty it has. The Union is older than any of the States, and, in fact, it created them as States. Originally some dependent colonies made the Union, and, in turn, the Union threw off their old dependence for them, and made them States, such as they are. Not one of them ever had a State constitution independent of the Union. Of course, it is not forgotten that all the new States framed their constitutions before they entered the Union—nevertheless, dependent upon and preparatory to coming into the Union. . . .

What is now combated is the position that secession is consistent with the Constitution—is lawful and peaceful. It is not contended that there is any express law for it; and nothing should ever be implied as law which leads to unjust or absurd consequences. . . .

The seceders insist that our Constitution admits of secession. They have assumed to make a national constitution of their own, in which of necessity they have either discarded or retained the right of secession as they insist it exists in ours. If they have discarded it, they thereby admit that on principle it ought not to be in ours. If they have retained it, by their own construction of ours, they show that to be consistent they must secede from one another whenever they shall find it the easiest way of settling their debts, or effecting any other selfish or unjust object. The principle itself is one of disintegration and upon which no government can possibly endure. . . .

It may well be questioned whether there is to-day a majority of the legally qualified voters of any State except perhaps South Carolina in favor of disunion. There is much reason to believe that the Union men are the majority in many, if not in every other one, of the so-called seceded States. . . .

This is essentially a people's contest. On the side of the Union it is a struggle for maintaining in the world that form and substance of government whose leading object is to elevate the condition of men—to lift artificial weights from all shoulders; to clear the paths of laudable pursuit for all; to afford all an unfettered start, and a fair chance in the race of life. Yielding to partial and temporary departures, from necessity, this is the leading object of the government for whose existence we contend. . . .

Our popular government has often been called an experiment. Two points in it our people have already settled—the successful establishing and the successful administering of it. One still remains—its successful maintenance against a formidable internal attempt to overthrow it. It is now for them to demonstrate to the world that those who can fairly carry an election can also suppress a rebellion; that ballots are the rightful and peaceful successors of bullets; and that when ballots have fairly and constitutionally decided, there can be no successful appeal back to bullets; that there can be no successful appeal, except to ballots themselves, at succeeding elections. Such will be a great lesson of peace: teaching men that what they cannot take by an election, neither can they take it by war; teaching all the folly of being the beginners of a war. . . .

DOCUMENT 5

HORACE GREELEY AND ABRAHAM LINCOLN ON EMANCIPATION,
AUGUST 19 AND 22, 1862

At the beginning of the secession crisis, Horace Greeley, in his immensely influential New York Tribune, had advocated letting the Southern states leave the Union in peace. But once the war broke out, he quickly threw his support to the radical anti-slavery men who were impatient with Lincoln's policy of conciliating the border states and holding back on emancipation. By the summer of 1862 Greeley's impatience had reached such a point that he felt impelled to give Lincoln a public scolding in this open letter. Lincoln, who had already decided to proclaim emancipation at what he regarded as an appropriate moment, was eager to hold the support of a publicist as widely read as Greeley—although Greeley's claim that he spoke for "twenty millions" was a gross exaggeration. Lincoln's answer to Greeley, which was universally reprinted, was an effective piece of propaganda, and it strengthened his position among conservatives. Greeley printed Lincoln's reply in the Tribune along with a lengthy answer of his own. Emancipation did not placate him. In 1864 he opposed the renomination of Lincoln, saying "we must have another ticket to save us from utter overthrow," but in September he rather belatedly gave the President his support.

THE PRAYER OF TWENTY MILLIONS

To Abraham Lincoln, President of the United States:
    DEAR SIR: I do not intrude to tell you—for you must know already—that a great proportion of those who triumphed in your election, and of all who desire the unqualified suppression of the rebellion now desolating our country, are sorely disappointed and deeply pained by the policy you seem to be pursuing with regard to the slaves

of rebels. I write only to set succinctly and unmistakably before you what we require, what we think we have a right to expect, and of what we complain.

I. We require of you, as the first servant of the Republic, charged especially and preeminently with this duty, that you EXECUTE THE LAWS. . . .

II. We think you are strangely and disastrously remiss in the discharge of your official and imperative duty with regard to the emancipating provisions of the new Confiscation Act. Those provisions were designed to fight Slavery with Liberty. They prescribe that men loyal to the Union, and willing to shed their blood in her behalf, shall no longer be held, with the nation's consent, in bondage to persistent, malignant traitors, who for twenty years have been plotting and for sixteen months have been fighting to divide and destroy our country. Why these traitors should be treated with tenderness by you, to the prejudice of the dearest rights of loyal men, we cannot conceive.

III. We think you are unduly influenced by the councils, the representations, the menaces, of certain fossil politicians hailing from the Border Slave States. Knowing well that the heartily, unconditionally loyal portion of the white citizens of those States do not expect nor desire that Slavery shall be upheld to the prejudice of the Union—(for the truth of which we appeal not only to every Republican residing in those States, but to such eminent loyalists as H. Winter Davis, Parson Brownlow, the Union Central Committee of Baltimore, and to *The Nashville Union*)—we ask you to consider that Slavery is everywhere the inciting cause and sustaining base of treason: the most slave-holding sections of Maryland and Delaware being this day, though under the Union flag, in full sympathy with the rebellion, while the free labor portions of Tennessee and of Texas, though writhing under the bloody heel of treason, are unconquerably loyal to the Union. . . . It seems to us the most obvious truth, that whatever strengthens or fortifies Slavery in the Border States strengthens also treason, and drives home the wedge intended to divide the Union. Had you, from the first, refused to recognize in those States, as here, any other than unconditional loyalty—that which stands for the Union, whatever may become of Slavery—those States would have been, and would be, far more helpful and less troublesome to the defenders of the Union than they have been, or now are.

IV. We think timid counsels in such a crisis calculated to prove perilous, and probably disastrous. It is the duty of a Government so wantonly, wickedly assailed by rebellion as ours has been, to oppose force to force in a defiant, dauntless spirit. It cannot afford to temporize with traitors, nor with semi-traitors. It must not bribe them to behave themselves, nor make them fair promises in the hope of disarming their causeless hostility. Representing a brave and high-spirited people, it can afford to forfeit any thing else better than its own self-respect, or their admiring confidence. For our Government even to seek, after war has been made on it, to dispel the affected apprehensions of armed traitors that their cherished privileges may be assailed by it, is to invite insult and encourage hopes of its own downfall. The rush to arms of Ohio, Indiana, Illinois, is the true answer at once to the rebel raids of John Morgan and the traitorous sophistries of Beriah Magoffin.

V. We complain that the Union cause has suffered, and is now suffering immensely, from mistaken deference to rebel Slavery. Had you, sir, in your Inaugural Address, unmistakably given notice that, in case the rebellion already commenced, were persisted in, and your efforts to preserve the Union and enforce the laws should be resisted by armed force, *you would recognize no loyal person as rightfully held in Slavery by a traitor,* we believe the rebellion would therein have received a staggering if not fatal blow. At that moment, according to the returns of the most recent elections, the Unionists were a large majority of the voters of the slave States. But they were composed in good part of the aged, the feeble, the wealthy, the timid —the young, the reckless, the aspiring, the adventurous, had already been largely lured by the gamblers and negro-traders, the politicians by trade and the conspirators by instinct, into the toils of treason. Had you then proclaimed that rebellion would strike the shackles from the slaves of every traitor, the wealthy and the cautious would have been supplied with a powerful inducement to remain loyal. . . .

VI. We complain that the Confiscation Act which you approved is habitually disregarded by your Generals, and that no word of rebuke for them from you has yet reached the public ear. Frémont's Proclamation and Hunter's Order favoring Emancipation were promptly annulled by you; while Halleck's Number Three, forbidding fugitives from slavery to rebels to come within his lines—an order as unmilitary as inhuman, and which received the hearty approbation of every traitor in America—with scores of like tendency, have never provoked even your remonstrance. . . . And finally, we complain that you, Mr. President, elected as a Republican, knowing well what an abomination Slavery is, and how emphatically it is the core and essence of this atrocious rebellion, seem never to interfere with these atrocities, and never give a direction to your military subordinates, which does not appear to have been conceived in the interest of Slavery rather than of Freedom. . . .

VIII. On the face of this wide earth, Mr. President, there is not one disinterested, determined, intelligent champion of the Union cause who does not feel that all attempts to put down the rebellion and at the same time uphold its inciting cause are preposterous and futile—that the rebellion, if crushed out to-morrow, would be renewed within a year if Slavery were left in full vigor—that army officers who remain to this day devoted to Slavery can at best be but half-way loyal to the Union—and that every hour of deference to Slavery is an hour of added and deepened peril to the Union. I appeal to the testimony of your ambassadors in Europe. It is freely at your service, not at mine. Ask them to tell you candidly whether the seeming subserviency of your policy to the slaveholding, slavery-upholding interest, is not the perplexity, the despair of statesmen of all parties, and be admonished by the general answer!

IX. I close as I began with the statement that what an immense majority of the loyal millions of your countrymen require of you is a frank, declared, unqualified, ungrudging execution of the laws of the land, more especially of the Confiscation Act. That act gives freedom to the slaves of rebels coming within our lines, or whom those lines may at any time inclose—we ask you to render it due obedience by publicly requiring all your subordinates to recognize and obey it. The rebels are everywhere using the late anti-negro

riots in the North, as they have long used your officers'
treatment of negroes in the South, to convince the slaves
that they have nothing to hope from a Union success—
that we mean in that case to sell them into a bitter bondage to defray the cost of the war. Let them impress this as
a truth on the great mass of their ignorant and credulous
bondmen, and the Union will never be restored—never.
We cannot conquer ten millions of people united in solid
phalanx against us, powerfully aided by Northern sympathizers and European allies. We must have scouts,
guides, spies, cooks, teamsters, diggers, and choppers from
the blacks of the South, whether we allow them to fight
for us or not, or we shall be baffled and repelled. As one of
the millions who would gladly have avoided this struggle
at any sacrifice but that of principle and honor, but who
now feel that the triumph of the Union is indispensable not
only to the existence of our country but to the well-being
of mankind, I entreat you to render a hearty and unequivocal obedience to the law of the land.

Yours,

HORACE GREELEY.

Washington, August 22, 1862.

Hon. Horace Greeley:

DEAR SIR: I have just read yours of the nineteenth,
addressed to myself through the New-York *Tribune*. If
there be in it any statements or assumptions of fact which
I may know to be erroneous, I do not now and here controvert them. If there be in it any inferences which I may
believe to be falsely drawn, I do not now and here argue
against them. If there be perceptible in it an impatient and
dictatorial tone, I waive it in deference to an old friend,
whose heart I have always supposed to be right.

As to the policy I "seem to be pursuing," as you say,
I have not meant to leave any one in doubt.

I would save the Union. I would save it the shortest
way under the Constitution. The sooner the National authority can be restored, the nearer the Union will be "the
Union as it was." If there be those who would not save
the Union unless they could at the same time *save* Slavery,
I do not agree with them. If there be those who would not
save the Union unless they could at the same time *destroy*

Slavery, I do not agree with them. My paramount object in this struggle *is* to save the Union, and is *not* either to save or destroy Slavery. If I could save the Union without freeing *any* slave, I would do it; and if I could save it by freeing *all* the slaves, I would do it; and if I could do it by freeing some and leaving others alone, I would also do that. What I do about Slavery and the colored race, I do because I believe it helps to save this Union; and what I forbear, I forbear because I do *not* believe it would help to save the Union. I shall do *less* whenever I shall believe what I am doing hurts the cause, and I shall do *more* whenever I shall believe doing more will help the cause. I shall try to correct errors when shown to be errors; and I shall adopt new views so fast as they shall appear to be true views. I have here stated my purpose according to my view of *official* duty, and I intend no modification of my oft-expressed *personal* wish that all men, everywhere, could be free.

> Yours,
> A. LINCOLN.

DOCUMENT 6

ABRAHAM LINCOLN, THE EMANCIPATION PROCLAMATION,
JANUARY 1, 1863

On the day it was issued, Lincoln was still working on the Emancipation Proclamation; he was not satisfied until he had consulted with the members of his Cabinet and carefully considered their suggestions for revision. In writing the final copy, he lavished ceremonial care on his penmanship. "I know very well," he said to Charles Sumner, "that the name connected with this document will never be forgotten."

Whereas, on the twenty-second day of September, in the year of our Lord one thousand eight hundred and sixty-two, a proclamation was issued by the President of the

United States, containing, among other things, the following, to wit:

"That on the first day of January, in the year of our Lord one thousand eight hundred and sixty-three, all persons held as slaves within any state or designated part of a state, the people whereof shall then be in rebellion against the United States, shall be then, thenceforward, and forever, free; and the Executive Government of the United States, including the military and naval authority thereof, will recognize and maintain the freedom of such persons, and will do no act or acts to repress such persons, or any of them, in any efforts they may make for their actual freedom.

"That the Executive will, on the first day of January aforesaid, by proclamation, designate the states and parts of states, if any, in which the people thereof, respectively, shall then be in rebellion against the United States; and the fact that any state, or the people thereof, shall on that day be in good faith represented in the Congress of the United States, by members chosen thereto at elections wherein a majority of the qualified voters of such states shall have participated, shall, in the absence of strong countervailing testimony, be deemed conclusive evidence that such state, and the people thereof, are not then in rebellion against the United States."

Now, therefore, I, Abraham Lincoln, President of the United States, by virtue of the power in me vested as commander-in-chief of the army and navy of the United States, in time of actual armed rebellion against the authority and government of the United States, and as a fit and necessary war measure for suppressing said rebellion, do, on this first day of January, in the year of our Lord one thousand eight hundred and sixty-three, and in accordance with my purpose so to do, publicly proclaimed for the full period of one hundred days from the day first above mentioned, order and designate as the states and parts of states wherein the people thereof, respectively, are this day in rebellion against the United States, the following, to wit:

Arkansas, Texas, Louisiana (except the parishes of St. Bernard, Plaquemines, Jefferson, St. Johns, St. Charles, St. James, Ascension, Assumption, Terre Bonne, Lafourche,

St. Mary, St. Martin, and Orleans, including the city of New Orleans), Mississippi, Alabama, Florida, Georgia, South Carolina, North Carolina, and Virginia (except the forty-eight counties designated as West Virginia, and also the counties of Berkeley, Accomac, Northampton, Elizabeth City, York, Princess Ann, and Norfolk, including the cities of Norfolk and Porstmouth) and which excepted parts are for the present left precisely as if this proclamation were not issued.

And by virtue of the power and for the purpose aforesaid, I do order and declare that all persons held as slaves within said designated states and parts of states are, and henceforward shall be, free; and that the Executive Government of the United States, including the military and naval authorities thereof, will recognize and maintain the freedom of said persons.

And I hereby enjoin upon the people so declared to be free to abstain from all violence, unless in necessary self-defense; and I recommend to them that, all cases when allowed, they labor faithfully for reasonable wages.

And I further declare and make known that such persons, of suitable condition, will be received into the armed service of the United States to garrison forts, positions, stations, and other places, and to man vessels of all sorts in said service.

And upon this act, sincerely believed to be an act of justice, warranted by the Constitution upon military necessity, I invoke the considerate judgment of mankind and the gracious favor of Almighty God.

In witness whereof, I have hereunto set my hand and caused the seal of the United States to be affixed.

Done at the city of Washington this first day of January, in the year of our Lord one thousand eight hundred and sixty-three, and of the Independence of the United States of America the eighty-seventh.

DOCUMENT 7

ABRAHAM LINCOLN, GETTYSBURG ADDRESS,
NOVEMBER 19, 1863

Edward Everett of Massachusetts, considered by many to be the greatest American orator of his day, was invited to give the main address at the dedication of the Gettysburg National Cemetery. Lincoln, though invited to be present, was not asked to speak, partly because, despite his acknowledged distinction as a political orator, it was felt that he was not adequate to this solemn commemorative occasion. Two weeks before the dedication, however, almost as an after-thought, those in charge of the ceremonies asked Lincoln to follow Everett with "a few appropriate remarks." About the occasion itself, Lincoln's Secretary, John Hay, wrote in his diary: ". . . Mr. Everett spoke as he always does, perfectly—and the President, in a fine, free way, with more grace than is his wont, said his half-dozen words of consecration. . . ."

Fourscore and seven years ago our fathers brought forth on this continent a new nation, conceived in liberty, and dedicated to the proposition that all men are created equal.

Now we are engaged in a great civil war, testing whether that nation, or any nation so conceived and so dedicated, can long endure. We are met on a great battle-field of that war. We have come to dedicate a portion of that field as a final resting-place for those who here gave their lives that that nation might live. It is altogether fitting and proper that we should do this.

But, in a larger sense, we cannot dedicate—we cannot consecrate—we cannot hallow—this ground. The brave men, living and dead, who struggled here, have consecrated it far above our poor power to add or detract. The world will little note nor long remember what we say here, but it can never forget what they did here. It is for us, the living, rather, to be dedicated here to the unfinished work which they who fought here have thus far so nobly advanced. It is rather for us to be here dedicated to the great task remaining before us—that from these honored dead we take increased devotion to that cause for which they gave the last full measure of devotion; that we here highly resolve that these dead shall not have died in vain; that this nation, under God, shall have a new birth of freedom; and that government of the people, by the people, for the people, shall not perish from the earth.

DOCUMENT 8

ABRAHAM LINCOLN, SECOND INAUGURAL ADDRESS,

MARCH 4, 1865

Near the end of February 1865, when this address was nearly finished, Lincoln said to the painter Francis B. Carpenter: "Lots of wisdom in that document, I suspect. It is what will be called my 'second inaugural' address, containing about six hundred words. I will put it away here in this drawer until I want it."

FELLOW-COUNTRYMEN:——At this second appearing to take the oath of the presidential office there is less occasion for an extended address than there was at the first. Then a statement somewhat in detail of a course to be pursued seemed fitting and proper. Now, at the expiration of four years, during which public declarations have been constantly called forth on every point and phase of the great contest which still absorbs the attention and engrosses the energies of the nation, little that is new could be presented. The progress of our arms, upon which all else chiefly depends, is as well known to the public as to myself, and it is, I trust, reasonably satisfactory and encouraging to all. With high hope for the future, no prediction in regard to it is ventured.

On the occasion corresponding to this four years ago all thoughts were anxiously directed to an impending civil war. All dreaded it, all sought to avert it. While the inaugural address was being delivered from this place, devoted altogether to *saving* the Union without war, insurgent agents were in the city seeking to *destroy* it without war —seeking to dissolve the Union and divide effects by negotiation. Both parties deprecated war, but one of them would *make* war rather than let the nation survive, and the other would *accept* war rather than let it perish, and the war came.

One eighth of the whole population was colored slaves, not distributed generally over the Union, but localized in the southern part of it. These slaves constituted a peculiar and powerful interest. All knew that this interest was somehow the cause of the war. To strengthen, perpetuate, and extend this interest was the object for which the insurgents would rend the Union even by war, while the Government claimed no right to do more than to restrict the territorial enlargement of it. Neither party expected for the war the magnitude or the duration which it has already attained. Neither anticipated that the *cause* of the conflict might cease with or even before the conflict itself should cease. Each looked for an easier triumph, and a result less fundamental and astounding. Both read the same Bible and pray to the same God, and each invokes His aid against the other. It may seem strange that any men should dare to ask a just God's assistance in wringing their bread from the sweat of other men's faces, but let us judge not, that we be not judged. The prayers of both could not be answered. That of neither has been answered fully. The Almighty has His own purposes. "Woe unto the world because of offenses; for it must needs be that offenses come, but woe to that man by whom the offense cometh." If we shall suppose that American slavery is one of those offenses which, in the providence of God, must needs come, but which, having continued through His appointed time, He now wills to remove, and that He gives to both North and South this terrible war as the woe due to those by whom the offense came, shall we discern therein any departure from those divine attributes which the believers in a living God always ascribe to Him? Fondly do we hope, fervently do we pray, that this mighty scourge of war may speedily pass away. Yet, if God wills that it continue until all the wealth piled by the bondman's two hundred and fifty years of unrequited toil shall be sunk, and until every drop of blood drawn with the lash shall be paid by another drawn with the sword, as was said three thousand years ago, so still it must be said, "The judgments of the Lord are true and righteous altogether."

With malice toward none, with charity for all, with firmness in the right as God gives us to see the right, let us strive on to finish the work we are in, to bind up the nation's wounds, to care for him who shall have borne the battle and for his widow and his orphan, to do all which may achieve and cherish a just and a lasting peace among ourselves and with all nations.

Note on Sources

THE following list locates the source of each item in the text. The references are given in the order in which they occur in the text and are numbered to correspond with document numbers.

PART I. REVOLUTION AND INDEPENDENCE. 1. E. S. and H. M. Morgan, *The Stamp Act Crisis* (Chapel Hill, N. C., 1953), pp. 106–7. 2. Soame Jenyns, *Miscellaneous Pieces in Verse and Prose* (London, 1770), 3rd. ed., pp. 421–6. 3. Daniel Dulany, *Considerations on the Propriety of Imposing Taxes in the British Colonies for the Purpose of Raising a Revenue by Act of Parliament* (London, 1766), pp. 4 ff. 4. W. S. Taylor and J. H. Pringle, eds., *Correspondence of William Pitt, Earl of Chatham* (London, 1888), Vol. II, pp. 369 ff. 5. P. L. Ford, ed., *The Writings of John Dickinson* (Philadelphia, 1895), Vol. I, pp. 312 ff., 328 ff. 6. W. C. Ford, ed., *Journals of the Continental Congress* (Washington, 1904), Vol. I, pp. 63 ff. 7. Daniel Leonard, *The Present Political State of the Province of Massachusetts Bay in General and the Town of Boston in Particular By a Native of New England* (New York, 1775), pp. 55–61. 8. C. F. Adams, ed., *The Works of John Adams* (Boston, 1851), Vol. IV, pp. 105 ff. 9. A. S. Cook, ed., *Edmund Burke's Speech on Conciliation with America* (New York, 1899), pp. 6 ff. 10. Adam Smith, *An Inquiry into the Nature and Causes of the Wealth of Nations* (London, 1843), Vol. III, pp. 391 ff., Vol. IV, pp. 419 ff. 11. W. C. Ford, ed., *Journals of the Continental Congress*, Vol. II, pp. 140 ff. 12. M. D. Conway, ed., *The Writings of Thomas Paine* (New York, 1894), Vol. I, pp. 84 ff. 13. Charles Inglis, *The True Interest of America Impartially Stated in certain Strictures On a Pamphlet intitled Common Sense, By an American* (Philadelphia, 1776), pp. 3 ff. 14. Carl Becker, *The Declaration of Independence* (New York, 1958), pp. 185 ff.

PART II. THE CONSTITUTION. 1. E. C. Burnett, ed., *Letters of the Members of the Continental Congress* (Washington, D. C., 1936), Vol. VIII, pp. 208–9. 2. H. P. Johnston, ed., *Correspond-*

ence and Public Papers of John Jay (New York, 1891), Vol. III, pp. 203 ff.; W. C. Ford, ed., *The Writings of George Washington* (New York, 1891), Vol. IX, pp. 53 ff. 3. A. T. Prescott, ed., *Drafting of the Federal Constitution* (University of Louisiana, 1941), pp. 277 ff. 4. E. S. Corwin, ed., *The Constitution of the United States* (Washington, D. C. 1953), pp. 19–54. 5. Max Farrand, ed., *The Records of the Federal Convention* (New Haven, Conn., 1937), Rev. Ed., Vol. III, pp. 128–9. 6. Julian Boyd, ed., *The Papers of Thomas Jefferson* (Princeton, N. J., 1955), Vol. 12, pp. 438 ff. 7. Jonathan Elliot, ed., *Debates in the Several State Conventions on the Adoption of the Federal Constitution* (Washington, D. C., 1863), 2nd Ed. Vol. III, pp. 29 ff., pp. 44 ff. 8. P. L. Ford, ed., *The Federalist* (New York, 1898), pp. 54 ff., pp. 88 ff.

PART III. FEDERALISTS AND REPUBLICANS. 1. H. C. Lodge, ed., *The Works of Alexander Hamilton* (New York, 1904), pp. 228 ff. 2. W. W. Hening, ed., *Virginia Statutes at Large* (Philadelphia, 1823), pp. 237 ff. 3. A. E. Bergh, ed., *The Writings of Thomas Jefferson* (Washington, D. C., 1907), Vol. I, pp. 270–9. 4. P. L. Ford, ed., *The Writings of Thomas Jefferson* (New York, 1895), Vol. V, pp. 284–9. 5. Lodge, op. cit., Vol. III, pp. 446 ff. 6. P. L. Ford, op. cit., Vol. IV, pp. 85–6. 7. Lodge, op. cit., Vol. IV, pp. 70 ff. 8. Elliot, op. cit., Vol. IV, pp. 528–9; N. S. Shaler, *Kentucky* (New York, 1885), pp. 409 ff. 9. Elliot, op. cit., Vol. IV, p. 533. 10. J. D. Richardson, ed., *Messages and Papers of the Presidents* (Washington, D. C., 1898), p. 322. 11. 1 Cranch, 137. 12. Bergh, op. cit., Vol. 15, pp. 312 ff.

PART IV. REPUBLICAN DIPLOMACY. 1. *Examination of the Treaty of Amity, Commerce, and Navigation, Between the United States and Great-Britain, in Several Numbers: by Cato* (n. p., 1795), pp. 3–8, 61–3, 95. 2. Lodge, op. cit., pp. 189 ff. 3. Richardson, op. cit., pp. 210 ff. 4. Bergh, op. cit., pp. 311 ff. 5. Henry Adams, ed., *Documents Relating to New-England Federalism* (Boston, 1905), pp. 338 ff., pp. 351 ff., pp. 377 ff. 6. *Annals of Congress*, 12th Cong. 1st Sess., pp. 425–7, 446 ff., 533, 457 ff. 7. Richardson, op. cit., Vol. I, pp. 499 ff. 8. *Proceedings of the Hartford Convention of Delegates; Report of the Commissioners While at Washington; Letters from the Massachusetts Members in Congress* (New York, 1815), pp. 13 ff.

9. Allan Nevins, ed., *The Diary of John Quincy Adams* (New York, 1951), pp. 300 ff. 10. Richardson, op. cit., Vol. II, pp. 209 ff.

PART V. THE JACKSONIAN ERA. 1. *Reports of the Proceedings and Debates of the Convention of 1821 Assembled for the Purpose of Amending the Constitution of the State of New York* (Albany, N. Y., 1821), pp. 219–22, pp. 178–80. 2. Richardson, op. cit., Vol. IV, pp. 313 ff. 3. Richardson, op. cit., Vol. II, pp. 483 ff. 4. Daniel Mallory, ed., *The Life and Speeches of Henry Clay* (New York, 1857), Vol. I, pp. 660 ff. 5. Daniel Mallory, ed., *The Life and Speeches of Henry Clay* (New York, 1843), Vol. I, pp. 441 ff. 6. Elliot, op. cit., Vol. IV, pp. 580–2. 7. R. K. Crallè, ed., *The Works of John C. Calhoun* (New York, 1855), Vol. VI, pp. 60 ff. 8. Richardson, op. cit., Vol. II, pp. 640 ff. 9. Thomas Cooper, ed., *South Carolina Statutes at Large* (Columbia, S. C., 1836), pp. 356–7. 10. Richardson, op. cit., Vol. II, pp. 576 ff. 11. Daniel Webster, *Works* (Boston, 1881), Vol. III, pp. 417, 423–5, 429, 446–7. 12. 11 Peters, 420. 13. 11 Peters, 420 at 582 ff.

PART VI. SLAVERY AND EXPANSION. 1. Chancellor Harper, Governor Hammond, Dr. Simms, and Professor Dew, *The Pro-Slavery Argument* (Charleston, S. C., 1852), pp. 451 ff. 2. W. P. Garrison, F. J. Garrison, *William Lloyd Garrison* (New York, 1885), Vol. I, pp. 224–5. 3 .T. D. Weld, *American Slavery as It Is* (New York, 1839), pp. 7–9, 164 ff. 4. Harriet Beecher Stowe, *Uncle Tom's Cabin* (Boston, 1879), pp. 397–9. 5. W. J. Grayson, *The Hireling and the Slave* (Charleston, S. C., 1854), pp. 49, 52–4. 6. *Niles' National Register,* Vol. LXVI, pp. 152–3. 7. Richardson, op. cit., Vol. IV, pp. 37 ff. 8. *Old South Leaflets,* Vol. 6, No. 132, pp. 137 ff. 9. *Congressional Globe,* 31st Cong., 1st Sess., Vol. XXII, Part 1, pp. 656 ff., 451 ff., 476 ff. 10. J. W. Shuckers, *The Life and Public Services of Salmon Portland Chase* (New York, 1874), pp. 140–7. 11. *The Nebraska Question Comprising Speeches in the United States Senate* (Boston, 1854), pp. 38 ff. 12. 19 Howard, 393. 13. R. P. Basler, ed., *The Colected Works of Abraham Lincoln* (New Brunswick, N. J., 1953), Vol. III, pp. 43 ff.

PART VII. SECESSION, CIVIL WAR AND EMANCIPATION. 1. Frank Moore, *The Rebellion Record* (New York, 1861), Vol. I, pp.

3 ff. 2. Basler, op. cit., Vol. IV, pp. 264–71. 3. J. D. Richardson, ed., *Messages and Papers of the Confederacy* (Nashville, Tenn., 1906), Vol. I, pp. 63 ff. 4. Basler, op. cit., Vol. IV, pp. 421 ff. 5. Moore, op. cit., Vol. XII, pp. 480 ff. 6. Basler, op. cit., Vol. VI, pp. 28–30. 7. Basler, op. cit., Vol. VII, p. 23. 8. Basler, op. cit., Vol. VIII, pp. 332–3.

The selection from Allan Nevins, ed., *The Diary of John Quincy Adams* is used with the permission of Charles Scribner's Sons.

✳ INDEX ✳

A NOTE ABOUT THE AUTHOR

Richard Hofstadter, who died in October 1970, was DeWitt Clinton Professor of American History at Columbia University. He received his B.A. from the University of Buffalo and his M.A. and Ph.D. from Columbia University. He taught at the University of Maryland from 1942 until 1946, when he joined the History Department at Columbia. He also served as Pitt Professor of American History and Institutions at Cambridge University in 1958–9. The first of his books on American History was *Social Darwinism in American Thought*, published in 1944, followed by *The American Political Tradition*, in 1948. *The Age of Reform* (1955) won the Pulitzer Prize in history, and *Anti-intellectualism in American Life* (1963) received the Pulitzer Prize in general nonfiction, the Emerson Award of Phi Beta Kappa, and the Sidney Hillman Prize Award. Mr. Hofstadter's other books include *The Paranoid Style in American Politics* (1965), *The Progressive Historians* (1968), *The Idea of a Party System* (1969), and *America at 1750* (1971). He also edited, with Michael Wallace, *American Violence: A Documentary History* (1970).

VINTAGE POLITICAL SCIENCE
AND SOCIAL CRITICISM